BRIGHT PARTICULAR STARS

Canadian Performers

*This book is dedicated to the memory
of Richard Monette*

Direction and script are important but in the end it is the acting that matters most.

You can have a theatre without design, without music even without text, but you cannot have theatre without actors.

When all is said and done theatre belongs to the actors.

It cannot be any other way.

BRIGHT PARTICULAR STARS

Canadian Performers

MARTIN HUNTER

DESIGN V. JOHN LEE

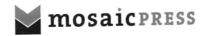

Library and Archives Canada Cataloguing in Publication
Hunter, Martin, 1933-, author
    Bright particular stars / Martin Hunter.
Includes bibliographical references and index.

Issued in print and electronic formats.
ISBN 978-1-77161-216-6 (Hardback).—ISBN 978-1-77161-217-3 (ePUB).—
ISBN 978-1-77161-218-0 (ePDF)
Entertainers—Canada—Biography. 2. Performing arts—Canada—Biography.
3. Celebrities—Canada—Biography. I. Title.

PN2307.H86 2016   791.092'2   C2016-901090-2
                                                          C2016-901091-

Published by Mosaic Press, Oakville, Ontario, Canada, © 2016.

Distributed in the United States by Bookmasters (www.bookmasters.com).
Distributed in the U.K. by Roundhouse Group (https://www.roundhousegroup.co.uk).

MOSAIC PRESS, Publishers
Copyright © 2016 Martin Hunter

Printed and Bound in Canada.
Cover design and layout by V. John Lee.
Interior design by V. John Lee. Interior layout by V. John Lee.

We acknowledge the Ontario Media Development Corporation for their support
of our publishing program

We acknowledge the Ontario Arts Council for their support of our publishing program

We acknowledge the financial support of the Government of Canada through the Canada Book Fund (CBF) for this project.

Nous reconnaissons l'aide financière du gouvernement du Canada par l'entremise du Fonds du livre du Canada (FLC) pour ce projet.

Canadian Heritage   Patrimoine canadien

MOSAIC PRESS
1252 Speers Road, Units 1 & 2
Oakville, Ontario L6L 5N9
phone: (905) 825-2130

info@mosaic-press.com

www.mosaic-press.com

CONTENTS

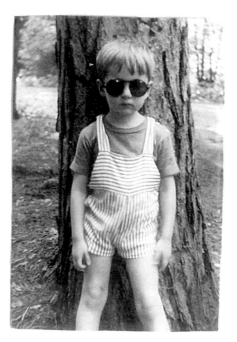

"All children are actors,
all actors are children."
Fran Lebowitz

"The important thing is to
keep on going."
James Cunningham

FOREWORD

This book is highly personal, for which I make no apology. I have been addicted to the theatre since I first attended a live performance at the age of five. Like many young hopefuls I attended stage performances whenever I could and supplemented these with excursions to the movies, initially every Saturday afternoon and later as often as several times a week. I became fascinated by various performers in both media, British and American stars, but above all a rising number of Canadians.

Like many of my generation, I went to London to try my luck, but I didn't much like England: the griminess of the 1950s, the bad food, the snobbery. I decided that the English were not going to change to please me and I had better go back to Canada where I belonged. In the years before and the years that followed I worked as an actor, a stage manager, a director, a playwright, and a producer. I was lucky enough to watch, to meet, and sometimes to work with many talented Canadian performers.

This book is an account of the performers that I have most admired. I saw their work many times over a period of more than seventy years. I had some personal connection with all of them, sometimes very slight, sometimes extensive. Although many of them are dead, they live vividly in my memory. This book is an attempt to share and preserve those memories.

Bright
Particular
Stars

Canadian Performers

This book has been made possible
by donations from

WALTER & LISA BALFOUR BOWEN

•

GEORGE & GLENNA FIERHELLER

•

JIM AND MARGARET FLECK

•

BILL & CATHY GRAHAM

•

BILL & DOROTHY HUNTER

•

NONA MACDONALD HEASLIP

•

WILMOT & JUDY MATTHEWS

•

DONALD & GRETCHEN ROSS

•

BILL & MEREDITH SAUNDERSON

I am grateful to Theatre Museum Canada
especially for the R.H. Thomson's interviews

THE FUNNIEST WOMAN IN THE WORLD

Beatrice Lillie

I first saw "the funniest woman in the world" at the Royal Alexandra Theatre when I was thirteen. I was with my friend Powell Jones, one of my fellow actors in the Toronto Children Players. His mother, Enid Ernestine, a tart-tongued North Toronto housewife, had actually gone to Gladstone Public School with Beatrice Lillie and remembered her putting shoes on her ears while singing "The Maple Leaf Forever," a now forgotten anthem written by their principal, Alexander Muir. Like Powell's mother, the famous comedienne was born in 1896. She was christened Beatrice Gladys, two names much in vogue at the time. (She would later appropriate another favourite late-Victorian name, Maud, and bend it to her own devilish devices.) Although most of the comics I held in reverence I shared with my friend Dick Williams, Beatrice Lillie was a separate discovery, and Powell and I maintained our enthusiasm for her distinctive brand of lunacy as a sort of shared passion.

Toronto in the first half of the twentieth century was a small provincial city culturally dominated by Protestant Ulstermen. The Lillie family was typical: Presbyterian, respectable, but with rising social aspirations undercut by a sense of mockery that could be characterized as "wicked." I knew this world intimately, dominated as it was by a rigid morality but also mitigated by a strong tendency to laugh at the pretensions and peculiarities of anybody who was in any way different. It had apparently not taken long for young Beatrice to figure out that everybody was in some way "different." She therefore learned early to mine idiosyncrasy, especially her own.

Beneath her individual peculiarities lay a solid framework of established routine. As Beatrice would later put it, "I was brought up on cod-liver oil, oatmeal, rice-pudding and church three times on Sundays." In Toronto this regimen would still be firmly in place thirty years later when I was growing up there, long after Miss Beatrice had become Lady Peel. Her irrepressible wit needed a recognizable social structure to bounce off, and Toronto provided her first experience of that—whether it was morning assemblies at Gladstone Avenue School, or her mother's musical soirées when she sent goose feathers plucked from a bed-pillow through the radiator grill onto the pomaded pate of a hapless tenor who was warbling "Oh, for the Wings of a Dove," or Sunday services in the vast neo-Romanesque interior of Cooke's Presbyterian Church, where she was expelled from the choir for exclaiming in a clearly audible voice as the leading soprano opened her mouth to sing and let out a loud belch, "Well, *really*."

Lillie's father, a former sergeant-major who left his native County Down and served with Kitchener in India before settling in Canada, called her, with pride and admiration, "pewerse wee Bea."

Perversity seems to be a feature of the Ulster personality, as clearly demonstrated by their politics. As a child I was very familiar with this phenomenon from my mother's family. All my uncles and aunts (two of whom, coincidentally, were named Beatrice and Gladys) were mimics who constantly made fun of each other and could twist almost any idea or situation to wring a laugh out of it, a skill I adapted to protect myself in the schoolyard and on the playing field. Nobody dared attack me as long as I could retaliate by making him look ridiculous.

We Ontario Ulstermen were actually displaced Scots who grafted onto a heritage of flinty stubbornness a peculiarly Irish delight in undermining the prevailing order and upending complacency. We were as committed to the rooting out of pretensions and weaknesses as any razor-tongued academic; we acted out our criticism, using the weapons of mimicry, exaggeration, and a keen nose for the ridiculous. Whether or not she was acting in self-defence, Beatrice Lillie took this perversity to supreme heights and soon became infected with a lifelong case of terminal silliness. From the moment we first saw her on stage, Powell and I loved her for this.

Bea Lillie's mother, Lucy Ann Shaw, was an Englishwoman with Irish antecedents and artistic aspirations. (She claimed to be a distant relative of George

Bernard Shaw, though as Beatrice put it, "she never mentioned the mileage.") She transformed herself into Lucie Anne Lillie, vocal artiste and teacher of singing, and trained the voices of her two daughters. Muriel, the elder, was the more musical and developed into a fine pianist, but Beatrice possessed a clear, high soprano voice that was to stand her in good stead throughout her career. "Mumsie," as her daughters called her, sent Beatrice for further "polishing" to a teacher and smalltime impresario, Harry W. Rich, who instructed her in "dramatic gesture, elocution and mime." He endowed her with a vocabulary of expressions, mannerisms, and poses, which she exploited with a vengeance for the rest of her life, fully justifying her father's early appellation.

These tics and quirks were apparently the result of a curious combination of calculation and spontaneity. She explained, "It's what I do after my lines that counts. Raise an eyebrow? Curl a lip? Flutter the eyelids? Tilt the chin? Someone once kept score of how many responses there might be, but I've forgotten the number of things he came up with, and I actually don't keep track of such things myself. I leave that to the audience, telling me what to do next. It's a clear case of osmosis, doctor. Believe me, I never calculate a gesture, inflection or movement in advance. If I were con-

sciously aware of what I was doing, I couldn't function at all."

This dependence on an audience made her unique in her immediacy. It also drove her colleagues crazy. In rehearsal she was often withdrawn and frequently grouchy. Her fellow performers never knew what she would do next, but they knew the audience would love it and that she would eclipse everyone else onstage. Noël Coward has written, "I have never really directed Beatrice Lillie any more than anyone else has…. Her instincts take command and her intuitive obedience to them is absolute." He concluded with qualified generosity, "I must say, Beattie is *usually* right."

Harry W. Rich also gave Beatrice Lillie a repertoire of songs, some of his

"Mad Dogs and Englishmen Go Out in the Noonday Sun"

3

own composition, including not only "Daddy's Sweetheart" and "The Strawberry Girl," but also a variety of ethnic numbers done with comic accents: "Mimosa San," "My Pretty Kickapoo," and an Italian ditty, whose lyrics went,

> Niccolini, he play da hand organ,
> He have-a da monk on da string.
> He catcha da coin from da window
> When songs of Napoli he sing....

Several of these songs are briefly recalled in a number she later trilled about the pathetic plight of the forgotten heroine Nanette:

> In China, the Chinkee
> No thinkee
> Of Nanettee.

Powell loved this song and frequently reprised it. He imitated Bea Lillie for years and mined her antics as a springboard for his own considerable gifts as a comic performer.

Of course the "Chinkee" number was "racist." Back in the days before political correctness reared its humourless head, Beatrice Lillie exploited racial caricatures quite unashamedly, as indeed we all did, although we knew our stereotypes bore no more relation to the actual nationalities being satirized than did W.S. Gilbert's depiction of Japanese nobles in

The Mikado, who are quite obviously Englishmen in fancy dress. In fact Lillie was not at all a master of accents but spoke always in what Kenneth Tynan characterized as "Berkeley Square Canadian," no doubt the result not only of her mother's ongoing lectures on "How to Behave like a Lady," but also of her insistent refrain, "Be natural. Be yourself. If you have talent it will be discovered." Lucie Anne Lillie, a stage mother in the grand tradition of Noël Coward's Mrs. Worthington, proved to be right.

The discoverer was the French producer and impresario André Charlot. Beatrice auditioned for him in London in 1914, singing a sentimental ballad as she sat on a battered suitcase:

> Though we're drifting apart
> And you're breaking my heart
> After all I've been to you.

At which point the suitcase collapsed and she fell over backwards. "I think perhaps I will let you do a comedy number in my next show," said Charlot, wiping the tears from his glasses. Indeed, Beatrice Lillie would play ever more prominent parts in the revues Charlot produced in London during the First World War. For a while she pressed for permission to try her hand at sad songs, but she soon came to recognize her producer's accurate per-

4

Beatrice Lillie

"If you know what I mean… and I think you do"

ception of her unique gifts as a performer: "From André Charlot I first learned that I was a natural born fool, one of those rare birds: a comedienne…. I was lucky enough to have Charlot give me that chance and I grabbed it."

Charlot, like "Mumsie," encouraged Beatrice to be herself. In fact she was not really an actress at all. Not for her the elaborate artifice by which Alec Guinness or Laurence Olivier transformed themselves into Arabian sheiks or hunchbacked usurpers, Edwardian suffragettes, Jewish merchants or boozy Scottish colonels. Lillie donned many a ridiculous outfit, appearing as a tottering Britannia or a washed-up mermaid, a fey Peter Pan tootling his pipes or Kabuki Lil sticking chopsticks in her wig, but the spirited performer within the costume remained always the same "pewerse wee Bea."

Beatrice Lillie spent ten years working with Charlot before she made her triumphant debut in New York in 1924. By then she had survived the war and begun to move in company with her co-star and great friend Gertrude Lawrence in fashionable London society, danced with the Prince of Wales, cruised off the south of France on fellow-Canadian Lord Beaverbrook's yacht, and broken her collarbone after falling from a horse in Rotten Row. This misadventure brought back to mind an early lyric she and her sister Muriel had composed back in Canada.

The next horse I ride on
I'm going to be tied on.

This social escalation culminated when in 1920 she married a dashing young

5

6

Britannia in Charlot's Revue *1924*

Beatrice Lillie

Guards officer, Robert Peel, grandson of the British prime minister in whose honour the London police are still called "bobbies." The wedding took place in Staffordshire and was followed by a sumptuous breakfast at the rambling family mansion Drayton Hall, soon to be lost to creditors. The couple honeymooned in Monte Carlo, where the groom lost thousands of pounds at the roulette wheel. It was a portent of what lay ahead, but the next year a son was born who would prove to be the great love of his mother's life.

"As far back as I can remember, I wanted to be slightly grand," confessed Lillie in her autobiography, significantly titled *Every* Other *Inch a Lady*. This sentiment was familiar to both Powell and me in our suburban North Toronto lives. It led Beatrice Lillie, on a return visit to Toronto after she had achieved Broadway fame, into posing for photographers in front of a white-pillared mansion she selected at random as her original Toronto home, before the irate owner came out and chased her away. When "Big Bobby," as she called her husband, succeeded to the title as fifth baronet, she became Lady Peel. The title sat on her close-cropped head "like a tiara on an emu," in Kenneth Tynan's words, or on another occasion "like a halo on an anarchist." Like Lillie, Powell and I would also enjoy the foolishness of our occasional attempted pretensions.

Lillie never really took to London society, much preferring the company of other stage people. Like them she was a gypsy, though an up-market gypsy to be sure, given to mink coats and an extravagantly long necklace she referred to as "the Peel poils," which she kept not in a vault but in her purse. When challenged as to their authenticity by a haughty dowager, her riposte was, "How can you evaluate real pearls with those false teeth?" She could assume an air of hauteur, but not for long. She blithely characterized herself as "A Lady in My Own Wrong."

Her cohorts and chums were almost all theatrical types: Gertrude Lawrence, Tallulah Bankhead, Fanny Brice, and Gracie Fields, all of them flamboyant comediennes, as well as such inspired

"The Peel poils"

male clowns as Bert Lahr, Clifton Webb, Bobby Clark, and of course Noël Coward, who provided her with some of her very best material, notably "Mad Dogs and Englishmen" and "I Went to a Marvellous Party," two songs she interpreted with a precision of individual nuance that rivals but is distinct from the Master's own renditions.

Beatrice Lillie's relationship with Coward was bumpy but ongoing. She managed to persuade Charlot to audition him when he was quite unknown; Charlot pronounced him to be utterly without talent. In the 1920s she starred in two of Coward's most successful

8

With Noel Coward on the Riviera

Beatrice Lillie

reviews, *This Year of Grace* and *Words and Music*. The two would maintain a slightly testy friendship as both went on to tour Europe, Africa, and the Mediterranean entertaining Allied troops during the Second World War and were taken up by the British royal family, Coward being especially close to Queen Elizabeth while "La Lillie" was a favourite of King George VI.

For thirty years Beatrice Lillie crossed and re-crossed the Atlantic, never quite at home on either side. It gave her for us an aura of glamour, though she made no secret of her Canadian origins, and perhaps because she didn't try to pass herself off as a Brit, the English accepted her as an eccentric, a concept they understood. Like Lawrence and Coward she was an upstart who dared to succeed by sheer talent and audacity. In America they would all find acceptance tinged with awe at their incisive mockery of everything they seemed to personify; their manners were impeccable and at the same time outrageous. Beatrice Lillie was, after all, a North American girl who had married up but not gone high-hat. Her title gave her a certain cachet she could undercut by sending it up. This allowed her to sail through Hollywood, charming everyone from Charlie Chaplin to Rudolph Valentino.

She accepted a three-year contract from MGM but never really adjusted to movies. Her unclassifiable humour was hard for film-makers to grasp, and they didn't know how to use her. Unlike Chaplin she never achieved the kind of control that might have allowed her to make a movie on her own terms. The lack of a live audience to bounce off meant that there was nothing to feed or inspire her invention. Her comedy had nothing to do with telling a story; it was all grace-notes and ornaments with no melodic or narrative line supporting it. Most of her films are no longer available, but the early *Exit Smiling* (1926) gives some idea of her comic inspiration. However, when the producers insisted on introducing a romantic storyline, her performance withered and died on the vine. Later films, such as *On Approval* (1944), have a few sublimely funny moments, and she does hold her own in *Thoroughly Modern Millie* (1967), where as Mrs. Meers she is allowed to go her own way. Her best lines are completely surreal, including "Sha-shoo" to indicate lofty dismissal, or her furiously indignant "Oh, *pook*."

Beatrice Lillie was to the dramatic actress what the parodist is to the novelist. Her effects were precise, pared down, unpredictable. Some of her funniest sketches involved no words at all. In *Madam Dines Alone* she sat at a well-appointed dinner table as a waiter set before her a large pink lobster. She then

9

took from her purse a nail file and scissors and proceeded with great care to manicure its claws. In a sketch in *Inside USA*, she entered a salon crowded with Chopinesque and Lisztian composers. In the manner of Camille she tossed one a flower from her décolletage and he immediately pounded out a polonaise on the piano. She lowered a shoulder strap and another took up his violin and began to fiddle furiously. She eyed them quizzically and stomped off in high dudgeon.

In *Kabuki Lil*, resplendent in the trappings of a geisha, she sat on patterned cushions, mewing like a stricken kitten, spiked her Japanese tea with Gordon's gin, and then suddenly got up and banged on a huge Oriental gong. It resonated sonorously and from the wings came the voice of Frank Sinatra singing "Three Coins in the Fountain," which seemed to give her enormous satisfaction. There was no logic to any of this; it was impure caprice but quite simply hysterical.

Although most of her routines involved a song, the best of which—like "Wind Round My Heart" and "The Yodelling Goldfish"—have clever lyrics, the words were never smutty or salacious, although occasionally the singer waxed a bit bibulous, like the society matron who informs her best friend,

"Maud, you're full of maggots and you know it;
Your soul's a bed where worms queue up to breed
You don't know what life's for, Maud,
You're rotten to the core, Maud...."

She goes on to extol the virtues of "high living and high thinking" until Maud hits back with "Get you, you're stinking."

Maud was one of her major characters, a sort of imaginary best friend, just as her favourite expression was "Get you" or, more often, "Get me." The use of slang was typical. Her skittish songs and smart cracks depended on a shared frame of reference rooted in the manners, idioms, and personalities of her era, juxtaposed in ways that were sly and unexpected: waxing philosophical, "Honi soit qui Lily Pons," or in another variation, "Honi soit can make a tree"; while holding a lily to her ear like a telephone receiver, "You're wanted on the gramophone," followed by "C'est lady Parle qui peel." The fun depended on a context that has disappeared, but at the time it was immediate, spontaneous, and riotous.

To a pigeon that landed on her shoulder in Trafalgar Square, "Any messages?" On winning 100.000 francs at Deauville, "Only the brave chemin de fer." On being interrupted by a fellow performer, "It's my ball, Maud." To a waiter who spilled hot soup down her front, "Never

10

darken my Dior again." Introducing herself to the audience, "I am known as Beyatrichay, the mezzanine soprano." After making some utterly inane pronouncement, "If you know what I mean and I *think* you *do*." She was the high priestess of ambiguity, the queen of the volte-face and the sphinx-faced goddess of the non sequitur. Powell and his future collaborator Rodney Archer would go on to exploit this erratic use of the unexpected quip in their plays the *Kitsch of Death* and *Foreplay and After*, just as I would when I began to write with my friend Robert Troop.

Lillie's signature number was "There are Fairies at the Bottom of My Garden," with its archly childish lyrics, delivered *almost* straight in the manner of a grandiose concert artiste modeled on her beloved "Mumsie," though she did allow herself the occasional sotto voce interpolation:

"Oh, the butterflies and bees
Make a lovely, little breeze
And the rabbits sit about and
hold the lights.

Isn't that *sweet?*
The King is very proud and very handsome.
And the Queen, well, can you guess who that may be?

Shhh, now this'll *kill* you...

She's a little girl all day
But at night she steals away.
Well, it's (rising to a mezzanine shriek)
MEEE...
Yes, it's *ME*."

And with an insouciant shout of "*Whee!*" she whirled the long string of pearls (the Peel poils?) around her neck so that they rotated around her body like a hula hoop until they reached her feet. She initially refused to do this number because she didn't think it funny. Her fans thought otherwise: for fifty years they would come back for this one routine and never fail to be convulsed. I saw it three times, the first being that Saturday matinee at the Royal Alex. I waited at the stage door till she appeared, and then I rushed forward. "You're the funniest thing I've ever seen," I blurted out. She eyed me critically. "Reahlly? Have you thought of looking in a mirror?" And she winked. I would never be as funny as Lillie, but in some *funny* way I began to see this as a challenge and almost a vote of encouragement.

Kenneth Tynan claimed that the key to Beatrice Lillie's success was that she ignored her audience, although we have her repeated declarations to the contrary, but his statement that "she is like a child dressing up in front of a mirror, amusing herself while the grown-ups are out....

11

[This] requires a vast amount of sheer nerve and more than a whiff of sheer genius, which is really another word for creative self-sufficiency" is spot on. Equally telling is Noël Coward's tribute, "She has subtlety, delicacy, wit and whether you like it or not, absolute truth. She is as incapable of a false note in her performance as her clear, fresh voice is incapable of singing out of tune." This was generous praise, in view of the fact that she frequently disregarded Coward's direction and sometimes his

"Shopping without stopping till my senses swoon"

words. But as Walter Kerr wrote, "Whoever hired Miss Lillie to do what a playwright put down on paper, of all things? ... if she does not always say 'Shoo!' to the plot right out loud as she comes on, it's only because that is no longer necessary; plots have heard of her and hide."

Critics have rarely had anything negative to say about her, and playwrights have even based characters on her. Noël Coward wrote Madame Arcati in *Blithe Spirit* with her in mind, but war and other commitments intervened. She did, however, play the role triumphantly in the musical version *High Spirits*. Similarly Patrick Dennis, though basing his character on his own relative, saw in his mind's eye Beatrice Lillie playing Auntie Mame on stage. She took over from Rosalind Russell partway through the run of *Mame* on Broadway and then crossed the Atlantic to play it in London. The film version opened on the other side of Leicester Square but slunk away after three weeks, but her stage version ran for over a year. Another writer, P.L. Travers, inscribed a copy of her book with the words "You *are* Mary Poppins." Beatrice Lillie declared that Julie Andrews played the role beautifully, but one cannot help but regret not seeing Lillie's quizzical expression as she unfurled her umbrella and sailed over the trees of Green Park peering down on its

inhabitants with beady-eyed curiosity.

Beatrice Lillie and her handsome, dashing, reckless husband drifted apart but never divorced. She needed to work, not only because of money but because that was her life; he needed adventure and found it climbing the mainmast of an Atlantic steamship, playing cricket at Lords, sheep farming in Australia, and leading a band in the Midlands, before he died in 1934. Friends tried to match her with a variety of suitors, from John Gilbert to Clark Gable, but her emotional life was increasingly centred on her son, Robert. Tall, handsome, and impetuous like his father before him, he enlisted as an ordinary seaman in the Royal Navy and was killed in action off the coast of Ceylon in 1942, when he was only 21. Beatrice Lillie received the news in her dressing-room but went onstage that night as usual, even though she was devastated by the loss. She would never enter into another close personal relationship, but her work was unaffected. Emotion was not an essential part of her theatrical territory.

She continued to light up theatres on both sides of the Atlantic with her own brand of lunacy well into the 1970s. She maintained a house, Peel Fold, at Henley-on-Thames, where "Mumsie" lived until her death at the age of 83. She took up painting, starting with china doorknobs. Her friend Winston Churchill once coun-

A New England Mermaid in Inside U.S.A

selled her, "Don't be afraid of the canvas." She took his advice until she realized, "I have now reached the point where the canvas is afraid of me."

She began to collect paintings, including a Modigliani that would be used to bail her out when she was nearing the end of her financial rope, and Pekinese dogs, some of whom she believed spoke to her in recognizable English phrases, including "I love you" and "Up yours." Sometime in the 1950s she struck up a friendship with a former lieutenant in

13

the United States Marines named John Philip Huck. He would soon drop the Huck and as John Philip performed with her and Reginald Gardiner in *An Evening with Beatrice Lillie*. He would become her close companion and eventually caregiver in her final years.

The last time I saw Beatrice Lillie was in the CBC studios in Toronto in the mid-1980s, when she was clearly a bit out of it, confused, uncertain where she was, not always able to respond to questions. John Philip was with her and said, "I have to keep a sharp eye out to make sure she doesn't misbehave." She flashed me a conspiratorial glance, "Get him." I went home and phoned Powell in England to report on this encounter.

At about this time she paid a final visit to Noël Coward in Jamaica. She insisted on going to a revival meeting in the vil-lage one evening and sang the hymns with great enthusiasm. The next evening she begged to go back but John Philip decreed she was to go to bed. Coward was awakened two hours later by a manservant who reported,

"Lady Bea, she gone down to the vil-lage."
"Oh, let her go."
"But sir, she naked."

John Philip hustled down to the village and strong-armed her into a raincoat. She turned her withering glance on him, "Aren't people *stuffy*." And there we shall leave her, delighted to the end at the resounding pop as she deflated one more balloon at the extended birthday party she had made of her life.

HANDS ACROSS THE SEA

Raymond Massey

"Actually Vincent was a more accomplished actor than Raymond." The opinion was put forward by their cousin Dorothy Goulding, herself an experienced theatre director. Vincent's finest theatrical moment was as the Pope; his preparation included borrowing the episcopal ring of the Bishop of Toronto. Raymond's most celebrated stint was as Abraham Lincoln; he was apparently cast at least partly because he looked uncannily like the American president. Of course Vincent's ultimate role was as Canada's first native-born Governor General; he not only looked the part but, in the way of all fine actors, disappeared into it. During his tenure it almost seemed as though the office should be hereditary. But actors, like other artists, achieve mastery by continual performance, and Raymond would become a prodigiously prolific performer.

Apart from an interest in theatre the two brothers were not much alike. Born almost ten years apart (Vincent in 1887,

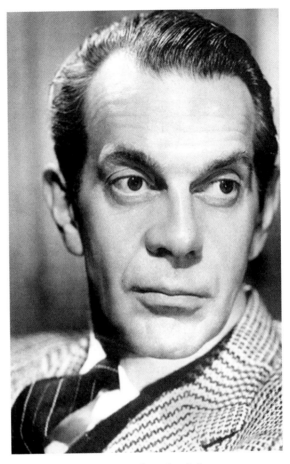

Raymond in 1896), they had few common friends or activities, although they grew up together in their father Chester Massey's formidable mansion on Toronto's Jarvis Street; its stately if faded elegance can still be seen today. In the early years of the twentieth century the Masseys were one of Toronto's most prominent and wealthy families, and their influence and affluence would continue well past the mid-century years, causing the poet Frank Scott to pen the lines

In Canada there are no classes,
Only the Masseys and the masses.

It had not always been so. A generation earlier the Masseys were shunned by the cream of Toronto society because they were "in trade." But the Jarvises, Ridouts, and other remnants of the Family Compact who had ruled the social roost in the nineteenth century were not exactly blue-blooded aristocrats tracing their lineage back to the Conqueror, and the city's relatively fluid social structure soon accommodated the members of this energetic family who built an international empire, manufacturing farm machinery in Toronto and selling it in the United States, Europe, and Asia. This change of attitude was no doubt influenced by the Massey family's generous donation of the entire cost of $150,000 for the construction of Massey Hall, the city's first real concert venue, as well as of the Fred Victor Mission, a home for derelict men, named for one of Vincent and Raymond's uncles.

The Masseys were devout Methodists, strict in their observance of religious and moral obligations though liberal in their social and political outlook. They contributed handsomely to the Metropolitan Church on Queen Street, sometimes referred to as Toronto's Cathedral of Methodism. The brothers' uncle Walter Massey, president of the farm implement company, conducted a Bible study class every Sunday at his house across the street from Chester's home. The classes were attended by 70 members of the family and their various servants and employees. Years later Raymond remembered these classes fondly.

Although the Massey children were not allowed to engage in frivolous activities on the Sabbath, they evolved a form of charades that took place on Sunday afternoons. Tableaux based on biblical stories that the Massey children acted out had to be identified by the adults. Walter's children Madeleine, Dorothy, and Denton participated in these dramatic scenarios along with their cousin Raymond. He became almost like a member of Walter's family and was particularly close to Madeleine and Dorothy, whose lively imagination sparked and complemented his own. He shared their games and their stories and particularly enjoyed performing in the biblical guessing games.

Raymond spent most of his summers at his uncle's farm at Dentonia Park. In the 1890s Walter Massey had purchased a sizeable tract of land east of Toronto where he tested the machinery made by the family firm and also established a dairy herd of some 200 head of Jersey cattle. His aim was to provide the city of Toronto with clean milk, and he founded the Pure Dairy

Young charmer at Dentonia c. 1900

Company to carry out this ambition.

After Walter's death in 1904, his widow, Susan Denton Massey, continued to run the farm, which had been named

in her honour. Her children vacationed there, riding on wagons and sliding down haystacks when they were young and later playing tennis and golf on the courts and nine-hole course that Walter had laid out. Raymond had his own pony, Aunt Fanny, and became a proficient horseman. Raymond also joined in the imaginative games devised by his cousins Madeleine and Dorothy. One game was called "Adventures" and involved forming teams and setting out through the woods trying to find the mysterious "Leaf Men," who arrived in "sky wagons" (space ships?) and had the power to stifle human breath as they slid through the woods disguised as leaves. This science fiction fantasy preceded any knowledge of Frank Baum or Ray Bradbury, never mind *E. T.*

In 1903, when Raymond was nine, he and his brother Vincent were taken to England by their parents. They travelled to France, Germany, and Switzerland, and Chester allowed his wife and Vincent to see a Shakespeare play and even to go to the opera, but Raymond had to content himself with a visit to the Regent's Park zoo. Raymond missed Dentonia and his cousins but was happy to be with his adored mother, the beautiful and spirited Anna Vincent. He was shattered near the end of their journey, however, when she was diagnosed with appendicitis. She died within a few days,

17

and Raymond returned home with his father and brother to face the prospect of life in boarding schools: Upper Canada, St. Andrew's, and finally Appleby College. His days at the first two schools were not particularly happy. He was a good student but hopeless at team sports, and his shyness prevented him from making many friends. At Appleby he was more in his element; he was befriended by one of the masters, Mr. Powell, who allowed him to stable his own horse across the road from the school and rode with him in the afternoons. He also cast Raymond as young Marlowe in the school play *She Stoops to Conquer.*

Raymond was already attending the theatre in downtown Toronto, where he saw the great American and British actors of the day: Otis Skinner, John Drew, Martin Harvey, George Arliss, and Johnston Forbes-Robertson in touring productions of *Hamlet* and *Romeo and Juliet,* Shaw's *Caesar and Cleopatra,* and the modern "classic" *The Passing of the Third Floor Back.* And he had a brief encounter after a horse show with a charming young woman from Buffalo who told him she was on her way to New York to become a professional actress. Her name was Katherine Cornell. Raymond apparently made up his mind that he would one day play opposite her on Broadway.

Raymond graduated, enrolled at

Victoria College, joined a fraternity, and dated a girl his father disapproved of. In the summer of 1914 he was travelling in France with Vincent when war broke out in August. The brothers returned to Canada and both enlisted in the army. Vincent would spend the majority of the war in Ottawa working with the war cabinet. Raymond thought that "soldiering would be more fun with a mounted unit" and so managed to have himself commissioned as an officer in the horse artillery. He trained in Kingston and was shipped to London in 1915. He underwent training in equitation from a warrant officer of the Household Cavalry, had a uniform tailored in Savile Row, saw shows starring Beatrice Lillie and Gertie Millar, and by January 1916 was attached to the Canadian Corps stationed in Belgium not far from Ypres.

In spite of the horrors of trench warfare, Raymond took to the life of a soldier. He was effective in obtaining intelligence of enemy positions, popular with his fellow officers, respected by his men, and scheduled for promotion before he was wounded when German shells hit his battery while they were advancing toward the front. His wounds were soon healed, but he suffered from severe shellshock. He was invalided home to Canada, where after a few months' rest he was described as fit to return to active duty. But a further two-week blackout

Raymond Massey

convinced his superiors that this was unwise, and he finished the war years as a gunnery instructor at Yale.

In June 1918 Raymond returned to Toronto where he learned that the Canadian army was sending troops to Siberia. Winston Churchill, determined to prevent the Bolsheviks from taking over the country, had persuaded the British and Canadian governments to support the White troops who controlled much of the eastern territory of the former Russian empire. Had their support been wholehearted they might have succeeded, but once the Armistice had been signed, the victorious governments were preoccupied with other priorities and the Canadian troops were never allowed to engage the enemy. To relieve their boredom the commanding officer commissioned Captain Massey to do something for their entertainment. He chose to do a minstrel show, which he wrote and directed and also played a prominent part in. It convinced him that this was where his future would lie.

He returned to Canada and was sent to Oxford on the recommendation of his anglophile brother. Vincent had been captivated by his experience at Balliol, and it coloured the rest of his life. Raymond also enjoyed his time there, but his major focus was on rowing and the social life of the many clubs and societies where he dined and listened to such celebrities as T.E. Lawrence and Rudyard Kipling. He went down from Oxford without taking his examinations and returned to Canada with a new bride, Margery Fremantle, whom he had married in 1921. His father and brother set him to work in the family plant, where he was bored and restless. The managers saw little promise in his work and treated him as a dilettante.

In his spare time he began performing at Hart House Theatre. Hart House had been given to the University of Toronto by the Massey family to be used for undergraduate activities: debating, recreational reading, music, and athletics. (It was named for Hart Massey, the founder of the family fortune.) Vincent oversaw its operation in what he considered a properly Oxonian manner and decided that a theatre should be created in an underground space that had been used during the war for rifle practice. The theatre was to be managed as a separate entity, partly because Hart House was an all-male preserve (following the Oxford model) whereas the theatre was to include female performers, and partly because Vincent wanted to control it.

The theatre was staffed by unpaid amateurs and run by a committee under Vincent's direction. Raymond played Marchbanks in Shaw's *Candida* and Rosmer in Ibsen's *Rosmerholm*. In both plays he relied heavily on his emotions,

Rosemer in Rosmerholm
Hart House Theatre

20

and he would later credit the director Bertram Forsyth with the advice that he must feel the emotion of the character but then draw back from it so that he remained in control of his performance: "emotion recollected in tranquility," in the words of Stanislavsky, echoing Wordsworth, though Massey would later decry "the Method," which was the American take on the great Russian's theories. At Hart House Raymond also played Smitty in O'Neill's *In the Zone*, his first experience with the American dramatist who was to be an important figure in his future career.

Raymond was increasingly dissatisfied with his work at the factory; the managers at the plant told him his prospects were dim. And his English wife did not like Toronto. So he went backstage one night at the Royal Alex and invaded the dressing room of the American actor John Drew, saying he wanted to be an actor. Drew asked, "Are you any good? If you don't know for certain, don't try it. And don't try to start in New York. Go to London. There is so much theatre there, you may have good fortune." Raymond went home and told his father of his decision to quit work at the plant and go to England to seek his fortune as an actor. His father made him get down on his knees and promise never to act on Sunday. Vincent came into the room, and when Raymond told

him of his intention, Vincent famously asked, "What name will you use?"

In London young Raymond called on actor-managers and agents and hung out in theatrical pubs. He turned up at stage doors and in rehearsal rooms. As a last ditch attempt he visited the tiny Everyman Theatre in Hampstead. They were rehearsing O'Neill's *In the Zone*, and one of their actors had just quit. George Carr, the manager, decided to hire Raymond as a replacement, as Raymond knew the play and had an American accent. They were to open the show in Liverpool a week later. The show ran three weeks and earned the young Massey a favourable notice in the *Times*. He continued to work at the Everyman and the Royalty, playing small roles and as an understudy, assistant stage manager, and assistant to the business manager. He also had a small role in the original production of Shaw's *Saint Joan*, starring Sybil Thorndike, in 1924.

His first West End role was in *Transit of Venus* playing opposite Athene Seyler as an Arab chieftain called Khan Aghaba. Raymond's dark and brooding aspect had earned him at school the nickname "Nig" (short for "Nigger"), and he would continue to be cast in ethnic roles including Reuben Manassa in *The Golden Calf*, Prince Ghul in *Drums* (1938), and Sheik Yousseff in *The Desert Song* (1953). His appearance was definitely not that of a leading man. He shared the distinctive features of the Massey clan: the beetling brows; the deep-set eyes, one slightly larger than the other; the prominent patrician nose. But his most telling physical attribute was his wide, sensual mouth, which could settle in a forbidding scowl or break into a sudden appealing grin, sometimes mocking, sometimes surprisingly vulnerable. Tall with a kind of awkward grace, his look was as individual as that of Laurence Olivier, Leslie Howard, Humphrey Bogart or Gregory Peck and just as sexy, as he would prove in the movies he made with them over the years.

Within the next few years Raymond was playing leading roles alongside Noël Coward, Ursula Jeans, Barry Fitzgerald, Cathleen Nesbitt, and C. Aubrey Smith. Then came a telegram from Gladys Cooper asking him to direct Somerset Maugham's *The Sacred Flame*. It was the beginning of a business partnership between the two that would last four years and involve them in six productions in which they both acted and Raymond directed, including two large-scale shows—*Late Night Final*, a play about newspapermen, with a five-part multiple set to allow for quick transitions and overlapping scenes; and *Grand Hotel*, with a 35-foot revolving turntable and a cast of 51. Massey often found himself directing rehearsals during the day at

21

one theatre and then skipping over to another to play in a different show at night. He frequently travelled "across the pond," recasting his London successes for a run on Broadway or picking up the rights to an American show that he would mount in London.

The luxury liners of this period were populated by a kind of floating "café? society" that included many American and British actors, writers, directors, composers, and playwrights. The members of this tight little artistic elite were famous, glamorous, creative, witty, often promiscuous, and frequently heartless. Their behaviour—and misbehaviour— was photographed, filmed, written about, and splashed across the headlines. California's Hollywood, New York's Broadway, London's West End, the French Riviera, and luxury liners were their hunting grounds, and they frolicked relentlessly. Raymond was accepted into this world, although his participation in their more outré activities was probably somewhat peripheral.

In 1931 Massey played Hamlet, his first role on Broadway, in an elaborate production directed and designed by the celebrated American scenic artist Norman Bel Geddes. In this production Raymond spoke the lines of the Ghost as well as the Danish prince and engaged in a spectacular duel in the final act. His deep baritone and articulate diction were

Hamlet *in New York 1931*

lauded, but his performance was naturalistic—to the surprise of the critics. Robert Benchley wrote in the *New Yorker*, "My only criticism of Mr. Raymond Massey… would be that he is not enough of a ham." Early on in his time in London, Raymond had been strongly influenced by Sir Gerald du Maurier, who had introduced the concept of "underplaying" to the British stage in contrast to the histrionic styles of Henry Irving, Beerbohm Tree, and Martin Harvey. The Massey *Hamlet* was

a moderate success, but Raymond returned to London to continue his partnership with Gladys Cooper.

Their next successful venture, in 1934, was *The Shining Hour*, which they rehearsed in England, opened in Toronto to caustic notices, and went on to play successfully on Broadway and in the West End. In Toronto Raymond's family turned out in force to support their cousin and were surprised to find him such a glamorous figure. They were very taken with his pretty young wife Adrianne Allen, whom he had married shortly after his divorce from his first wife in 1929 and who was playing a leading role opposite him. They were titillated as they caught a whiff of the sophisticated ambience of the London theatre world and the realization that Raymond and Adrianne were very much caught up in its social whirl.

The young couple mixed freely not only with Noël Coward and his set but also with socialites from Princess Marina of Kent to Mrs. Wallis Simpson. Raymond lunched at the Garrick Club and had supper at the Ivy or the Savoy. They lived in a smart house on fashionable Wilton Crescent, where Adrianne entertained lavishly. Such were her social ambitions that Noël Coward nicknamed her "Plannie Annie." Coward was godfather to their son Daniel and cast Adrianne in his smash success *Private*

Lives, playing opposite the young Laurence Olivier, who was rather dazzled by their glitter and later wrote, "Everyone knows that Ray Massey is as rich as Croesus."

It is not clear to what extent Raymond used his own money to help finance his career as a manager. He was certainly shrewd where money was concerned. He bargained with playwrights, including Shaw, to get reduced royalties and, whatever Adrianne's extravagances might have been, retained some of the frugality that had been instilled in him by his Methodist forbears. Thanks to his experience in the army and at Oxford he had the manners of a gentleman and some very good connections. And in spite of a certain amount of innate shyness and even a stammer when he was uncertain of himself, he got along wonderfully well with women. Throughout his stage career he had strong professional liaisons with Gladys Cooper, Gertrude Lawrence, and especially Katherine Cornell, whom he referred to affectionately as "Miss Kitty."

But it was Ruth Gordon who persuaded him that he should follow up his Hamlet with another role on Broadway. She had bought the rights to Edith Wharton's novel *Ethan Frome* and commissioned a dramatization. She was determined to play the heroine Mattie Silver and to have Raymond play the title role. He agreed to

23

take it on and sailed to New York to begin rehearsals. On the first day he overheard one of the producers exclaim, "My God, Ruthie's hired a Goddam Englishman to play the lead." But Raymond's ancestors had been New England farmers, and he slowly but successfully managed the transition from English gent to rural Yankee. The play might easily have become a burlesque of stereotypical rubes, but in the sensitive hands of Raymond, Ruth, Pauline Lord, and director Guthrie McClintic it emerged as a deeply moving drama. Raymond had discovered a vein from which would flow his finest performances.

On the final day of his performance of Hamlet the playwright Robert Sherwood had come to Raymond's dressing room and after sitting in silence for a few minutes said, "I think Abraham Lincoln was a lot like Hamlet. Would you like to play Abe Lincoln?" Before Sherwood had his script ready, Massey would play the seedy song-and-dance man Harry Van in Sherwood's *Idiot's Delight* in London. The role had nothing in common with the character of Lincoln, but Sherwood was confident of his casting. When it was announced the American icon would be played by a Canadian, there was widespread critical skepticism, but so successful was Raymond's portrayal that acclaim was universal. The role tapped into many aspects of Raymond's own personality: the reserve, the underlying neediness,

the awkward sincerity, the self-questioning, the defensive device of using a quick sardonic retort to fend off unwanted advice or involvement, the gradual building up of confidence and assumption of authority. The fact that he struggled with the role so much that he asked to be released from the production after the Washington tryout provides both evidence of his commitment and a strong indication of why his portrayal was so vividly real.

Raymond would play this role on Broadway and on tour across North

Abe Lincoln in Illinois *on Broadway*

Raymond Massey

America for over two years, and his performance is admirably captured in the film version of *Abe Lincoln in Illinois* (1940), in which he is provided with an excellent foil by the strong-willed Mary Todd of Ruth Gordon. It was unusual at the time for a stage actor to be cast in the film version of even his greatest success, but Raymond had already established himself as a capable film actor. He first acted in films in Britain for the Hungarian producer Alexander Korda, his most notable role being that of the suave but ruthless French diplomat Chauvelin in *The Scarlet Pimpernel* (1934). He proved a most effective adversary to the handsome, foppish but cunning Sir Percy Blakeney of Leslie Howard, with whom he enjoyed a great sense of camaraderie, although he was fond of telling how the set had to be provided with built-up walkways so that he and Howard could appear to be the same height on screen.

With Raymond's success as a French villain, Hollywood came calling and he was cast as Black Michael in the costume drama *The Prisoner of Zenda* and then in a South Sea spectacle *Hurricane* (both 1937), but *Abe Lincoln in Illinois* established him as a major Hollywood actor and earned him an Oscar nomination. From then on pictures would dominate his career, and it was as a Hollywood actor that he would be best remembered.

with Ruth Gordon in the film of Abraham Lincoln

Raymond's decision to spend the majority of his time in the United States was influenced not only by the higher economic rewards but also by a strong personal consideration. The many months when he and Adrianne were apart when they were working on different sides of the Atlantic put a strain on their marriage. At some point during his Broadway years Raymond met and fell in love with Dorothy Ludington, an American theatrical lawyer. Adrianne came to New York to work out a reconciliation, but Raymond asked her for a divorce. She sought the advice of a New York lawyer, William Whitney, who after listening to her tale said, "Mrs. Massey, I'm afraid I cannot represent you. Dorothy Ludington is my ex-wife."

Nevertheless, the divorce was agreed upon and shortly thereafter Adrianne married—in an interesting twist—William Whitney. In his later autobiography Raymond suggests that the divorce was perfectly amicable but his daughter Anna, who was one year old when her father defected, tells a different story. She and her brother Daniel were brought up by Whitney. When Anna married, Raymond flew to England to give her away, but Anna told him not only that Whitney was paying for her wedding but that she regarded Whitney as her real father. Although Anna had a successful career as an actress, father and daughter never reconciled, and Anna's resentment is vividly recounted in her 2006 memoir *Telling Some Tales.*

Raymond would remain with Dorothy until her death shortly before his own. She was a shrewd, tough businesswoman and handled his financial affairs with dispatch, gaining a good deal of animosity from agents and producers in the process. Although Anna characterized her as "The Wicked Witch of the West," Raymond's Canadian relatives seem to have accepted her. She could be charming and amusing, as I discovered when I had dinner with her and Raymond at Massey College in the 1970s. Although Raymond continued to be susceptible to attractive women, she kept him in line. A relative remembers her saying, "I may kill you, Ray, but I'll never divorce you."

Raymond and Dorothy established themselves in a brownstone in New York, and then at a farm in Connecticut. Raymond did not abandon the stage but achieved his dream of playing opposite Katherine Cornell in two Shaw plays, *Candida* and *The Doctor's Dilemma*, as well as opposite Gertrude Lawrence in *Pygmalion*. His ability to provide an air of British urbanity and intellectual authority made him an effective foil for Shaw's dazzling heroines, and his easygoing amiability endeared him to his leading ladies.

But it was in film that he did his more interesting later work. The persona of Lincoln contributed to his shaping of performances as the wild-eyed abolitionist John Brown in *Santa Fe Trail* (1940), later in *Seven Angry Men* (1955), and finally in the staged reading of Stephen Vincent Benét's *John Brown's Body*, in which he toured with Judith Anderson and Tyrone Power. Brown could hardly have been more different from Lincoln in his outward personality, but the fervour and passion, the underlying streak of fierce determination and ruthless commitment to a cause, linked the two. In *John Brown's Body* Raymond was able to play both characters in the same evening and gave an admirable display of his versatility. Two other major film roles would provide opportunities for Raymond to build on the roots of his flinty New England ancestors. One was

Raymond Massey

John Brown's Body

the severe but troubled general Ezra Mannon in Eugene O'Neill's grim retelling of the Oresteia trilogy *Mourning Becomes Electra* (1947). The scene in which he opens his heart to his faithless wife is moving for its simple honesty and deep-felt injury.

His direct experience of combat in the trenches in 1916 would be useful to Massey when he played in war films such as *Action in the North Atlantic* (1943), which rises above its propagandistic purpose thanks to Massey's ironic grittiness and the laconic humour of his co-star Humphrey Bogart. It provides a vivid sense of the dangers of allied convoys facing torpedoes launched by German submarines and strafing from the Luftwaffe, in spite of the fact that the picture was made entirely on the back lot

An AWOL soldier in Michael Powell's The 49th Parellel *in 1941*

of a Hollywood studio, which meant that Ray and Bogey could retire after a day's shooting to the Polo Lounge for martinis and cigars.

After the Great War, Raymond had continued to take his patriotic obligations seriously. As a volunteer he drove a bus in London in the General Strike of 1926. During World War II he spent several months attached to the office of the Adjutant-General of the Canadian Army. After pushing papers around, an activity for which he had neither a taste nor a talent, his superiors admitted that they didn't know what to do with him and released him. He returned to the United States and before long was leading a company of actors in a production of Thornton Wilder's *Our Town*, entertaining allied troops in Europe. He played the Stage Manager, a role that he settled into with ease.

Adam Trask in East of Eden
with James Dean as his son Cal

The last of Raymond's great film roles was as Adam Trask in Steinbeck's *East of Eden* (1955). Here Raymond creates a father figure who is stern and unrelenting and yet has an underlying layer of rectitude and repressed gentleness. It is possible that this is in part a portrait of his own father Chester, the lovable, slightly eccentric scion of the Massey clan who presided over the decline of the family empire. The film is illuminated by the fresh and vigorous performances of two young actors, Julie Harris and James Dean. Dean and Raymond developed an instant antipathy while Harris tried to mediate between them. The director, that arch-manipulator Elia Kazan, exploited this offstage triangle to goad the three actors into achieving some of the best performances of their careers, as he freely confesses in his autobiography.

As an actor Raymond had another string to his bow: he was an accomplished comedian. When I first met him at a party for student actors at Hart House when he was playing in a touring company at the Royal Alex in the 1950s, I was impressed not only by his capacity to consume whisky without showing any visible effects, but also by his skills as a raconteur who kept us chuckling for over an hour. Not all his films exploit this quality, but two that do are *The 49th Parallel*, the propaganda film he made in Canada in 1941 for Michael Powell, where he performs with a kind of loose-limbed goofiness, and the now venerable comedy *Arsenic and Old Lace* (1944), in which his deadpan portrayal of the psychopathic Jonathan far outshines the eye-popping overkill of Cary Grant's Mortimer. Both films underscore the versatility of this first-rate character actor.

Raymond would go on working in films until the late 1960s, appearing in many television series from *Alfred Hitchcock Presents* to *Dallas*. Inevitably much of this work involved retreads of earlier successes. His most celebrated television role was in the long-running series *Dr. Kildare*, where he played Dr. Gillespie, a seasoned senior physician

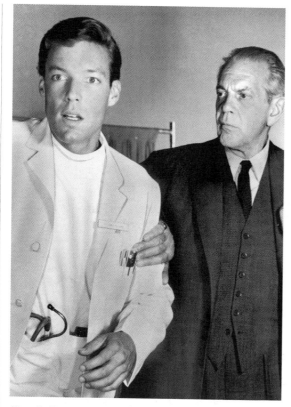

Dr. Gillespie with Richard Chamberlain as Dr. Kildaire.

who mentors the young Richard Chamberlain. The crusty old curmudgeon with a heart of gold made use of all the skills Massey had built up over the years. He was once again the shrewd realist, but mellower now and, as he aged, more handsome and more likeable. Perhaps this reflects the fact that he was by now successful and respected, or perhaps the comfort of his settled married life with Dorothy, or a combination of both.

But also as he aged his health deterio-rated. He suffered from arthritis, and in the last Western he made he could no longer mount a horse but had to be tied on, riding sidesaddle. Eventually he had to give up his favourite hobbies, golf and woodworking. But he didn't give up live theatre. He played opposite Grace Kelly in Strindberg's *The Father* in New York in 1949; as Prospero in *The Tempest* at Stratford in Connecticut in 1955; as the argumentative, self-absorbed business-man Tom Garrison in *I Never Sang for My Father* at the Duke of York Theatre in London in 1968; and finally as the aging poet Nonno in Tennessee Williams's last great play *The Night of the Iguana* at the Ahmanson Theatre in Los Angeles in 1975. At 79 he was so crip-pled with arthritis that he could not get out of his wheelchair, but his gallant spirit prompted the playwright to praise his performance for its simple beauty.

The most impressive of his late stage appearances was in Archibald MacLeish's *J.B.*, a reworking of the biblical story of Job. His impressive stature, stern demeanour, and sonorous vocal tones provided the necessary authority for the godlike character of Mr. Zuss, pitting his implacable will against the snarling quicksilver cunning of Christopher Plummer as Nickles, the devil-figure in this modern morality play. It ran for two hundred performances and was the most talked about show on Broadway in the

30

Mr Zuss with Christopher Plummer as Nickles in J.B. *by Archibald McLeish*

1958–59 season. During the run, Raymond and Plummer solidified the friendship that had begun a few years earlier at Stratford, Connecticut. Both men enjoyed good talk, good whisky, and above all a good laugh. Plummer would describe him as "gregarious, generous, gentle and a hell of a lot of fun."

Raymond served as a mentor and father figure to several young actors he worked with, notably Plummer and Richard Chamberlain, whose emotional tribute in a biographical documentary completed shortly after Raymond's death showed how much the older actor had meant to him. Like many vigorous and ambitious men, Massey was too busy building his own career to spend a lot of time with his own children and made up for it in his later years by becoming a surrogate parent to talented young men who were learning to practice the art to which he had devoted his life.

As for his brother Vincent, the two remained friends, though at a distance. Raymond came to Ottawa to be with Vincent when he was installed as Governor General of Canada in 1952. He showed his brother how to get into his dress uniform and rode beside him in a landau, gazing with slightly mocking approbation at Vincent's braided and beplumed splendour as he proceeded from Rideau Hall to Parliament Hill. Raymond briefly became titular head of the Massey Foundation, but by then he had become too crippled to take an active part in its work, and in any case Vincent had spent the bulk of the foundation's capital establishing Massey College.

Raymond had by then become an American citizen like his Yankee ancestors and the great American political fig-

ures he had portrayed so successfully. But the Canadian arts community remained proud of his achievements, and the next generation of performers would follow in his footsteps. Not only Christopher Plummer, but Richard Easton, Donald Harron, William Hutt, Richard Monette, and Donald Sutherland all sought to make their names in London and New York. Some worked mainly outside their native country, while others returned and achieved success at home. But it was Massey who showed the way and set the pattern.

portrait by Grant Macdonald

32

COMIC CRONIES

Jane Mallett and Donald Harron

The last time I saw Jane Mallett, she was buying olives and cheese for one of her many parties at the "Five Thieves" on Yonge Street just south of Summerhill. Her hair was immaculately coiffed, her eyelashes carefully mascaraed, a brilliant scarlet smile on her face. Her head seemed to rest on the windowsill. Never very tall, she shrank as she got older, the result of osteoporosis. I went in and was greeted with, "Like Alice, I'm smalling," said with a throaty chuckle. But it was emphysema that did her in a few months later. At her funeral at St. James the Less, the theatre world of Toronto turned out in force. She was said to be eighty-five, born in 1899. A prominent lawyer said, "Nonsense, she was ninety." She would not have been the first actress to shave a few years off her age.

Whatever the date, she was born and christened Jean Dawson Keenleyside in London, Ontario, the daughter of an entrepreneurial father whose family had emigrated to Canada a generation earlier, in the 1850s, from Cumberland in northern England. Clifford Keenleyside was a colonel in World War I, a staunch Methodist and writer of religious tracts, who moved his family to Saskatchewan, where he drilled for oil and undertook various other ventures before being wiped out financially in the crash of 1929. Young Jean was the eldest of six children and her father's favourite. He indulged her and encouraged her to read, especially Shakespeare, but he also imbued in her a sense of responsibility for her younger siblings, which was something she never forgot. Colonel Keenleyside was ambitious for his children, and they would all end up having significant careers. Ed became a medical doctor, Pat an architect, and Isabel a high-ranking official at UNRA, delivering powdered milk to starving children in Europe at the end of World War II. Another brother, Paul, was killed in the war. Helen, the youngest sister, married an American theological student who later became an advertising executive and settled in Rye, New York. They remained a close-knit family, visiting back and forth, exchanging opinions and barbed quips. Ed in particular enjoyed teasing Jane:

"I can't come to your party."
"It's the whole family."
"I've got to catch up on the last three issues of Readers Digest."
"I suppose that's where you get your medical information."

Jean Keenleyside came east to study at Victoria College in Toronto in the early 1920s, and it was there that she became a lifelong friend of her fellow student Lester "Mike" Pearson. She was soon involved in productions at Hart House Theatre, which had recently been opened with the patronage and active participation of Vincent Massey. It is not exactly clear why she changed her name

from Jean to Jane at around this time, although for some time she used Jane Aldworth as her stage name. Her earliest success was as Portia in *The Merchant of Venice*, which began at Hart House and toured Ontario, playing in such theatres as the Opera House in Orillia and the Grand Theatre in Kingston. Jane apparently initially saw herself as a tragedienne, but it was as Portia and Viola in *Twelfth Night* that she scored her greatest Shakespearean successes. These young, spirited women disguised as boys and playing tricks on the young men they woo with wit and charm were admirably suited to Jane's gifts of shrewd observation and not so gentle mockery.

Before long Jane became involved in professional theatre, which was still fairly lively in Toronto. She worked in stock at the Victoria Theatre, playing a variety of roles. Young, pretty, and vivacious, she was well suited to the ingénue roles in the light comedies and farces that were popular with the audiences of the day. The producer George Heppy saw her and contracted her to play in his season at the Empire and to go on tour. He also encouraged her to try her luck in New York, where she went in 1926 and played on Broadway. She came back to Toronto to deal with family problems; her son John believes she somewhat resented this in later years, though not enough for her to return to New York. She was in fact

something of a homebody, fastidious as a housekeeper and a dedicated shopper. I sometimes met her at the liquor store, where she would greet friends and neighbours, murmuring as she looked around her, "Ah, the great communion."

In 1925 she had been asked to play the female lead in a production of Arnold Bennett's *The Great Adventure* at Upper Canada College, and it was there that she met Frederick Mallett, who was also in the cast. He was a chemistry master at the boys' school, "an Englishman of the old school," in the words of a contemporary. Mallett had served as a major in the British army in the Great War and may have reminded Jane of her beloved father. They were married in 1926, and although Jane saw no reason to give up her acting career, she rarely worked out of Toronto for any extended period after her marriage. Instead she continued to work at Hart House Theatre as the professional theatres in Toronto melted away with the advent of "the talkies" and the coming of the Great Depression. From that point on she would work professionally as Jane Mallett. Her husband appeared occasionally with her in minor roles; Robertson Davies remembered that he had a certain charm but "a limited bag of theatrical tricks." Jane, however, had plenty of tricks. She and "Freddie" set up house at 81 Lonsdale Avenue, near his school, and Jane briefly did some teaching at the nearby girls' school, Bishop Strachan. Their son John was born in 1932.

In the early 1930s, Jane began performing in a series of revues with the title *Town Tonics* at Hart House Theatre. Originally this was a two-person show featuring Jane and Freddy Manning, an English master at Upper Canada with a strong musical bent. He played for Jane, who wrote most of her own material and occasionally added other performers as needed. The show, which first appeared in 1934, became an annual event and ran into the early 1940s. The shows were directed by Dorothy Goulding, a cousin of Vincent Massey who was just beginning to develop the Toronto Children Players. Her daughter Dorothy-Jane acted as Jane's dresser and prop master and remembers that Jane was a meticulous performer who worked to get every gesture and intonation precisely right, as well as being extremely fastidious about her costumes, right down to wearing the perfect shade of lipstick for every number. But although she could be finicky she was generally good-tempered, and both her colleagues and her audiences loved her.

Revue was to become Jane Mallett's most successful medium. During World War II she used to entertain servicemen at various bases near Toronto and at the Heliconian Club on Hazelton Avenue, a

35

36

Jane as Nature Woman in Town Tonics

centre for artistically inclined women that roughly corresponded to the all-male Arts and Letters Club. When it was obvious the audience wanted more, Jane would run out on stage and reprise an old *Town Tonics* number dredged up from memory on the spur of the moment. It was here that she was first seen by a young RCAF serviceman who was to become an important collaborator, Donald Harron.

When the indomitable Dora Mavor Moore started up her New Play Society, Jane took part in the first season in the tiny 300-seat theatre in the basement of the Royal Ontario Museum. The company led off with an ambitious program of six British and American plays performed for two nights each. Jane's most successful role was Shaw's Candida, with Harron playing her husband, Mavor Morell, although she also played in *Charley's Aunt* and *The Importance of Being Earnest*. In spite of encouraging notices at the end of the season, the financial picture was dire. Nevertheless Dora persevered until, at the end of their third season, her son Mavor came up with the notion of a satirical revue. He cobbled together some of Jane's recycled skits from *Town Tonics*, along with undergraduate sketches written by Harron, bits stolen from *The Army Show* by Peter Mews and Connie Vernon, lyrics written by Tommy Tweed and Lister Sinclair for

radio, and a couple of new numbers, including one about a crusty old farmer visiting "Th'Ex"—the Canadian National Exhibition or CNE.

In the words of its creator Mavor Moore, "*Spring Thaw '48* was a sensation. It was a misbegotten *omnium gatherum* of a show, derivative, gauche and manic, but it was a sensation…. What we had done, as accidentally as we had stumbled into the show, was to provide a whistle for a head of steam. Somehow I must have known that Canadians were bursting to laugh at

37

Jane as a Society Belle in Spring Thaw

themselves." *Spring Thaw* broke attendance records in the 1950s, toured nationally in the 1960s, and became "the longest running annual topical revue in the world."

Jane became the acknowledged star of *Spring Thaw* alongside such comic talents as Eric Christmas, Peter Mews, and later Dave Broadfoot, Rich Little, and of course Don Harron. Jane played a native woman, Nellie Freefoot, and satirized the accents of the country people around her summer cottage near Parry Sound with their talk of "It'ly" and "Yerp" (Europe). The salty wit and sheer stubborn cussedness of these rural characters have provided a rich source of humour for Canadian writers and performers for over a century, and Jane has earned a place at the centre of a chain that stretches from Sam Slick and Stephen Leacock through to Walt Wingfield and the Trailer Park Boys.

It was Jane who told Don that he was

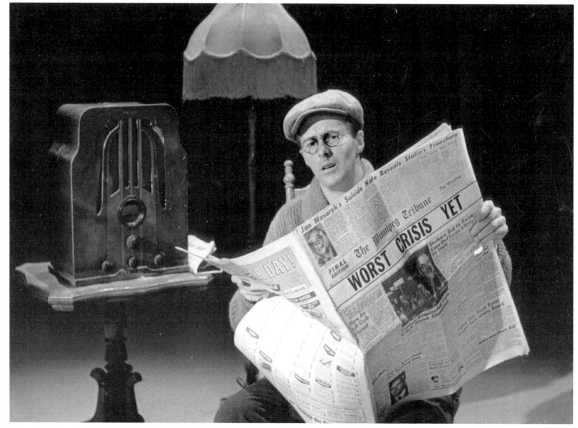

Don Harron in an early incarnation of Charlie Farquharson

38

too young and charming to be a successful comic and advised him to develop a more eccentric character. The result was Charlie Farquharson and later Valerie Rosedale, two personalities that Don inhabited until his recent death. (Or did the two characters inhabit *him*?) Jane continued to collaborate with Don, who wrote sketches for both of them. When a New York engagement fell through, Don suggested they do a revue called *Fall Freeze*, but Dora, whose ambitions were highly classical, nixed the idea.

Don was handsome and quick-witted. He came from a lower-middle-class family but had been a brilliant student at Victoria College, where he participated in theatre and wrote a revue before he enlisted in the Air Force. At the age of ten he was doing stand-up comedy. He began working as a radio actor at age twelve and would go on to work with Andrew Allan. He married a classmate from Vic, Gloria Fisher, and took her to England, where he worked as a BBC comedy writer, played a clown in the film *The Red Shoes* (1948) and acted with both Vivien Leigh and Ralph Richardson. He returned to Canada and played the leading role of Bertram in the first season at Stratford, opposite Irene Worth. He would play a number of other Shakespearean roles: Gremio in *The Taming of the Shrew*, in which he appeared with a set of false buck teeth, as

Don Harron with William Shatner in The Taming of the Shrew *at Stratford 1954*   39

well as Octavius Caesar, Bassanio, and Christian in *Cyrano*, before he was assigned to the minor role of Scroop. He sent a letter to Michael Langham saying "scroop you," and moved on. On Broadway he played leading roles in *Home is the Hero* and *Look Back in Anger.* He adapted *Anne of Green Gables* as a musical for the Confederation Theatre in Prince Edward Island, which is still playing to enthusiastic audiences after fifty seasons.

In spite of their age gap, Jane and Don bonded as a comedy team. Jane's comic skills were based on more than eccentric speech patterns, sudden shifts of inflection, and deft timing. She used her knowledge of human vanity to expose the underlying desires and drives of her characters—to the delight of her audiences. Not that she herself was free of vanity, just that she understood how to exploit it for its comic potential. After the decline of *Spring Thaw* she continued to mine this territory, going into partnership with Harron and Robert Christie to produce *Fine Frenzy* at Hart House Theatre and then starring in *The Crest Revue* at the refurbished movie house on Mt. Pleasant Road.

In the early 1930s, Jane had met Andrew Allan, who described their initial encounter thus: "She was propped up in bed being an adorable convalescent from an attack of pneumonia. The room was filled with admirers, mainly young men. I started being nervous and ended up her slave. I am still her slave." Jane's surviving colleagues, such as William Needles and Joseph Shaw, have similar recollections: "She was magical," or "I adored her." As her nephew David Keenleyside put it, "She had a lot of people in her thrall."

Foremost among these were her husband Freddy, her brother Pat, and her son John, who lived with her and provided physical and emotional support. But although the general impression was that they worshipped her, her son John remembers that she could be critical, caustic, and even vicious in her assessment of others. Like many actors she alternated between "I can't wait till this show closes" and then two days later moaning, "I'll never work again." This would bring on a spate of frantic housecleaning, an activity that always put her in a temper until the phone rang with another offer. The family was expected to tolerate her volatile moods and adapt to her sometimes eccentric schedule. John remembers visiting with his daughters after his marriage and his father saying to the little girls, who were having a fit of giggles, "Shhhh, you don't want to wake the Dragon."

From the earliest years of her marriage, Jane became famous for her parties, first in her house on Lonsdale Road and later at 26 Chestnut Park Drive in Rosedale. In effect she operated a salon in her chic living room, with its elegant French period chairs and a portrait of Jane by Grant Macdonald dominating the forest green walls. The food was excellent, casseroles whipped up by Jane or Pat, who remained living with them, salads made by John. Freddy was rarely in attendance; when he was teaching he insisted that he had to go to bed early, a practice he continued after he retired. There was always plenty of drink; in those days almost everybody drank fairly heavily and smoked even during meals. The guests were mostly actors and mostly men. Andrew Allan, John Drainie, Arch McDonnell, and Max Helpmann were rarely accompanied by their wives, although Jean Tweed, Tommy's wife, was

40

a good friend and could be found on the sofa trading barbs with Jane.

Talk was the principal entertainment and the theatre a central topic, along with politics and a good deal of gossip. Jane was a compulsive talker who emitted a sort of verbal stream-of-consciousness, going off on elliptical tangents, never stopping to explain, assuming her listeners were familiar with the entire cast of characters who peopled her life. Those who couldn't keep up were pronounced "clunks" and dropped, although occasionally Jane would pick out one or two completely random names from the phone book, saying that she didn't want her parties to become "too cliquish." And there was often music provided by one of the guests, particularly Andrew Allan, who was an accomplished pianist.

In the 1940s Andrew stood at the centre of the Toronto theatre world. Born in Scotland, the son of a clergyman, he had traveled to Australia as a child and then spent his teenage years in Peterborough, where he worked for the *Examiner* under Robertson Davies, before coming to Toronto to work as an actor and radio announcer. He then spent several years in England before returning to Canada in the early days of the war, during which his ship was torpedoed in the North Atlantic. Soon after his arrival he went to Vancouver, where he began working for the CBC as a radio produc-

er. In 1943 he was sent to Toronto to begin producing "definitive radio drama," and the next year he inaugurated a Sunday-night series called *Stage 44.*

This program would continue for twelve years. Early recognized as original and indeed ground-breaking by the intelligentsia, it became in time highly popular and second only to the Saturday-night hockey games in attracting an audience. Although there were adaptations of classical plays, much of the material was original. Allan developed a stable of writers that included Budd Knapp, Fletcher Markle, Len Peterson,

41

Jane tears her hair out

Joseph Schull, Lister Sinclair, and Tommy Tweed. Allan's idea was to do a mixed bag of work, alternating hard-hitting dramas of social concern with satiric comedies, mysterious fantasies, and even the occasional melodrama. He fought skillfully and tirelessly with his political and bureaucratic masters for the freedom to handle whatever topics he wished, and one of his last dramas, *The Investigator*, was such an obvious take on the American witch-hunting senator Joseph McCarthy that it may have contributed to the decline of the *Stage* series. In his heyday Allan was looked up to by his colleagues for his wide-ranging intelligence and articulate conversation. Like Jane he was exceedingly sociable and a great attender of parties. He could often be seen late at night at his special table at the Bloor Street bistro *Chez Paree*, surrounded by friends and acolytes, pronouncing on a variety of topics.

For his *Stage* series Allan built up a repertory company of fine actors. From Vancouver he recruited Bernard Braden, John and Claire Drainie, Larry McCance, and Aileen Seaton. In Toronto he quickly gathered together Lorne Greene, Frank Peddie, Ruth Springford, Tommy Tweed, and of course Jane Mallett and Don Harron. Members of this highly accomplished group met every Saturday morning at the old Margaret Eaton Hall on McGill Street

to begin rehearsing a new show that would be broadcast live to air the following evening. In addition to the actors standing in front of microphones reading from scripts, there was an orchestra providing music from an original score written and conducted by Lucio Agostini. Allan recalled in his memoir that there were very few glitches and that the group was highly disciplined. They became comrades-in-art, adept at covering for each other. But Larry McCance told me there were sometimes high-jinks; on one occasion he looked away from his script for a minute only to discover that John Drainie had put a match to it and his lines were rapidly going up in smoke.

In 1940, Jane had an operation on her larynx to remove a node. She was warned that she must not talk for at least two weeks. This proved impossible, of course, and she developed the characteristically husky timbre that her listeners will vividly remember, a sound once described by Aileen Seaton as being like "whisky running over broken glass." Although initially horrified by this phenomenon, Jane accommodated herself to it with her usual ability to see the funny side of her predicament. In fact, this throaty voice became one of her greatest assets, particularly for radio work, because it allowed the listener to be sure which character was speaking.

In the early 1950s, the CBC decided

to venture into television. This involved a new hierarchy of producers and directors. Not all of the actors whose skills had been developed in radio made the transition to the new medium as easily as Jane. She had continued to do stage work throughout the 1930s at Hart House Theatre, winning awards at the Dominion Drama Festival. Jane earned money for her radio work but kept a foot in the amateur camp when it came to the legitimate theatre. She continued to work wherever there were opportunities. In the early years of Dora Mavor Moore's New Play Society, Jane, like all the other actors, was paid five dollars a performance. This may have allowed her to call herself a professional, but even in the 1940s it was hardly a living wage.

By the late 1950s she was too long in the tooth to play ingénues, so she took to doing character roles. She had a natural

Jane with Jack Creley in Spring Thaw

quality that made her ideal for playing farmwives and middle-class mothers. She had already become a CBC radio fixture as a farmwife on the daily soap opera *The Craigs* and as Aunt Mary on *John and Judy*, two extremely popular series. But she could also command the aristocratic air required for Oscar Wilde's Lady Bracknell, Julia in T.S. Eliot's *The Cocktail Party*, Lady Kitty in Somerset Maugham's *The Circle*, and Mme. Desmermortes in Jean Anouilh's *Ring Round the Moon*, all of which she would play for television. In these roles she emerged not as a formidable harridan, but instead she attacked them with a sort of good-natured but mischievous glee. One of the things that made Jane such an attractive performer is that she always seemed to be enjoying herself. Between 1960 and 1980 she played dramatic roles for producers Robert Allen, Daryl Duke, David Gardner, Mario Prizek, and Ronald Weyman, had an ongoing role in W.O. Mitchell's *Jake and the Kid*, made guest appearances on *The Time of Your Life* and *The King of Kensington*, and had a sitcom written for her called *Travels with Aunt Jane*. And as if that weren't enough she did commercials for everything from Bell Canada to Tums.

A trademark of Jane's public persona was a sort of lovable ditziness. Don Harron compared her to Beatrice Lillie, but in many ways she was closer to

Travels with Aunt Jane *CBC television.*

Lucille Ball and, like that canny businesswoman, her organizational skills were considerable. Don had returned to Canada after making several films and television shows, including *Twelve O'clock High* (1949) and *The Man from U.N.C.L.E.* in Hollywood, and 17 years of performing in *Hee Haw* on U.S. television. He hosted the CBC radio show *Morningside* for five years and appeared in Canadian films such as *The Hospital* (1971). He had divorced Gloria and married first Virginia Leith and then Catherine McKinnon, a singer whom he

met when she was playing in *Anne of Green Gables.* The marriage was stormy; Catherine complained that she never knew whether she was married to Don or Charlie.

As she grew older, Jane became more interested in working to help her fellow actors. Early on in the 1930s she was one of the principal organizers of RATS (Radio Artists of Toronto Society), a rudimentary trade union that eventually evolved into ACTRA (Association of Canadian Radio and Television Artists), which Jane continued to support as an executive and advisor. In New York she had become a member of Actors' Equity, but she was convinced that Canada needed its own separate organization, and so she was instrumental in helping set up Canadian Actors' Equity in the early 1950s.

Jane also founded the Actors' Fund of Canada, which was designed to help members of her profession who were in financial need. Each year she organized a benefit in support of the Fund, cajoling her many talented friends into donating their services. Initially she managed the fund herself, and when asked how she managed to keep track of the finances she said, "Oh, it's very simple, dear. You see, whatever comes in goes right out again." Like ACTRA and Equity, the Actors' Fund is still active and was responsible for establishing PAL (the Performing Arts Lodge) on Toronto's Esplanade, which today houses many aging thespians. Jane used her craftily cultivated personality as a bubbly scatter-brain to override nay-sayers and bureaucrats, often arriving a bit late for meetings and excusing herself with some such explanation as "I'm sorry but I was cornered by a squirrel in Queen's Park." Whimsy to combat the chronic whiners.

Neither Don nor Jane was active in politics, although Charlie often commented on the national scene: "Every guvmint estimit incloods an extry estimit of how much more it's gonna cost than yer ferst estimit. That's how come they always leeve this big deficit on the floor of yer House. And a deficit is what you've got wen you haven't got as much as if you jist had nothin'. If we tried any of this, we'd end up in jail. But the guvmint gits rid of its detts by Nashnullizing them. That's like the alky-holick who solved his problem by poring the booze in all of his bottles into one big container. Himself."

Jane was a whole-hearted supporter of Canadian organizations and Canadian independence. She eventually became quite anti-American, deploring the antics of Senator McCarthy and Richard Nixon, which led to some major squabbles with her American relatives. Jane continued acting into her early eighties on radio and television and in films. She

45

was honoured as "the first lady of Canadian theatre," received the John Drainie Award and the Order of Canada, more for her "humanitarian" work than her artistic prowess. If she was sometimes cranky at home, she never let up on appearances.

Don continued to embody Charlie Farquharson to the point that anyone meeting him might have thought that he really was that character. He published nine books supposedly written by Charlie, which sold well and earned him the Order of Canada. In 2012 he published an autobiography, *My Double Life*, in which he discusses not only his career but his three unsuccessful marriages and pays tribute to his fourth and final wife, Claudette Garneau, whom he had married that year. At 90 he had slowed down

Don Harron and his alter ego Charlie Farquharson

Jane Mallett and Donald Harron

somewhat but was still vigorous and full of wisecracks until his death in early 2015. ("I was born in bed with a naked woman and hope to exit the same way.")

As Jane grew older the parties became less frequent, the circle of actors who had surrounded Andrew Allan in "the golden age of radio" gradually melted away, but Jane continued to dress stylishly, usually in beige, brown or green, the colours she felt suited her best. She would say that she couldn't afford all the accessories needed to complement other colours. Appearance had always been important to her. Photographs show her dressed up for radio broadcasts as though she were appearing as a guest on television. Her golden hair was always carefully coiffed, her makeup meticulously applied, even when she was relaxing at her cottage on Blackstone Lake near Parry Sound. "You never know when somebody's going to recognize you," she would say. A family friend once said, "I

Jane glamorous to the end

doubt if even Freddy ever saw her without her maquillage." She was an actress to the core and to the end.

After her death in 1984, a Toronto theatre was named after her. The city refused to support this initiative, but the money was raised by her peers. At a benefit, such as she herself might have organized at her old stomping ground the Heliconian Club, tributes were given by Ontario's first female lieutenant-governor Pauline McGibbon, as well as by her old friends and colleagues Araby Lockhart and Don Harron. "I don't expect any Canadian will ever have a fuller theatrical career than Jane Mallett." "She had a heart like a hotel." "She taught us to laugh at ourselves."

48

COMEDIEN CANADIEN

Gratien Gélinas

When I was a teenager acting with the Toronto Children Players, our director Dorothy Goulding would sometimes recommend that we go to see a play that was currently being presented at the Royal Alexandra Theatre on King Street. These recommendations were infrequent, but the first one I remember was to see a French-Canadian actor who was playing in *Tit-Coq*, a piece he had written himself and originally played in Quebec in French, but now it was touring across Canada in an English version.

It was unlike anything I had ever encountered, funny and sad at the same time, with a special flavour that I would come to understand later was quintessentially French. It concerned a young soldier, a very ordinary little guy, a bastard (in the literal sense) who had been brought up by nuns and later Catholic brothers. As a young man he is ashamed of his illegitimacy but meets a young girl, Marie-Ange, and falls in love with her, which brightens his life. Having no par-

ticular prospects, he enlists in the army during World War II, thinking it might be a way to better himself. He is defensive but enterprising, with a cocky attitude covering his underlying insecurity, hence his nickname, Tit-Coq (literally "little rooster"). He returns home from the war to find that Marie-Ange, under pressure from her family, has married an older man. He is heartbroken and bitter, all the more so because he realizes that Marie-Ange is still in love with him. He faces up to a lonely and solitary future.

In the French text Tit-Coq speaks in the accents to be heard in the streets of

50

'Tit-Coq, the little rooster

Montreal, a sort of precursor of *joual*. Gratien Gélinas, the writer and leading actor of *Tit-Coq*, pioneered the use of Québécois French in his work at a time when most of the actors in Montreal performed in classical French, imitating the elevated language used at the Comédie française in Paris.

Gélinas picked up on the work of the chanteuse La Bolduc, who wrote and sang songs in a racy French idiom and became the first Québécois singing star, a sort of French-Canadian cross between Bessie Smith and Kate Smith, but with a tarter and more immediate sense of humour than either of them. She grew up in the Gaspé, came to Montreal and worked as a maid, married a plumber, and had six children. When her husband could not work because of a back injury, she began performing songs of her own invention, dealing with the most ordinary aspects of her life: shopping at the grocery store, advising her young daughter on how to please her husband, commenting on current events, the Dionne quintuplets or the current elections. She started singing on Sunday evenings at the Monument national in Montreal and eventually toured most of French-speaking North America: Quebec, New Brunswick, Northern Ontario, Windsor, northern New York state, and Maine. She began in church basements but eventually sold thousands of records and had her own radio show before her untimely death in 1944.

When Gélinas took *Tit-Coq* on the road in English-speaking Canada, he found a way of rendering this speech in colloquial English that paralleled the slang of the plateau in Montreal. *Tit-Coq* was an enormous hit first in Quebec and subsequently in major cities across the country. He then took it to New York. There had already been a successful play about a Quebec family, *The Happy Time*, in a Broadway theatre, based on the novel by Robert Fontaine. It was considerably more sentimental than *Tit-Coq* and was eventually turned into a musical. Gélinas's play ran for some weeks in Chicago and then decamped to the Broadhurst in Manhattan's theatre district, where it closed after a few performances, largely due to problems of financing exacerbated by a dispute between the William Morris Agency, which represented Gélinas, and the Shubert organization, which owned the theatre. Gélinas returned to Montreal with a deep sense of failure and sank into a depression. However, in 1953 he succeeded in making a movie based on his script, which he co-directed and starred in with a cast of French- and English-speaking actors that included Corinne Conley, Juliette Béliveau, Jean Duceppe, Monique Miller, and Denise Pelletier.

Gratien Gélinas was born in the town

51

of St-Tite in 1909. Not long after his birth his parents decided to move to Montreal. Their life there was precarious and their earnings meagre. But they found ways to amuse themselves: Gratien's mother Genève had a lively wit and engaged in salty repartee while his father was a storyteller. She encouraged Gratien to learn snatches of poetry and short monologues that he would recite whenever he had the opportunity. Already at an early age he evidenced a deep need for approbation and sought attention wherever he could get it. One Sunday afternoon his parents entertained a notary, Jean-Pierre Laframboise, who encouraged Gratien to recite his entire repertoire. He praised the young man, and it is probable that this was the moment when he decided to become an entertainer.

His parents had many bitter disagreements, and Genève eventually demanded a legal separation. In order to avoid paying for her upkeep, Gratien's father ran away to the United States. Genève insisted that her children tell everyone their father was dead. Gratien's sense of insecurity over this lie, not the only one he would perpetrate during his lifetime, made him introverted and solitary as a teenager. His sense of shame would haunt him and surface in the actions of some of the characters he created in his plays.

His attitude brightened when he enrolled at the Collège de Montréal. He began in a program of classics, but when the Depression hit in 1929 he switched to commercial studies. While at college he began appearing in amateur productions. With some of his fellow students he fell under the influence of Père Legault, a curé who encouraged and directed young would-be performers. Gratien's professional career began as a radio actor in 1936 in Robert Choquette's serial *Le curé de village*, going to the studio at nights while he still worked during the day. At about this time he married Simone Lalonde, a young teacher who was pious and soft-spoken. Their marriage was harmonious at the beginning. Simone understood Gratien's need for approval and praise and supported him, although he was often impatient and had terrible temper tantrums.

Before long he was appearing on radio in the character of Fridolin, a young handyman, a sort of *naif savant* who stood up to and exposed the corrupt and self-serving people in the *Grande Noirceur* era of Maurice Duplessis, the premier of Quebec, who pretended to be amused by these critiques of his autocratic regime. Wearing knee-socks and suspenders over a faded *Canadiens* hockey sweater, Fridolin encountered a constant barrage of problems and setbacks but was

texts were his own handiwork.

The shows were an annual event from 1938 to 1946. In that latter year Gélinas went to Chicago to join other comics in a show, *Pharmacie St. Lazare*, which confirmed and consolidated his own self-confidence and his reputation as an accomplished comedian. Some of the Fridolin sketches were revived in the 1950s when I was able to see Gélinas himself perform in this by then famous persona. I didn't get all the topical references, but I enjoyed the antics and *drôlerie* of this inventive performer, part clown, part stand-up comic, a sort of Québécois Charlie Chaplin as he punctured the hypocrisies and chicaneries of his compatriots.

53

Fridolin, the street-smart orphan of the Plateau

incurably optimistic. He came to be seen by his compatriots as a kind of emblem of the *"survivance"* of the downtrodden but indomitable *habitant*. His targets included politicians, moneymen, Anglos, and clerics. By 1938 he was performing regularly in a series of revues, *les Fridolinades*, at the Monument national in Montreal. Gélinas not only played the main character but also directed other actors in sketches, songs, and monologues. He collaborated with other writers but always claimed that the

Fridolin holds a political rally

Essentially Gélinas created a single character for himself, one that he would play in various incarnations throughout his career as a stage actor. This personage was complex, although he seemed simple. He was a shrewd observer of the world around him, curious and clear-eyed, accepting but not uncritical. Underlying this was a belief in a divine order that was questioned but never abandoned, that combined both doubt and wonder, a recognition that not everything that happened could be explained or justified, but had to be accepted.

In the early 1940s Gélinas inaugurated a film company, Excelsior, and in 1942 produced his first feature, a parody version of Dumas's *La dame aux camélias*, in which he turned the story into a comedy; the characters were not aristocrats but spoke in Québécois patois. Although the film was not a financial success, it was the beginning of cinematic comedy in Quebec and would pave the way for such comic masterpieces as *Mon oncle Antoine* by Claude Jutra and *Les Barbares* and *The Decline of the American Empire* by Denys Arcand. However, Gratien soon abandoned cinema and took the *Fridolinades* on tour.

Encouraged by his success with the *Fridolinades*, in 1957 Gélinas founded a theatre company, *la Comédie-Canadienne*, which played in the Théâtre Gayety in Montreal and was initially funded by Dow Brewery. The company was dedicated to doing original plays by Québécois authors and was designed to contribute to the growing sense of a national sensibility. Gélinas's timing was auspicious, for the Quiet Revolution was waiting in the wings and a number of up-and-coming playwrights provided new scripts, beginning with Marcel Dubé's *Un simple soldat*. Other original creations followed: *Le gibet* by Jacques Languirand, *L'auberge des morts subites* by Felix Leclerc, *Le cri de l'engoulevent* and *Les temples* by Guy Dufresne, *Double jeu* and *Medium saignant* by Françoise Loranger, *Moi et l'autre* by Gilles Richer, and *L'Osstidcho King Size* by Yvon Deschamps and Robert Charlebois.

In 1956, Gélinas, in company with Jean Gascon, led a company of Montreal actors to the Stratford Festival in Ontario, where they embodied the elegance and hauteur of the French court in their dazzling blue and silver finery facing the scruffier, more down-to-earth English led by Christopher Plummer as the young King Henry V. In reviewing the production I wrote, "the opposing armies were like water and oil, ale and champagne, roast beef and pheasant under glass." Gélinas played the ailing, half-mad French king, a figure proud but pathetic in his dotage. In the same season he did a hilarious turn as Doctor

54

'Tit-coq with Huguette Oligny as Marie-Ange in the film version

Caius in *The Merry Wives of Windsor*, skewering an imaginary adversary on his twirling rapier and bringing down the house. Gélinas never returned to Stratford, but Gascon would go on to lead the company, infusing it with a strong dash of Gallic élan and introducing it to the comedies of Molière, who soon became established as its second major playwright.

Back in Montreal, Gélinas was influential in helping to set up the National Theatre School to train students in both French and English. Originally all students took classes together and the hope was that graduates would combine the verve of the French and the precision of the English theatrical traditions. But not long after its founding this dream was shattered by the separatist sentiments of many of the faculty members, and the school was split into two sections which from then on would have little contact with each other.

In 1959, Gélinas debuted his new play *Bousille et les justes*, in which he played another simple soul, an orphan, religious, handicapped, a former alcoholic, confronting the rigidity and malevolence of the members of a violent family dominated by the Catholic church and led by an hysterical mother, a forerunner of the formidable women that would soon after people the work of Michel Tremblay. Gélinas apparently got the idea for the

Gratien as the French King in Henry V *at Stratford*

Dr. Caius in The Merry Wives of Windsor

piece sitting in a restaurant listening to the squabbles of a duplicitous and bad-tempered family. In the play, Bousille has witnessed a fight in which a man is killed and is forced to lie to the court in order to prevent his bullying cousin from being convicted. Under extreme pressure he does so, but after the trial is over he commits suicide. The play is highly melodramatic but was a huge success, in large measure because of Gélinas's complex and sympathetic performance. Again the play was translated into English and achieved over 700 performances on a tour from Charlottetown and Halifax to Vancouver and Seattle.

During the run of *Bousille*, Gratien's wife Simone underwent a serious operation in the United States. Although she recovered, it left her weak and fragile. She had devoted her life to providing a home for Gratien and their children. She was well aware, however, that Gratien had many mistresses (including one of my cousins, who was a script assistant at the CBC in Toronto; he was apparently a gentle and accommodating lover). Gratien revived his fading union with Simone for a time but also maintained an ongoing relationship with the actress Huguette Oligny, to whom he had given the role of Marie-Ange in *Tit-Coq*, replacing Muriel Guilbault. In 1967 Simone died and Gratien and Huguette became a couple, not living together but spending a great deal of time in each other's company. Their relationship was stormy but passionate, and after Huguette divorced her husband they would eventually marry.

When Radio Canada began producing television shows, Gélinas soon became involved in *Les quat'fers en l'air*, in which he played a barber in a working-class neighbourhood in Montreal. Always a slow study and a perfectionist, he could not acclimatize himself to the rapid pace and constant pressure of this new medium, and his career in it was short-lived. He returned to the stage and wrote and performed in a new play, *Hier les enfants dansaient*. In it he played a father who was a federalist confronting his sons who were engaged in terrorist activities. It was the era of the FLQ, whose members were blowing up mailboxes in the streets of Montreal, while in Ottawa Pierre Trudeau was combatting them with the War Measures Act.

For the first time, Gélinas's new play was not a critical success. Although it was dealing with contemporary issues, his former audience was aging and the young people of Quebec were looking for new forms of expression. Once again Gélinas translated his play and took it on the road to English Canada, where it was more enthusiastically received than in his home province, probably because the English-speaking population was curious

57

Gratien as the father confronts his real-life son Yves in Yesterday the Children Were Dancing

58

about the violent actions in a province that they had always thought of as backward and subservient.

Gélinas continued to be the director of la Comédie, but it went into deficit, partly because the audience was turning more and more to the newly formed Théâtre du nouveau monde, led by Jean Gascon and Jean-Louis Roux. Meanwhile la Comédie became more of a rental space, and many of the rising chansonniers of the time, Claude Léveillée, Gilles Vigneault, Pauline Julien, and Claude Gauthier, performed there to an enthusiastic audience.

Discouraged and bitter at the lack of

enthusiasm for his latest play, Gratien decided to quit the theatre and took up a post at the newly instituted SDICC (Société de développement de l'industrie cinématographique canadienne), which would eventually evolve into Telefilm Canada. As president he worked assiduously at his new job and did much to encourage emerging actors and writers. But the theatre was in his blood. He contemplated a revival of the Fridolin revues but instead turned to writing a new play, *La passion de Narcisse Mondoux*. It was a somewhat sentimental piece about the love affair between a widow and a retired plumber, a character who was a sort of aged Fridolin who was beginning to lose his memory. Of course Gratien would play Narcisse, and he had written the part of the widow for Huguette, who he felt was slipping away from him. He would reconquer her affections by writing a wonderful role for her. Although the new play was considered somewhat slight, he was happy to be back onstage. But this work proved to be somewhat prophetic: Gratien began to lose his memory and eventually succumbed to senile dementia. He died at his home in Oka in 1999, at the age of 89.

Before his death much of his work was revived by other performers in both French and English Canada. He was acknowledged as the grandfather of Québécois theatre, a brilliant actor who was a true pioneer in working onstage in radio and film and television, speaking the language of ordinary people. Not only did he show the way by creating theatre that reflected the realities of the life of his compatriots, but his vision was marked by complexity, humour, skepticism, and above all humanity. His contribution to the vibrant artistic cultural scene in Quebec was enormous and lasting, and in his heyday his public adored him.

Sometime in the 1980s I was invited to a lunch by the Toronto Critics' Circle to honour Gratien Gélinas. He sat at a table with Huguette Oligny, smiling benignly. He spoke briefly and simply about his love of the theatre and the pleasure it had given him to be able to perform throughout his long career. Not long after, he wrote in his notebook the following lines, which express both his humility and his awareness of his own God-given talent, as well as the deep-seated Christian belief that, in spite of his criticism of the venality and repression he saw in many clerics, permeated his perception of the world he inhabited:

« ... j'ai jeté un coup d'œil sur le tableau de ma vie, et j'ai vu, dans la colonne des péchés d'omission, les œuvres que je n'ai pas écrites, mais que vous m'aviez donné le talent et la mission d'écrire. C'était magnifique, Mon

Dieu. Ça m'a donné comme un coup dans le ventre !

C'est pas le moment de me vanter devant vous, Mon Dieu, mais sans le savoir, j'avais presque du génie... Savez-vous, j'aurais jamais pensé que ça pouvait arriver à un Canadien. »

"Glancing over the picture of my life I saw in the column of my sins of omission, the works that I didn't write, but that you gave me the talent and the mission to write. That was magnificent, my God. It gave me a punch in the gut.

This is not the moment for me to boast to you, my God, but I have almost touched genius. Do you realize I would never have thought this could be accomplished by a French-Canadian?"

Fridolin surrounded by a bevy of girls

GREAT KATE

Kate Reid

In her elegant Forest Hill sitting room, Sis Bunting Weld, Kate Reid's friend from early childhood, hands me a silver-framed photograph of some dozen little girls who attended Miss Lightbourne's School in Oakville, circa 1936. I fail to recognize Sis, but in the back row, the huge brown eyes peering provocatively from beneath lowered brows, and the slightly pouty mouth, belong unmistakably to Kate Reid. "Flirting with the camera, even then," laughs Sis. "She always knew how to get attention."

Kate Reid was the product of a passionate affair between Babby Moore, the daughter of a prominent London, Ontario, family and Colonel Walter Reid of the Bengal Lancers. As a result he left his English wife and his position in the Indian Army. Kate was born in 1930, and soon after her parents settled in the town of Oakville on the north shore of Lake Ontario, a small upscale community peopled mainly by British people of sporting interests, particularly equestrian. They lived in a house on Second Street, a few doors from the Bunting family. She and Sis, who was slightly younger, became friends in early childhood and visited each other's houses, often staying overnight. Their frequent companion was Sis's older brother Pierce, who would follow his father into the brokerage business and eventually become president of the Toronto Stock Exchange.

Kate's father died when she was ten, and afterwards she spent even more time with the Buntings, becoming almost one of the family, even after they moved to a farm, the better to indulge Alf Bunting's passion for horses. Kate did not share this enthusiasm, and indeed a club foot ruled out participation in most sports, even after it was successfully corrected by surgery. But Kate loved to be part of the Buntings' family outings. "Kate always loved to shock people," Sis recalls, "Once, I remember, we went on a sleigh ride and Kate fell off the back of the sleigh. She pretended to have amnesia and had everyone in a high old state before she confessed it was just a trick."

When Sis's mother became increasingly incapacitated by arthritis, the two girls went into boarding at Havergal College in north Toronto. At one point they were not supposed to speak to each other, because Kate was in a higher grade, but they went home for weekends, driven by their parents and those of their friends Judy Blaikie and Sheila Dunwoody, who formed a carpool, so they had plenty of opportunity to giggle and gossip. "Kate often teased me," Sis remembers. "She really knew how to get at me. But she was like an older sister and I was devoted to her." The devotion would prove to be life-long. At school there was not much drama, but Kate acted in classroom plays while Sis stage-managed. "I knew I couldn't compete, but I wanted to be part of it." Sis would go on supporting and befriending artists, sitting on boards,

and giving fabulous parties for the next fifty years.

Both girls began to have active social lives, initially dating the brothers of friends. Because Kate's father was dead, and Sis's mother was an invalid, their headmistress bent the rules to allow them to attend fraternity parties, sometimes even in midweek. They would both continue to follow the call of romance in the years ahead. Kate left Havergal and a life bounded by the niceties of the upper middle class at the age of fifteen, to study speech at the Royal Conservatory of Music, then housed in an elegant Italianate building at College and University. She came under the influence of the elocution teacher Clara Salisbury Baker and worked with Robert Gill, the newly appointed director of Hart House Theatre, who offered lessons in acting, the first serious professional theatre training in Toronto since the end of the war.

Gill was impressed by Kate's seriousness and intensity, and although she was not really a university student he cast her as a member of the Roman mob in *Julius Caesar*. The cast included Donald Davis, David Gardner, William Hutt, and George McCowan. Gardner, who was playing Mark Antony, remembers that she told him he stepped on her toe in the middle of his funeral oration. "I didn't want to spoil your big moment so I kept my mouth shut." Utterly charmed, he embraced her. "It was

our first hug, but not our last." His eyes twinkled mischievously.

Kate must have stood out even in this crowd of student luminaries, because soon afterwards, the adventurous and enterprising young actress Anna Cameron organized a group of Gill's students—including William Hutt, Eric House, and Ted Follows—to form an ad hoc company, and under Henry Kaplan's direction they mounted a production of Lillian Hellman's *Another Part of the Forest*, which they entered in the

Kate as Mme. Ranevskaya with Frances Hyland as Varya in The Cherry Orchard

Dominion Drama Festival at the Royal Alexandra in 1949. The D.D.F. was then the biggest event in Canadian theatre, and all the drama buffs of Toronto turned out for it. Kate appeared as Birdie and greatly impressed the British adjudicator Phillip Hope Wallace, who gave her the award for best actress.

In his next season Gill cast Kate in *Crime and Punishment*, an adaptation of the Dostoievsky novel by Rodney Ackland, which John Gielgud had produced with great success in London. She took on a role that had been played by Edith Evans in London and Lillian Gish on Broadway and carried it off with panache. Michael Tait, who played in the production, remembers Kate "thrashing around in the wings, getting ready to perform. She was playing the consumptive mother. She coughed a good deal and even spat blood." I saw Kate for the first time in this play and was struck not only by her bravura performance but also by her sad, haunted eyes and the sense of utter hopelessness she projected.

This performance led Gill to cast her as Nina in *The Seagull*, the most complex and volatile of all Chekhov's disappointed young women. In this role she travelled from a keen and spirited anticipation of life to a state of forlorn and damaged determination, exhibiting an extraordinary range for a girl still in her teens. She won the hearts not only of her

63

audience but also of the actor playing Treplov, David Gardner, who admits to having had "a huge crush on Kate" and would remain her friend for life. Again I was struck by her bravery and vulnerability. She was the finest Nina I have ever seen, including Vanessa Redgrave. In this performance Kate foreshadowed the whole arc of her own career, the eager appetite for life, the headlong throwing of herself into the maelstrom of the artists' world, the fierce and desperate drive to keep going, no matter what obstacles and reversals rose to block her. Over the years she would memorably portray most of Chekhov's women, notably Masha in *The Three Sisters* and Ranevskaya in *The Cherry Orchard*. Gill saw her potential, and although his own taste embraced the "glamour acting" that was exemplified by Katherine Cornell, Lynn Fontanne, and Maria Callas, he recognized the raw talent of Kate Reid and showcased it right at the beginning of her career.

At the same time Kate performed in a radio play written by Ronald Bryden and James Eayrs and directed by Henry Kaplan. Bryden remembered her quick, intuitive take on her role and the tremendous energy with which she threw herself into it. She had gained confidence from her work on campus, though she still had little formal training. She relied on instinct and native wit, as she would

do throughout her career. Most of Gill's actors had limited technique in those early days. After his first year in Toronto the director was too busy mounting four shows a year to continue giving students instruction, and many of them were not overly enthusiastic about extracurricular workouts for which they got no academic credit. William Hutt once remarked, "Gill threw us in at the deep end and those who needed reassurance turned to alcohol." Kate would follow this path, but not just yet.

Instead she joined forces with Anna Cameron and Barbara Hamilton and headed to New York to work with Herbert Bergdorf, a guru following the Stanislavsky tradition. She attracted the attention of his wife, Uta Hagen, who took her on as a student. Hagen was demanding and outspoken, given to telling her students they were lazy, sloppy, and had no place in the theatre. Her classes were conducted with a strict Teutonic rigour that often left students in tears or sent them away to try their luck in other spheres. Kate was less than a devoted disciple, but she soon began to get work in American television and stopped taking classes. But Hagen must have seen something in the young Canadian that she respected, for Kate would later play the matinees when Hagen created the character of Martha in the enormously successful Broadway

run of Edward Albee's *Who's Afraid of Virginia Woolf?* in 1962.

Kate returned to Toronto, where she already knew many of the key actors who were bringing professional theatre to life in the 1950s. She was invited to work in summer stock in Peterborough, where she acquired a husband, Michael Sadlier, the young Irish producer of the company. She also bagged a major role in a new play by Robertson Davies, *At My Heart's Core*, considered by many critics his most successful theatrical work. With Sadlier and a group of fellow Canadian actors she traveled to Bermuda, where they mounted a season of comedies and Broadway hits: Sherwood's *The Petrified Forest*, in which she played the tough barmaid Gabby; and Synge's *The Playboy of the Western World*, in which she proved a fiery and passionate Pegeen Mike. Kate enjoyed the civilized British ambience of the island and the company of fellow actors Barbara Hamilton, Charmion King, Eric House, and the young Christopher Plummer, who remembers her as "a combination of finishing-school deb, tomboy, Mother Earth and imp." Kate and her mother Babby hung out with Plummer at "21," a smart seaside restaurant in Hamilton, where they consumed quantities of vodka and sang into the wee hours of the night. One morning Kate and Chris engaged in a passionate embrace until she broke out laughing

and Chris retreated, his libido deflated. But they would remain close friends and playmates. This was a happy time for Kate, even though her marriage was short-lived; Sadlier and Kate divorced when he took up with Maxine Samuels.

Kate played in other summer theatres, taking the title role of the ditsy wife in the Broadway hit *Claudia*, directed by Brian Doherty, at Niagara-on the-Lake and in a variety of plays for the Straw Hat Players when Murray and Donald Davis set up shop in the cottage country of Muskoka. Like the Davis boys, Kate could rely on some financial support from her family and so was not forced to wait on tables but could instead keep acting, even when financial rewards were minimal. Brought up in polite society, she could portray aristocrats and debutantes; because her family had a close connection with England, the speech patterns and vocabulary of Shaw, Coward, and Rattigan were easily manageable. (It is interesting to note how many of the most successful Canadian actresses in Kate's generation had English parents: Jackie Burroughs, Clare Coulter, Fiona Reid, Janet and Susan Wright.) But Kate's immediacy, her gritty sense of humour, and her gutsy appetite for life were all her own. She also had a broad range: she could be light and sparkling or soft and sensual. In one summer season she tackled the poet-

65

ic invalid Elizabeth in *The Barretts of Wimpole Street*, the edgy heroine Ruth Gordon had created for herself in *Year Ago*, and the dim flapper Jackie in Noël Coward's *Hay Fever*.

During the winters Kate worked regularly at the CBC. The late 1950s marked a turning point in the Corporation's evolution; their justly admired productions of radio drama were beginning to be superseded by the tenuous efforts of early Canadian television. Kate worked for the legendary radio directors Andrew Allan and Esse Ljungh but also appeared in early TV dramas. The stable of ambitious young directors included Robert Allen, Paul Almond, Mavor Moore, George McCowan, Silvio Narrizano, and Mario Prizek, and Kate worked for all of them. She played roles in original Canadian dramas but also in the works of classical and contemporary writers from Ibsen to Giraudoux, Brecht to Montherlant. These live productions were usually broadly histrionic and often technically shaky, but they afforded Kate the opportunity to extend her craft. Over the years she would take on a broad range of roles, from Mother Courage in 1965 to Nellie McClung in 1978. One of her most notable creations was the matriarch Adeline Whiteoak in Timothy Findley's confusingly chopped-up screen version of Mazo de la Roche's family saga. Kate played this sharp-

tongued, domineering Irish aristocrat from her arrival in Canada as a young wife to her final days as a centenarian with the salty vigour and perverse relish that were among her specialties, and she gave the series a tang of emotional truth it badly needed.

During the early 1950s Kate performed regularly in productions at the Crest Theatre, run by the Davis brothers. Her first appearance was in September 1956 in the title role in Colette's *Gigi*, before the musical starring Leslie Caron surfaced. Kate played opposite the Halifax-born actor Austin Willis, and their onstage romance was paralleled by an offstage courtship, which would soon lead to marriage. Willis was a handsome actor and a man with a great deal of easy-going charm. Kate lured him from the arms of the flamboyant and much-courted Montreal actress Joy Lafleur, a romantic victory that no doubt buttressed her sometimes shaky self-confidence. Anna Cameron remembers that Kate was "often disparaging of her own looks." This may have been rooted in her childhood deformity, even though it had been corrected, or simply in the fact that she was not a conventional beauty. It certainly steered her toward roles in which she could display an active and sparky personality rather than being a passive recipient of adoration.

Kate and Austin set up house on

In The Rainmaker *with Robert Sherriff at the Crest Theatre*

Chaplin Crescent, then on Douglas Drive, and later on Binscarth Road as their fortunes grew. They produced two children, Reid and Robin, and entertained the theatrical community, their hospitality rivalling that of the Davises and Jane Mallett, though the Reid-Willis house was more a place to drop in for a cocktail at sundown than an artistic salon. Many of us dropped in unannounced and stayed on for a drink and a good gossip. Louis Negin remembers, "They were so glamorous, especially Kate. She was at her most beautiful then. She had incredible sex appeal but at the same time she was intelligent, witty, quick on the uptake … you couldn't fool her about anything. She would challenge anyone. And on stage she could always break me up. Once she had to look out a window and I was standing there nude; and she didn't even blink. Afterwards she said, 'You think you can shock me with that little thing?' We had so many laughs. And terrible fights. But I loved her. Everybody loved her."

Her sense of fun and her extravagance were legendary. She bought people ridiculously expensive presents. When Barbara Hamilton opened as Merilla in *Anne of Green Gables* in Charlottetown, Kate's opening night present was a horse, which she had led into Barbara's dressing-room at intermission. Delighted, Barbara guffawed and had to be dissuad-

ed from riding it onstage in the second act. She reciprocated by delivering to Kate's dressing-room at her next opening a large gift-wrapped box of manure.

The performance that gained Kate major critical attention in this period was Lizzie Curry in Nash's *The Rainmaker*, which she performed first at Vineland for Brian Doherty, the only Canadian producer at that time who had any real theatrical savvy. It was repeated at the Crest and garnered praise from the often censorious but highly influential Nathan Cohen, who encouraged Kate to try her luck in Britain. She followed his advice. She and Austin set off for London, where he would play in Lesley Storm's *Roar Like a Dove* in the West End while she explored the intricacies of British society, still a very hierarchical world in the late 1950s. For Kate it was, in a sense, going home.

One of Kate's greatest assets was her curiosity. She was always game for a new experience, attending a *seder* at the house of Jewish friends (which in the 1950s her WASP acquaintances considered decidedly peculiar), putting her ear to the wall to eavesdrop on neighbours in her New York apartment, visiting a kindergarten in an inner-city school to meet underprivileged children. Kate was a keen observer and a committed listener. She once told me the secret of good acting was to listen to the other actors. She was curious about

the activities of all her friends, including their sexual adventures. It is typical that while she was rehearsing for *The Rainmaker* in London she sought out and became friends with her father's first wife. She wanted to learn whatever she could about other aspects of his life. Her newly found stepmother looked forward to Kate's opening with keen anticipation, but as it turned out Kate did not get to play Lizzie in the West End. The sudden illness and death of her mother Babby brought her back to Canada (the role was taken over by Geraldine Page, who would

also play it in New York.) However, in London Kate attracted the attention of Alec Guinness and this would pay off for her handsomely.

But not until she had found a new platform for her developing talent. In 1959 she was invited to Stratford to play Emilia in *Othello*, the first production of the newly fledged Canadian company to be directed by Canadians, a collaboration between Jean Gascon and George McCowan. Kate found the dual director-ship confusing and had great misgivings about her ability to pull off this classical

69

As the Nurse in Romeo and Juliet *with Julie Harris and Bruno Gerussi, Stratford 1962*

role. She tried to back out of the production, but her portrayal of this passionate, mistreated woman was acknowledged to be one of the strongest things in the production. She was partnered by Douglas Rain playing Iago and formed an attachment to him that was to be of primary importance in her emotional life.

70

As Katherine of Aragon with Douglas Campbell as Henry VIII

The next year she went back to Stratford to play the nurse in *Romeo and Juliet.* Her earthy, knowing, all-too-human interpretation providing an excellent foil for the sweet innocence of Julie Harris's Juliet and Bruno Gerussi's hot-blooded Romeo. Christopher Plummer, who played Mercutio, describes her Nurse: "Coarse, vulgar, big-hearted and caring—Falstaff as a woman." Kate responded strongly to the demanding direction of Michael Langham, who, she later claimed, taught her more about acting than any other single director. Throughout her life, the free-wheeling, spontaneous, and often disorganized Kate would be attracted to stern martinets and tough authoritarians. As for Langham, he acknowledged her innate gift: "She doesn't know why she does it, but when she says she's right, she *is* right, and I hate her for it." His words echo Noël Coward's on the experience of directing that other wayward but consummate Canadian performer Beatrice Lillie.

The next three Stratford seasons featured alternating triumph and disappointment. Her Katherine of Aragon in *Henry VIII* had dignity, weight, and heartsore immediacy but in the opinion of some critics "lacked variety and majesty." Her Lady Macbeth opposite Christopher Plummer was spirited and intense, but the two actors never quite

Kate Reid

connected and Kate was dissatisfied with her own performance. She announced one afternoon to stage manager Jack Hutt, "I'm not going on today as Lady Macbeth," to which he replied, "Very well, darling, what role will you play?" Still grinning she made her first entrance on cue. But her performance as Katherine in *The Taming of the Shrew* was masterly. Ably paired by John Colicos as Petruchio, they sparred with caustic wit and violent horseplay, challenging and encouraging each other. The mutual attraction was clear, and these may have been the most accomplished comic performances of both their careers.

Kate would go on to give striking life to Cassandra in *Troilus and Cressida* and Adriana in *The Comedy of Errors*, but her Ranevskaya in John Hirsch's production of *The Cherry Orchard* in 1965 was the crowning glory of her early years with the Stratford company. As Nina in *The Seagull* she had foreshadowed the pattern of her early life; now this production epitomized the conflict and stresses of her mature years. The generosity, the loyalty, the impetuous candour and bittersweet humour, the irrational extravagance and sudden spurts of anger and affection and self-ridicule all contributed to this portrait of a woman who was at once infuriating, captivating, and heartbreaking. In this role Kate still looked wonderful, but we somehow knew (per-

The Macbeths: Christopher Plummer and Kate

haps only instinctively) that the road ahead would be bleak.

In between seasons she played opposite Alec Guinness in *Dylan*, a play about the sonorous-voiced, hard-living Welsh poet. As Caitlin, Thomas's passionate young wife, Kate was the perfect foil. Guinness was wonderfully articulate, sensitive, and cerebral, but Kate as his tempestuous and willful consort gave the production the fire and spontaneity that were not in Guinness's range and contributed substantially to their success in New York. Guinness found her engaging

71

personally and made a habit of involving her in an hour-long game of cribbage before the curtain went up, which he confessed to a friend was partly designed to keep her away from the bottle.

With this production Kate gained the attention of the major dramatists of America, and several of them wrote roles for her. In 1966 she appeared as the tough and ambitious mother of Natalie Wood in the film version of Tennessee Williams's *This Property is Condemned* and also as the outspoken Molly in Williams's *Gnadiges Fraulein*, easily holding her own in the company of Margaret Leighton and Zoe Caldwell. She would also play the passionate and impulsive Serafina in the1963 Granada television version of *The Rose Tattoo* for Canadian director Paul Almond, and Big Mama in the first major Broadway revival of *Cat on a Hot Tin Roof* in 1974, rounding out her gallery of brash, hard-edged, strong-willed Williams women.

For Kate, Arthur Miller created the role of Esther Franz in *The Price*, a role she played on Broadway with Arthur Kennedy and Pat Hingle. Rehearsals were filled with argument and acrimony, especially after Miller took over the direction himself. But it was a notable success on Broadway, Miller's last. Kate would go on to play Linda Loman in a major revival of *Death of a Salesman* opposite Dustin Hoffman in 1984. Miller

72

as Linda Loman with Dustin Hoffman as Willie

acknowledged this as the ideal production of his work, and Kate played with a simplicity and warmth as she charted a path of deepening disillusion and disappointment that paralleled Hoffman's painful journey as Willy. I went back to see Kate after the show, because she had insisted I should. It was a matinee and she had another show to do in the evening. She was welcoming but distracted, jumpy and uneasy when not actually involved in her character onstage, a fish out of water. Even the prospect of martinis at Sardi's didn't hold any appeal.

Following her vigorous attack on the role of Martha in *Who's Afraid of Virginia Woolf?*, Edward Albee wrote a part specifically for Kate: the alcoholic sister in *A Delicate Balance*. Unable to take on this assignment on Broadway, Kate

Kate Reid

73

In Tennessee Williams's This Property is Condemned *with Charles Bronson*

played the role in the 1973 film, catching the pain underlying this mean-mouthed woman, just as she would nail the desperate bravery of Henny in the tragicomic *Bosoms and Neglect* that John Guare wrote for her. Though not acclaimed on Broadway, this play achieved a notable critical success when she played it at Stratford in 1980. To this considerable gallery of women in major American plays must be added Lavinia in O'Neill's *Mourning Becomes Electra*, which she played at Hart House Theatre in 1969 under the direction of Leon Major. The production was uneven, but the intensity that Kate brought to the repressed emotions of this determined and frustrated woman swept across the tiny stage and propelled the drama through its seven hours of performance.

After Kate's marriage with Austin Willis dissolved, she continued to care for their two children, son Reid and daughter Robin. She and Austin remained on friendly terms and she visited him in Los Angeles from time to time. She maintained an apartment in New York during much of this time, and her earnings were enough to support a reasonable lifestyle but, as is so often the case with busy and successful actors, her finances were mishandled by irresponsible or incompetent managers who neglected to pay taxes, did not keep accurate records, and probably dipped into the

till. Kate travelled a good deal, although she disliked moving around and hated flying. She would sometimes hire a limousine to go to the Toronto airport and end up getting the driver to take her all the way to Manhattan.

It was also during this period that she began drinking heavily. What had started as a social habit in the late 1950s had by the end of the 1960s become an addiction. She drank not only before but often during a show, sometimes needing a stage manager to walk her to the wings. But she seemed to be able to go on and give a performance. She was unpredictable, but that had always been true of her work. Frances Hyland recalled that during the run of *The Cherry Orchard*, in which she was playing Varya, she and Kate agreed one day that they would not

as Claire in A Delicate Balance

go to the bar before the show. Frances stuck to her side of the bargain but she realized when she arrived at the theatre that Kate had not. "I gave a terrible performance that night but Kate was brilliant. So much for good intentions."

I had a similar experience when I asked Kate to dedicate a plaque in the lobby of Hart House Theatre to Robert Gill, not long after his death. I had asked her to lunch. She arrived with Barbara Hamilton and promptly insisted we drink martinis. She barely touched her food and when she ordered her fourth drink, Barbara left in disgust. Fearing the worst I propelled her downstairs to the theatre where she sat in ominous silence. But when I introduced her, she rose, a bit unsteadily, and spoke clearly and movingly of her affection for Bob. She turned to me with a charming smile and said, "Now get me into a cab and get me home."

Barbara walked out on Kate that time but she remained a firm friend, as did Frances Hyland, Charmion King, and Roberta Maxwell. They were as loyal to her as she was to them, loaning them money on occasion and exchanging gossip and confidences. If Kate liked you, she liked you and that was that. The same was true of a number of gay male actors—Roland Hewgill, Tom Kneebone, and Louis Negin. Kate loved to laugh and tell raunchy stories until the wee hours. Mornings were another story.

David Gardner remembers casting Kate in a scene in Timothy Findley's TV drama *The Paper People*. Kate turned up at CBC half an hour late and looking terrible: tousled, hung-over, and bleary-eyed. "I haven't learned any lines," she confessed. Gardner ordered breakfast brought in and the make-up artists set to work. By two in the afternoon Kate looked presentable, and she and David made their way to the studio where Marigold Charlesworth, the other actress in her scene, and the crew had been waiting four hours. "I've got cue cards for you," David announced, and decided to have Marigold stand behind the cards and shoot cutaways later. "Kate played the whole scene to the cue-cards as though they were actors. I don't think she ever even looked at Marigold. And her scene was brilliant. She was the best thing in the film."

Kate continued to give vibrant performances and kept on working, but not all directors were as tolerant and forgiving as Gardner. In 1967 Kate had scored a success at the Shaw Festival as the ruefully frivolous Lady Kitty in Somerset Maugham's *The Circle*. She went back to the Shaw again in 1976 and gave another strong performance as the hard-headed former prostitute in Shaw's *Mrs. Warren's Profession*, in which she was at once warmly sympathetic and defiantly unyielding. This was followed two sea-

76

As Mrs. Warren at the Shaw Festival

sons later by a bittersweet cameo turn as Rummy Mitchens in *Major Barbara* and a luminous and sensitive Ella Rentheim in Ibsen's late play *John Gabriel Borkman*. The critic Ronald Bryden remembered it as "probably the finest work she ever did and possibly the most warmly human portrayal of any Ibsen heroine I can remember. Her rapport with the fellow actors and with the audience was extraordinary. We felt so deeply for her." But by this time her behaviour on and offstage had become so erratic that Shaw's artistic director Christopher Newton had had enough. In spite of the enthusiasm of the audience and the critics she was never again asked to play in Niagara.

But there were other outlets: film and television. In the late 1970s Kate played roles in the largely forgettable films *Shoot, Plague, High Point*, and *Double Negative* and the television dramas *Loose Change*

and *Happy Birthday to Me*. Most of the roles were small, but Kate's friend Anna Cameron remembers, "By that stage Kate didn't want to do big roles where she had to carry the show. She couldn't handle that kind of responsibility."

Meanwhile, at Stratford, Robin Phillips was determined to lure Kate back for another season. She had not appeared at the Festival since 1970, the year she played Gertrude to Brian Bedford's Hamlet at Stratford, Connecticut. She then appeared in short runs of two plays, Arnold Wesker's *The Friends* and Slawomir Mrozek's *Vatzlav*, in a short season of modern work organized by Tom Hendry at Stratford, Ontario's Third Stage. During the period of Jean Gascon's artistic directorship Kate was notable by her absence. She had not responded well to Gascon's direction in his commedia-inspired *Comedy of Errors*, the precision demanded by this style not being comfortable to such a spontaneous performer as Kate.

She had become involved emotionally with the actor Douglas Rain. It was in some ways a curious pairing: Rain was an actor who planned everything in advance and was notorious for refusing to take direction other than the six words upstage, downstage, left, right, louder, softer. He was a fine comic and had a certain icy authority, the exact opposite of Kate's warmth and immediacy.

Nevertheless they had an extended and passionate relationship. Kate's friend Sis Weld said simply, "He was the love of her life."

Both professionally and in her personal life Kate seemed to need strong-minded and highly organized people to play off against, and some of her best work was done with actors and directors who possessed these qualities: Gill, Langham, Bedford, Rain. Douglas Rain was already married. He decided to divorce his wife, but when the decree came through, he married Martha Henry. Kate was shattered but with typical generosity she told stage manager Ann Stuart, "I was very much in love with Douglas, but I wish them happiness."

In 1977 Robin Phillips offered her

77

As Fonsie in The Gin Game *with Douglas Rain*

Mrs. Alving in *Ghosts*, Queen Margaret in *Richard III*, and the Countess of Rousillon in *All's Well that Ends Well*. It was a fine season and she would no doubt have acquitted herself well in all three roles, but she turned them down, believing that it was simply too much for her to take on. For the 1980 season Phillips approached her again. This time the offer was for a shorter season and more tailored to her needs: Maria in *Twelfth Night*, a remount of Guare's *Bosoms and Neglect* with her original Broadway director Mel Shapiro, who would also direct her in Coburn's *The Gin Game* opposite Douglas Rain. It was a relatively short season but featured Kate alongside the other stars Maggie Smith and Peter Ustinov.

Phillips recalls their first meeting, which he approached with some trepidation. "I wasn't sure how she would respond. Whether I should mention Douglas … Martha. She brought up the subject herself and was very frank and open. I remember at the end of our meeting she smiled at me and said, 'There now… it wasn't so difficult, was it?'" He also recalls that although she often came into rehearsal having spent the night before in the bar, "she would sometimes do something that would just … astonish us. Her electricity could fill the whole room." Kate gained splendid notices in both the modern plays, and

although *Twelfth Night* got fewer critical plaudits it was a hauntingly muted production with a mature cast that included a worldly-wise Feste from William Hutt and a deliciously self-regarding but vulnerable Malvolio from Brian Bedford. Barry MacGregor played Sir Toby with a Scots burr (a last minute Phillips inspiration just before the first preview). Richard McMillan was a loose and limber Sir Andrew, and Kate's sharply intelligent Maria rounded out the comic contingent that offset the bittersweet tang of Phillips's subdued and intimate realization of the text.

The season proved to be Phillips's last. Kate was approached to play in the next season, being offered a chance to revisit her interpretation of Martha in *Who's Afraid of Virginia Woolf?* as well as a role in John Murrell's *Waiting for the Parade*. But Stratford went into crisis mode when the directorate set up by Phillips was dismissed and the board elected to turn the theatre over to John Dexter. In the end John Hirsch was appointed, but by that time Kate had agreed to appear in a production of *Stevie*, a play about the English poet Stevie Smith, with her friend Roberta Maxwell and directed by Richard Monette. He recalls that she resisted his direction and then decided to leave the show before the run was completed because she had an offer to appear on Broadway in *Mornings at Seven* and

needed a break before she went into rehearsal in New York. It left him not only disappointed but out of pocket, as he needed to rehearse a replacement and mount a fresh publicity campaign.

In fact, Kate was becoming increasingly unpredictable in her behaviour. Sis Weld remembers getting into an elevator with Kate at a function and discovering they were standing beside Donald Sutherland. Although Kate knew Sutherland, who greeted her, she refused to speak to him. On another occasion Kate and Sis were asked to a weekend house party. Kate remained in her room until Sunday-night dinner, when "she made a very grand entrance dressed to the nines and sporting her Order of Canada."

A streak of perversity had always been there, but it became more pronounced in the last decade of her life. She had always liked to shock and now she gave this inclination free rein. It coloured her portrayal of Adeline in the TV miniseries *Whiteoaks of Jalna* and gave dimension and edge to her remarkable performance as the aging mistress of Burt Lancaster in Louis Malle's *Atlantic City* (1980). This film shows Kate in fine form: touchy and vulnerable, salty, tough, and tart-tongued. Set against *This Property is Condemned* they book-end her film career, not in the end as memorable as her stage work but peopled by characters

with a strong emotional presence like the outspoken country woman in Peter Pearson's *The Best Damn Fiddler from Calabogie to Kaladar* (1968). She would go on to do further work in television, appearing on *Gavilan* for two seasons and *Dallas* for four, but her important work was over.

By the mid-1980s she could no longer sustain a major stage performance. Her old friend Louis Negin mounted a production for her of *Arsenic and Old Lace* at Hart House Theatre. She and her friend Charmion King played the old ladies who poison their roomers with elderberry wine, but the script seemed tired and faded and Charmion recalls that many nights she had no idea what Kate would say or do next. I went to the opening and realized there wasn't much sign of the

Mistress Overdone in Measure for Measure *with Nicholas Pennell as Lucio and Bernard Hopkins as Pompey*

79

old magic. Her friends rallied round and went to an opening night party at Sis's. We talked and drank and sang till three in the morning, but the show closed after a couple of weeks.

There were no more offers from New York, but there was still some television work. Then David William invited Kate to Stratford to play in two Michel Tremblay plays, *Les Belles-Soeurs* and *Bonjour, là, Bonjour.* The roles were small but meaty and Kate acquitted herself with gusto. She bonded with fellow actress Janet Wright and bought a little house in Stratford. Richard Monette conceived the idea of adapting *Whatever Happened to Baby Jane* as a stage piece and asked me to work on the script with him. On a snowy day in January 1993 I drove to Stratford, and we went to Kate's house to read the script, the other roles being taken by Janet Wright, Bernard Hopkins, and Sheila McCarthy. It was slated for production at the Grand Theatre in London. Kate read slowly, but every so often there was a glimmer of what she might bring to the part—the sly humour, the petulance, the childish self-indulgence, the pathetic need for one more moment in the limelight.

Six weeks later she was dead; they found six brain tumours. Sis flew back from San Miguel de Allende to attend the service at St. Paul's. The acting com-munity turned out in force and went to Sis's house on Farnham Avenue for the wake. The wine flowed and so did the stories. Tom Kneebone, Barbara Hamilton, and Roly Hewgill all had tales to tell. But there were no speeches, no one to say, "This woman was Canada's greatest actress. Kate Reid had the range, the depth, the variety, the originality, the ability to surprise, to move, to make you laugh and cry and hold your breath." Once, when I was talking with Richard Monette, he said, "You know, we have some very good actors now at Stratford. Young up-and-comers, mature talents, wonderful old stagers. But what we don't have is an actor of immense raw natural talent. We don't have a Kate Reid."

As Katherina in The Taming of the Shrew *with John Colicos as Petruchio*

HELDENTENOR

Jon Vickers

Shortly after World War II, the church my family attended decided it could afford to hire four paid soloists. I have forgotten three of them, but the tenor was a blond young man with a barrel chest and a huge voice that filled the entire church. Many in the congregation thought the voice was too big, unbecoming to the sacred music he was given to sing. "He just swamps the whole choir," was one comment. The young man's name was Jon Vickers.

It turned out he was boarding in a house that lay on the route I took going to and from my high school. I would sometimes see him mowing the lawn of that house or a neighbour's, I suppose to earn some pocket money. I would stop and we would talk for a few minutes, I don't remember exactly about what— probably not the church but maybe about music. I learned that he was studying at the Conservatory. I also learned that he had been a farm boy out west but had come to Toronto with a few bucks in his pocket. He hoped for a career as a singer and had given himself two years to see what he could accomplish in the world of classical music.

He stayed as a soloist at Glenview Presbyterian for only one season, and I lost touch with him. Then, on the advice of my music teacher I went to hear *Messiah* performed at Massey Hall by the Toronto Symphony and the Mendelssohn Choir led by Sir Ernest MacMillan. Jon Vickers was the tenor soloist. His rendering of "Every Valley Shall Be Exalted" was exciting in its jubilation and vigour. I had learned in my earlier conversations with Jon that he had been influenced in his youth by American gospel singers who had visited his native Prince Albert, and some of their emotional fervour carried over into this aria. The emotional quality of his singing would always stay with him.

Vickers would sing a good deal of oratorio in his early career: Mendelssohn's *Elijah*, Handel's *Samson*, and Stainer's *The Crucifixion*. He had been brought up in a pious family; all of his brothers and sisters sang in church choirs, and arias from oratorios were performed in church services. Their stories were based on scriptural material, and the wording of their texts in English was derived from the King James version of the Bible. In mid-twentieth-century Toronto the enthusiasm of key musicians such as Sir Ernest and Healey Willan was focused on sacred music. Vickers would later confess, "As a young singer I was a snob. I thought opera was an inferior art form." He would continue to sing as a church soloist and in larger musical productions for fees ranging from $75 to $300; these were booked by Ezra Schabas, who ran the Conservatory's Concert and Placement Bureau.

Messiah would continue to be an important part of Vickers's repertoire. In 1959, after he had begun singing opera in London, he was approached by Sir Thomas Beecham to take part in an RCA recording of the oratorio, with original orchestral embellishments by the famous conductor. Jon was surprised by the invitation but was told that Beecham had heard him sing Samson; Beecham told Vickers he was the only one in that performance who understood Handelian style. The two hit it off, and after Jon sang a ringing version of "Comfort Ye My People," with its long run over a top A natural, Beecham exclaimed, "You're damn good, Vickers." Beecham declared the take a keeper and Vickers told the technician, "I'll give you half my fee, if you leave that in."

Vickers had been discovered by the singer Mary Morrison when, in his early 20s, he was working in retail, first for Woolworth's and then for the Hudson Bay Company in Winnipeg. She arranged for him to get scholarship money to study at the Conservatory in Toronto, where he came under the influence of George "Papa" Lambert, a baritone who arranged for him not only to study singing but to learn French, German, and Italian as well. He must have had a good ear, because from his earliest recitals he was praised for his clear diction. During his early years in Toronto he was very poor and worked nights driving taxis and beer delivery trucks. As he began to get gigs singing in churches and in small-town concerts, his financial situation improved.

Always a man with an eye for the

Jon Vickers

ladies, he had had several girlfriends out west, whom he charmed with his blond good looks, amiable manners, and ready sense of humour. In Toronto he met and fell in love with Henrietta Outerbridge, a very pretty young woman who taught English at Forest Hill Collegiate. David Lewis Stein remembers that he and his fellow students were attracted to her and that she encouraged them in their early attempts to write poetry. Hetty, as she would be called by Jon and his friends, also painted and awakened Jon's interest in visual art. They wasted little time in getting married in 1953 and settled into a cramped third-floor apartment in a house in south Rosedale. Jon acquired a large car, a second-hand Chrysler, and within the space of three years their first two children, Allison and William, were born. Jon proved a fond and boisterous parent, but his household was patriarchal; he made the rules and saw to it they were obeyed.

After World War II, the teachers at the Conservatory included a number of Germans: Greta Kraus, Nicholas Goldschmidt, Franz Kramer, and the man who would become the first artistic director of the Canadian Opera Company, Herman Geiger-Torel. They told Jon his voice would not mature until he was thirty and encouraged him to sing oratorio and lieder in the meantime. However, they saw Jon's potential as an operatic performer, not only because of his big voice and distinctive timbre but also because of his flair for the dramatic. Handsome and barrel-chested, with the physique of an athlete, he looked like a leading man even though he was only of medium height and bow-legged, something he would endeavour to camouflage by insisting on knee-length tunics and leggings when cast as a Roman or Viking hero.

Geiger-Torel pursued him to sing in some of his early productions at the Royal Alexandra Theatre, most notably Don José in *Carmen*, opposite the sultry soprano Regina Resnik as the flirtatious gypsy girl. Resnik recalled, "He did two kinds of singing. He either sang with his huge voice … or he sang *pianissimo*, crooning, a kind of *mezza voce*. He already had a big boisterous temperament, and then as now he was very impulsive." Don José would become one of his signature roles, and he would later credit Geiger-Torel with teaching him a good deal about stage acting, especially the use of his hands.

Jon sang a *Messiah* and Florestan in Beethoven's *Fidelio* in a concert in New York, and the Male Chorus in Britten's *The Rape of Lucretia* in Stratford, as well as Alfredo in Verdi's *La Traviata* in Toronto and Jason in Cherubini's *Medée* in Philadelphia. He acquired a New York agent, William Stein, through the good

84

Siegfried in Die Walküre

offices of Resnik, who also told him he should approach Wieland Wagner at Bayreuth. She predicted that he would be a wonderful Siegmund and Parsifal, and although Vickers was skeptical she would be proved right. Meanwhile Vickers told his wife and Papa Lambert that he intended to leave singing and return to the business world in the spring of 1956.

About this time the young director Irving Guttman visited Covent Garden, attending a production of *Carmen* with English tenor James Johnston as Don José. He met the general manager, David Webster, afterwards and told him that he knew of better tenors in Canada. Webster replied that he was going to New York with the Sadler's Wells ballet, and Guttman offered to set up auditions in Montreal. He invited Vickers, who refused to go to Montreal, saying if Webster wanted to hear him he could come to Toronto. Already he was beginning to adopt the somewhat arrogant attitude for which he would become famous. Webster marvelled at Vickers's audacity, but he did travel to Toronto and heard Vickers sing, among other things, an aria from Handel's *Judas Maccabeus*. He went up on stage and then had a long talk with Vickers in the green room of Massey Hall. He said he was prepared to offer the young tenor a contract, to which Vickers evidently replied,

"It had better be a good one." Webster concluded their interview by saying, "I can see you're a young man who knows the value of a dollar."

In early May 1956, Vickers received a cable from Webster asking him to come to London to discuss future engagements. Stein, Vickers's agent, phoned Webster, who confirmed that he was prepared to offer him a place in the company. Stein arranged for Vickers to go to New York and work with Leo Taubman, a respected accompanist and vocal coach. Vickers stayed at the YMCA and worked several hours a day, polishing his repertoire for the next month, and then flew to London. He sang a big audition for Webster and conductor Rafael Kubelik. Webster offered him a three-year contract, but Vickers would only agree to eighteen months. He then returned to Canada to sing in Britten's *Lucretia*. When the contract arrived he went over it carefully himself, as would be his invariable custom in the future. His London agent John Coast reported that Jon rarely signed a contract without crossing something out.

It happened that I was in London that spring. I attended a performance of Verdi's *Un Ballo in Maschera*. I don't know why I picked that particular opera but was surprised to discover that Vickers was singing Gustavus. I had not looked at the program, but the clear,

85

ringing, almost metallic tone was immediately recognizable to me. I went back afterwards and he was welcoming and agreed to go out, not for a beer but for coffee. I don't know if Vickers was a life-long teetotaler; I'm reasonably sure his parents would have been. Jon possessed a strong moral sense, bound up with his religious faith. Many years later he accepted an invitation to sing at a private party in Dallas, with the proviso that no one was to have anything to drink until after he had sung.

Jon told me that night that he had been offered the leading role of Enée in Berlioz's *Les Troyens*. When Webster had suggested it to him he admitted he had never heard of it and would have to study the score. It was not only extremely long but also complex, ranging from a strong *spinto* opening scene, to a delicate, lyrical love scene with the Carthaginian queen Didon, and a resolute final section where the hero leaves his lover and sets out to found the city of Rome. The opera is a great sprawling work and had never been done in its entirety. Critics were already writing that the managers of Covent Garden must be insane to think they could stage the complete work or find a tenor who could handle the leading role. When the opera was presented, critics and musicologists, thinking they would never have a chance to see the complete work again, came from

all over the world. It was a triumph for Vickers, who brought virility, passion, and virtuosity to his portrayal. It made him a star, and not just in Britain but on the international opera scene as well. He would continue to sing Enée at Covent Garden, and some fifteen years later at the Met in New York.

Offers poured in from San Francisco, Barcelona, and Miami. But Stein wanted to orchestrate Vickers's career carefully. Meanwhile, Hetty and the two children moved to London and set up house in suburban London, near Harrow. Before he left, George Lambert took Vickers aside: "Always remember that your voice is like a big, juicy orange. And every conductor and every producer and every impresario who can get his hands on you will suck every bit of juice out of it if he can. And you know what they do with the peel." Vickers never forgot this piece of advice.

Within the next four years Vickers would debut in Vienna, Bayreuth, San Francisco, Buenos Aires, New York, and Milan. He met with Herbert von Karajan in Salzburg and with Wieland Wagner, the composer's grandson, who invited him to sing *Lohengrin*. Vickers declined, but he agreed to play Siegmund in *Die Walküre* in the summer of 1958. The following year he sang Radames in *Aida* and Don Carlos, in addition to repeating his roles in *Carmen*, *Ballo in Maschera*, and

Jon Vickers

Pollione in Norma

Die Walküre, and finished up with Canio in *I Pagliacci*. This would become one of his most affecting portrayals, the first of a string of tormented outsiders cheated in love. This quality was already evident in his Don José and would eventually include a string of dramatic personages: Samson, Hermann in Tchaikovsky's *The*

Queen of Spades, Luca in Janáček's *Jenůfa*, and his three greatest roles: Tristan, Otello, and Peter Grimes.

Some critics would say that Vickers was not really much of an actor, but his portrayals of these anguished, thwarted men had force and intensity of emotion that his audiences found tremendously moving. Subtlety was not his forte. He did not often play comic roles, but he possessed the stature and the passion to play tragic figures. His stage presence undoubtedly stemmed not only from his physical attributes but also from his belief in himself as the possessor of a God-given talent. His ability to portray the hurt and anger of a man deceived may have derived from his own strong attraction to women, something he forced himself to rein in.

Vickers was flirtatious with many of the women he sang with, as well as some of his female admirers. He would sometimes pick them up off the ground and whirl them around in his arms. In the course of his career he sang opposite almost all the major opera divas of the era: Teresa Berganza, Grace Bumbry, Montserrat Caballé, Maria Callas, Victoria de los Angeles, Maureen Forrester, Marilyn Horne, Gwyneth Jones, Roberta Knie, Christa Ludwig, Birgit Nilsson, Regina Resnik, Teresa Stratas, Kiri Te Kanawa, Astrid Varnay, and Teresa Żzylis-Gara, among

Samson in Samson and Delilah

many others. He never sang with Joan Sutherland, perhaps because she was two inches taller than he was. There has been speculation about whether he ever acted on his romantic, not to say carnal, desires, but his Christian morality obliged him to resist temptation, and the tension he must have experienced in wrestling with his erotic impulses no doubt fed into his dramatic portrayals.

Vickers first sang Otello in Buenos Aires in 1963, and then in Manchester and Montreal before performing it in Salzburg, London, and New York almost a decade later. To prepare for it he read

Jon Vickers

Shakespeare and saw Olivier's production at the National Theatre. Like Olivier he was flamboyant and carried a stick. His love duet at the end of the first act was lyrical and sensual. Later, as his suspicion grew, his pain was largely internalized until he erupted in a sudden outburst of rage in Act III. In the final act he was both pitiful and violent. His interpretation continued to develop as he performed it over the years, trying to find new shadings in each performance. Eventually he would say that Otello was too much concerned with himself and should have trusted Desdemona if he really loved her.

I saw Vickers's Otello in New York in 1974 in a production designed and directed by Franco Zeffirelli. Vickers was both impressive in his majesty and pathetic in his childlike trust in Iago. The sumptuous production had been built around James McCracken. Zeffirelli did not attend Vickers's rehearsals, which were conducted by Fabrizio Melano. He tried to get Vickers to adopt some of the stage directions that had been set on McCracken, and before long the two men were screaming at one another. Vickers's friend and fellow Canadian Louis Quilico, who was playing Iago, burst out, "Shut up, you're wasting our time with your tantrums. Jon, we know you're going to do what you want. Do me a favour. Just do it."

But not everyone was prepared to stand up to Vickers's demands and outbursts of temper. The genial, good-humoured farm boy had become untrusting, overly sensitive of slights, demanding not only financially but also of the respect he considered his due, a real divo in his immaculately tailored blazer and bowler hat. Many of his leading ladies, though they found him attractive, were terrified of him. And he didn't hold back from quarrelling with them or his con-

89

Otello

ductors. At the Met he discovered Zubin Mehta was sight-reading the score during rehearsal and burst out, "Son of a bitch, you haven't studied it, have you? Go back to your hotel. I'm going home. Call me when you've learned the score." Vickers had great loyalty and respect for certain conductors, Beecham and von Karajan in particular, but there were others he continually tangled with, particularly Georg Solti at Covent Garden.

By the mid 1970s Vickers had a large and varied repertoire of widely contrasting roles, greater in their range and diversity than most of his peers: Florestan in *Fidelio*, Don José in *Carmen*, Gustavus/Ricardo in *Un Ballo in Maschera*, three of his earliest successes; Siegmund in *Die Walküre*, Parsifal, Canio in *I Piagliacci*, Samson in both Handel's opera and Saint-Saëns's *Samson et Dalila*, Radames in *Aida*, Don Carlos, Don Alvaro in *La Forza del Destino*, Enée in *Les Troyens* along with Aeneas in Purcell's *Dido and Aeneas*, Luca in *Jenůfa*, and the comic role of Vašek in Smetana's *The Bartered Bride*.

He sang in all the great opera houses of the day: Covent Garden in London, the Metropolitan Opera in New York, the Lyric Opera of Chicago, the San Francisco Opera, the Dallas Civic Opera, the Houston Grand Opera, the Teatro Colón in Buenos Aires, the Paris Opera, the Salzburg Festival, Bayreuth,

the Deutsche Oper in Berlin, the Hamburg Staatsoper, the amphitheatres at Epidaurus in Greece and Orange in Provence, the Vienna Staatsoper, Teatro alla Scala in Milan, the Grand Théâtre de Genève, the Israeli Opera in Tel Aviv, and with the Royal Opera on tour in Seoul and Tokyo. There were also a good number of one-time appearances in smaller centres in Europe and North America.

During his time living in England, Vickers managed to run afoul of the BBC, who accused him of arriving unprepared at a rehearsal for Strauss's *Salome*, and of the government's Department of Inland Revenue, who claimed he was now a British resident and was subject to punishingly high taxes. Vickers decided he would establish his residence in Canada and appealed to John Diefenbaker, the prime minister, for help. Vickers had known Diefenbaker when both were resident in Prince Albert. Diefenbaker and his wife Olive were childless and had apparently suggested to Vickers's parents that they would be willing to adopt young Jonathan. This never transpired, but the two men remained in touch and the prime minister did help the singer settle his tax problems. Always loyal to those he considered his real friends, Vickers stayed in touch with Diefenbaker, and when the prime minister died Vickers

90

Jon Vickers

flew to Ottawa to sing at his funeral.

Jon bought a farm in the rolling hills of Caledon, west of Toronto. He enrolled his older children in local schools and settled into a Victorian red-brick house, which he restored and enlarged. He decided to set up a working farm, raising beef cattle, a 300-strong herd of Aberdeen Angus and Herefords. He rode a tractor to plough his fields, stooked hay, and dug holes for fence posts, just as he had done on the White farm in Saskatchewan in his teens. He became a skilled woodworker and made furniture for his farmhouse. He tried to spend at least six months of the year on the farm and was on friendly terms with his neighbours, even though he drove a Cadillac to the nearby airport. He sang in a local choir and donated a pipe organ to his church.

Living in Canada did not lead to Vickers singing more engagements in this country, however, especially in Toronto. In 1960 he agreed to appear at the Grandstand show at the Canadian National Exhibition along with the Canadettes, a mini-chorus-line imitative

Canio in I Pagliacci

of the New York City Music Hall Rockettes and the American comic Phil Silvers. The show was disparagingly reviewed, and Vickers was told in the press that he was wasting his talents. He had already received highly critical notices in Toronto papers, including some personal comments by critic William Littler about his pudgy physique. He felt that Canada was happy to be what Margaret Atwood labelled at the time "a kind of hopeless cultural backwater." Seeing himself as a prophet without honour in his own land, he refused to sing in Toronto, reporting that he was often asked to sing for "a bucket of sentiment and half my usual fee," although he did perform in Ottawa in *The Queen of Spades* for Mario Bernardi, a friend from his Conservatory days, and in *The Rape of Lucretia* in Guelph for his old friend and mentor Nicholas Goldschmidt.

Vickers was considered by many to be a Wagnerian tenor, but he himself never wanted to be labelled in this way. He had many reservations about Wagner, whom he considered an immoral adulterer under the philosophic influence of the atheist Nietzsche. When they first met in 1958, Von Karajan said to Vickers, "You will be my Tristan next year," but Vickers declined, saying he was not ready. During the next few years he refused the role of Siegfried when it was offered to

him, and plans for him to sing Lohengrin fell through. Though he considered Tristan "a thoroughly despicable person," he knew he would eventually sing the role. Plans were made for him to debut the role in San Francisco, but he balked when Birgit Nilsson received superior billing. He waited until 1971, when he first sang it in Buenos Aires with Nilsson as Isolde.

One critic reported, "Those who watched him had the feeling they were seeing the incarnation of Wagner's hero, something that had not been felt since the golden days of Max Lorenz and Lauritz Melchior." Elijah Moshinsky, who would stage Vickers's *Tristan* in London, commented that Vickers always offered a subtext: under the apparent horror at the ravages wreaked by passion, "sexuality was always there, the underside, waiting in the darkness to be revealed. In America Vickers' portrayal of Tristan would cause his audiences embarrassment in a way that Sinatra never did. He caused embarrassment in the way Billie Holiday did in night clubs, from the sheer authenticity of the sexual-emotional event."

Vickers would sing Tristan in major opera houses over the next decade: in Salzburg, Berlin, Munich, Chicago, Rio de Janeiro, and London, where I saw a performance in 1978, when his Isolde was Roberta Knie. He radiated a sense of

Jon Vickers

a man torturing himself, suffering a passion beyond his control, who somehow manages to achieve a sort of transcendence in death. Although it became one of Vickers's greatest portrayals, he only twice sang it at the Met. By the mid-1980s his popularity was being eclipsed by two younger tenors: Plácido Domingo and Luciano Pavarotti.

Apart from his Handel roles, most of Vickers's work was centred in the nineteenth-century repertoire: Beethoven, Berlioz, Bizet, Leoncavallo, Saint-Saëns, Tchaikovsky, Verdi, and Wagner. But perhaps his most fully realized characterization was to be in the masterpiece of the twentieth-century British composer Benjamin Britten, *Peter Grimes*. The opera is not melodic, in spite of the wonderfully impressionistic seascape interludes. In this work Vickers declaimed as much as sang, his speaking voice, which was sometimes said to resemble that of James Cagney, rising in anguish and terror. Vickers studied all of his roles in depth. To portray Grimes he went to the work of George Crabbe, upon which the libretto is based, and read and reread it. He realized that Britten had written the work to gain understanding and acceptance of homosexuality, but Vickers's interpretation was not based on the composer's intention. Rather he saw Grimes's story as a powerful study of human rejection and lack of compassion. In the final

act Vickers's Grimes is so much not mad as "smashed," destroyed by the lack of understanding of the people around him.

Vickers first performed *Peter Grimes* at the Met in 1967, in a production directed by Tyrone Guthrie with a simple but evocative setting designed by Tanya Moiseiwitsch. He played Grimes in London in 1969 and in Buenos Aires, Milan, and Paris, but he was the foremost interpreter of the opera in America, where he played it in Chicago, San

Peter Grimes

Francisco, Houston, Dallas, and Seattle and on a Met tour of Atlanta, Minneapolis, Detroit, Cleveland, and even one performance in Toronto. Vickers believed that Britten did not fully comprehend the depth of his own work and that the original production in which Grimes was sung by Peter Pears did not do justice to the work. Britten, for his part, did not accept Vickers's portrayal and walked out of the performance he attended at Covent Garden. Because of their homosexual content Vickers declined to appear in Britten's later operas, *Billy Budd* and *Death in Venice*.

In the mid-1970s, Covent Garden and the Staatsoper in Vienna laid plans for a production of *Tannhäuser* starring Vickers. Plans proceeded until, unexpectedly, Vickers informed his agent that he would not sing the opera because in his view the character was immoral and the story was sick. As a Christian steeped in Old Testament morality he could not accept the idea that Tannhäuser was redeemed in the eyes of the Church of Rome by the love of Elisabeth, when what he really wanted was to sport with Venus. However, it was widely bruited in opera circles that when Jon had studied the part he realized he couldn't sing it, since the tessitura was too high. He had always had trouble singing above a high A, and his upper range became weaker as he got older, a not uncommon develop-

ment for tenors and indeed all singers. He sometimes had the music transposed down and, although he denied it, sometimes resorted to falsetto. Vickers dismissed what he considered groundless gossip, however, and remained adamant that he had refused the role on moral and philosophical grounds.

In spite of his objections to *Tannhäuser*, Vickers sang two characters possessed by lust. The first was Herod in *Salome*, which he performed in Orange in 1974. He almost slobbered and slopped wine on his costume as he watched Leonie Rysanek perform the dance of the seven veils. Then in 1979 in Paris he sang the notorious Nerone in Monteverdi's *L'Incoronazione di Poppea*, an opera that depicts the Roman emperor as a total libertine who orders the death of his tutor Seneca, discards his aristocratic wife, and ends up singing a duet with his paramour Poppea, who is about to be crowned empress. Presumably Vickers regarded these two historical figures as the embodiment of evil, and it is true they are not presented as heroes in their respective operas.

In 1973, Vickers and Hetty had moved with their five children to Bermuda, an island with which Hetty's family had a longstanding connection. The move was motivated by a change in Canadian tax laws. Vickers kept the farm in Ontario and visited it frequently, but Bermuda

94

became his official residence. He bought a small estate with a large house known as Blue Horizons that had formerly belonged to the Greek shipping tycoon Stavros Niarchos. Vickers, ever canny about money, was able to get it at a good price because of its run-down condition. His skills as a carpenter would come in handy in renovating the house, and he and Hetty would live there for the next 14 years. The children were enrolled in local schools, and Vickers sang in the choir of the Presbyterian church. Hetty no longer travelled with him, and he was away a good deal.

After Hetty was diagnosed with cancer, Vickers sold the big house and bought a smaller one at Random Rocks on the island. Hetty endured a number of operations but was able to be present at his final performance at the Met in March 1986, in *Samson et Dalila* opposite Marilyn Horne. He would repeat this opera in Denver, his final stage appearance. Vickers continued to sing at occasional concerts: opera arias, the song cycle *Die Winterreise*, and Mussorgsky's *Songs and Dances of Death* in Guelph, Kitchener, Toronto, and Montreal. He also gave a series of lectures at the Conservatory in Toronto. I went to the first of these and was shocked by his right-wing views, racial prejudices, and sexist views on birth control and abortion; apparently I was not the only one.

Vickers returned to Bermuda in order to spend as much time with Hetty as he could, but she finally succumbed in 1991. She was a woman of great warmth and spiritual fortitude who had devoted her life to her husband and family.

Vickers had always studied the libretto of any work he was performing. He always knew what the words meant and was capable of distorting the tempi of the music to make sure their meaning came across. Indeed, he was much criticized in some quarters for his liberal use of *rubato*, a tampering with the strict rhythm that the composers had indicated. After he had stopped singing he would recite a Tennyson poem *Enoch Arden*, for which Richard Strauss had written a light piano accompaniment, and his presentation was a clear and forceful delivery of the poet's words.

Vickers could no longer endure the cold of a Canadian winter. He had developed severe arthritis and had operations on both his knees. Then, to the surprise of many of his friends, in 1993 he remarried. Judith Stewart was a stewardess with United Airlines; they had met some years before on a flight, and she would continue to fly until she reached the retirement age of 55. Vickers travelled with his new wife to Italy to be a judge in Giuseppe di Stefano's voice competition, to London for a gala before the renovation of Covent Garden, to

95

Toronto to appear on Stuart Hamilton's CBC Opera Quiz, and to Ottawa to receive the Governor General's Performing Arts Award at the hands of his friend and colleague Teresa Stratas. By this time he had also been awarded eleven honorary degrees. However, he had begun to show the symptoms of Alzheimer's disease. Eventually his wife Judy left him, but not before she had managed to get her hands on a chunk of his fortune. He spent his last days in a home near Niagara, close to where his oldest son William is an actor at the Shaw Festival, and died in 2015. It seems an end as tragic as that of any of the characters he portrayed so vividly on the operatic stage.

96

Tristan *with Maureen Forrester as Brangane and Roberta Knie as Isolde*

FIRST POSITION

Celia Franca

As a teenage actor in the Toronto Children Players I was impressed by the strong influence of ballet on our director Dorothy Goulding. I purchased tickets for the Ballets Russes and on a Saturday afternoon sat in the top balcony of the Royal Alex to watch a group of not-so-young women in tatty tutus and pale men in Buster Brown wigs cavort about the stage to the recorded strains of Chopin. I didn't get it.

Right after the war, the Sadler's Wells Company visited Toronto for two weeks. Tickets were almost impossible to come by but I discovered that if I went to the theatre about forty minutes after the first curtain I could mingle with the smokers on the pavement in front of the theatre during intermission and go in with them to catch the second and third acts. This is how I managed to see Robert Helpmann's ballet *Hamlet.* The sheer theatricality of it bowled me over. Helpmann himself with his gaunt, heavily shadowed eyes and crimson mouth was the dramatic embodiment of pain and madness. Two female dancers matched his histrionics. I had heard of Margot Fonteyn but was unprepared for the delicacy and pathos of her descent into insanity as Ophelia. And then there was the compelling drama of Hamlet's tortured relationship with his overpowering mother, danced by a ballerina I had never heard of. Her name was Celia Franca.

Not long after that first North American tour of Sadler's Wells, three Toronto women, Sydney Mulqueen,

Pearl Whitehead, and Eileen Woods, decided it was time that Canada should have its own ballet company. They sent an envoy Stuart James to approach Ninette de Valois, the artistic director of the renowned British company to see if she could suggest someone who might come to Canada to make this dream a reality. De Valois considered the matter for a few moments and then recommended Celia Franca, "if you can get her." Franca came to Canada in 1950, saw a ten-year-old in a Montreal dance school in toe shoes desperately trying to perform *en pointe* and said, "I think you need me here." She would stay for several months, travelling across the country doing a "feasibility study" before she committed herself to taking on the challenge.

Celia Franks was born in 1921 into a Jewish family living in the east end of London. Her father was a ladies' tailor working in a sweatshop. Her parents were not particularly cultivated or interested in the arts, but young Celia loved music from an early age and used to dance around the family flat. At a wedding she danced spontaneously around the tables of the guests as a band played. The leader suggested to her mother that she should train for the ballet. Neither Celia nor her mother had ever heard of ballet, but Celia pestered her mother until she was enrolled in a dance class and later at the Guildhall School of Music.

She completed the Royal Academy of Dance senior certificate at the age of thirteen. Soon after she learned of auditions at the Saville Theatre and was hired as a chorus girl in a revue called *Spread It Abroad*, starring Ivy St. Helier, Michael Wilding, and Hermione Gingold. Every week she brought home her earnings and plunked them down on the dinner table to counter the objections of her father, who had insisted she could never earn a living as a dancer.

The principal dancer in the revue was Maude Lloyd, who recommended Celia to the artistic director of Ballet Rambert, for which she auditioned in 1936. Marie Rambert was contemptuous of her background as a chorus girl and refused to teach the girl herself, instead assigning her to the class of Anthony Tudor. Tudor was quick to appreciate Celia's dramatic flair and created the role of the Mistress for her in his masterpiece *Lilac Garden*. Rambert was skeptical: "She probably doesn't even know what a mistress is," to which Tudor replied, "She will by the time I've finished with her." It was Tudor who introduced her to the idea that each new role required a specific colour and personality based on character analysis.

It was about this time that she changed her name to Celia Franca, inspired apparently by the example of Alice Marks, who had become Alicia Markova. Celia played a number of

Celia Franca

highly dramatic roles including a drug fiend in the ballet *Paris Soir*: "I had no idea what a drug fiend was but I made a lot of weird faces." She also married at age nineteen a young dancer, Leo Kersley. Like Celia he was a Cockney but he would later say that Celia had gone to a good school and learned to "speak posh." But his family had an interest in the arts and Celia was happy to move into their household, which she found more congenial than living with her parents in Golders Green.

Celia soon attracted the notice of the critics and appeared on the cover of *The Dancing Times*. Kersley was asked to join the company of the Sadler's Wells Ballet, and soon afterwards Ninette de Valois invited Celia to become part of the company as well. She became a principal dancer, beginning with the role of the Queen of Willies in *Giselle*. Other major roles followed, and Celia rapidly learned not only the ballerina's steps but the parts of the corps and the male dancers as well, which would stand her in good stead when she mounted these ballets in Canada a few years later.

When war was declared, the company continued to dance even during the blitz. "Air raid sirens would go off in the orchestra pit if the planes were coming over from Germany and it was always so satisfying to find that really nobody in

Lilac Garden *with James Ronaldson*

that audience ever got up to go to the shelter." Kersley was a conscientious objector and was sent to prison. Celia asked de Valois for permission to visit her husband one Sunday, and although her request was refused she went anyway. Clearly Celia was not easily dissuaded from getting what she wanted.

Sadler's Wells not only staged the great classical ballets *Swan Lake*, *The Nutcracker*, and *Cinderella*, but also new ballets created by choreographers Robert Helpmann, Frederick Ashton, and de Valois herself. With her innate dramatic instincts Celia was a favourite of these choreographers, especially Helpmann, who cast her as everything from Queen Gertrude in *Hamlet* to the prostitute in *Miracle in the Gorbals* and an arachnid predator in *The Spider's Banquet*. Ashton used her in a *pas de trois* in *Les Masques* and a leading role in *The Quest*. Celia's own debut as a choreographer came when she set *Khadri*, a ballet with an oriental flavour, on the young dancers of Sadler's Wells, among them John Cranko and Kenneth MacMillan.

In 1947, because she didn't want to perform *The Sleeping Beauty* for three straight months, she left Sadler's Wells and joined the Metropolitan Ballet as a soloist and ballet mistress. She then joined the company of Kurt Joos to learn something about modern dance, performing in his signature work *The Green Table*. Soon

Franca arrives in Canada

100

afterwards she created two ballets for BBC television, the first dance works they had ever commissioned. Prints of these works, *Eve of St. Agnes* and *The Dance of Salome*, survive; through the blurs and scratches on the film it is still possible to get a sense of the drama she brought to these performances.

Restless, curious, energetic, adventurous, Celia was ready for a fresh challenge, and Canada provided it. With the example of Marie Rambert and Ninette de Valois to guide her, she would stake out a territory of her own in the cultural wilderness. She approached the new country as a pioneer, a kind of latter-day cultural Champlain, crisscrossing the country in search of talent. While she pulled together her "feasibility study" she was given a job at Eaton's as a file clerk. She opened her first season of the new National Ballet of Canada at Eaton Auditorium, and coincidentally it was there that she met her second husband, Herbert Anderson, who worked in the box office; she had previously divorced from Kersley.

Celia gathered together a mixed company of young dancers from across the land. She was well aware that many of them were not really ready to dance professionally; in spite of the enthusiasm of such local teachers as Boris Volkoff and Bettina Byers, their training had been somewhat hit and miss. Celia worked tirelessly for six weeks with the dancers she had chosen to prepare them for their opening season. Celia would be the prima ballerina, playing Giselle and a one-woman dance-piece she choreographed to Rachmaninoff's second piano concerto.

After their performances at Eaton Auditorium, Celia took the dancers on tour, playing one-night stands in smaller towns and cities in Canada and the United States. The dancers earned less than a living wage, but at least they were dancing and getting paid something for it. Celia took on the administrative duties of getting bookings, casting, and

101

Coppelia

preparing programs and publicity. She danced principal roles, and when someone was sick she filled in for them in the corps. Everywhere and always she begged for more funds, from board members and corporations, from individual enthusiasts, from sponsoring organizations like the Kiwanis and the IODE. On one occasion at a Canadian Club luncheon she approached my brother, an economist and philanthropist, and said, batting her mascaraed eyes, "I am so fascinated by your trigonomics." The company pianist Mary McDonald has said, "In those early days she was disciplined, she was tough; she had to be. She had nothing going for her but sheer guts." Celia herself would say her time at the National Ballet was "one long fight." But as she said it, her eyes were alight with the joy of combat.

"I was always good at spotting talent." What did she look for? Determination, personality, musicality. When she first arrived in Canada she encountered Betty Oliphant, who had been sent by a suspicious Ballet Teachers' Association to find out what Franca was up to. Celia quickly won her over and co-opted her as her ballet mistress. Betty had a no-nonsense attitude and thorough grounding in the Giachetti method. The two women would fight for and eventually succeed, in 1959, in setting up a school to train young dancers, in an abandoned church

Giselle as a simple peasant girl

on Maitland Street. Betty would run the school—the National Ballet School—with a firm hand for over twenty years.

Another early recruit was pianist Mary McDonald, a strong-minded and outspoken but endlessly patient young woman. Mary confessed she was "utterly terrified" of Celia in the early years but she would be the company's principal pianist for over two decades and a sort of den mother and confidante to many of the company's young dancers. In the early days the company danced to the accompaniment of two pianos, both in Toronto and on tour. Then Celia found George Crum, who built an orchestra as soon as

103

Lady Capulet in Romeo and Juliet

Karen Kain and Frank Augustyn

the company could afford one and continued to lead it during Celia's artistic directorship. She also discovered Kay Ambrose, who made all the costumes in the early years. To the people who delivered the goods, Celia was intensely loyal.

Celia also found dancers who had magnetism, style, and grace. Although she engaged visiting Russian dancers Irene Alpine, Yuri Gottschalk, and Galina Samtsova, she sought out Canadian dancers and gave them incredible opportunities. Foremost in the early years were Lois Smith and David Adams. They danced the principal roles in all the major ballets and were warmly appreciated by audiences and critics. The fact that they were husband and wife not only enhanced their work but had a popular

appeal when a lot of the public thought of male dancers as "sissies in long underwear." David choreographed a number of ballets, such as *Pas de Chance*, which although slight were whimsical and charming. Other dancers shone in the company, including Angela Leigh, Lillian Jarvis, and Earl Kraul, but Lois and David were the stars of the early years.

Celia was convinced that the most important thing for her company was to master the great classical ballets. Drawing on her own knowledge, she led her dancers through two acts of *Giselle*, four acts of *Swan Lake*, *Les Sylphides*, the

Polovtsian Dances from *Prince Igor*, and of course *The Nutcracker*. She was also interested in new work and commissioned original ballets from Adams, Grant Strate, and Ray Muller, but she understood that her audience wanted the proven and familiar works of the existing repertoire.

During this period Celia was highly visible both backstage and out front for the company and at the school, which she visited frequently. Her striking profile and flamboyant dress made a strong impression on the young dancers. James Kudelka remembers, "She smoked like a fiend, Craven A menthol, at the same time as she lectured me about smoking too much. She was right but I didn't want to hear it. And of course we were all terrified of her." The same word has been used by everyone from Mary McDonald to Karen Kain. Celia was commanding and critical, but witty too, with a bawdy sense of humour that she shared with even the youngest students. They would sometimes hide in the stalls of the lavatory to escape her scathing criticism, but they knew that at the same time she could be compassionate if they were in trouble. And she gave them not only sharp rebukes but also images that provided a vivid context for their work. Karen Kain recalls, "After one rehearsal she took my hand and we went for a little walk. She told me that I must think of the moonlight and the rustling of the leaves in the trees overhead. I went back there whenever I was dancing that particular piece."

Celia was outspoken and critical with her dancers, never failing to let them know they could do better. She would later say she treated different dancers in different ways, gently admonishing those whose confidence she perceived to be fragile while giving others, whom she considered lazy, a "good kick up the derriere." She realized that some were more talented than others, but she never betrayed confidences or spoke behind people's backs. As one dancer said, "She levelled with you and that begat confidence." And the sting of her sharp tongue kept her dancers psychologically, as well as literally, on their toes.

Celia had already drawn on her British connections to expand the National's repertoire, calling on Anthony Tudor to teach the company *Offenbach in the Underworld*, which became an immediate favourite. In 1964 she took on a much more ambitious project, bringing John Cranko from Stuttgart to stage his vigorous and highly romantic version of *Romeo and Juliet* to the vivid Prokoviev score. It was a splendid spectacle, with sumptuous costumes in a stunning combination of reds, oranges, and magentas by the German designer Jürgen Rose, and became an immediate crowd-pleaser. Franca herself sunk her teeth into the

Celia Franca

meaty role of Lady Capulet, which she performed with unabashed gusto, tearing her hair as she wept over the body of the slain Tybalt.

The ballet proved so popular that it was revived the next year, but Franca was unable to obtain the participation of Galina Samtsova, who had danced Juliet the previous year. So she took a deep breath and cast Veronica Tennant, the youngest dancer ever to be invited to join the company. Franca had noticed Veronica's intense dedication when she was her first examiner at the age of ten, and had followed her progress through the school. Like Celia she was small of stature with a strong profile and a flair for the dramatic. Did Celia see herself in the young Veronica? Was she the daughter that Celia never had? With her youth, her emotional commitment, and her dark Mediterranean looks, Tennant was perfect casting as Juliet, and she was immediately hailed as a bright new star. She would soon be dancing all the major classical roles: Odette/Odile, Giselle, Cinderella. Celia's next acquisition would be Erik Bruhn's *La Sylphide*. She had danced with Bruhn in London with the Metropolitan Ballet, and he agreed to perform the leading role of James himself, partnered by Veronica.

Celia was ambitious enough to have her ballets televised, and she formed an alliance with producer Norman Campbell at CBC to produce TV versions of *Romeo and Juliet* and *Cinderella* in the early 1960s. Over the years Franca and Campbell would produce a total of 14 telecasts, broadening the National's audience across the country and winning many awards.

Celia also decided it was time to seek international recognition. She took her dancers on tour to London, where they danced at Covent Garden, opening with a gala attended by Princess Anne. There followed performances in Paris, Stuttgart, Brussels, Lausanne, and Monte Carlo. The notices ranged from favourable to ecstatic. The National Ballet of Canada had established itself in Europe as a company to be reckoned with, and Celia's plan to attract major dancers and repertoire had taken shape. She was not about to abandon the Canadian dancers, but she rightly thought they would benefit by working with a wider range of partners, just as she had learned from working with the Russians Stanislas Idzikowski and Léonide Massine.

And it would be another Russian who would propel the company in its next big leap forward. Rudolf Nureyev, recently defected from Soviet Russia, came to Canada to visit his friend and lover Erik Bruhn and to see *La Sylphide*. Celia met him and offered him a chance to choreograph a new *Sleeping Beauty*. With alacrity

105

he accepted. The 1972 production would be a lavish one, with sets and costumes designed by the Russian Nicholai Georgiadis. Veronica would dance the Princess Aurora, and the cast would include two newcomers to the company, Karen Kain and Frank Augustyn. Their charm and vivacity gained them immediate attention, and publicist Mary Jolliffe remembers that the company christened them "The Gold-dust Twins." Kain and Augustyn gained international recognition in 1973 when they danced the Bluebird *pas de deux* at the second international competition on the stage of the Bolshoi theatre in Moscow and brought home the first prize.

Nureyev's production was very well received, and of course he was the principal attraction, so much so that Celia was able to cut a deal with the American impresario Sol Hurok for a tour of major American cities, beginning with a gala opening at the Metropolitan Opera House in New York. Hurok wanted to bring in well-known American ballerinas to dance opposite Nureyev, but Celia insisted that the company would be made up entirely of Canadian dancers with Nureyev as the headliner. Veronica Tennant danced Aurora at the Met opening and was hailed as a star. The tour was a critical success and a big moneymaker. Finally Celia proved to her board that she was not only had

artistic vision but also financial smarts.

Soon after the tour, another celebrated Russian dancer defected, this time in Toronto. Mikhail Baryshnikov was almost immediately taking class with the company. He danced *La Sylphide* with Veronica Tennant, which was televised for CBC. The participation of the two ballet superstars Nureyev and Baryshnikov enormously enhanced the company's reputation. Of course they

Franca watching her dancers

106

Celia Franca

could not be expected to remain with the company once major American and European companies came knocking, but their presence had bolstered the confidence and profile of the Canadian dancers. They all felt that they had learned a great deal working with Nureyev. "It changed everything," Karen Kain recalled. "Although I was terrified of him, I would do anything to please him." Nureyev's obsessive attention to detail was both invigorating and exhausting, and he insisted that he get his own way in everything. This was difficult for Franca, and there is no doubt there was tension between the two, but Kain recalls, "Celia stepped back and let it happen. She understood that this was a major step forward for all of us."

Now that the company was on a

Carabosse in The Sleeping Beauty

stronger financial footing, criticism began to surface about Celia's artistic vision. The Toronto critics, always anxious to take aim at a successful institution, attacked Franca as a "cultural colonizer" whose only interest was in recreating an imitation of Britain's Royal Ballet. Celia's early career in England suggests that she was in fact very open to innovation, but in Canada she had been faced with financial constraints and an essentially conservative audience. She commissioned over 30 new ballets, but the Canadian choreographers available to her in the beginning were neither groundbreaking nor daring innovators. But in 1972 a promising new choreographer had joined the company as a young dancer. With her eagle eye for talent, Celia had spotted him as a shy, bespectacled twelve-year-old at the school. Soon afterwards, James Kudelka was choreographing a new work for Veronica Tennant, *Sonata*. He would carry on to stage *Apples*, *The Party*, and the critically praised *Washington Square*.

Celia had stopped dancing principal roles in 1959. She was then still at the top of her form and was known for her graceful femininity. "She had a great jump and wonderful arms; her arabesques were incomparable," remembers Lorna Geddes, a member of the corps in the early years. She would continue to dance character roles into the early 1970s, notably Lady Capulet, which was the signature role of her mature years. Then in 1976 she decided to step down as artistic director. She was tired of the endless battling, but there was a more personal reason. She had married the musician Jay Morton in 1960, and when he was appointed principal clarinet of the National Arts Centre orchestra they had to live apart. For several years Celia would travel to Ottawa every weekend to be with him. Now she wanted a taste of domestic life.

Betty Oliphant let Celia know she was ready to take over the directorship. Celia decided against this, for whatever reasons, some of them obviously personal. Celia would say that Betty was jealous of her authority and position. Would Betty have been an effective artistic director? It seems likely that her rather more rigid attitude and less impartial view of the potential of individual dancers would have led to a more turbulent era for the company. Perhaps Celia understood this, perhaps not. In any case, the friendship of the two women was at an end. At a gala tribute, Celia spoke afterwards to thank the many people who had helped her over the years. "And finally there is one more person…." Betty Oliphant was already making her way down the aisle when Celia said, "Ninette de Valois." It was a moment of intense drama that shocked the audience and that Celia

undoubtedly enjoyed to the full.

Celia's immediate successor was the New Zealand–born dancer from the Royal Ballet, Alexander Grant, who continued to pursue her policy of giving his principal attention to classical work. The two were friends and Celia was still a presence. "Although I had stepped down, I still considered it my company and I will till I am in my grave," she had said on the occasion of her retirement. Her influence on such up-and-coming dancers as Peter Ottmann and James Kudelka is obvious from their later tributes to her. And they, as well as other young dancers, would get ample opportunities to spread their wings when Erik Bruhn succeeded Grant as the artistic director in 1983. In spite of his classical training and reputation as the ultimate *danseur noble*, he was responsible for the most experimental period the company had known up to that time, including new works by Kudelka, David Allan, David Earle, and Robert Desrosiers.

Not surprisingly, Celia's new life in Ottawa was far from reclusive. She did some coaching and before long was a co-founder, along with Merrilee Hodgins and Joyce Shietze, of the School of Dance. She returned to the National to restage *Offenbach* and *The Nutcracker*. Film clips of her in her 70s show her still lithe and limber, wiggling her hips as she coaches Karen Kain and Rex Harrington

in a jazz duet or dancing the Tango from *Façade* with Alexander Grant. She served

Franca with Ninette de Valois

109

on the board of York University and the Canada Council. She made two trips to China, one for three weeks and another for three months, to work with young dancers there and introduce them to the techniques of Western dance.

After the death of her husband in 1997, she seemed for the first time lonely and out of it. One day she called Mavis Staines, who had taken over the direction of the National Ballet School, to say she had heard that Mavis was ruining the school. Mavis replied, "You'd better come and see what I'm doing." Celia visited soon after, and the two became good friends. Celia would continue to make regular visits.

In 2005 the National Ballet School opened its new building on Jarvis Street, a bold design created around an historic edifice that had been the original Havergal College and then the broadcast headquarters of the CBC. The project was realized by the concerted efforts of Mavis Staines and Robert Sirman. At the grand opening, Celia was there to inaugurate the Celia Franca atrium. Still majestic with her abundant gray hair swept up in a French roll, sporting the

dramatic eye make-up of a prima ballerina and a vivid slash of scarlet on her lips. She was asked to light the enormous fireplace that extends along the northern wall. She gestured with her expressive hands and flames leaped up. She turned to the assembled spectators with a throaty cackle, "There, you see. The old witch can still do some magic."

Franca in her dancing prime

ACTOR, SOLDIER

William Hutt

In the fall of 1954, the Trinity College Dramatic Society obtained the rights for the first Canadian production of Arthur Miller's *The Crucible* at Hart House Theatre. A British director was chosen. He cast the play and had an initial read-through and announced that the cast was not up to the task of performing it. This came as a bit of a shock, as many of those chosen were quite proficient and even accomplished student actors by the standards of the day. Determined to carry on, I approached Jimmy Hozack, the manager of Hart House Theatre, to try to find another director. He suggested we approach a recent graduate of Trinity who was starting a career as a professional actor. I contacted him and he immediately agreed to take on the project for the lordly fee of $500. His name was William Hutt.

We began rehearsals immediately. William Hutt turned out to be tall and willowy, with a very distinctive, though not exactly handsome, face and a sonorous voice. The most striking thing about him was his hair, which was dyed a vivid shade of yellow. He had just finished playing Hamlet and was letting his flowing locks return to their natural colour. At the time this was as extraordinary as if he had appeared wearing a sequined dress. It immediately established him as a figure of high theatricality, and we would-be Thespians quickly took to him. He used expressions like "too frightfully twee," "going for a burton," and "one swell foop." He had been in the original Stratford season, played with Christopher Plummer, starred on

Broadway with Raymond Massey, and dated Kate Reid. He obviously moved in the most recherché theatrical circles. But in fact this was probably his first professional (paid) engagement as a director.

We read the play for him and he accepted the cast as it stood, with one minor switch. Rehearsals were organized and stayed on schedule, probably as a result of his experience with Robert Gill, who was something of a martinet, and also his years as a corporal in the army. We learned that he had served in Italy, but he could not be induced to speak about the experience, which added to his enigmatic air.

As a director he was well prepared, blocked the show confidently (he had acted in a number of shows there under Robert Gill's direction and knew the stage), and made generally encouraging comments. Sometimes he demonstrated how to do things. I was playing Danforth, and when I first walked on stage, he said, "No, no. I have given you a splendid entrance and you must make the most of it." He then strode, stopped to take in the whole scene so that everyone had to look at him, and then took a long pause at centre stage before speaking. Many years later, at the launch of my book about Stratford with Bill in attendance, I said, "Bill Hutt taught me how to make an entrance. Unfortunately he didn't tell me how to stay downstage

centre for the rest of my life." Bill chuckled appreciatively.

Throughout rehearsals Bill was companionable and friendly, sometimes drinking with members of the cast after rehearsal and regaling us with theatrical stories and jokes. This was not the custom with older directors such as Bob Gill. Our producer Juliana Gianelli christened him "Slutsie," partly because of his dye-job and also because of his bonhomie; we used this nickname behind his back but did not dare use it to his face. When I told him many years later, he was tolerant but not particularly amused. Even as a young man Bill had a certain reserve that bordered on hauteur.

I understand now that this quality was the result of a somewhat repressed middle-class upbringing not unlike my own. In "Toronto the Good," Sunday was observed with rigorous decorum: Church, followed by Sunday school and then family dinner, but no drinking, no movies, no frivolous games. Along with this went an ingrained sense of duty and a belief in acceptable behaviour. When Bill was a teenager he formed a strong attachment to a younger boy. His mother pointed out that this was not normal, and so he dropped his young companion. When war came, Bill enlisted in the Ambulance Corps from a sense of duty both to his country and to his older brother Mountain. He did not take easily

to army life but stuck with it and was decorated for bravery while on a reconnaissance mission near Cassino. Bill would later say, "As a teenager I was very much at loose ends. The army gave me a sense of structure that I realize now was to stay with me." He would carry a sense of hierarchy and a commitment to discipline into his theatre work.

He also held the conviction that everything British was somehow superior. Canada in the 1940s was focused on helping to defend gallant little England and her far-flung Empire. The opinion was widely held, at least in Toronto, that the English way of doing things was the right way, whether it be table manners or style of dress or formal speech patterns. Bill Hutt, like most of the rest of us, absorbed this attitude both consciously and unconsciously, and it affected his offstage manner as well as his stage performances, which were usually in British plays directed by Brits. (Timothy Bond remembers working backstage and being summoned into the office by Marigold Charlesworth and Jean Roberts and told, "We hear you want to be a director. You must realize, dear boy, that it won't happen. You're not English." Bond proved them wrong and would some years later direct Hutt and Robin Phillips in *The Dresser*.)

I saw only a few of Hutt's performances at this time. His Archbishop of Canterbury was authoritative and forceful and was typical of a number of impersonations of English worthies: Blunt, Brackenbury, Warwick, Worcester. But as Hortensio in Guthrie's flamboyant Western staging of *The Taming of the Shrew* he was a deliciously vain and silly young dandy, expertly captured in Grant Macdonald's drawing of him and hinting at comic portraits that were to come.

The other performance I recall was self-consciously brittle and mannered

113

Hortensio in The Taming of the Shrew (*drawing by Grant Macdonald*)

performance, "jagged with sophistication," as Elyot opposite the Amanda of Charmion King in *Private Lives*, in summer stock at Niagara Falls. Hutt would later say of his years in summer stock, "What comes to mind is not what it did for me, but what it did to the poor bastards who had to watch. We learned by doing. And there we were standing in front of all these people, probably giving despicable performances because we didn't have that much technique." But Charmion King remembered Hutt as an accomplished Coward actor even then, and certainly the night I saw them we laughed long and loud.

Noël Coward was one of Hutt's early idols. He went to England on the proceeds of a Tyrone Guthrie award in 1959 and had a very thin time of it, although he did play his first James Tyrone at the Bristol Old Vic, a Viennese bachelor in a musical version of Schnitzler's *Anatol* for BBC-TV, and Ross in a television version of *Macbeth* starring Maurice Evans and Dame Judith Anderson. When he learned that Coward was mounting a production of a new play, *Waiting in the Wings*, he was determined to audition. At the Duke of York's Theatre he read the part of a young Canadian with the director Margaret Webster and sensed that the scene had gone reasonably well. Then out of the shadows stepped Coward himself, and Hutt sprang to his feet. "The real pleasure for me this morning, sir, was the distinct honour of meeting you." Coward evidently beamed with pleasure, and Hutt was cast.

The show premiered in Dublin, played Liverpool and Manchester, and then opened in London to generally dismissive notices. Coward was seen by the critics as passé, although Hutt received commendation for his scene with Dame Sybil Thorndike and the audiences in the early few weeks were enthusiastic. Hutt shared a dressing-room with Coward's longtime companion Graham Payn and soon found himself included in the master's intimate inner circle, going to lunches and after-theatre pub-crawls in Dublin and later London. He loved being in London, rented an apartment, which Graham helped him decorate, and settled in.

When the show closed, Coward offered him a part in his next venture, the musical *Sail Away*, which was to be mounted in New York with Elaine Stritch and Jean Fenn, a west-coast actress who was 'breathtakingly beautiful and had a voice like an angel's ... but couldn't act the role at all." Hutt was to play her husband, but day by day his part shrank. Then he got an offer from the Canadian Players to play Lear as well as Thomas Mendip in Fry's *The Lady's Not for Burning*. Hutt remembered, "I went to Noël and was quite frank about it. He

Gary Essendine in Nöel Coward's Present Laughter *at the Crest Theatre*

was absolutely wonderful and said, 'You must go back, darling, and do Lear.' Two days later he called the entire company on stage—I was still playing in it—and announced that he had just cut Jean Fenn out. Everybody gasped."

In 1970, Bill was in England playing a season at Chichester when he was invited to a gala party shortly after Coward received his knighthood. The evening was star-studded and champagne flowed. Bill remembered, "He was effervescent and jolly as always, but I knew the evening was a strain. At the end of it I went up to him and said, 'I've just been to the most marvellous party and it was yours. And I love you very much.' He said, 'I love you too, Bill. I always have.' Those were the last words we exchanged."

The "Eskimo Lear," the first of Hutt's four incarnations of the role, was the brainchild of director David Gardner and designer Herbert Whittaker. Their conceit was to make Shakespeare's drama into a uniquely Canadian experience. The fact that there were many elements in Shakespeare's script that did not fit

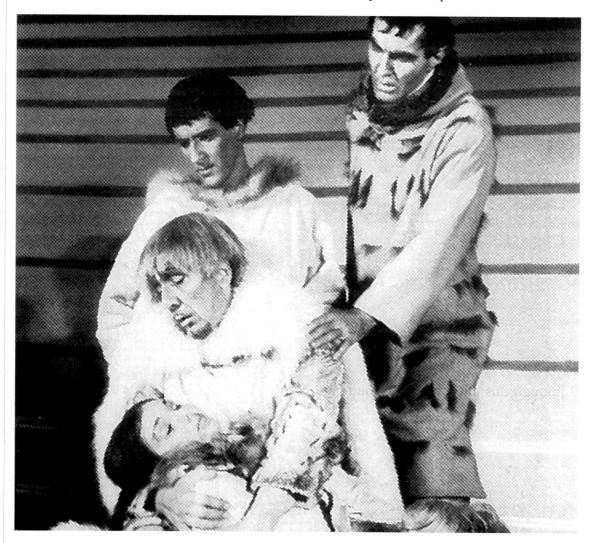

The Eskimo Lear *(1961-62) with Judith Coates, David Renton and Kenneth Pogue*

and that neither of them (nor their actors) knew anything about Inuit life did not deter them. It was an adventurous experiment in "high concept" before the term was in general use, at once bold and far-fetched. Hutt bought into the concept and gave a performance that was powerful and commanding. His howls of pain and rage were shattering to his fellow actors and audiences alike. His vulnerability at the end was touching. But critic Wendy Mitchener condemned it as "rank nationalism … Shakespeare's characters don't fit that easily into becoming Canadian citizens." But Hutt's friend and protégé Timothy Findley commented, "It was hysterical and how Bill got through it, I just don't know."

This production has become the stuff of theatrical legend. Whittaker in particular loved to tell the story of its performance at a small community on the edge of James Bay, where astonished natives sat in a circle surrounding the actors and others pressed their noses against the windows in awestruck amazement. Although this did occur, Rex Southgate, who was a member of the company, paints a somewhat different picture. The bulk of the stops in the tour were at American colleges. There were long bus-rides and everyone was expected to pitch in to erect the set—except Hutt, who sometimes tinkled out cocktail music on a nearby piano while the others worked.

He was travelling with his current companion, a young French Canadian, who dispensed drinks from Hutt's travelling bar to the lesser actors while his lover roared and howled onstage.

This early Lear prepared the way for Hutt's later conceptions of what was to become perhaps his greatest role. He would play Lear again at Stratford in 1972 and lead the company on a European tour the next year. This was a more traditional realization of the play, and Hutt turned in a performance that was acknowledged for its ferocious power, fury, and ultimate defeat, though it was still a highly controlled and technical performance. But it was roundly praised in Denmark, Poland, and the Soviet Union and was a concrete manifestation of the desire for cultural exchanges promoted by Pierre Trudeau and Leonid Brezhnev.

Hutt had by now achieved his goal of becoming a leading actor at Stratford, an ambition he had confided to his more skeptical schoolboy friend Eric House when they were beginners at the festival. In his early years under Michael Langham's direction, before going to London, Hutt had portrayed a wildly jealous Ford in *The Merry Wives of Windsor*, a thoughtful, concerned Polonius, and an observant, alienated Jacques. Good character roles, but not leads. He had also acquired a formidable

117

vocal technique, working with Robert Gill and then Esmé Crampton, experimenting with inflection and phrasing, sometimes emphasizing an unexpected word, even a connective or an article instead of the received wisdom of "going for the verb." Possessed of a naturally rich and resonant vocal instrument, he treated it with the care a musician would accord a Stradivarius. And he had learned something about simplicity: "I never believe in speaking unless it improves on silence. I never believe in moving unless it improves on stillness."

The year after the "Eskimo Lear," Hutt played his first Prospero. Rex Southgate remembers that he did a little dance of triumph when he received a wire offering him the part. But it was the next year that he achieved what his biographer Keith Garebian described as a significant breakthrough in the role of Pandarus in *Troilus and Cressida*. A vain, lecherous, flattering old voyeur with his clanking bracelets and swishing flywhisk, this was the first role in which Hutt publicly let the lid off and exploited the feminine side of his nature. His simpering delivery of "Honey-sweet queen" to the langorous Helen, his coy praise of Troilus to the innocent young Cressida were sycophantic in the extreme, and yet underneath there was the touching pathos of a libertine no longer young but still wracked by sexual desire.

Prospero (1962 drawing by Grant Macdonald)

Hutt remembered, "I began to think like a woman, and the final flash of inspiration was literally just before I went on the opening night. I suddenly took a deep breath and said, 'My God, I've got tits.'" As Garebian has written, "It was not simply that Hutt delivered an absolutely fresh, comic, touching performance, but that he released some secret wellspring of character in himself that fed his interpretation and released him from anxieties about his

Pandarus in Troilus and Cressida
with Martha Henry

own psyche and talent." Ann Casson recalls, "he is able to take a character and get all the comedy out of it, but the pathos at the same time … he was a tragic figure, a sort of lost soul, really but incredibly funny."

Hutt had realized his homosexuality as a teenager but had not come to terms with it. To retain the respect of his parents and his older brother Mountain, he suppressed his instincts. It was a time when society did not tolerate sexual deviance, which indeed was punishable by law. Hutt realized that there was no place for such activity in the military, though he did go to an Italian brothel for a "Christmas fuck." As a young actor he kept his secret, although he let it be thought he was madly in love with Kate Reid, who at the time was married to Michael Sadlier and so functioned as a plausible beard. After his time in London he acquired a French-Canadian lover who traveled with him when he went on tour, and one cast member described Hutt's offstage manner as "really quite queenly," but he was not willing to expose this quality onstage.

After Hutt's success as Pandarus, he would feel free to make use of the liberated femininity of his own nature, not with the crude lasciviousness of Pandarus but as an element in the make-up of the characters he created, or, in the words of Timothy Findley, "sank into." He was volatile and aggressive as Elyot opposite the rapacious Amanda of Zoe Caldwell, but, like Coward himself, suddenly sentimental. He and Caldwell scrapped as much offstage as on. It is an interesting phenomenon that many of the best

119

actors more or less turn into the characters they are playing onstage in their private lives. (An extreme example would be Don Harron, who more or less disappeared into the character of Charlie Farquharson.)

Langham cast Hutt as Don Armado in *Love's Labour's Lost* for the tour to Chichester on the quadricentenary of Shakespeare's birth in 1964. His performance was described by Clive Barnes as "a silver shadow composing a living ode to his own absurdity." Langham insisted Bill not play the role for comedy: "The comedy will come of its own." Bill thought this advice misguided, but after the show opened to favourable reviews, he apologized to Langham. Then came the Restoration fop Sparkish and Richard II. As the doomed king, Hutt again tapped into the feminine side of his nature. His movement had never been more graceful, his manner more gracious. The poet-king was eloquent and tender, delicate but weak. Jackie Burroughs, playing his young queen in her Stratford debut, was nervous and uncertain, but he inspired her. "If another actor grabs your attention, it takes you where you have to be, which is right in the moment. He will grab whom he needs. That's what acting is to me.... That's when I fell in love with him." Many actresses fell at least a little bit in love with Bill Hutt: Charmion King, Zoe

Caldwell, Frances Hyland. Presumably they did not expect consummation, just mutual attraction and admiration.

Also in 1964, Hutt was invited to go to New York to play the lawyer in the premiere of Edward Albee's *Tiny Alice* alongside Sir John Gielgud and Irene Worth. Albee was enjoying the height of his early acclaim following *Who's Afraid of Virginia Woolf?* But the new piece puzzled critics and public alike. Certainly it caused a buzz around town. Albee refused to explain his work even to the actors. "Talking to Edward Albee is like chasing a rabbit down a labyrinth," Hutt concluded. He was lonely in New York, and although he got on with Gielgud they never developed the rapport he had with Coward. He left the run early to return to Stratford.

In the remaining three years of Michael Langham's long reign at Stratford, Hutt gave three utterly contrasting and original performances. Leonid Gayev in Chekhov's *The Cherry Orchard* was, like both Pandarus and Richard II, a lost soul, and as different from either of them as they were from each other: dreamy, sentimental, full of half-realized fantasies. As Gayev, Hutt moved in a world of his own, his incapacity for life complementing the reckless gaiety and sudden passionate outbursts of his equally doomed sister Lyubov, played by Kate Reid. This was

the last great triumph of the two old friends, in a moving production by John Hirsch, who made magical use of the many talents in his cast.

Next came Khlestakov in Gogol's *The Government Inspector*, a petty clerk mistaken for an important government official by the inhabitants of a small provincial Russian town. Hutt had a crafty innocence, always on the verge of being found out, although his confidence never quite toppled as his ego swelled under the attentions of the deluded townspeople. Amelia Hall as the mayor's wife coquettishly responded to Hutt's amorous advances, "Well, I'm sort of married already," while she swatted flies off her homely, simple-minded daughter. The town police were as tightly choreographed as the chorus in *The Pirates of Penzance*, as they strove to keep up with Hutt's impeccable timing. Hutt had always been a natural comic, and in Shakespearean comedy he knew how to wring a laugh from an Ontario farmer in a way that such English imports as Paul Scofield or Jeremy Brett would never understand.

The same year Hutt was cast as Feste in David William's first production at Stratford. The cast included the young Martha Henry and Richard Monette as the twins. Feste in this production was a lonely old man, an observer with an acute sense of his own failure. William recalled at the first rehearsal, when Feste comes into the scene having been away for a few days, Hutt asked, "Have I had a good weekend?" "On the whole, probably not," replied William. From this one directorial suggestion Hutt constructed a complete psychological portrait, and as William pointed out, "drew his circle around the whole concept. The incarnation that followed was, to me, very powerful." Hutt's description of his method was "Build a shell, then fill it." In other words, find an image and then accumulate the appropriate details that will make the character vivid and true for an audience. This production of *Twelfth Night* was generally conceded to be "Feste's show."

In 1968 Michael Langham was succeeded as artistic director by Jean Gascon and John Hirsch as joint artistic directors, the first of several unsuccessful attempts at sharing the position. Gascon soon emerged as sole artistic director. He and Hutt developed an immediate rapport. I recall Hutt saying on one occasion, "The French Canadians can teach us so much about passion. It's simply part of their nature." Hutt's lover on the Lear tour had been a young French Canadian, and he would soon embark on an affair with an ambitious young French-Canadian actress, Louise Marleau, per-

121

haps the most serious relationship he would ever have with a woman. Initially it was she who pursued him, but he was ready to make a life with her. However, she opted out of the relationship before he could propose to her. And then at the end of his career there would be Monette. Somehow the vigorous, exuberant Québécois connected with the well-bred Anglo side of Bill Hutt to work to their mutual advantage.

Gascon accepted Hutt's position as a star actor and proceeded to promote the idea that Hutt should plunge into the French repertoire, starting with Molière's *Tartuffe*. It proved a wonderful role for Hutt. Though from a cultivated and privileged background himself, Gascon encouraged a broad, not to say vulgar, approach. "Physically, you have to be heavier and uglier. I think his balls are so big he cannot put his legs together." Hutt's expression was pious, his voice quaveringly sententious, but his splay-footed walk betrayed his sexual intent and his heavy breathing before the seduction scene was unmistakably carnal. Herbert Whittaker, not one of Hutt's greatest admirers, thought it the perfect realization of Molière's comedy. Gascon would also direct Hutt as Argan in *The Imaginary Invalid* in a production that would play in Stratford and then tour Australia. It drew laughs but was condemned for its vulgarity. Stratford audi-

ences, after their initial enthusiasm, were beginning to tire of Gascon's Gallic flamboyance, even as he was running out of steam in what was not his native environment.

Gascon encouraged Hutt to play two of Ben Jonson's most extreme characters, Volpone and Sir Epicure Mammon in *The Alchemist*. In both plays Hutt relished the opportunity to use his vocal skills to brilliant comic effect, inflecting Jonson's arias with the skill of an operatic diva. By now he had established himself as the acknowledged king of comedy at the Festival, but his tragic portrayals still lacked the warmth, compassion and pathos the roles demanded. And yet he had tapped into these qualities as Gayev and Feste, and even Pandarus. The question was whether he could adapt his sensibility to the playing of tragedy. For all its grandeur, his portrayal of Lear on the European tour did not quite manage it.

Gascon also gave Hutt the opportunity to direct at Stratford. In his production of Beckett's *Waiting for Godot* with Powys Thomas and Eric Donkin, his approach was pragmatic, rather than academic. "I'm not Professor Higgins. I watch what the actors do and then encourage them to expand it. They must surrender themselves completely to every second. That's all." Hutt was not an intellectual but he was highly intelligent, as his program notes indicate. "The two

Moliere's Tartuffe

main characters in the play are not waiting for Godot; he's waiting for them…. One starts off wanting to be perfect, and then good, and then fair, and then just to be recognized. It's the final confirmation of our existence."

Offstage, Bill Hutt's life was far from satisfying. He was elegant and grand, but behind this façade he was lonely. "Everything worked well for me once I went through the stage door. Once I left the stage door, nothing went well.... I began to understand failure, not that I was necessarily failing, but I began to understand human failure.... I was beginning to search not so much for love, but for *how* to love." Like many middle-aged homosexuals, Bill was enamoured of younger men and he had a number of liaisons with people who were attracted by his growing fame and enjoyed being pampered, given presents, and taken on trips. But there was no real parity in these relationships. Bill was the dominant partner, and one by one his lovers left him.

The arrival of the Englishman Robin Phillips as artistic director at Stratford in 1975 provoked outcries from the Canadian nationalists. Phillips immediately sought Hutt as an ally. The two men had dinner and got drunk together and an artistic partnership was formed. Hutt directed the opening production of Shaw's *Saint Joan* in Phillips's first season, but it was not well received. His production of *Oscar Remembered*, a one-man show featuring Hutt's protégé Maxim Mazumdar playing Wilde's lover Bosie Douglas, got better press. But the season was dominated by Phillips's *Measure for Measure*, in which Hutt played the Duke Vincentio as a benign manipulator, seemingly detached and watchful, but at the same time sensual and curious. It was a splendidly complex creation.

Hutt readily took to Phillips as a director. His intuitive insights, his direct and suggestive communication with actors, his intolerance of anything that he saw as false, lazy or vulgar encouraged Hutt to achieve a new restraint and simplicity. Phillips, for his part, appreciated Hutt's unique quality: "He's the best I know at being able to control his power. You must have power to withhold. When you see him restraining himself, you feel that if he let the lid off, the result would be lethal. It would be a tidal wave. His habit of saying 'Not yet!' makes you shake."

In 1974 Phillips suggested that a production of *The Importance of Being Earnest* would bring a lighter note to the festival.

"Why not? I've always wanted to play Lady Bracknell," Hutt said.

"I think that's a wonderful idea."

And so it turned out. Hutt reversed his earlier tactic and sought the masculine side of the character. Costumed to look like Queen Mary, walking on nurse's heels and crowned with a plumed toque, he sailed through the play with a regal hauteur that camouflaged basic insecurity, an act Hutt had already perfected offstage. After Edith Evans's famous reading of the handbag line, Hutt felt he had to find something else and eventually came up with an extended quadruple take that

124

"A handbag?" Lady Bracknell with Nicholas Pennell as John Worthing

brought down the house every night.

Although this was one of Hutt's most celebrated roles, he also created an achingly vulnerable Vanya, another Feste, and another Prospero. But the creations that stick in the mind are his Titus Andronicus, with its outpouring of inner pain, and the Fool in *King Lear*.

Peter Ustinov's Lear was a doddering, shuffling old fellow whose sense of humour never deserted him, even as he approached madness. Hutt stated, "I saw from the first rehearsal that Ustinov was going to be the fool, so I would be the wise one." Hutt's wise fool perfectly complemented Ustinov's foolish king.

The production garnered a great deal of attention and was to transfer to London, but the collapse of this ambitious plan led to a string of events that ended Phillips's regime at Stratford.

During the late 1970s, while Robin was at Stratford, Hutt was asked to become artistic director of Theatre London. This proved to be a happy arrangement. He was able to perform a number of plum parts: James Tyrone, Martin Dysart in *Equus*, and John A. Macdonald in a play written especially for him by Timothy Findley. He established a Young Company and discovered the enormous pleasure and satisfaction to be gained by encouraging and mentoring young actors, with whom he felt a special rapport. Two of his protégés in London were Tom McCamus and Stephen Ouimette, who had his first major professional role in *Equus* playing alongside Hutt as the psychiatrist. Hutt would continue to help young actors throughout the rest of his career: Maxim Mazumdar, Albert Schultz, his nephew Peter Hutt, Michael Therriault, Jordan Pettle. Most of these actors were not gay; Hutt's relationship with them was not sexual. They were the sons he never had, and his feeling for them transcended infatuation.

But his closest and most devoted disciple was Timothy Findley, whom Hutt had met in his very first year at Stratford when Findley was a young actor who had not yet found his true vocation as a writer. Over the years they remained friends and often got together and enjoyed each other's company. Bill was a fairly serious drinker, but Tiff, as his friends called him, became a drunk. Tiff told me of an evening when Bill was visiting at Findley's farm when Tiff became incoherent. Bill suddenly rose from his chair in a rage. "You have enormous talent and you're pissing it away. Unless you pull yourself together, I don't want to have anything more to do with you." He strode to his Cadillac and drove off into the night. Tiff did pull himself together and eventually repaid Bill by writing *The Stillborn Lover* for him.

The years after Robin Phillips left Stratford were chaotic. Bill was considered a possible successor but he was edged out by John Hirsch. Bill played Anton Schill in *The Visit* in Hirsch's first year opposite the faded movie star Alexis Smith, but the offer he received from Hirsch the next year he considered insulting. He left Stratford and played Sir in *The Dresser* with Robin Phillips in Vancouver, before joining Phillips's company at the Grand Theatre in London, Ontario, for its ill-fated, financially disastrous 1983–84 season. He played a number of roles, but the stand-out was his interpretation of *Timon of Athens*. Timothy Findley wrote: "There in the midst of all that Edwardian elegance and poise and all those panels of glass … the unbearable grace, the restraint…. The golden leashes at the end of which everyone is let out to walk, the sinister quiet, the structure in jeopardy, shimmering—the rage, the fury—the heartbreak. I shall never see the like of it again."

Hutt would go on to play in Vancouver, London, Toronto, and Ottawa before being invited back to Stratford by Hirsch's successor, John Neville. He played Cardinal Wolsey in *Henry VIII*, Sir Thomas More in *A Man for All Seasons*, and Sir Peter Teazle in *The School for Scandal*, but the most important role was Lear in a small, intimate production mounted at the Tom Patterson Theatre by Robin Phillips with his young company. Hutt experimented with the role he had played twice before and found a whole new interpretation. Keith Garebian recalls him as "a choleric old man, tethered by age and folly, yet capable of unpredictable spasms of anger…. On the heath it was deep madness rather than towering passion … there was a real, battered, frightened yet exalted human being … the frailer he grew the more affecting he became. Fatigue, disillusionment, scalding sorrow—all the residue of the private life of a shattered king—were revealed in a production that was virtually filmic." It would be Phillips and Hutt's last collaboration; their artistic partnership had been incredibly rich and fertile.

In 1994, Richard Monette became artistic director of the Stratford Festival and he immediately invited Hutt to return. They had always been on friendly terms ever since Hutt had crossed to Monette on his first day in the theatre to say, "Welcome home, Richard." Stratford was to be home to Monette over the years as much as it was for Hutt. They shared many things: a deep love and knowledge of Shakespeare and splendid vocal resources for interpreting his work, a quick wit and delight in repartee, a taste for martinis and fine wine, strong egos combined with an expansive generosity. Hutt had long since abandoned any ambition to be the Festival's artistic director, so this was no impediment to close collaboration with Richard.

Monette and Hutt quickly became verbal sparring partners. Monette has said, "When other people are around us, they are simply aghast at the way we talk to each other…. I continually puncture his bubble. It's sport. I bait him. He just rises to it." Although Richard was often outrageous, Bill could give as good as he got. His incisive wit was celebrated. Some examples:

"The soul of acting is honesty, and the quicker you can fake it, the better."

On being interviewed by the English director Clifford Owens, who said, "Unfortunately, Mr. Hutt, I don't know

127

128

Sir John Falstaff in The Merry Wives of Windsor

your work." "Mr. Owens, we're both in the same boat. I don't know your work either."

Upon hearing that Walter Learning of the Canada Council, who had denied him a grant, was embarking on a course in French immersion, "I hope he drowns."

To firefighters when a fire broke out onstage at the Grand Theatre in Kingston and they asked. "How do I get onstage?" "Like the rest of us, you'll have to audition."

On Zoe Caldwell: "She projects more femininity across the footlights than other actresses can pack into a Maidenform bra."

On Stratford's leadership: "Guthrie gave the Festival its inspiration, Langham its style, Gascon its lust, Phillips its soul, Hirsch its deficit."

On Monette's tenure. "Richard has brought the theatre to the people and the people to the theatre."

In his first season Monette was determined to mount a production of *Hamlet* for Stephen Ouimette, who had been promised the role in 1980 and then deprived of it when Hirsch took over the Festival. Hutt wanted to be in the production and readily accepted the cameo roles of the Ghost and the First Gravedigger. But it was as James Tyrone that he gave perhaps his most affecting performance to date, in Diana Leblanc's

wonderfully modulated production of *Long Day's Journey into Night* with Martha Henry, Peter Donaldson, Tom McCamus, and Martha Burns.

At the heart of Hutt's performance was his tender, regretful concern and love for his ruined wife, as embodied in the fluttery, pained, and distant Mary Tyrone of Martha Henry. These two remarkable actors, working together as instinctively as they had in *The Stillborn Lover*, again playing a flawed couple, were intimately connected and yet unable to live down the errors of the past. Hutt's performance eschewed histrionics yet encompassed a vast range of emotions—drunken regret, lingering vanity, sudden gestures of extravagance, pathetic helplessness that gave way to overblown anger—all the time covering a deep sense of his own failure.

The performance was widely hailed in the press: "There is a scene near the end … that is simply magnificent theatre. Hutt delivers his lines with such clarity and luminous simplicity that the 500-seat Tom Patterson Theatre became completely silent—except for the faint snuffling of people struggling to hold back tears. It is one of those rare timeless moments when a great performer combines with a great play to catch something of life's elusive mystery." The production was revived the next season and then recreated as a film that caught all

129

the intensity and muted passion of the stage presentation.

Although Bill had no official administrative position, Richard would consult him frequently and in building his seasons would always see that there were good roles for the "Big Three": Hutt, Martha Henry, and Brian Bedford. All three appeared in his revival of *The Little Foxes*, but many of Bill's roles were those he had played before. I remember thinking that one of the reasons that many of the great British actors' performances were so richly detailed was that they had the opportunity to play the big parts several times. Bill was the first Canadian actor to have the advantage of this: he would play Prospero, Falstaff, and Feste three times; Leonato, James Tyrone, and Lear four times, always reinventing the roles, coming at them from a fresh perspective, adding detail, discovering fresh and subtle nuances but at the same time both simplifying and digging deeper.

Most exciting was his final interpretation of Lear, directed by Monette. More than ever before Hutt wrung unexpected humour from the role, modulating his vocal attack as he made his way through the many emotional changes to final self-understanding and reconciliation with the circumstances in which he found himself. This Lear was Hutt's final exploration of the foolish, fond old man who was not only Lear but Hutt himself.

Hutt had once observed, "acting is a very deeply personal experience because you are dealing constantly with yourself in a variety of circumstances. I don't believe that when you are onstage you are a different person. You are the same person in a different set of circumstances."

In most of these late performances Hutt was directed by Monette, whom he came to trust as he had trusted Phillips. "Robin demands your best performance, Richard allows you to give your best performance." The mutual respect and admiration between these two grew as Hutt's performances continued to grow. Monette, who was an excellent cook, often invited Hutt to dinner and the two talked far into the night. Monette hoped to find a play that they could act in together, but it never happened. I had suggested Beckett's *End Game*, but instead Hutt opted to play in *Waiting for Godot* at Soulpepper in Toronto with Jordan Pettle, who had been the Fool in his last Lear, playing Vladimir to Hutt's Estragon. It was a stunning performance in its simplicity and verbal command, the last of the many lost souls that Hutt interpreted over the span of years.

In his personal life Hutt was now happier. He had encountered Matt Mackey, an intelligent, questioning teenager who was ushering at the Festival Theatre when Hutt first met him at a party. The two men saw each other sporadically, and

James Tyrone with Martha Henry in Long Day's Journey Into Night

With Jordan Pettle in
Waiting for Godot *at Soulpepper*

The last King Lear

132

Matt rather shyly showed Hutt some of the things he had written. Hutt encouraged him to go to university and to travel. Hutt had bought a substantial house at 4 Waterloo Street North, backing on the river, and in time he suggested Matt move in with him. Matt acquiesced in the summer of 1975. "Contrary to a lot of outside perceptions, I haven't found it all that easy," Hutt confided, about adjusting to living with another person. Matt and Hutt were connected by an ongoing exploration of ideas, emotions and a search for the meaning of wisdom. Hutt said, "We are more than friends and less than lovers…. With patient urging he has constantly turned my mind to the future, as if to say, 'There will always be something still to discover.'… He has brought me tranquility and beauty." With Matt as his companion, Hutt began to feel truly at home, perhaps for the first time in his gypsy life. Although only a minority of the Stratford actors are gay, there is a sufficiently strong presence that they are mutually supportive. Some have longtime partners, some not, but they form a kind of brotherhood and at

least within the theatre community they are not only tolerated but accepted. And beyond that there was a strong sense in Monette's time that all the actors were part of a family.

Gradually Bill Hutt became more relaxed and assured. I remember turning the corner from William Street onto Waterloo and seeing Bill sitting in a peacock chair on his front verandah. He asked me to come and join him and we had a half-hour chat. "You know the older one gets, one's priorities in life become more and more simple. You throw away a lot of baggage that really bugged the hell out of you fifteen years ago and you begin to realize it simply doesn't matter any more." Stephen Ouimette rode by on a bicycle and waved. Hutt cocked his head at me, "I don't suppose you'd care for a martini?"

"Why, Bill, I thought you'd never ask."

In a few moments he came back out of the house with two ice-cold glasses filled to the brim and I toasted him. He smiled and said, "As time goes on, your thoughts become much more simple and direct—at least mine do. Much more to the heart of the matter." As on his front porch, so on stage. Bill's final performance of Prospero on the Festival stage was simple, stark, but filled with an underlying warmth. Like Shakespeare he was saying goodbye to his craft and art. In the pavilion behind the theatre Bill sat enthroned while the country's theatre people came up one by one to pay him tribute.

The next year Bill was a central figure in the television series *Slings and Arrows*, as an aging actor playing his final King Lear. Not only did he get a chance to play a somewhat mocking version of himself, but much of his virtuoso interpretation of the role has been preserved for posterity. He enjoyed a few months of retirement but was reminded by Monette that he had promised to return to the stage in Monette's final season. He was offered a choice of two small parts but opted instead to take on the leading role in Albee's *A Delicate Balance*, once again playing opposite Martha Henry and directed by Diana Leblanc.

A few weeks before rehearsals were to begin, he was diagnosed with leukemia; he had only a month or two to live. He withdrew from the cast. Letters poured in from friends, fellow actors, former students, strangers. His funeral was held at St. John's Church on a hill above the river on a blisteringly hot day in July. The church was packed. Speeches and readings brought to the podium Richard Monette, Martha Henry, Peter Hutt, and Albert Schultz. He had asked that on his tombstone they carve two words:

Soldier   Actor

133

Bill Hutt's career spanned over 60 years. He was a hugely complex man. On stage he was able to explore and expose many aspects of his personality that he would not have had a chance to realize in private life. And he did this primarily in his own country. This was his choice. He wanted to do it on his own terms and his own turf. And underlying this was belief and pride, not only in his own talent, but in Canada.

Soldier Actor Patriot

Feste in Twelfth Night: *"The rain it raineth every day"*

134

DOWNHOME DIVAS

Maureen Forrester and Lois Marshall

When I was seventeen I had my first experience of Handel's *Messiah* conducted by Sir Ernest MacMillan at Massey Hall with the Toronto Symphony, the Mendelssohn Choir, and four soloists. One of these was Jon Vickers, who was the tenor soloist at my family church. And it was because of him that I was there. I had heard him sing "Every Valley Shall Be Exalted," and I knew the Hallelujah Chorus, but the full performance of this oratorio was staggering in its splendour and emotional impact. Kenneth Clark of the TV series *Civilisation* would later write that certain masterpieces have such power that they immediately grip the imagination of anyone exposed to them: Michelangelo's frescoes in the Sistine Chapel, Beethoven's ninth symphony, Shakespeare's *King Lear*, and *Messiah*. Certainly I was mesmerized by this musical pyramid. But the most moving moment was the aria in the third part: "I Know that my Redeemer Liveth." It was sung with such a depth of feeling and emotional fervour by a small woman whose eyes were closed but whose face was lifted up as if to the heavens. I carried her image and the sound of her clear pure voice with me long afterwards. If I close my eyes I can still hear it today.

At the time I was studying piano with a young woman named Mary McDonald. Every Saturday morning my brother Bill and I would make our way to her house on Playter Avenue, north of the Danforth. While one of us thumped our way through the simpler compositions of Mozart and Bach, the other would sit in the kitchen eating cookies baked by

Mary's mother. I told Mary about the young woman who had sung so passionately and it turned out that Mary knew her. Her name was Lois Marshall, and she lived with her brother and sisters a few blocks away on Ellerbeck Street. Both Mary and Lois were members of large Catholic families, and they had sung in the choir together at Holy Name Church a few blocks away. Lois had been recognized by the congregation as a remarkable talent and had received some financial support from them when she began her serious musical studies.

I had noticed that Lois walked with a limp, and Mary explained that she had contracted polio at an early age and had spent a good deal of her childhood in the Hospital for Sick Children, where she had undergone a number of operations to strengthen her leg. While there she had entertained the other children and the staff by singing. Later she attended Wellesley Street Public School, where she continued to sing. Her mentor was a woman called Elsie Hutchison, who persuaded her to enter a number of contests singing a piece titled *The Fairy's Lullaby*. Although Lois was put off by the sentimentality of the piece, she mastered her aversion and won the competition. It led to the beginning of serious study at the Conservatory of Music with the pianist and accompanist Weldon Kilburn. One of his sons Nicholas was in my class at

high school, but when I asked him about Lois, he was not very forthcoming.

I continued to attend performances of *Messiah* every year. Vickers and Lois Marshall were the soloists, along with James Milligan and Mary Morrison. But in 1954 there was a new contralto. She was a statuesque redhead with a much fuller sound than Morrison, her voice rich and creamy as she tackled "Oh Thou, That Tellest Good Tidings of Zion" with vigour and a strong sense of rejoicing. I would learn from Mary that she was from Montreal and, like Lois, a member of a large family of working-

Lois Marshall with her mentor Sir Ernest MacMillan

136

class people. She had quit school at the age of thirteen and worked as an operator for Bell to finance her musical studies. Ezra Schabas, who had headed up the Toronto Conservatory, would later explain to me that Sir Ernest was determined to have the best singers he could find for his annual performances of *Messiah* and the *St. Matthew Passion* and didn't hesitate to hire young singers if he believed they possessed the quality he was looking for.

These two women were destined to become the leading Canadian classical singers of their generation. They both began by singing whenever and wherever they had the opportunity: in churches, in community halls, in school gymnasiums, for weddings, ladies' musical societies, and men's service club dinners, usually for low fees. Maureen Forrester began her professional musical career touring for the *Jeunesses Musicales* in Quebec; Lois sang with the Eaton's musical comedy society in operettas by Gilbert and Sullivan, which whetted her appetite to sing opera. Both women won awards on the national radio program "Singing Stars of Tomorrow," which gave them national exposure. Both women would tour extensively in Canada with their accompanists: Lois with Weldon Kilburn, Maureen with John Newmark.

Canada was fortunate to have a musician of the stature of Sir Ernest

MacMillan, the only artist to receive a knighthood before titles were banned in Canada by the government of Mackenzie King. Recognition by him gave talented musicians a great boost in Canada, but in the 1950s, as today, real prestige depended upon acclaim from outside the country. Both Lois Marshall and Maureen Forrester received accolades abroad fairly early in their careers.

In February 1953, Lois received a phone call while touring in New Brunswick, asking her to go to New York to audition for Arturo Toscanini, the legendary 86-year-old conductor of the NBC Symphony. He was looking for a soprano for a concert featuring Beethoven's *Missa Solemnis* that would be broadcast and also recorded. Toscanini hired her and she appeared to his astonishment without a score, although he himself was conducting from memory. The concert was memorable, as the reviews acknowledged:

"In a performance that even Toscanini has rarely equaled for fire and devotion there was no single standout. But Marshall's soprano as the highest solo voice could be heard floating magnificently above even the massed ensemble … her tone was pure and well-rounded, her florid passages had a liquid sound and her phrasing a natural warmth that her colleagues, for all their greater experience, never quite matched."

In her 20s, Maureen studied in Berlin and then returned to Montreal in 1956 to learn that an agent, Monni Adams, had written to all the major conductors in the United States about her. She received a reply from Bruno Walter that he would be willing to audition her. He suggested several dates, only to find she was engaged. Finally he said to her with some exasperation, "Well, my dear, you're obviously much busier than I am. When can you come?" Walter had been an assistant to Gustav Mahler in Vienna before he emigrated to the United States. He had been closely associated with the great British contralto Kathleen Ferrier until her untimely death, and had been searching for a singer with a similarly distinctive voice. Maureen sang an aria from Bach's *St. John Passion* for him. He immediately offered her the contralto part in Mahler's *Resurrection Symphony*, which he was to conduct the following winter. Maureen had never heard of Mahler and was disappointed to discover that the alto part in the second symphony lasted only four minutes. But she accepted the engagement, even putting off a tour to Morocco in order to do so.

Maureen would sing twice more following Walter's baton: the Mozart *Requiem* and Brahms's *Alto Rhapsody*. Maureen spent time with Walter in his home in Beverly Hills, and he coached her in several Mahler works: the

*Maureen Forrester in recital
at the Pablo Casals Festival in Puerto Rico*

Kindertotenlieder and *Das Lied von der Erde*. He told her, "Think masculine. Sing dark." Maureen always said that Walter had given her the gift of Mahler. His song cycles were to become her signature works. In the 1950s Mahler was not well known in North America, but in the next decade he would be rediscovered, and Maureen played an important part in bringing his work to a wider public. She had hoped to record all the Mahler repertoire with Walter, but there

was a problem of conflicting recording contracts, and before she was free from them he died, in 1962.

Meanwhile Lois's career was progressing. She gave a recital in New York's Town Hall, singing Purcell's *Divine Hymn*, Brahms's *Four Serious Songs*, and Ravel's song cycle *Shéhérazade*. In Stratford, Ontario, she sang Bach and Handel arias and Purcell's *Ode on St Cecilia's Day*, as well as more modern repertoire, Alban Berg's *Seven Early Songs* and Paul Hindemith's *Marienleben*, accompanied by Glenn Gould. In Chicago she sang Purcell's *Elegy on the Death of Queen Mary II* and *The Queen's Epicedium*, and "In questa reggia" from Puccini's *Turandot*. Then in 1955 she was auditioned by the flamboyant British conductor Sir Thomas Beecham, who signed her for two recordings: the Queen of Sheba in Handel's *Solomon* and Constanze in Mozart's *Die Entführung aus dem Serail*. In 1956 Lois made her first trip to England, where she sang, in a concert at the Royal Festival Hall conducted by Sir Thomas, Mozart's *Exsultate, Jubilate* and "Martern aller Artern" from *Die Entführung*, as well as Manuel de Falla's *Seven Popular Spanish Songs*, which exercised her lower register and would become one of her signature pieces. While in England she sang with The Halle Orchestra under Sir John Barbirolli and at the Welsh Eisteddfod.

She also sang in Hamburg, where she was completely unknown but garnered ecstatic reviews.

Although there are some early pictures in which they are made to look almost glamorous, neither woman was a beauty. Maureen Forrester was a large, robust woman with an animated face that would in time become not only imposing but almost craggy. Lois Marshall was small and delicate with a serious, sensitive mien, though she could flash a radiant smile at her friends and sometimes her audience. Maureen's daughter Gina remembers her:

"Lois was like a kid. The first time I saw her, in fact I thought she was one. Her back was turned and I tapped her on the shoulder, excited to find someone my own age in a grown-up crowd, so I was shocked that a grown woman turned around…. She was fun and funny but never treated me like the child I was. I felt like a peer. Her hairstyles were even higher than mom's; bun upon bun upon bun. But like mom, she supported that look so regally."

At the age of twenty-one, Lois began an affair with her teacher Weldon Kilburn, which would last throughout much of her professional career. He was married with four children, but because he and Lois toured together they spent a great deal of time with each other. Although people in musical circles knew

139

about this liaison, it was never reported in the press. Eventually, after Kilburn's wife died, they would marry and live in a house that Lois had bought in north Toronto. However, the marriage was not to last. Kilburn was a philanderer, and when Lois returned from a tour to find he had moved another woman into her house, she ended the relationship and they divorced.

Maureen's romantic life was equally complicated. She had agreed to sing in a high-school auditorium in Ottawa. "Whap—it hit me—the smell of overripe gym socks. It had a stage that was too high and lights that were too bright. You couldn't have missed a yawn at 300 paces. I looked out and thought to myself, what an audience. And then I noticed a face in the second row to the left. I took one look and in one of those psychic flashes of mine—that's the man I'm going to marry." The man was Eugene Kash, a violinist who at the time was the conductor of the Ottawa Philharmonic. He came backstage after the concert with his friend Karl Weiselberger, the music critic of the *Ottawa Citizen*. Maureen was holding a nosegay that had been given to her at the end of her concert. She greeted Eugene saying, "Well, I've got the flowers. Now all I need is the man."

They would not meet again for several months when Eugene asked Maureen to join him for dinner on New Year's Day with his friend, folk singer Alan Mills, and Alan's partner. Slowly they began dating. Eugene made occasional visits to Montreal, and after a bit he took a small apartment there. Maureen was happy cleaning and cooking in the tiny kitchenette. But Eugene tried to keep his distance: "I'm not the marrying kind. And I'm older." Nineteen years, in fact. But there was another reason. Eugene was Jewish, and he was under considerable family pressure not to marry outside his religion. Maureen's mother would also have disapproved, but her daughter was impulsive and determined to get what she wanted.

Maureen had been a favourite singer with *Jeunesses Musicales*, and in 1955 they offered to send her on a tour of Europe with a special grant they had received from UNESCO. She started in Paris, where she sang a mixed program ranging from Beethoven to Richard Strauss. She included some songs that Schumann had composed to letters written by Mary, Queen of Scots. The lyrics Schumann had set were in German, but Maureen had obtained copies of the originals written in French and she sang them in that language at the Salle Gavreau on St. Valentine's Day. The critics were as delighted with this initiative as they were with the rich golden tone of her voice. The tour was off to a rousing start, and

Maureen Forrester with her husband Eugene Kash and their children Daniel, Gina, Susie, Paula and Linda

Maureen was feted in a variety of cities in France and Spain. But towards the end she began to experience sickness and exhaustion and before long she realized she was pregnant. She phoned Eugene, but he wanted no part in this development and flatly refused to consider marriage.

Headstrong as ever, Maureen decided she would have the baby anyway. She had considered studying in Berlin and decided to proceed with this plan. With the help of the Canadian Embassy, Maureen got in touch with Michael Raucheisen, who had accompanied Fritz Kreisler and been closely associated with Richard Strauss. She learned to speak German with the accent of a Berliner and acquired an extended repertoire of Schubert and Schumann lieder. In October the baby was born and there were complications that required surgery.

However she survived and was delighted with the child. She called Eugene and they agreed to call her Paula. Maureen had bookings lined up in Paris, London, and Canada. She left the baby with her landlady and set out to fulfill her commitments.

Lois's experience recording Mozart's *Die Entführung* further whetted her appetite to perform in opera. She had managed to sing the high coloratura arias of the Queen of the Night in *Die Zauberflöte* at the Royal Alexandra in Toronto, but Herman Geiger-Torel, the director of the Canadian Opera Company, adamantly refused to cast her in anything where she had to move, because of her limp. Then an offer came from Sarah Caldwell, the highly idiosyncratic American conductor, for her to perform in Boston. The roles chosen were Mimi in *La Bohème* and the heroine in *Tosca*. Both roles were highly dramatic, but Lois did not manage to completely convince as the Roman diva. However, as the frail, passionate, young seamstress who dies of consumption in a Parisian garret she created a character whose experience paralleled her own. Her success in Boston led to a tour, which eventually visited Hamilton, but although Lois shone, the supporting cast was second rate.

Lois's only other major operatic experience came with the 1959 broadcast by the CBC of Benjamin Britten's *Peter Grimes*, in which Lois played Ellen Orford, another role to which she was eminently suited by her personality as well as her vocal range. Although Lois would sing in concert several Wagner arias from *Tannhäuser*, *Lohengrin*, and *Die Meistersinger*, she would have needed a heavier voice and greater physical stamina to perform these operas onstage. In the early 1960s she developed nodules on her vocal cords, which meant that she needed to take time out to rest and restore her voice. Following her return to the stage she was considerably more cautious in her choice of repertoire.

In 1958, Lois had made her first appearance in Russia in the Great Hall of the Moscow Conservatory. Her youth, vigour, and vocal elegance captivated those in attendance, and in the second half of her program the audience was considerably larger than at the beginning. She would go on to give concerts in Riga, Leningrad, and Kiev. The Russian musical fraternity loved her: Lois would visit the Soviet Union seven times and was enthusiastically received each time. During this period the Russians gave a warm reception to several Canadian visitors, including Glenn Gould, Maureen Forrester, and the National Ballet of Canada. Peter Roberts and Doris Crowe at the Canadian Embassy were knowledgeable about

142

Lois Marshall as the Queen of the Night with the Canadian Opera Company

music, and they helped arrange concerts and receptions for their compatriots.

On her return to Canada, Maureen began seeing Eugene again. She toured in Canada with John Newmark from coat to coast giving recitals and sang the Mozart *Requiem* with the Montreal Symphony. But she became increasingly concerned by letters she received from Berlin which indicated that her former landlady had become very possessive of baby Paula. On a sudden impulse she flew to Berlin, retrieved her child, and set up house in London. For the next few months she flew back and forth between London, New York, and Montreal. Before long she realized she was pregnant again. Regretfully she took the practical course of having an abortion. She was ready to give up on Eugene and stopped telephoning him. Although this was not a tactic she had devised, to her surprise he phoned and proposed marriage. The couple were married in a civil ceremony in London, and shortly afterwards Maureen converted to Judaism.

Maureen and Eugene would go on to have four more children, three daughters and a son. They eventually became established in Toronto, moving to ever bigger houses. Although Eugene continued to work, he became a househusband since Maureen was on the road most of the time and had become the principal

144

"FEEDING THE FAMILY — KIWI STYLE"

Mama Maureen and her nestlings

breadwinner. She demanded and got sizeable fees but was always in debt. She insisted the children have private lessons and go to summer camps. She employed managers in both London and New York and a publicist. She spent a small fortune

on hairdressers and gowns, often specially constructed to hide her frequent pregnancies. And she redecorated their various houses with the help of an interior designer. She was constantly going to the bank with her signed contracts to arrange loans and a line of credit. She continued to sing Bach, Handel, Schubert, Schumann, and of course Mahler, on two continents. As she herself would put it, "Perugia, Pittsburgh, Vienna, Vancouver, Warsaw and Walla Walla." In the 1960s she sang for almost every major conductor in North America and Europe. In 1962 she added trips to Australia and Israel.

Maureen first sang with the Bach Aria Group in 1958, and Lois joined the Group in 1965 as soprano soloist. This was a small ensemble of vocalists and instrumentalists: violin, cello, flute, oboe, and piano. The Bach Aria Group had been founded in 1946 by William H. Scheide, a wealthy American musicologist and philanthropist, who wanted to explore all of Bach's 249 cantatas using musicians and singers of the highest calibre. This gave the Group's members ongoing employment at competitive salaries while still allowing them time to

145

The Bach Aria Group Maureen, Lois and musicians with Bill Scheide, seated at right

accept other engagements. They prepared three programs each year, which they performed in New York and on a touring circuit in the United States and Canada. As time went on, Lois became increasingly nervous singing the soprano arias. One night in El Paso, Helen Watts, who had replaced Maureen as the alto soloist with the Group, was indisposed. Lois offered to take on her arias in addition to her own. Soon afterwards she became the alto soloist and continued in that capacity until the Group was temporarily disbanded in 1980.

Maureen has written about touring with the Bach Aria Group. She most often took the wheel of the car herself. When they checked into a hotel she would ask for a room as far way from Lois as possible, because Lois vocalized for two or three hours every morning starting at 7:00. Maureen, on the other hand, rarely exercised her voice before performing, believing that if she did she would sacrifice spontaneity. The two were rivals but also friends. Stuart Hamilton, who accompanied both of them, especially toward the end of their careers, has commented, "They admired each other but Maureen resented Lois's spirituality and Lois resented Maureen's commercial success."

The Group, which was all male except for Maureen and Lois, often indulged in rather coarse humour and even on one occasion wrote a parody cantata that was full of lewd double entendres. They loved good food and drink, which in time caused both female soloists to put on weight. They also shared a sense of humour. Maureen's daughter Gina recalled, "Lois brought out the silly in mom. Of course my favourite was the cat duet." This piece of musical whimsy was written by Rossini, and the lyric is a repeated meow as the two singers go up and down the scale. Maureen described herself as zany, whereas Lois loved dirty jokes and sometimes composed bawdy limericks. Stuart Hamilton remembered one:

> There was a young man from Sparta
> Who was a prodigious farter.
> He could blow out his ass
> The B minor Mass
> And for an encore La Traviata.

William Scheide usually toured with the Group. He became very fond of Lois and on one occasion invited her to be a guest in his house in Princeton. He showed her the collection of rare and valuable musical manuscripts he and his father had collected and donated to the university library. They included signed and dated copies of works by Bach, Beethoven, Schubert, and Wagner. He then took her to his house where he played for her on his own pipe organ. He

146

asked Lois to marry him and share his beautiful home. "Oh, I couldn't," she replied. "I'm just a singer." She and Scheide remained close colleagues and friends until she left the Group.

During the later years of their careers, both Lois and Maureen sang a similar repertoire: Handel's *Messiah*, Beethoven's *Ninth*, lieder by Mozart, Schubert, Schumann, Brahms, Strauss, and Mahler. Both women had specialties, and both sang works by Canadian composers. Maureen performed the *Songs for Dark Voice* that were written for her by Harry Somers and works based on Jewish themes by Srul Irving Glick. Lois sang works by John Beckwith based on the poems of e.e. cummings, and by Godfrey Ridout based on hymns by John Donne. They also sang folk songs: "Go Way from My Window," "Blow the Wind Southerly," and "Ae Fond Kiss." Lois's voice deepened from the silvery ethereal timbre of her youth to a richer, fuller sound; Maureen claimed that with every new baby she could sing both a half-tone higher and a half-tome lower. Her mature voice was less golden than bronze in colour. Stuart Hamilton accompanied both of them in Schumann's *Frauenliebe und Leben* during their farewell tours. He said that Lois treated the character as Everywoman and her performance had tragic power; Maureen had the down-to-earth directness and honesty of a simple

German peasant girl. He was so moved by her performance that he had difficulty playing the postlude to the cycle.

When Lois gave up singing she taught at the Royal Conservatory. Maureen had already spent three years teaching in Philadelphia. Both had pupils who would go on to have successful careers: in Maureen's case Florence Quivar, who would eventually sing at the Met; Lois trained Monica Whicher, who would have the operatic career that Lois had hoped for, largely in Canada.

Late in her singing life Maureen also had a career in opera. She was surprised one day when she picked up the phone and was asked by Mario Bernardi if she would consider singing in *Hansel and Gretel*. She expected to be offered the rather uninteresting minor role of the mother but leaped at the chance to play the Witch. For CBC television, through the use of technology, they created the effect of her flying, and when she later reprised the role onstage in Calgary and San Diego she insisted on repeating the effect and, strapped into a harness attached to wires, she soared above the stage. She felt the role brought out the crazy side of her personality; she went on to sing the Queen of the Fairies in Gilbert and Sullivan's *Iolanthe* and the title role in Giancarlo Menotti's *The Medium* at Stratford. In Toronto she undertook *Fricka* in *Die Walküre* and

147

Mistress Quickly in Verdi's *Falstaff*. Later she would sing Klytemnästra in Strauss's *Elektra* and, by way of contrast, the Stepmother in Massenet's *Cendrillon*. She surprised her serious music fans by showing a distinct flair for the comical. Perhaps it is not so unnatural that one of

Bloody Mary in South Pacific *in Edmonton*

her daughters Linda has had a career as a comedienne onstage and in film. Her mother nicknamed her Sarah Heartburn.

Maureen was flying to New York when she met a man with whom, in her impulsive way, she immediately fell in love. She divorced Eugene and embarked on a three-year affair before she realized that her new lover was primarily interested in being seen with her in smart restaurants where she would usually be expected to pick up the bill. She came to her senses and dumped him.

In December 1983 Maureen received a phone call from Francis Fox, a cabinet minister in Pierre Trudeau's government, asking her to become Chairman of the Canada Council. She somewhat reluctantly agreed to take on the job when she realized that as a successful artist in her own right she could stand up to the government without whining or begging. As she toured the country giving concerts, she gave receptions where she met hundreds of artists. Backed by Tim Porteous, the chief administrator at the Council, who wrote her speeches, she successfully fought to get tax exemptions for artists to deduct their expenses and fended off an attempt by the government to take over the direction of some of the country's major cultural organizations, including the National Arts Centre, the CBC, Telefilm Canada, and the Canada Council, preserving their arm's length

148

Maureen as the Wicked Witch in Hansel and Gretel *with Judith Forst and Christine Anton*

relationships. She was the first artist to be made a Companion of the Order of Canada, an honour Lois Marshall received soon after.

By this time Lois was in a wheelchair. She no longer sang in public but sometimes recited. Her friend the musicologist Carl Morey remembers her reading of "On Bredon Hill" in a voice that was strong and vibrant. Her phrasing and intonation made the poem come across clearly and powerfully for the audience. He already knew she had always been a great reader, often saying the words out loud. This practice had made a major contribution to the clarity of her singing; her carefully worked-out articulation underlay the purity of her singing voice. She had begun her creative life as a storyteller, making up tales for her sisters on Ellerbeck Street, and she would retain her narrative powers to the end. Her many students always spoke of her fondly after she was gone.

Even after she retired from the Council, Maureen would continue to lend her name and presence to a variety of good works. I was approached by Nona Macdonald Heaslip to produce a benefit for CANFAR, an organization dedicated to AIDS research, with Maureen as the chairman in charge of programming. She was easy to work with, full of good ideas herself but receptive to the contributions of others, good-humoured if sometimes a bit imperious. Many of the performing artists contributed their time and talent merely because Maureen was the headliner, and the fundraiser was a great success.

I learned a few years later that Maureen was suffering from Alzheimer's disease and was living at the Performing Arts Lodge in greatly reduced circumstances. One Saturday I had helped to organize a program at the Arts and Letters Club and had persuaded Robert Gage, a fashionable hairdresser, to speak.

149

When he finished his highly amusing talk a smartly dressed woman came up to him and offered to sing a song to him. It was Maureen. For years he had fashioned her coiffures. The song was a sentimental ballad interpreted with both humour and warm feeling. The voice was still rich and warm, and she received a standing ovation. I think it may have been the last time she sang in public.

HIGH FLYER

Richard Williams

Dick Williams and I met playing in a mud puddle in a vacant lot in North Toronto. We were five years old. Dick asked me to his house and I readily agreed. We went around to the side door and climbed the four steps up to the kitchen where his mother was laying out cookies on a sheet. She gave us milk and her freshly baked cookies and let us go up to Dick's room to play with his electric train.

Even at that young age I think I recognized that Dick's mother, Kay, was a beauty, with her dark hair parted in the middle and caught up at the nape of her neck, ballerina-style, and her wide slanting eyes, which gave her a rather exotic air. Later I would hear her compared to Wendy Hiller. She shared with the famous actress a slightly elfin appearance. Dick had the same large, slanting eyes as his mother and something of her pixyish look. Kay's whole family had it. They were the children of a carpenter from Yorkshire, who worked till he reached a ripe old age in a shop at the back of his house on Dufferin Street and instilled in his children a respect for craftsmanship which they applied to various fields, most of them arts-related. The best known was Kay's brother Ken Bell, who became a celebrated photographer.

That October afternoon I must have passed Kay's workroom as she sat at her drawing board, outlining the figure of a stylish matron wearing one of those fanciful hats that women sported in the 1930s. I learned that Kay was a commercial artist who worked at home, creating illustrations for advertisements in magazines. I had never before encountered a real, working artist.

I don't know when I first realized that Dick could draw. According to the prevalent psychology it was natural enough; he took after his mother. Certainly Kay taught and encouraged him. His early efforts were almost always cartoon figures: Donald Duck, Bugs Bunny, and Goofy were favourites. Dick's drawings of them were just as good as those in the comics and Big Little books we went through by the dozens. Kay took us to see all the Walt Disney features as soon as they came out: *Pinocchio*, *Bambi*, *Dumbo*, *Fantasia*.

Dick and I were also hooked on comedy, some of it sophisticated, much of it not. Kay introduced us to Danny Kaye's *Up in Arms* and *The Secret Life of Walter Mitty*. At Saturday matinees we discovered the Marx Brothers in *A Night at the Opera*, and Olsen and Johnson's *Hellzapoppin'*, both of which we saw several times. We spent a lot of time making faces and doing weird voices. We competed, egging each other on to see who could be the silliest.

But we did not limit ourselves to cartoons and comics. We followed the adventures of Superman, Batman and Robin, and an underwater superhero called Submariner. We went to all the Tarzan movies and followed the adven-

tures of Terry and the Pirates and the Lone Ranger on radio. We both identified with Terry, living a life of ongoing danger unencumbered by parents. But Dick, always ahead of me in his commitment to imaginative fantasy, became convinced his uncle was Superman. For a while he wore a blue cape Kay had made for him everywhere, even to school. Eventually on a dare he climbed up on a rose trellis and announced he could fly. He leaped into the air and crashed to the ground, breaking his wrist. "Serves him right," said one of the local mothers.

As soon as we learned to print we wrote a play. It was called *Cat and Dog* and was a comic adventure story for two actors (us). Sadly, the manuscript of this early masterpiece has not survived. It was the first of many dramatic entertainments we devised. Wherever we went, whatever groups we belonged to, we immediately put on a show. We joined the Cub Pack at the church my parents went to. Dick's parents didn't go to church but Ken Williams, Dick's father, became Cubmaster and encouraged our theatrical efforts. As well as performing playlets at Cubs, our weekly outings involved daring each other to commit ever more outrageous pranks on our way home. We went into apartment buildings along the way, ringing doorbells and pitching snowballs at whoever answered, then running away before the irate ten-

Dick and the author as wolf cubs c. 1942

ants could catch us. Or we pretended to be spastics (as we called them then), walking out into traffic and laughing hysterically as cars swerved and screeched to a stop.

Sometimes Dick and I were in the same class at school, sometimes not. In grade seven we were both in the class of Mr. Martin, the school's art teacher. He taught us to make marionettes using a light bulb and plasticine to fashion the heads, coating them with papier mâché and painting them. We made bodies of

cloth stuffed with tissue paper and attached articulated arms and legs manipulated by strings attached to the head, hands and knees.

Not surprisingly, Dick's first puppet was Donald Duck. His mother made and clothed the body; Kay was a gifted seamstress who made all her own clothes. Kay's puppet bodies were extremely skillful concoctions, and before long Dick and she had created a range of Disney characters. Dick and I worked on a script based on various comic-book scenarios. Once again we were in show business together. We were joined by a classmate, Richie Brown, who had a strongly idiosyncratic sense of humour and a gift for doing cartoon voices, especially Donald Duck. We were asked to perform at a birthday party and put on a show. Before long Dick and Richie had a business going that was to keep them in pocket money for the next five or six years. I was only briefly involved in this venture, because it was decreed by our parents that we should go to different high schools.

About this time Dick went away to summer camp, where he learned about what were then called "the facts of life" in a somewhat garbled version. This information fascinated us, although we were not yet old enough to put our new-found knowledge to the test. At camp Dick also became a strong swimmer. He

153

continued to swim at the YMCA and before long he became a daredevil diver and performed in water shows as a kind of aquatic clown. For several years my father had taken a bunch of the neighbourhood kids to the Shriners' Circus. We both loved the clown acts and imitated many of them on our way home from school. Dick's aquatic clown act incorporated various aspects of these antics into a sophisticated if not exactly subtle comic act. He was a natural performer.

In our early high-school years we became interested in what was then called Dixieland jazz. We discovered Bessie Smith, Louis Armstrong, Johnny Dodds, Sidney Bechet, Billie Holiday, and Bix Beiderbecke: all the great jazz performers of the 1920s and 30s. Their early recordings were being re-released on the newly invented LPs and we bought as many of them as we could afford. We listened to them late at night, mainly in the basement room at the Williams house, which Dick now occupied. It had a separate entrance through the garden shed, and consequently he could come and go as he pleased.

Just as Dick borrowed routines from *A Night at The Opera* and *Hellzapoppin'* and made them his own, so too he wanted to make jazz himself. He acquired a cornet and taught himself to play, crudely at first, but with great energy and verve. He found some other would-be musicians at

his high school, Northern Vocational, and formed his own band. They played at noon-hour or after school. Dick took on an invented persona as the leader of the band, calling himself Ivan Yurpee, and it was inevitable that he would decide to produce a full-length evening of music and skits. We stole some gags from Olsen and Johnson and Milton Berle, whose show we watched on television at an appliance store on Yonge Street, long before our families bought their own TV sets.

The Ivan Yurpee Show included a Sherlock Holmes skit and a mock game show. We enlisted the help of a couple of sexy girls, one of whom ran across the stage in a grass skirt pursued by a guy with a lawnmower. She also walked across the stage with a handsome young guy, both of them in pyjamas; when they reappeared they had exchanged pyjama bottoms. There was a skit in which Dick entered a beauty contest wearing an outrageous blonde wig and exaggerated lipstick. And of course he led the band, tooting his own horn for all he was worth. Dick had become a celebrity at Northern Vocational.

But he was also having problems. He started to hang out with some fairly rough characters, learned to shoot pool and devoted more time to his cornet than his schoolwork. His grades slipped and he was in danger of failing. I had

154

already learned that Ken was not Dick's biological father. Kay had married at a young age another artist, Leslie Lane. Once she became pregnant with Dick, Lane abandoned her. Kay sued for divorce and soon after was courted by Ken. They married and Ken adopted Dick, who took his surname. For a while this seemed like a good arrangement all round. Dick benefited from Ken's support and Ken was proud of Dick's talent. But when Dick became a teenager, conflicts bubbled up.

It was sometimes said by the local gossips that Dick had inherited bad blood from his real father. Far from being hurt by this judgment, I think Dick set out to live up to his reputation. And at the same time he was determined to escape. The summer he turned fifteen, he climbed on a bus and went to California. He looked up a connection of his parents who worked as a draughtsman for Walt Disney. Disney was not about to put a teenaged kid on the payroll but allowed Dick to stay for the summer and learn whatever he could. He came back in the fall and told his parents he wanted to apply to go to the Ontario College of Art. This prestigious institution did not open its doors to anyone who did not have a high-school diploma, but when they saw Dick's work they allowed him to enroll in commercial art.

Dick flourished at art college. He was skilled, quick, and hard-working. His outrageous humour and gifts as a mimic made him popular with other students. He liked to party and hang out with the guys; he was also attractive to women. Under the influence of Jim Burke, an aspiring writer he met at the Y, he began to read a wide variety of modern work: Joyce Cary's *The Horse's Mouth*, Truman Capote's *Other Voices, Other Rooms*, and J.D. Salinger's *The Catcher in the Rye*. He also began to listen to classical music: from Bach to Stravinsky, but above all Beethoven. Encouraged by Jim he began to tackle the big figures in the arts: Beethoven and Brahms, Shakespeare and

155

Dick with animator Richard Kelsey at Walt Disney Studios, 1948

Tolstoy, Michelangelo and Rembrandt and especially Goya, whose savage depiction of war and madness Dick found especially powerful. Not that he abandoned telling jokes or listening to jazz. He rapidly became a more skilled musician and soon was part of a small combo of art-college students, which included Michael Snow on piano and Graham Coughtry on trombone.

Dick continued to live at home. He still earned pocket money doing puppet shows for kids' birthday parties, but a new source of income opened up. Television production was beginning in Toronto. There was a demand for animated commercials, and Dick knew how to animate, thanks to his summer at Disney's. He began to work for Graphic Associates, a studio north of Toronto at Kleinburg that was led by George Dunning and Jim McKay. These two had been recruited by Norman McLaren to be part of his stable of animators at the National Film Board before setting up on their own.

Their studio was an unusual building with separate living quarters for each of them radiating from a central work area. They employed various artists like Dick, Michael Snow, and Joyce Wieland, who all came and went. The studio was presided over by a gnomic octogenarian houseman with the improbable name of Yet Yung. It was a hangout for artistic types who lived nearby: a young but already somewhat pontifical Pierre Berton, and a straggly-bearded polymath named Lister Sinclair. There was also a striking, sharp-tongued, carrot-topped woman called Steve. Underneath the intellectual sparring and edgy repartee of this little society we sensed the throb of sexual dalliance.

Dick began to make real money animating commercials and soon acquired a car: a red mini Morris. It was a second-hand convertible with no heater and extremely cold in the winter. He also acquired a girlfriend, Stephanie, known as Tep. She had a sort of Botticelli delicacy of features, with corn-gold hair and china-blue eyes. Although superficially demure in the style of the time, she was sharply observant and quite capable of barbed comments. She helped Dick with his puppet shows and had a shrewd appreciation of his artwork. Not an intellectual, she was nevertheless able to keep pace with Dick's musical and literary interests and won the respect of his friends.

The summer before his last year at the art college, Dick went with a fellow student to Mexico for part of the summer. He stayed with his friend in the third-oldest house in North America and soaked up the strange flavour of a culture new to him but with ancient roots. He was strongly influenced by pre-

156

The Revival Meeting lithograph

Colombian art but also by the great Mexican muralists, particularly the social realist José Clemente Orozco and the brilliant colourist Rufino Tamayo. He went back to school and transferred from commercial to fine art, having decided he wanted to become a serious painter. He worked closely with Fred Hagan and produced some very complex lithographs, particularly two large-scale works, one of a Mexican brothel and another of an evangelical revival in downtown Toronto. He began to paint portraits and revealed a particular gift for getting a likeness and catching the essence of a sitter's personality. This would be another source of income in the next few years.

Because he had switched courses, Dick didn't graduate from the Ontario College of Art with a diploma, a point he rammed home when the college held a tribute dinner in his honour many years later. (Dick was always one to get his revenge when the time was ripe.) However, when he finished at the OCA we celebrated his non-graduation at Old Angelo's, the only Italian restaurant in Toronto at the time. We drank Chianti with our spaghetti and meatballs and thought ourselves very cosmopolitan. Dick went off to Spain with his friends Mike and Graham, where they painted all morning, swam every afternoon, played jazz in the evenings, and lived for a dollar a day on the tiny island of Ibiza. A year later he came back for a month and married Tep at her parents' summer cottage. Dick looked very respectable in

Dick with some of his paintings done in Ibiza

blue blazer and white flannels but made a predictably outrageous speech.

Dick and Tep stayed in Ibiza for a couple of years, but by 1957 they had moved to London. Dick had given up on his goal of being the next Goya: "I was trying to paint a masterpiece to hang in the Tate, just between a Matisse and a Picasso, and I suddenly thought, what am I doing here? I should get back to doing what I know," he explained as we drank beer and ate fresh prawns in a pub. In London by happy chance Dick met up with George Dunning, who had just arrived to set up a studio for UPA (United Productions of America.) Dunning immediately hired Dick and they began working on commercials. They also found time to develop two animated shorts.

Dunning created *Flying Man* while Dick produced *The Apple*, based on the story of William Tell. They took these two films to the first animation festival at Annecy in France in 1960 and won first and second prizes. Thus emboldened, Dick began work on two more films. Tep, who had learned how to colour the animation cells Dick drew, worked alongside him. He produced *Love Me, Love Me, Love Me* about a little man with an insatiable need for attention. It was both funny and iconoclastic; it retained the spirit of some of Dick's socially concerned lithographs, but the style was

158

The Little Island: *Good, Truth and Beauty*

more primitive and the humour had the savage edge of Dick's more outrageous stage performances.

Then came *The Little Island*, about three men committed to Truth, Good, and Beauty. Each man has an ideal, but only one. The ferocity of their single-minded commitment results in a conflict as side-splitting as it is devastating. It invokes the anarchic spirit of his hero Goya and translates it into another sphere. I saw *The Little Island* in Toronto and recognized a few of my own idiosyncrasies in the figure committed to Beauty. The film featured a score composed by Tristram Cary, son of the novelist Joyce Cary whom Dick had so admired as a teenager. This film not only charmed the juries at Annecy and Venice but actually changed the look of animation, introducing a new style whose hallmark was draughtsmanship of vigorous, almost primitive simplicity, powered by an impudence that was perfectly in tune with the emerging "swinging London" of the 1960s.

Dick was right at home in this world. After he and Tep separated, he lived and worked in a bachelor pad, putting up visiting pals from Toronto, drove a sports car, dated models and actresses, and painted huge and colourful murals of circus clowns or Lautrec-inspired chanteuses for fashionable restaurants when he needed some ready cash. For a while Dick and George Dunning worked together amicably enough, but it was inevitable that their competitive egos would clash. Dick continued to respect Dunning's ability: "George had judgment, vision and above all taste," he would later say. "Half the time he couldn't be bothered to finish what he started. He could also be pretentious; his last project was to animate Shakespeare's *Tempest*. At the end of his life he used to sit up all night drinking Nuits-Saint-Georges and pontificating. But he had incredible curiosity; he was willing to try anything, open any door, no matter what was behind it." Eventually Dunning would crown his career with his masterpiece, *The Yellow Submarine* (1968).

By then Dick had moved on. He set up his own studio in Soho Square, in a forest-green Georgian mansion rented from Lord Rothschild. He continued to make commercials and began to do titles for a number of hot new movie directors:

Woody Allen, Mike Nichols, Richard Lester, and Tony Richardson. My first awareness of this work came when I went to see *What's New, Pussycat?* in 1965 and the screen filled with bold, outrageous figures in bright neon colours. I turned to my wife and said, "That has to be Dick's work," and of course it was.

He created equally inventive titles for the *Pink Panther* films and *A Funny Thing Happened on the Way to the Forum* (1966) that established his style as slick, sharp, and sly. "The fact is," Dick would say later, "we were willing to do anything they asked for. We were totally eclectic, and the ironic thing is, this is now seen as *my* style." His work was widely appreciated, though when he did the logo for Mike Nichols's 1967 film *The Graduate* they fell out over the terms of payment. Dick still refers to the director as "Mike Dimes."

He had a happier collaboration with Tony Richardson. He did not only titles but also internal sections for *The Charge of the Light Brigade* (1968). Picking up on the cartoons of George Cruikshank allowed him to give this work a strong Victorian flavour, which he continued to exploit in a half-hour animated version of Charles Dickens's *A Christmas Carol* (1971), using the voices of prominent English actors led by Alastair Sim as Scrooge. This film won Dick his first Academy Award in 1972. I remember

160

The Charge of the Light Brigade: *The British Lion attacks the Russian Bear while the French Coq looks on*

seeing him on television clutching his Oscar, giving a triumphant chuckle and thanking his mother. I pictured Kay in front of her set, dry-eyed but smiling a little private smile. Her years of patient encouragement had paid off.

I visited London in 1971 when Dick was making this film and we went with our kids to a screening at Soho Square. My son Ben picked up that they had used the same background for two different sequences. Dick shouted at his staff, "There. You see. I told you. Even a ten-year-old can spot it. We'll have to do it

Jacob Marley and Scrooge in The Christmas Carol

over." His rebukes were legendary. Always sharp-tongued, he now had no reason to hold back, but on the other hand there could be no doubt his staff not only feared but respected him. By this time he was married to his second wife, Cathy, a beautiful American socialite, and together they had two children, Alex and Claire. They lived in fashionable St John's Wood, and Cathy gave us useful information about renting a flat, smart restaurants, and shopping. Two or three years earlier Dick had come back to Toronto to see Kay and had spent an evening at our house. I had a sense that he was impressed by my domestic set-up and perhaps been motivated to emulate it, a conjecture I've never confirmed.

Dick had already begun to work on a project that would dominate his thoughts for the next three decades. *The Thief and the Cobber* was an Arabian Nights fantasy, inspired perhaps by our childhood experiences of Alexander Korda's *The Thief of Bagdad* (1940), a book called *The Great Road* by Frederic Arnold Kummer that Dick and I read as kids, and maybe even by *Terry and the Pirates*. It also reflected Dick's friendship with Idries Shah, who translated the sayings and folktales of the Persian sage Nasruddin, a trickster philosopher who lived in the great days of the Baghdad Caliphate. The sensibility of Nasruddin, outspoken, devious, utterly irrepressible, appealed to Dick—he was a fellow spirit from an exotic world whose wit illuminated our own disjointed times. Dick travelled in the Muslim world, learning sayings from the Koran so he could gain access to mosques and absorb the intricacies of Islamic art. He was particularly taken with the medieval city of Fez in Morocco, which he visited in the late 1960s before it became crowded with tourists.

Dick was determined to improve his skills: "The way you learn is by working with the best. So I began to import some of the great Hollywood animators and I went back to school to learn from them. Like the late Milt Kahl. The world's best

162

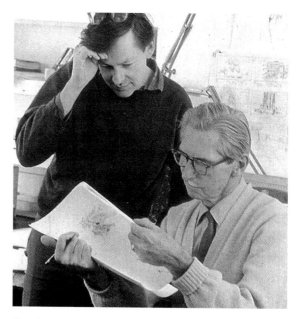

Dick with animation master Ken Harris

animator. The tiger sequence in *The Jungle Book* proves it. Milt was that tiger. The only way you can make an animated character come to life is to be that character. I brought Ken Harris (a Warner Brothers animator) to London and he created the character of the Thief, while I did the Grand Vizier. The desperate battle between these two characters is at the centre of the film. Let me show you." He screened a sequence in which the characters are caught in a sort of destructive death machine that draws on the complex invention of Leonardo's drawings and at the same time invokes the comic madness of Charlie Chaplin's *Modern Times*.

The Thief and the Cobbler was a hugely complex and expensive undertaking. Dick would work round the clock making commercials for six months, and then turn the studio over to producing perhaps five or ten minutes of *The Thief*, until he had exhausted his resources and had to turn around and make some more money. For a while he operated studios in both London and Los Angeles, flying back and forth, always concerned when he was in London that the people in Los Angeles were slacking or ripping him off; when he was in Los Angeles that the London studio was not operating at full tilt. He sought investors wherever he could find them, from New York bankers to Saudi princes, but costs kept escalat-

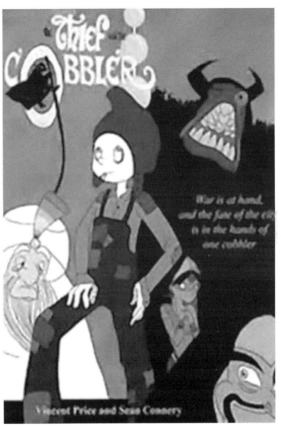

Poster for The Thief and the Cobbler

163

ing and his affairs were further complicated when he divorced from Cathy. He faced personal and financial chaos, but Dick always thrived on challenge and seemed to be stimulated by adversity.

In his attempt to find funding for *The Thief*, Dick spent an increasing amount of time in the United States. His third wife Margaret was American and preferred to live in Los Angeles where she could be close to her parents. She and Dick had two children, Holly and Tim, and they took up an increasing amount of Margaret's time and interest. Dick would be at his drawing board every day from 9 in the morning till 9 at night, and then go out for dinner and play two sets with a band until 1 a.m. Margaret asked, "Do you intend to do this for the rest of your life? Seven days a week?" "Yes. Why not?" Understandably she felt there was not a great deal of room for her in this schedule.

In the 1980s Dick agreed to work on a full-length animated feature *Raggedy Ann*. He was wooed by composer John Reposo, who had written songs for the

Record cover for Dick's Six Jazz Combo: *Dave Chandler, Brian Chadwick, John Ferguson, Malcolm Harrison, John Lee, Dick Williams*

film. There would be less acerbic edge in this movie than in any of Dick's other work, but he gave it his customary full-out commitment. He put *The Thief* on hold, moved to New York, took an apartment in the old Carnegie Hall building, and began studying trumpet with Rudy Braff. He made an effort to accommodate himself to the wishes of his producers, but there was a falling out when his insistence on maintaining quality clashed with their economic and scheduling imperatives and he left the project before it was completed. The picture came out but did not receive either critical acclaim or wide audience acceptance. Dick went back to his London studio to make commercials and resumed his work on *The Thief*. He abandoned his studio in Los Angeles and left it to Margaret to bring up their children.

"I've been discovered again," he said with a wide grin, when I visited him in London in 1986. He was in the process of hammering out a deal to make a combined live-action and animated film for Steven Spielberg and Walt Disney, tentatively titled *Who Framed Roger Rabbit*. It involved a metre-high bunny that functioned by a process especially developed by Williams, director Robert Zemeckis, and George Lucas's company ILM (Industrial Light and Magic). It was so effective that at the screen test the head of Disney studios thought the character

RICHARD WILLIAMS
FRAMES ROGER RABBIT

Who Framed Roger Rabbit?

was actually an actor in a rabbit outfit. "I'm diving in with the killers," said Dick, with the distinctive chuckle that betrayed his appetite for the big challenge. "They're sure to get me in the end, but if I can complete *The Thief*, it's worth it." He signed a two-picture deal: first *Roger Rabbit*, then *The Thief*.

Dick had a genuine respect for

Spielberg: "He's captured the fantasy market that used to belong to Disney. He's reinvented the genre with *E.T.* and *Indiana Jones* and *Star Wars*. The thread that connects *Alice* and *Peter Pan* and *Pinocchio*. There'll always be an audience for fantasy that is truly magical." *Roger Rabbit* had some of this magic but it also had satirical edge. It drew on the wise-cracking, hard-boiled outrageousness of Hollywood in the 1940s, the time when Dick first went to learn at the Disney studios. It also celebrated the heyday of Groucho Marx and Mae West and Betty Boop, who actually puts in an appearance in his film. And it reflects the raucous spirit of that era. Its irreverence and unpredictability won it an eager audience. It won Dick two Academy Awards, one for animation and another for lifetime achievement—and the chance to complete *The Thief*, or so he thought, though by now he was both an inveterate optimist and a confirmed skeptic. "They keep saying, 'Don't you see, don't you see, now you can do whatever you want?' I've heard that before."

The Thief was completed, but not by Dick. His insistence on his own high standards and his unwillingness to come to terms with the commercial demands of his producers eventually led to the film being taken away from him. It was released without the necessary publicity budget to gain it widespread public

165

acceptance. Disney's executives saw it as unwelcome competition for their *Aladdin*, which appeared at much the same time. Some thought that the character of the Grand Vizier in that film was a rip-off of the character Dick had created in *The Thief*. Although it is available on video, Dick feels it is truncated, sabotaged by the moneymen for their own insidious reasons. Nevertheless, Walt Disney's nephew Roy is keen to have Dick go back and restore the film on his own terms. Is this a real possibility? Time will tell.

The Thief can now be seen on the Internet in a cut that is more or less true to Dick's original intention. The songs of the Disney-released version have been eliminated and replaced by the soundtrack that Dick had recorded. Some sequences are incomplete, rough drawings not yet coloured, but this version gives an idea of the narrative shape Dick envisioned. It is visually both witty and spectacular, combining often stark simplicity with the intricate detail of Islamic architecture and Persian miniatures. The backgrounds are a complex miasma of patterns, chequered and striped, spirals and swirls, brilliantly lit or darkly obscure. The camerawork alternates long shots, medium shots and close-ups, jump cuts, and sudden segues, often in surprising juxtaposition. Many of the sections involve intricate machinery,

166

especially in the monumental final war sequence, which betrays the influence of Leonardo da Vinci, Rube Goldberg, Monty Python, and *Star Wars*. The colours are opulent, often startling combinations of simple strong hues. (I remember that on the wall of Dick's studio over his drawing board hung only one motto. "Simple is Best").

The Thief is a fairy tale and contains elements of those highly imaginative stories: witches and sorcerers, magic animals, and the magical ability to fly through the air. In folkloric fantasy, anything can happen, and the same is true of animation, making it perhaps the perfect visual medium for the filmic expression of this genre. The characters are vivid if not particularly complicated; both the compulsive Thief and the duplicitous Vizier are obsessive, which provides drama and suspense. The heroine Princess Yum-Yum and her cobbler Tak are simple, big-eyed cartoon figures:

Tak the Cobbler and the Princess in The Thief and the Cobbler

Snow White as an Arabian dancing girl; her Prince Charming becomes a character part Pinocchio, part Dopey. The Vizier, voiced by Vincent Price, owes something to the Wicked Queen in Snow White, but the most original character is the Thief slithering across the scene in his shapeless gown, his head crowned with a circle of buzzing gnats. The soundtrack is eclectic, based primarily on Rimsky-Korsakov's *Scheherazade* but incorporating bits of Mussorgsky, Richard Strauss, Vaughan Williams, and Verdi, interspersed with popular tunes from "I'm Forever Blowing Bubbles" to the Army Airforce Hymn, from snatches of Beatles tunes to Argentinian tangos and circus marches.

In the early 1990s Dick closed his studio in London and moved with his fourth wife Mo (short for Imogen) to Saltspring Island on the west coast of Canada. He had retained his Canadian citizenship and a love of the land, though his comments about Toronto remained scathing. ("Living in Toronto is like being in an attic above an apartment where a wonderful party is going on. You hear the music and the noise and open the door and somebody staggers halfway up the stairs and pukes on your shoes.") He and Mo produced two children, Natasha and Lief. They made friends with their bohemian neighbours and enjoyed the redwood forest. Dick found some like-minded musicians and they played together several nights a week. Dick began to work on a new film. Like *The Little Island* it would be entirely his own work. It would be based on Aristophanes' comedy *Lysistrata*, about Athenian women deciding to hold out on their husbands until they agreed to stop making war. It had all the elements of Dick's signature work: satire, bawdy humour, and an underlying moral concern.

Dick had spent over thirty years on *The Thief* so it did not faze him that his new work would inevitably take a long time, perhaps the rest of his life. Mo is also a filmmaker, and she came to see that she could not realize her ambitions in a place as isolated as Saltspring. She began to campaign for a return to England and eventually her wishes prevailed. Dick moved with Mo and the children to a small village on the west coast of Wales. He set up a studio and continued to work on *Lysistrata*. And he found some local musicians to play with at the local pub. To augment their shaky finances he agreed to write a book, *The Animators' Survival Kit*. It was published by Faber and Faber in 2001.

In February of that year Dick and Mo came to Toronto on a tour to promote the book. We met for a drink at the Park Plaza. Dick looked the same as ever: the big blue elfin eyes, the hair thinning a little bit hanging in a lock over his forehead, the irrepressible grin, the sudden

167

chuckle, the hands gesturing expressively, the barbed quips about Toronto, the Americans, the British, though he had surprisingly pleasant things to say about the Welsh. Mo joined us and it was obvious she was in charge of this outing. She was brisk and efficient but also warm and protective. Dick, like Henry VIII, had made some bad choices in the consort department. And also like Henry he didn't repeat his mistakes; he made different ones. Yet it seemed to me that Mo wasn't a mistake. She drew Dick's attention to the time. He explained, "I'm giving a little talk somewhere. I don't know whether anyone will show up. I'll set aside some tickets for you if you like."

Thank goodness he did. The Bloor Theatre, one of the few surviving old movie palaces left in Toronto, was surrounded by buses bringing students from Ryerson, OCAD, the Film Centre, Sheridan College, wherever animation is taught. Kids were hanging from the rafters. Dick came out on stage and spoke for ninety minutes, supported by clips from *The Little Island*, *The Pink Panther*, *the Light Brigade*, *Guinness* commercials, and *Roger Rabbit*. In one minute he grabbed the attention of his youthful audience. He moved about the stage with energy and grace, gesturing extravagantly and cracking jokes. It was a performance

168

worthy of Groucho or Milton Berle.

More recently he has moved to Bristol, where both he and Mo have access to the filmmaking facilities they need. Dick survived heart surgery, and his work on the Lysistrata film continues. Several nights a week he plays with a group of musicians who are known as Dick's Six. Ivan Yurpee is still alive and well and leading the band.

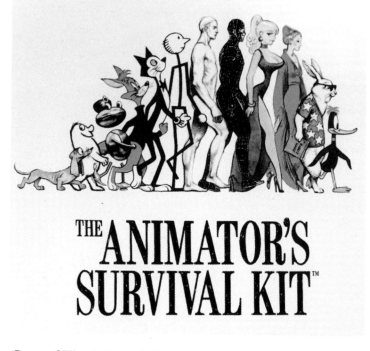

*Cover of The Animator's Survival Kit
- Faber and Faber*

SISTERS IN ART

Martha Henry and Diana Leblanc

One winter evening I was rehearsing *Johnny Bananas*, a play about Italian immigrants in Toronto in the early years of the twentieth century. I happened to look over my shoulder and see a woman watching the proceedings with intense concentration. She smiled at me enigmatically and I thought her face seemed familiar. I have never minded people sitting in on my rehearsals and so I turned back to watch the actors. Then it dawned on me; the woman was Martha Henry. What was she doing there? Was she researching some project that involved Italian Canadians? Was she scouting talent for some show she was about to direct? (She was at the time artistic director of the Grand Theatre in London.) When the rehearsal was finished it became clear. She was there to meet the one WASP actor in the cast, Rod Beattie. She and Rod joined us when we had a drink at a local pub after the show. I had had a nodding acquaintance with Martha for a good many years, but I had always seen her as a

rather distant, indeed remote, figure and here she was, pursuing her man almost like some infatuated schoolgirl. I had admired her elegance, her air of distinction, but suddenly she was humanized.

I first saw Martha in the 1950s when she was acting at the Crest Theatre in Toronto. She was a strikingly beautiful young woman, and I was told she was an American who had recently come to Canada from the Detroit area. She was still using her birth name, Martha Buhs. Over time I would gradually learn a little bit of her early history. Her parents had divorced when she was five. Her mother, who had serious ambitions to become a concert pianist, began to work playing accordion in cocktail lounges in order to support herself. Because she worked nights, Martha was sent to live with her maternal grandparents. She was shy but imaginative. Influenced by her grandmother, who had a love of fun and a sharp sense of humour, she read extensively. She began to play dress-up games, pulling costumes from a trunk that was kept in the dining room. One day at the bottom of the trunk she found two little books, which contained the scripts of plays. She read them with avid interest and imagined herself playing one of the characters. The seed of her ambition to become an actress had been sown.

170

As a teenager Martha was a good student and won a scholarship to Kingswood, a girls' private school with a strong theatre program. One summer she joined her mother on tour with a somewhat down-at-heel band of vaudeville performers. Vaudeville had been pronounced dead, but this group did a summer circuit playing in seaside towns. There was a dancer, a clown, even a snake-charmer. They were very welcoming to young Martha. She in turn felt she had a found a place where she fitted in, not just as a child, but as a member of a family. Encouraged by her mother from the age of 14, she began working in summer stock, playing small parts and doing backstage work.

Martha had always been a good stu-

Isabel in The Enchanted *at the Crest Theatre*

dent, and her family wanted her to go to college. She chose and was accepted by Carnegie Tech in Pittsburgh, at that time and even now considered one of the foremost theatre training schools in the United States. While there she worked

as an apprentice at a summer stock company where George C. Scott was a guest star. He and a colleague had started a small summer theatre in Leamington, Ontario, which he invited her to join as resident ingénue at the princely salary of twenty dollars a week. She spent three summers in that company, which provided her with invaluable experience in plays as varied as *Goodbye My Fancy, Night Must Fall, Macbeth*, and *Under Milk Wood*, as well as an introduction to Canada. With her mother she had visited the Stratford Festival in Ontario to see Christopher Plummer in Michael Langham's groundbreaking production of *Henry V*, in which the French court was composed of the leading French-Canadian actors from Montreal, most notably Gratien Gélinas and Jean Gascon. Martha knew she wanted to be part of this theatre.

She went to Toronto, auditioned for the Crest Theatre, and was hired for a season. Both freshness and beauty were in her favour, but so was the fact that she had trained at Carnegie. Many of the actors at the Crest were alumni of Hart House Theatre at the University of Toronto, notably the Davis brothers and their sister Barbara Chilcott. Their mentor there was the artistic director Robert Gill, who had not only trained but taught at Carnegie during the war, and who sometimes directed at the Crest

under a pseudonym. He may well have been a factor in Martha's acceptance into the company.

While at the Crest Martha came under the influence of Powys Thomas, the dynamic Welsh actor who had made his mark at Stratford and was currently crisscrossing the country looking for young would-be actors to be students at the National Theatre School, which would open the next year in Montreal under the joint direction of Thomas and Jean Gascon. Martha remembers that Powys would come back and rave about someone he had seen: "She has hair down past her waist and she auditioned in bare feet. She's been taught by nuns and has a wonderful purity. I wonder if we have anything to teach her."

It's possible Powys was teasing Martha—although it was also possible he was talking about Diana Leblanc. Thomas must have realized that Martha was intrigued by the idea of the school, not just the chance to improve her skills but the prospect of working with some of the French actors and teachers she had seen at Stratford. During the season she played relatively small roles such as Ermengarde in Thornton Wilder's *The Matchmaker*. (She recalled, "She cries a lot; I could manage that.") But at the end of the season she found herself cast as Nina in *The Seagull*: "It was beyond me. I understood it intellectually and good-

171

172

Nina in The Seagull *with Henry Hovencamp as Trigorin*

ness knows I was full of a tangle of feelings but I couldn't call them up at will. I knew I needed more training."

Martha was a student of the National Theatre School in 1960, its first year, when it was housed in the top of an old legion building on Mountain Street in Montreal. The students had classes in mask, movement, voice, and improvisation led by Thomas, Gascon, Eleanor Stuart, Guy Hoffmann, and Michel and Suria Saint-Denis. Martha remembers

the camaraderie between the French and English students who took all their classes together and would walk down St. Catherine Street hand in hand, jabbering excitedly in both languages. "We thought we were going to change the world," she remembers. "We were going to create something new and unique, a new kind of theatre that combined the passion of the French with the discipline and precision of the English." It was a dream shared by their early instructors, though it would never be realized, as the aspirations of the separatists and the reaction of the Anglos drove a political wedge between the two linguistic groups, although traces of the dream surface now and again in the multilingual work of Robert Lepage and the occasional bilingual production such as Stratford's recent *Don Juan*.

Martha remembers that first-year group contained many promising students who would make their mark in English-language theatre, including Suzanne Grossman, Heath Lamberts, and Neil Dainard. But there were two students who would play a major role in Martha's future.

One was the bilingual actress Diana Leblanc, who was to become Martha's close friend and collaborator. Diana was the daughter of a French-Canadian father and an Irish mother. She had gone

to a convent school from which she emerged completely bilingual. Her early ambition was to be a dancer but, realizing she would never be a prima ballerina, she joined the French section of the National Theatre School after an audition in which Jean Gascon leaped up on stage to respond to her first speech. Luckily she had memorized the lines in the whole scene, which they played out together. She was immediately accepted as a student.

Also at the school was a handsome young actor, Donnelly Rhodes, who would become Martha's first husband in 1962. She did not take his surname but instead adopted the name of his mother, the poet Anne Henry. "I don't quite know why we thought we wanted to get married, but we liked each other a lot." Richard Monette recalled, "They were young and foolish but for awhile they were happy. As the song goes, 'we had some fun and no harm done.'" They divorced amicably a few years later when Martha's stage career was blossoming in Canada and Rhodes decided he wanted to go to Hollywood and have a film career. Which he did.

In their second year at the NTS, the students went to Stratford for a month to work on the new thrust stage and have the advantage of instruction from some of the actors in the company. Michael Langham was immediately impressed

173

with Martha. "She had a wonderful honesty and directness about her. Absolutely no bullshit," he recalled. He offered her a position in the company, including the leading role of Miranda in *The Tempest*. She felt she couldn't turn it down, and the instructors at the school agreed with her. Although she had completed only eighteen months they offered her a certificate, making her the very first graduate of the National Theatre School.

Meanwhile Diana had decided to switch to the English stream of the school. Gascon told her she was making a big mistake and pleaded with her to reconsider. But he had not reckoned

Diana as Princess Katherine with Douglas Rain as Henry V

on Diana's determination, and she made the move anyway. She would graduate from the English section and soon after make her debut at Stratford as Princess Katharine in *Henry V*. But Gascon's warning that she would be seen by her Québécois compatriots as *vendue aux Anglais* proved to be prophetic. She recently said, "Nowadays I work mainly in French in Toronto and in English in Montreal."

The highlight of Martha's first season at Stratford was her Miranda opposite William Hutt's Prospero. She and Hutt formed a bond that would last until his death. Over the years they would play together many times as husband and wife, brother and sister, lovers and co-conspirators. They shared an affection enriched by all of these relationships, and never was it more evident than in the experience of *The Tempest*: "I adored him and I was his love, the love of his life, his daughter." Martha brought to the role not only intelligence and a certain simplicity, but a genuine naïveté as well, which at the time was part of her own character, though certain subsequent events would cause her to outgrow it.

Her next major role was the doomed heroine in Langham's production of *Troilus and Cressida*. She admits to having been terrified of Langham, not only because he could be impatient and

Miranda in The Tempest *with William Hutt as Prospero*

demanding but because she couldn't seem to get the quality he wanted. It was an era when directors were all-powerful and thought to be all-knowing, and Martha at the time bought into this notion. Again she was playing with Hutt as her foolish, foppish uncle, and perhaps she picked up on his tone. When they were rehearsing the early scene where she and Hutt are watching the parade of Trojan soldiers go by, she jumped up on a bench and giggled. Langham squeezed her hand as he passed in front of her, and she knew she was onto something. Her Cressida was a girl beneath whose wit and sensuality lay a certain shallow vacuity that made her fate not just pathetic but inevitable.

In 1966 Martha was cast as Viola in *Twelfth Night*, David William's first

Stratford production. Her twin, Sebastian, was the young Richard Monette, who remembered that they made up together in order to look as much alike as possible, which even involved Martha drawing a cleft in her chin to match Richard's. These two would also have a lifelong and mutually supportive relationship. Also in the cast was Douglas Rain, playing Sir Toby Belch. He would become Martha's second husband.

Martha's Viola was audacious as well as rueful, poised but vulnerable. It was the only one of Shakespeare's "trouser" roles that she would attempt, but in these three early characterizations she had already shown an enviable range that would broaden as she progressed to more mature parts. This maturity was evidenced in her performance of Elmire, the canny wife in Jean Gascon's splendid production of Molière's *Tartuffe,* in which Douglas Rain played her husband Orgon and William Hutt played the title role. The *New York Times* critic Walter Kerr wrote, "Martha Henry plays her as a woman who cannot be surprised. She is herself reserved, immaculately self-contained, gently delicate. But she is informed. … she is too supple and intelligent to engage in affectation … she stands her ground, cool, worldly, and in her worldliness as generous as a woman may be." Kerr admirably describes the

Viola in Twelfth Night *with Richard Monette as Sebastian*

complexity and command that Martha Henry would bring to her work in the next decade.

Martha and Douglas Rain took time off from the Festival to visit England for two years, but they returned in the final years of Gascon's regime to appear as a gutsy Desdemona in *Othello* and a serene Thaisa in Gascon's highly original and

moving production of *Pericles*. But Gascon was running out of steam. He had brought his own distinctive flair, colour, and comic invention to the Festival, expanding the repertoire and mining the talents of many of its players, but the strain of working in a language that was not his mother tongue and captaining the ever-expanding Festival, which included a winter season in Ottawa, was wearing him down. Martha was feeling the need for a new stimulus, and the Stratford board felt it was time for a change. Major change would indeed be brought about by the Festival's next artistic director, Robin Phillips.

Martha Henry was already aware of Phillips. "An actress friend from England had said to me, 'I'm working with this wonderful director, and you simply must work with him because he's absolutely brilliant'… My first impression was—how beautiful, shy and gentle he was. He showed great care for us, and came to every table [in the Green Room] to shake our hands."

Robin quickly galvanized the Stratford company. His rehearsals have been called magical: a mixture of games and improvisation, challenging and questioning, rooting out old habits, seeking new answers, plumbing unexplored depths, leading actors into territory they had been afraid or unwilling to enter, paring away extraneous detail. It was, in Martha's own words, "terrifying and funny and shocking and whimsical." It was also hard work, scary, unnerving, and exhilarating. Some of the older company actors did not take to it and left; Robin replaced them with fresh, often untried newcomers. But both Martha and William Hutt bought into Robin's methods, and he quickly accepted them as stars in his Stratford firmament.

Both actors had leading roles in *Measure for Measure*, his first main-stage production, in 1975. As the Duke, Hutt was a devious, worldly prankster in a cor-

177

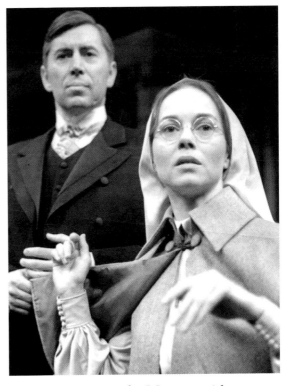

Isabella in Measure for Measure *with Brian Bedford as Angelo*

rupt world. Martha was a naïve recluse, drawn into a rancid, festering society out of family obligation. She dominated the action as she journeyed from the seclusion of a cloister to an acceptance of a tangled, imperfect world. Her finest moment occurred as she waited alone in the office of the seducer Angelo and cooled her brow from the water pitcher on his desk, silently weighing the bitter alternatives that faced her. This was the kind of acting Phillips was seeking, where the actor silently manifests the thought process taking place in her head.

178

The next season would see Martha playing Olga in *The Three Sisters*, alongside Maggie Smith as Masha and Marti Maraden as Irina, directed by John Hirsch. Martha had already worked with Hirsch in Winnipeg, where she played Catherine in *Mother Courage* with Zoe Caldwell, and in New York, where she played both Elizabeth Proctor in *The Crucible* and Sophocles' Antigone. Hirsch had wanted her to play Antigone as a sexual young woman in a flaming red wig. Martha resisted him but later regretted it, saying if she had worked with his idea she realized she could have given a much more interesting performance.

Three Sisters was the second Chekhov Martha had done with Hirsch. She had previously played the maid Dunyasha in his 1963 production of *The Cherry*

Martha as Olga (centre) in The Three Sisters *with Maggie Smith and Marti Maraden*

Orchard. Both productions were proclaimed as brilliant. In *Three Sisters* Martha gave a restrained performance, at the same time bleak and full of warmth. Along with her Isabella it established her as the foremost Canadian actress at the Festival. However, because Phillips and Hirsch became engaged in a slanging match that was widely reported in the papers, Martha would not have an opportunity to work with Hirsch again.

Phillips's introduction of foreign actors Keith Baxter, Jeremy Brett, Brian

Bedford, Stephen Macht, Maggie Smith, Jessica Tandy, Margaret Tyzack, Kathleen Widdoes, and ultimately Peter Ustinov gained critical attention for the Festival and gave Canadian actors the opportunity of working with some of the foremost stage artists in the English-speaking world. Martha appreciated this and made the most of the opportunity. Robin was anxious that his Canadian stars—Martha, Hutt, Monette, and Rain—should get equal billing and treatment as the visiting celebrities, but there was tension among the Canadian performers that was voiced by William Needles and Rain. Rain was a fine actor but a cryptic and crusty personality; he could be charming but also obdurate, as his relations with both Kate Reid and Martha illustrate. Still, in 1972 Martha produced a daughter, Emma, to the delight of both parents, and they stayed together longer than they might otherwise have done.

In 1976 Robin recruited as dramaturge the *Toronto Star* critic Urjo Kareda, who quickly became his *éminence grise*. Highly intelligent, articulate, and perceptive, Kareda would have enormous influence on Robin's choices of repertoire. He was already a great fan of Martha's work, and they would become friends and for a time collaborators. It was Kareda who suggested that Martha should play Sister Jeanne in John Whiting's *The Devils*, Elena in *Uncle Vanya*, and Hecuba in Edward Bond's *The Woman*. The last two were co-directed by Kareda. All three roles exploited Martha's innate sexuality in different ways, as well as demonstrating her developing vocal power as her voice expanded to encompass the ringing contralto notes that would become a hallmark of her mature performances.

Kareda would later say that knowing Martha was like having a good friend and at the same time feeling he really didn't know her at all. He confessed he had no idea how she developed her performances. Her friend Diana Leblanc would say, "She arrives on the first day of perform-

179

Hecuba in The Woman *with Clare Coulter*

ance with an elaborate character already formed, and you can't imagine how she could get any better, but she does."

Indeed, Martha is assiduous in preparing for a role; in discussion with R.H. Thomson she talked about her method. She will reach down inside herself to discover "touchstones," the strands of her personality that seem appropriate to the character she will be playing, often unused or undeveloped aspects of her own inner being that she can explore in the role. She is also a keen observer who collects and stores away impressions of people she comes in contact with. She has an intuitive empathy with many people, to the point where she knows what they are thinking even if they don't voice it. ("That's my job.") She also has the ability to focus strongly on the people she is playing with. Does she become the character? "I'm the character but I'm still Martha." Geordie Johnson, an actor who worked with her frequently, says, "When you look into her eyes, you see the character she's playing. You're looking into the eyes of Mary Tyrone or the Princess or whoever."

Martha works on her character not just in rehearsal but in whatever she is doing: eating dinner, brushing her hair, shopping for clothes. She doesn't find it difficult to work on several characters at once but finds that one character feeds another, just as at school she would take

a technique learned in one class and apply it in another class. This internal interaction gives her characterizations greater richness and complexity. At the same time she is not oblivious to external appearances. She has said that she sometimes learns more about a particular role in the fitting room than in rehearsal. Designer Astrid Janson has said she is very particular about her costumes and props: "But once she accepts them, she has a special ability to make them her own." Offstage, too, she is always elegantly turned out: in one of her houses she had a whole room in which to store her extensive wardrobe. Her immaculate appearance is part of her public persona and her sense of her responsibility as a senior artist. And although she is willing to give us a glimpse of her method, her ultimate process and indeed her *persona* retain an air of mystery.

Meanwhile, Diana had been living in Montreal. She married her fellow NTS student Gary Learoyd and then divorced him. She left the school to work at the Neptune Theatre in Halifax. Her mother died and she felt she had to take responsibility for her sister Victoria, who had a young daughter. She played in the film *Lies My Father Told Me* (1975) and a television series of *Swiss Family Robinson*. For a while her career languished. She had a number of affairs; she waited on tables and went into therapy; she did scene

180

study work with students at the National Theatre School. Then things began to pick up. She moved to Toronto and played in several English-language versions of the plays of Michel Tremblay at the Tarragon, notably *Albertine en cinq temps*. She and Martha had remained friends, and it was probably through Martha's influence that Phillips invited her to Stratford, where she would again play Katharine in *Henry V* and Hero in *Much Ado About Nothing*, with Brian Bedford and Maggie Smith as Benedick and Beatrice.

In Phillips's last years Martha was less in evidence, partly because of the demands of motherhood, but she did give two memorable performances, as the bedraggled, syphilitic whore Doll Tearsheet in *Henry IV, Part II*, and the relentlessly ruthless Goneril in the remount of *King Lear* with Peter Ustinov. That year the Festival was in disarray; partly because of his unstinting efforts, Phillips was exhausted. He decided to step down from the sole artistic directorship of the Festival and suggested an elaborate three-tier directorate involving several major players. After a good deal of negotiating in which most of the projected co-directors bowed out, four remained: Pam Brighton, Martha Henry, Urjo Kareda, and Peter Moss. They set about putting together a season for 1981, creating an

181

Diana as Hero in Much Ado About Nothing

interesting roster of plays and players.

Unbeknownst to the quartet, who were dubbed the "Gang of Four," the Board of Directors of the Festival were secretly negotiating with the British director John Dexter to become the next artistic director. Their cover was blown when Martha telephoned Christopher Plummer in New York to offer him a role in their projected season and he told her he understood Dexter had been offered the job. Martha sent the board members a note, which they refused to answer. Instead they summoned the Gang to a special meeting and fired them. In a state of shock Martha and Urjo retired to a bar, but not before she had told her husband, Douglas Rain, who promptly phoned the Toronto papers and broke the story.

A huge uproar ensued, as the media and the Canadian theatre community rallied in support of the Gang of Four. Neither its members nor the Stratford board had thought the public would care, but they misjudged the nationalistic temper of the time. There were public protests and stormy meetings. Canadian Actors' Equity brought pressure to bear on the federal government, who denied a work visa to Dexter. Just in time to save the 1981 season, John Hirsch was appointed artistic director. Martha might have expected to work for Hirsch, but she had stated that she would not come back to the Festival unless the board sent her a formal apology. None was forthcoming and so she stuck to her guns.

This was a time of major re-evaluation for Martha. She was shocked at the brutality of her treatment after years of being praised and even courted. She had thought of the theatre as her family but now realized this was something of an illusion. "The theatre is not your family, it is where you go to work," she would later say. Kareda explained that it was awkward to be in Stratford, a small

Diana in Further West *with Diego Matamoros and Mary Haney*

town where everybody knew everybody else and gossip was rife. He rapidly moved back to Toronto. Martha also moved on, leaving Stratford and her husband Douglas as she searched for new opportunities.

For the next two or three years her financial situation would be somewhat precarious. She decided she wanted to direct. She had begun her directing career in 1980 with the one-man show *Brief Lives,* starring Rain: "One does not direct Douglas Rain, but in my next show I remember saying in the first day of rehearsal to Diana Leblanc, 'Do you think you could move down right as you say that line?' and she said, 'Sure,' and I suddenly thought: I can do this."

182

Her first major assignment as a director was Timberlake Wertenbaker's *The Grace of Mary Traverse* at the Toronto Free Theatre on Berkeley Street. She had a strong cast including Rod Beattie, David Fox, Diana Leblanc, and the young Christina Nichol. It was a major critical and financial success. There followed a production of O'Neill's *Moon for the Misbegotten* at the Tarragon Theatre, where Kareda was now artistic director. And she would play the rich socialite in *Pal Joey*, which gave her an opportunity to sing "Bewitched, Bothered and Bewildered" to a young Morris Panych.

At about this time Diana was offered the artistic directorship of *Théâtre français de Toronto* by John Van Burek. Initially she turned the offer down, but on the advice of friends, including Martha and Urjo, she reconsidered. She would head the company from 1991 to 1996, directing productions of Molière and Tremblay and acting in a number of plays, including Cocteau's *La Voix humaine*, with Martha directing, Tremblay's *Damnée Manon, sacrée Sandra* and *La Maison suspendue*, and Simon Fortin's *Le Pays dans la gorge*. Having established herself in this theatre she would go on to direct at the Manitoba Theatre Centre, the Citadel in Edmonton, and the National Arts Centre in Ottawa.

Soon after the financial debacle of Robin Phillips's season at the Grand Theatre in London, Martha was offered the artistic directorship. She would spend six happy years in London, directing one or two shows a season, appearing usually in one show herself, and finding and encouraging new young actors to work with seasoned professionals. She became an accomplished programmer, providing her audience with the right mix of entertainment and drama, comedy and experimental work, much of which took place in the Undergrand, the small house beneath the main theatre. During her years in London, Martha worked closely with two women: Diana, her longtime friend, and Astrid Janson, who had first designed for her in *Mary Traverse*. Astrid has described how the three shared ideas and concepts. Their collaboration would be ongoing, as both Diana and Martha honed their directorial skills and relied on Astrid to give them visual definition.

Martha has said that directing and acting call for the use of different parts of the brain or psyche. The actor must focus on her own character, while the director must step back and see the play as a whole, understanding the interplay of various characters and the arc of the dramatic action. Although she has been successful as a director, she would ultimately consider herself primarily as an actress: "At the Grand I realized I must

183

184

Gertrude in Hamlet *with Donna Goodhand as Ophelia*

keep the wheels greased by playing at least one role each season."

She would also act in several films in this period, most notably *Dancing in the Dark* (1986), in which she played an ordinary housewife with stunning simplicity and emotional openness and for which she won a Gemini award. Then came Robin Phillips's version of Timothy Findley's *The Wars*, produced in 1981, in which she was the neurotic upper-middle-class mother of the confused young soldier who goes to meet his fate in the trenches in France. Although Findley was not pleased with the finished film, which had to be sanitized to meet the demands of the investors, he was delighted with Martha's performance and the two became friends.

This would result in one of Martha's finest performances as the wife of a bisexual diplomat, a brave but troubled woman suffering from the early ravages of dementia in *The Stillborn Lover*. Arguably Findley's best play, the leading roles were written for Martha and William Hutt, with whom Findley also had a long-term friendship dating back to the first year of Stratford. The two would reprise these roles a few years later at Stratford. This was followed by Findley's *Elizabeth Rex*, which Martha directed in 2000, starring Brent Carver and Diane D'Aquila. It was a huge critical success and was later filmed by Rhombus Media in 2003.

Before working in London, Martha had been assistant to director Robin Phillips on his 1986 main-stage produc-

Marion Raymond in The Stillborn Lover *with William Hutt*

tion of *Cymbeline* at Stratford. "He was incredibly generous. We met months before rehearsals began and he showed me his sketches of sets, costumes, even wigs and make-up. He had everything worked out—everything. In rehearsal he would suggest, pare down but almost never dictate. And yet the final result down to tiny details reflected his early intentions. It was uncanny. I came away thinking—how does he do it?"

Both as a director and as an actor

Martha has moved a long way from the dictatorial method of Michael Langham. She allows her actors a great deal of freedom. "She loves actors and acting," comments Geordie Johnson. "She's prepared to let you just wing it in the early stages. She takes whatever is given to her and uses it." She values inventiveness and has a taste for eccentricity, sometimes leading to work that is distinctly "over the top." Her casting choices often seem bizarre but can turn out to be inspired, as when she chose a young Sandra Oh to play the student opposite Rod Beattie's professor at the Grand in David Mamet's *Oleanna*.

When Richard Monette took over the reins at Stratford in 1994, he was determined to attract Martha to act again at Stratford. No public apology was made

185

Mary Tyrone in Long Day's Journey into Night *with William Hutt*

for her earlier treatment, but Martha came on board and again appeared opposite William Hutt, along with Peter Donaldson, Tom McCamus, and Martha Burns in O'Neill's *Long Day's Journey Into Night*. Under the direction of Diana Leblanc, the cast bonded to form a perfect ensemble, a family whose pain and illusion were deeply intertwined; they knew each other intimately but did not know themselves. Martha's Mary Tyrone showed us the ghost of the romantic young lover she had been, now encased in a cunning, charming, manipulative drug addict. This was a triumphant return of the actress to her old territory. The play would be repeated the next season, when Martha's performance would be undercut by a number of embellishments, emphasizing her arthritic hands, which detracted from rather than enhanced the power of her performance. When the production was filmed she was persuaded by director David Wellington to go back to her original interpretation, which is preserved in this highly acclaimed 1996 screen version.

Diana seems to have known instinctively how to handle these actors, allowing them to explore and interact, making an occasional telling comment or suggestion. Martha remembers that at one point Diana said to her, "Just sit in that rocking chair and rock." It not only gave her an action with which to vent her repressed emotion, but also unlocked the powerful anger that underlay her often gentle words. After this highly successful experience, Diana and Martha would continue to work together frequently, building upon their intuitive understanding and deep personal friendship. They both appeared in Richard Monette's production of *The Little Foxes*. Martha was the ambitious, scheming, and ultimately ruthless Regina, Diana her battered and broken sister-in-law Birdie, contrasting characters that still somehow depended on and fed off each other.

Martha made a specialty of uncompromising women: the proud, unyielding Volumnia in *Coriolanus*; the wise and weary Eleanor of Aquitaine in *King John*; the possessive, disappointed Mrs. Alving in Ibsen's *Ghosts*; the grief-stricken but indomitable Hecuba in Euripides' *The Trojan Women*; the self-deluded, interfering Amanda of Tennessee Williams's *The Glass Menagerie*; the terrified, drug-addled aging Princess in Williams's *Sweet Bird of Youth*; the drunken and destructive Martha in Albee's *Who's Afraid of Virginia Woolf*? Indeed Martha would play a whole gallery of Albee's savage, unsatisfied women, from the caustic 90-year-old protagonist of *Three Tall Women* to the autocratic Agnes in *A Delicate Balance*. These women were unmistakably Martha but were all separate creations, with distinctive quirks and indi-

vidual idiosyncrasies. Martha's range has proved to be enormous and her invention seemingly limitless.

Although Diana and Martha have had a number of triumphs, they have also been responsible for some less successful ventures. One was Chekhov's *The Seagull*, in which Martha's mannerisms as the vain, self-absorbed actress Arkadina, including a silly little dance, became tiresome. Even more unfortunate was a production of *Macbeth* with Martha playing the Lady opposite her husband Rod Beattie. At one point Rod appeared in an apron, presumably indicating he was barbecuing some steaks for the forthcoming "banquet," and the couple sang and danced to a verse of Gershwin's "Our Love is Here to Stay." Experimental perhaps; foolish certainly. Yet when Diana and Martha are at the top of their game, as they were in *Ghosts* and *A Delicate Balance*, they produce nuanced and textured work of extraordinary power and complexity.

While at Stratford Martha has directed a number of productions. Two of the most successful were Ibsen's *An Enemy of the People* and *Richard II* starring Geordie Johnson. The first was richly detailed and somehow made the rather pompous and rigid world of Ibsen's nineteenth-century bourgeoisie seem relevant and vital. Her *Richard II* was remarkable for its simplicity and clarity, allowing

Johnson full range to explore the character's vanity and self-pity and at the same time give full value to Shakespeare's soaring words. And in 2009 she unveiled a beautiful production of *The Three Sisters*, with a strong cast ranging from the young Dala Badr to the veteran James Blendick. At the centre are the highly nuanced and passionate performances of Lucy Peacock as Masha and Tom McCamus as Vershinin. The range of emotion, from sudden gaiety and high spirits to wistful regret and disappointment, encompassed the quicksilver volatility of the Russian psyche that so many English-language productions of Chekhov fail to deliver and reinforced Martha's status as a director of the first rank. She would follow this with a gritty, hard-nosed production of Brecht's *Mother Courage*, dominated by Seana McKenna's tough and indomitable Anna Fierling.

During the late 1990s Martha lived with Rod Beattie in his elegant Victorian house on Mornington Street. She appreciated his sardonic wit, which complemented her own more restrained sense of humour. He obviously adored her. The success of his one-man Wingfield shows gave him financial security and artistic status so that he was not perceived merely as Martha's consort. But he was away on tour a good deal. Martha calculated that some years they were together for

187

four months and apart for eight. This inevitably put a strain on their relationship. They built a summer house on the shore of Lake Huron but spent less than two weeks a year there. They went on tour together in A.R. Gurney's two-hander *Love Letters*, and Martha matched her playing to Rod's rather broader comic style. Eventually they decided that the only way to preserve their relationship was to live apart. So Martha moved into a house with her daughter Emma, while she and Rod continued dating. One wag said, "Isn't that what you do before marriage?" but the arrangement seems to work for them.

As Richard Monette's long reign drew to a close, there was much speculation about who would succeed him, and Martha's name was often mentioned. She was acknowledged to be the company's leading actress. She had successfully run the Grand Theatre in London, putting it back on the rails after several disastrous seasons, and she was acknowledged to be an accomplished director. She was appreciative of the work of others and particularly concerned to see young people were given a chance. And she was not an egomaniac. But she was rapidly approaching the age of seventy. Would she be able to muster the stamina the job required?

When the triumvirate of Marti Maraden, Des McAnuff, and Don Shipley was announced, Martha was

pleased, seeing it as a reincarnation of Phillips's idea for a joint directorate. But as somebody said, "Didn't Shakespeare write a play about this?" Perhaps predictably the triumvirate fell apart within the first year, following in the footsteps not only of the Gang of Four but of the doomed shared directorate of Jean Gascon and John Hirsch in 1968. Martha had already accepted the leadership of the Birmingham Conservatory, the training program that Monette had inaugurated. She therefore managed to avoid internal squabbles.

Diana and Martha continue to interact. Diana was a founding member of Toronto's Soulpepper Theatre and has directed productions there in every season, usually modern classics like *Who's Afraid of Virginia Woolf?*, *A View from the Bridge* or the Canadian classic *Doc*. She also directs in Montreal at the Segal Centre, where she made her debut with *Rose*, starring Martha, and followed up with such comedies as *Fallen Angels*, *The Odd Couple*, *Same Time Next Year*, *Harvey*, and most recently *Guys and Dolls*, her first production of a major musical, which she characterized as "a fairy tale for adults." Next she directed two plays by John Murrell, a revival for Soulpepper of *Farther West*, a play in which both Martha and Diana have acted in the past, and a new play at Stratford, *Taking Shakespeare*, written especially for

188

Frosine in The Imaginary Invalid
with William Hutt

Diana in The Road to Mecca *at Soulpepper*

189

Martha. And she continues to teach every year at the NTS.

Martha was a natural choice to train young actors at Stratford. She has had plenty of experience in such a role, especially at the National Theatre School. Judith Thompson remembers her as one of the best teachers she had, because she allowed her students to develop in their own way and at their own pace. This lack of rigidity, along with a genuine sensitivity to her students' need and an appreciation and enjoyment of their individual personalities, makes for a warm and responsive connection with the young people she is training. She has innate authority as well as compassion,

and her meticulous and conscientious preparation has impressed everyone who works with her.

Carmen Grant, one of Martha's protégées, who has spent two years at the Conservatory, characterized her as "relentless, but not like a hurricane or a storm at sea; more like water constantly flowing over rocks, wearing down the sharp edges." Carmen reports that Martha looks at her actors as individuals, finds a thread that leads to their emotions and gently pulls on it to see what it will reveal: "She guides the various individuals she has cast along their various paths towards the same destination. As a mentor, she is the definition of grace." She has a strong staff who teach voice, movement, improvisation, and text and has been able to attract some experienced directors to work with the young actors, from Michael Langham to Richard Monette, Christopher Newton to Stephen Ouimette. As I write she is touring the country in search of fresh talent.

It is heartening to know that these two women—Martha Henry, the pre-eminent Canadian actress of her generation, having played virtually all the great roles in classical and modern drama, and Diana Leblnac, a skilled actress and arguably the most accomplished Canadian female director—are passing on their skills, their understanding, and their profound knowledge of their art to the most promising young actors of the rising genera-

190

tion. It bodes well for the future of the theatrical art in Canada.

Martha as Regina and Diana as Birdie in The Little Foxes

BON VIVANT

Christopher Plummer

While I was still an undergraduate I went to see a production of Christopher Fry's *The Lady's Not for Burning* at the Museum Theatre in Toronto. I was encouraged to do so by Herbert Whittaker, the Montreal director and designer who had recently taken up the post of film and drama critic at the *Globe and Mail*. He let it be known that the state of dramatic art in Montreal was far superior to what was available in Toronto. He championed actors whom he referred to as the Four Horsemen of the Apocalypse: John Colicos, Richard Easton, Richard Gilbert, and Christopher Plummer.

Plummer was playing the lead. Fry was the hot playwright of the day; we all thought he was bringing back to English theatre the glories of Elizabethan verse drama. The cast featured some of the best actors in Toronto: David Gardner, Eric House, Jane Mallett, Rosemary Sowby. Plummer brought to the role of Thomas Mendip a dashing appearance, virile energy, sly, self-deprecating wit, and the ability to speak Fry's verse with clarity and style. At Herbie's invitation I went to a cast party at Jane Mallett's house. (It turned out he had designed the set and costumes for the production.) It was, like all Jane's parties, a lively affair featuring good food and plenty of drink. I recall that Plummer partook liberally of the latter, and then sat down at the piano and played popular songs of the day with both skill and élan.

In his autobiography *In Spite of Myself*, Plummer gives a lively account of his privileged boyhood in Montreal. His mother, Belle, was a member of a distinguished Anglo family and he spent summers with her friend Polly at a cottage at Lac des Deux Montagnes, at that time in the wilderness. As a young teenager he sailed, skied, and played tennis, partied and engaged in several outrageous pranks, having begun drinking at an early age. He also went to the theatre

192

Montreal schoolboy

and the movies at every opportunity. Whittaker saw him in a high-school performance playing Darcy in *Pride and Prejudice* and was immediately struck by his talent.

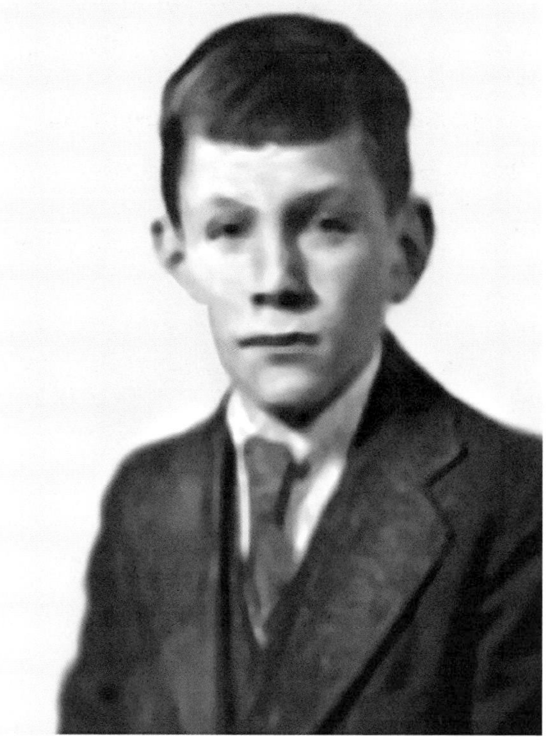

Plummer did not attend university but went straight from high school into the theatre. He played Posthumus in a production of *Cymbeline*, directed by the visiting Russian superstar director Theodore Komisarjevsky, played opposite a young Elaine Stritch at the Mountain Playhouse, essayed the role of Oedipus in Cocteau's *La machine infernale* (the first of his three portrayals of the Greek hero) for the Montreal Repertory Theatre, and spent a season in Ottawa working for Amelia Hall's company, for which he played everything from an octogenarian in Jerome K. Jerome's *The Passing of the Third Floor Back* to the sensitive young pianist Finch in Mazo de la Roche's *Whiteoaks*. He also had his first serious love affair with a married actress, a brief fling after which she sensibly returned to her husband. For Plummer it would be the first of many liaisons. Shortly thereafter he moved on to a demi-mondaine seductress, Joy Lafleur, whom he had met in one of the city's louche bars.

During this period Plummer had roles in many radio plays, including Rupert Caplan's weekly Bible series where he first encountered William Shatner, and

Andrew Allan's prestigious Stage series, produced in Toronto, which Plummer described as a city of incomparable dullness and Protestant rectitude that was definitely not to his taste. (Although born in Toronto in 1929, Plummer grew up in Montreal.)

In the late 1950s, Plummer joined the year-round repertory company run by Michael Sadlier in Bermuda. There were several Canadians in the company: Sadlier's young wife Kate Reid, Barbara Hamilton, and Eric House, as well as the American actress Marian Seldes. Together they sailed, played tennis, and went to parties and drank prodigious amounts at the local Bar 21. Plummer and Kate both imbibed heavily, a habit that would eventually impact both their careers.

The company brought in visiting American stars to play the leading roles and attract an audience, among them Constance Cummings, Zachary Scott, and Ilka Chase. Plummer got to play the juvenile in a number of plays, most notably *The Royal Family*, in which he impersonated a character based on John Barrymore. In *The Petrified Forest* starring Franchot Tone he played Duke Manatee, the role made famous on stage and screen by Humphrey Bogart. Two of these visiting luminaries would have an important role to play in Plummer's career. One was Edward Everett Horton, a comedian who owned the rights to a

vehicle called *Springtime for Henry*. Following the season in Bermuda, Horton invited Plummer to tour with him in this light comedy across the United States, thus introducing him to American theatre. Ruth Chatterton, who had played Regina in *The Little Foxes* in Bermuda, introduced Plummer to Jane Broder, who became his agent and launched his career in New York.

Plummer acted in a number of American television shows, which in those days were broadcast live from the studio. He played in an adaptation of Kipling's *The Light That Failed* and opposite Sylvia Sidney in *Dark Victory* and *Kind Lady* before reprising his role as Thomas Mendip opposite Mary Ure in *The Lady's Not for Burning*. But his most memorable work was opposite Julie Harris in *The Doll's House* and *Johnny Belinda*. At about that time he teamed up with Jason Robards Jr. and the two became drinking buddies; on one occasion they turned up at the studio totally sozzled five minutes before the show went on air but managed to stagger though the performance.

Television kept Plummer from starving, but he was ambitious to work on stage and with Jane Broder's help he managed to get cast with three of the leading actresses of the period: Eva Le Gallienne in *The Starcross Story*, a British play of no particular distinction, and as

193

Jason in *Medea*, opposite Judith Anderson, when she took her already famous production to Paris, playing at the Châtelet, where the great nineteenth-century French actress Sarah Bernhardt had also played the vengeful sorceress who kills her children to spite her husband. Plummer's performance was lambasted by the critics, but he had gained the support of the producer Guthrie McClintic, who saw in Plummer a promising classical actor. As a result he was cast in *The Dark is Light Enough*, the last of Christopher Fry's successful verse dramas, starring McClintic's wife Katharine Cornell as a Hungarian countess. The cast included Tyrone Power playing opposite Cornell, and a fellow Canadian, Donald Harron.

This Broadway exposure led to Plummer being cast in the two plays that opened the new Shakespearean theatre in Stratford, Connecticut: *Julius Caesar* and *The Tempest*. The company was led by Raymond Massey and Jack Palance and included Roddy McDowall, a fellow playboy with whom Plummer formed an immediate bond. Plummer also entered into an easy-going relationship with Massey, a fellow Canadian of similarly upper-class background. The two would work together and remain friends over several decades. Plummer was an engaging Ferdinand in *The Tempest*, but it was as Mark Antony that he impressed audi-

194

ence and critics alike: handsome, eloquent, slippery, and cynical, the first of a number of Shakespearean roles he would inhabit that fitted him as though they had been written especially for him.

Christopher Plummer made his delayed entrance at the Stratford Festival in Ontario in 1956. In its first year Tyrone Guthrie had sought out the best Canadian actors he could find. Plummer auditioned for him with his friend Richard Gilbert. But radio producer

Henry V at Stratford 1956

Rupert Caplan, apparently motivated by the suspicion that Plummer had enjoyed a dalliance with his longtime mistress, reported to Guthrie that Plummer was "a womanizer, a libertine and a drunk, totally irresponsible, and a black influence on any company." Guthrie did not hire Plummer for the first season, and he had to wait three years until Michael Langham had the inspiration of casting him as the young king in *Henry V*, battling against the decadent and arrogant French, as played by the leading actors of French Canada, foremost among them Gratien Gélinas and Jean Gascon.

This brilliant stroke of casting brought the play to vivid life for the Canadian audience, drawing on the 200-year rivalry of the Anglos and French Canadians of Montreal. As I wrote in my 2001 book *Romancing the Bard*, "The opposing armies were like water and oil, ale and champagne, roast beef and pheasant under glass. The emotions suppressed for two centuries bubbled up." Plummer as Henry exerted charm, a dash of danger, and great curiosity. His brashness, his confidence, and his energy were irresistible. In victory he retained his sense of humour as he savoured the delight of conquering a decadent court and winning a fresh young beauty, Princess Katharine of France. This performance made him an instant star in his own country.

In the following season he played Hamlet, revelling in the character's sardonic wit and razor-edged anger. His pain was masked, his violated nobility set aside, but his whole performance was shaped by his wonder at the unfolding events. His director Michael Langham suggested that before each speech Plummer should say to himself, "isn't it extraordinary." Plummer has acknowledged that Langham taught him more about acting than any of his other mentors. That quality of discovery, coupled with the intensity of his frustration, was brilliantly complemented by the fragile instability of Frances Hyland, hailed by critics as "the Ophelia of her generation." During the run Plummer broke his ankle and had to go on wearing a cast, which was painted inky black to match his costume. He realized that this immediately gained him the sympathy of the audience, and so he continued to wear it even after his ankle healed.

Plummer would return to Stratford to play a playful, mocking Benedick, whose witty exchanges with the equally sharp-tongued Beatrice of Eileen Herlie in *Much Ado About Nothing* would suddenly give way to unexpected passion and then swing back to raillery. This romantic performance would establish Plummer as a strong comic actor, and he would reprise the role several times in the future. Next came his flamboyantly

195

196

Hamlet

Mercutio

In the early years the Stratford season lasted only six weeks. Plummer would then return to New York, where he continued to appear in soaps and on stage. He played Christian to José Ferrer's Cyrano, for once tongue-tied but picking up tips for his own impersonation of the romantic Frenchman later on. He was also cast in Jean Anouilh's *The Lark*, starring Julie Harris as St. Joan, in which he gave a solid portrayal of the English nobleman Warwick who captures Joan and insists on her trial.

During these years Plummer would

197

extravagant and caustically inventive Mercutio in the 1960 production of *Romeo and Juliet* that featured Julie Harris as an incandescent Juliet, Bruno Gerussi as a recklessly capricious Romeo, and Kate Reid as a garrulous, salty-tongued nurse. Plummer made his mark as one of a group of exceptional players who put Stratford on the map, gaining it international recognition.

Cyrano de Bergerac:
drawing by Grant Macdonald

continue to have affairs with a variety of young women from both within the theatre and without. His steady girlfriend was a sexy and outspoken young actress called Tammy Grimes. When she discovered she was pregnant, Plummer married her, and not too long afterwards, in 1957, she produced a baby girl whom they named Amanda. Plummer would prove to be a neglectful father, following in the footsteps of his own father, whom he first met after a matinee in Ottawa in his early 20s.

J.B., Archibald MacLeish's poetic drama based on the book of Job, was Plummer's next assignment. The director was the famous Elia Kazan, who had shepherded the early plays of Tennessee Williams and Arthur Miller to Broadway acclaim, and the cast was headed by Pat Hingle as J.B. (the Job figure), Raymond Massey as Mr. Zuss (God), and Plummer as Nickles (the Devil). It would be the first of Plummer's roles as a scheming villain and he took to it with delight, revelling in the chance to play the quintessence of evil. Plummer asked Kazan who the most exciting actor was that he had ever worked with and was told, "Marlon Brando. I never knew what he would do next." Plummer had some of Brando's charisma but not his spontaneity. Unlike Brando he would go on acting into old age, but he would never quite achieve

Brando's stature as the greatest actor of his generation.

Plummer returned once more to Ontario to play Macbeth opposite Kate Reid as the Lady. She was splendid in boldly taking over Duncan's murder and her pathetic, lost-soul delivery of the sleepwalking scene, but Plummer was disappointing in managing his transition from confident general to ghost-ridden tyrant. However, in the same Stratford season Plummer played Cyrano in a splendidly rich production directed by Michael Langham, and this proved to be a great role for him: Cyrano is sharp-witted, dashing, inventive, and deeply romantic without being sentimental. Plummer accepted Langham's direction that at the end Cyrano has achieved his destiny and the love of Roxanne; he is ecstatic and this is what makes his death so moving. The production was televised for the Hallmark Hall of Fame, and Plummer achieved his dream of having this production, which he believed was the highlight of his career so far, seen by an international audience.

Meanwhile, Plummer managed to find time to play in Shaw's *Captain Brassbound's Conversion*, with Greer Garson, and Anouilh's *Time Remembered*, with Dame Edith Evans, on Broadway. His invitation to join the Royal Shakespeare Company in England's Stratford-on-Avon may have been partly

due to Evans's recommendation. There he reprised the role of Benedick opposite the brilliant English comedienne Geraldine McEwan, in a production directed by the young Peter Hall. He followed this with another villainous role: Richard III. During the rehearsal period he suffered from a bronchial condition. Plummer would have his fair share of medical problems, in fact: a broken ankle when he was playing Sir Andrew and Hamlet at Stratford, a knee injury when he was Pizzaro in Peter Shaffer's *Royal Hunt of The Sun*, and periocarditis while recording *Much Ado About Nothing* with Dorothy Turin for a CD. This latter disease was nearly fatal, but Plummer with his usual resilience managed to survive.

Plummer's next assignment for the RSC was Henry II in Anouilh's *Beckett*. He thoroughly enjoyed this role, which was to have been played by Peter O'Toole if he had not been still shooting *Lawrence of Arabia* in the desert. The play transferred to London, and Plummer would like to have played the role in the film, but by the time it was ready to shoot O'Toole had completed his desert duties and was available. Plummer believes that the film lacked the theatricality of the stage version with its prop horses manipulated by the actors, and having seen both versions I think he was right.

Plummer would spend most of the swinging 60s in London. He had a new companion, Patricia Lewis (Trish to her intimates), an entertainment columnist who drove a Triumph Herald convertible through the streets of London at breakneck speed and dined with Plummer and her former lover Peter Finch at all the best restaurants in the English capital. Trish was acquainted with a bevy of London luminaries, from Judy Garland to Noël Coward, Sean Connery to Princess Margaret. Inevitably, one night after a drunken party Trish crashed her car into a lamppost just outside Buckingham Palace. Plummer was not seriously injured, but Trish had a broken jaw and a blood clot on the brain. Plummer nursed her through her convalescence and then married her.

Through Trish's influence with the producers, Plummer was cast in a huge epic, *The Fall of the Roman Empire*, which was filmed in Spain. The cast included Alec Guinness, Sophia Loren, James Mason, Eric Porter, and Anthony Quayle. The film demanded that the actors spend much of their time riding or reining in horses pulling their chariots, and eventually it ran out of money although it was released in 1964. Plummer fell in love with Spain, though, thoroughly enjoying the whole experience, and a few years later he signed on for another epic, *The Battle of Waterloo*, in which he played

199

Wellington. This time the film was shot in Ukraine, where the railway cars were filthy and the food even filthier. Plummer would never again undertake to film outside the "civilized" world.

Two other films made in this period were more satisfying. In 1964 he played Hamlet in a film shot at Kronborg castle in Denmark standing in for the Elsinore in Shakespeare's text. Michael Caine played Horatio, Robert Shaw was Claudius, and Alec Clunes was Polonius. Plummer's second take on the role, strongly influenced by his director Philip Saville, was less exuberant, more thoughtful than his earlier impersonation at Stratford. Four years later he would play his third Oedipus, this time set in Greece, again directed by Saville. The cast included Lilli Palmer as Jocasta and Orson Welles as Tiresias. Plummer was overawed as the famous actor held forth with his accustomed magnetic account of his life in the theatre. Also in the cast were Roger Livesey, Cyril Cusack, and the young Donald Sutherland, whom Plummer had already met when Sutherland played Fortinbras in the Kronborg Hamlet. In both productions, according to Plummer, Sutherland mumbled. After the shooting he hit Plummer up for a loan to finance a flight to Los Angeles for an audition. Plummer obliged and, in his own words, "I got my money back and he got M*A*S*H," the

film that kick-started his movie career.

Halfway between *Hamlet* and *Oedipus*, Plummer made the film that over the years he has most denigrated (but for which he is often most popularly known): *The Sound of Music.* He would later refer to it as "S&M" and "The Sound of Mucus." It was definitely not the work he most wanted to be associated with, but in spite of his protestations he was perfectly cast as Baron von Trapp, his natural hauteur, coolness, and elegance giving the film just the right ingredient to mitigate against its sentimentality. In his memoir he plays down his distaste for this project and generously compliments Julie Andrews on her freshness, optimism, and spontaneous humour. The film became one of the all-time hits of the movie industry and made Plummer into a sought-after star in Hollywood.

In between his various appearances onscreen he found time to work on the legitimate stage in New York, playing a blustering Pizarro in *The Royal Hunt of The Sun* and Arturo Ui in Brecht's satire on the rise of fascism, in which he modeled his performance on Adolf Hitler, adopting a scratchy vocal sound and an accent that was a mix of Bronx, Brooklyn, and Chicago. He was particularly proud of this characterization, having been greatly impressed by the work of the Berliner Ensemble when he saw

With Julie Andrews in The Sound of Music

them on tour in London some years earlier. However, the production was panned and soon closed.

In 1967, Plummer returned to Stratford to play Antony opposite the bravura performance of Zoe Caldwell as Cleopatra. The Australian actress pulled out all the stops in a role that had defeated Vivien Leigh, Tallulah Bankhead, and Edith Evans. Her vulgarity and her frank sensuality, coupled with her extraordinary vocal range, made her performance electric. Though perhaps too young for the part, Plummer proved a worthy consort: lithe, sensual, and fun-loving. The highlight of his performance was a drunken dance that he did while carousing with his shipmates on the way to Alexandria. This ruin of a man—brought down by drink, wenching, and fatally infatuated with the Egyptian witch-queen—was familiar territory for Plummer. The production went to Expo 67 in Montreal, where it was seen by a wider audience, including Queen Elizabeth II.

Plummer's next assignment was Lord Foppington in a 1969 film shot in Ireland titled *Lock Up Your Daughters!*, which tried to cash in on the success of *Tom Jones*. Plummer's performance was decidedly over the top. Although he liked to demonstrate his versatility by taking on eccentric character roles, he was not really convincing as Foppington,

Sir Andrew Aguecheek or Atahualpa (in the 1969 film version of *The Royal Hunt of the Sun*). He seemed to lack the ability of an Alec Guinness to internalize and inhabit these outlandish personalities.

While in Ireland, he met and became enamoured of a pretty young actress, Elaine Taylor. He courted her and eventually she became his third wife, after making it a condition that he reform his errant ways, particularly his by now heavy drinking. Plummer admits he was more or less a wreck at the age of forty and credits Elaine with helping him clean up his act. The couple were married in Provence in 1968. For a while Elaine continued to act, but they longed to have a home of their own. Over the course of the next few years they bought houses in London, Provence, Hollywood, and eventually Connecticut, where they acquired a property at Wampum Hill. They also acquired dogs; Plummer had had a canine companion as a boy, and the animals that he and Elaine took on were close to both their hearts.

While living in London, Plummer became involved in a project to replicate Shakespeare's Globe Theatre on the south bank. On one occasion he hosted a fundraiser for this theatre in Toronto, where a number of eminent actors performed speeches. At the last moment Claire Bloom arrived, and she and John Neville announced that as the finale they

203

Antony and Cleopatra *with Zoe Caldwell*

would perform the balcony scene from *Romeo and Juliet*, which they had played years before in London. Plummer, who had expected to be the star of the evening, left the stage in a moment of pique. On another occasion, after he had been negatively reviewed by Brooks Atkinson, he was offered a role in a play by Atkinson's wife Jean Kerr. Plummer, feeling he was being blackmailed, turned it down. When stung, he was not without a certain vindictive streak.

Also when he was in London at that time, Plummer accepted two film roles: in *The Battle of Britain* (1969) he played a British air ace in World War II, almost immediately after having played Rommel in *The Night of the Generals* (1967). Soon afterwards, Sir Laurence Olivier offered him a chance to act with the National Theatre. He was to have played Coriolanus, but he turned it down when he discovered it was not Shakespeare's version but Brecht's, to be directed by a pair of Germans. He then appeared in Georg Büchner's *Danton's Death*, directed by Jonathan Miller, whom he greatly admired. The play, though a respected classic, is long and tedious and was pulled from the National season to make way for Olivier's performance as James Tyrone in *Long Day's Journey Into Night*.

Moving to New York he played Cyrano again, this time in a musical adaptation by Anthony Burgess. The previews in Toronto and Boston were greeted with enthusiasm. Plummer's singing, while not of operatic calibre, was clear, and his articulation of the lyrics masterful. But although the translation was trenchant, the songs tuneful, the cast skilled and the sets by Desmond Heeley gorgeous, the show failed to capture the imagination of New York audiences and had only a limited run.

Plummer followed up with an appearance as Chekhov in *The Good Doctor*, Neil Simon's most serious dramatic script up to that point. Plummer enjoyed working in a contemporary comedy, in spite of the fact that Simon rewrote every day and sometimes even during the run. He then returned to film, playing his longtime hero Rudyard Kipling in *The Man Who Would be King* (1975) with Michael Caine and Sean Connery and directed by John Huston. In the same year he appeared in *The Return of the Pink Panther* with Peter Sellers. Other roles later that decade included a murderous psychotic transvestite in the 1978 Canadian thriller *The Silent Partner* with Elliott Gould and Susannah York, followed in 1979 by a rather low-key Sherlock Homes with James Mason as Dr. Watson in *Murder by Decree*.

Just when it seemed that his future lay in the movies, he returned to the stage to play Iago to the Othello of James Earl Jones. This blackest of Shakespeare's vil-

lains was a perfect role for Plummer. He relished the wit of the opening scenes, which made the revelation of his malevolence all the more shocking. His controlled anger and at the same time relish of his own duplicity gave the role complexity and an element of surprise. Zoe Caldwell, who took over as director halfway through the rehearsal period, rapped his knuckles "until they bled," forcing both him and Jones to abandon any hint of nineteenth-century "hamminess" but rather to play with conviction and restraint. Jones's stature and nobility and Plummer's malevolent drive were well matched in their duel to the death, but it was Plummer who won the Tony.

During his long run on Broadway, Plummer tuned into the fact that his daughter Amanda, who had grown up without much attention from her father,

Colonel Chang in Star Trek

205

Iago in Othello *with James Earl Jones*

had received excellent notices for her portrayal of a visionary but demented nun in *Agnes of God.* She would go on to play roles that benefitted from her intensity and eccentricity, most notably Alma in Tennessee Williams's *Summer and Smoke* and St. Joan in *The Lark* at Stratford, a gig that her father brokered. Plummer became inordinately proud of this child that he had not had the trouble of bringing up. Father and daughter bonded as she took her place in his world of theatre and later film.

Having had a success with one Shakespearean tragedy on Broadway, Plummer signed on for another: *Macbeth*, this time playing opposite the formidable British actress Glenda Jackson. In an early rehearsal following his delivery of a soliloquy, Jackson shouted, "You're not going to play it like that, are you? For God's sake Plummer, where are your balls?" The rehearsals got off to a poor start when the original director defected; shortly thereafter, Robin Phillips was brought in. Plummer asked a Canadian actor about Phillips and was told, "There will be a steam bath scene with a lot of naked young men, Glenda will masturbate and she will take over the show." When I saw it in Toronto, this prophecy proved to be right on the nose. Plummer gave a listless performance that, as the saying goes, he might well have phoned in. Phillips resigned and Zoe Caldwell took over, but she couldn't save the day. Plummer's notices varied from a gentle reprimand to an outright pan, and the show closed. Jackson moved on to the world of politics and Plummer moved on to another show: Pinter's *No Man's Land*, with his old drinking pal Jason Robards Jr. Pinter himself attended some rehearsals, but when asked what some of his more obscure lines meant, he replied, "I haven't the foggiest." The show played at the Roundabout and gradually attracted a good audience. Plummer enormously enjoyed playing with his old friend, their last appearance together.

Plummer accepted a television series and took parts large and small in many films, but he was not through with the stage. His old friend Robert "Ratty"

Whitehead brought him a script by William Luce, who had written a number of other one-person scripts for Julie Harris and Whitehead's wife Zoe Caldwell. The subject was John Barrymore. Early in his career Plummer had met Diana Barrymore, an attractive and talented actress, but like her father an alcoholic. Plummer had from his earliest days in the theatre been fascinated

John Barrymore on Broadway

206

by the figure of Barrymore. When offered the chance to play him he couldn't resist. Barrymore's wit, his volatile moods, his drunken forgetfulness, his endless fund of stories, and his compulsive reciting of Shakespeare were all familiar territory to Plummer. The role fit him like a glove, and he inhabited it with total conviction. With the help of director Gene Saks, Plummer also plumbed the emotional depths of a man who realizes that for all his fame he is not going to recover his former glory at this late stage in his life. The show ran for nine months and gained Plummer his second Tony. He would later write, "It was for Diana in a way that I'd done it…. How I wished she'd been there to see it. I hope she might have been proud."

Barrymore had opened at Stratford in 1996. Richard Monette, who had played Eros with Plummer in the 1967 *Antony and Cleopatra*, was keen to lure him back to play at the Festival Theatre. When offered King Lear in 2002, Plummer readily accepted. He managed to persuade Jonathan Miller to direct, and the cast included many of the company's best actors. Plummer was impressive as the ruined king, proud but forgetful, ironic in his exchanges with the Fool when faced with his daughters' disloyalty, pathetic when he discovers Cordelia's death. By the end of the play he sometimes slurred his speech, as though suf-

King Lear

207

fering from early Alzheimer's, until he sounded the trumpets for a final burst of strength at the end. Miller ignored the fact that it was being played on a thrust stage, which caused some problems with sightlines. He may be a genius, as Plummer insists, but he was also arrogant. Because of some fabulous notices the production was transferred to Lincoln Centre in New York. I saw it a second time there and it worked much better on this more conventional stage. A few actors were replaced by stronger players, which added strength and variety to the production. There was talk that Plummer would be awarded his third Tony, but this did not transpire.

Stratford was keen to find another vehicle for Plummer after his recent successes. His next choice was *Caesar and Cleopatra*, which he had always wanted to do. His performance was astonishingly athletic as he brought to life Shaw's pragmatic, energetic and hard-headed tactician, susceptible to Cleopatra's sex-kitten charms but more concentrated on his political ambitions. Again there was a strong supporting cast and the show sold well.

Plummer next appeared at the Festival in *The Tempest*. He was less forbidding than some actors who have played the role, relishing the verse and speaking it with obvious enjoyment. Once again Stratford backed him up with some accomplished actors, but the most remarkable casting was Julyana Soelistyo as Ariel, a tiny blue sprite who brought a special magic to the proceedings. Both this production and *Caesar* were filmed and had brief commercial runs, as had *Barrymore* before them. Plummer's final Stratford appearance was billed as *A Word or Two*, a series of excerpts from his favourite poems, novels, and plays. Though not an intellectual, Plummer is literate and well-read, and his selection was eclectic, from Winnie the Pooh to Nabokov, the Bible to Kipling, Lewis Carroll to Herman Melville, and of course Shakespeare. He has performed these pieces often and always donated the proceeds to various charities, usually to do with the arts.

Following his stage success Plummer received many film scripts from his

Prospero in The Tempest *at Stratford*

208

Count Leo Tolstoy in The Last Station

agents, most of them of a much higher calibre than before. Shooting was sometimes in Europe or even North Africa. Plummer frequently travelled with Elaine, whom he has nicknamed Fuff. They enjoyed staying in the best hotels and eating in the finest restaurants: the Elysées Matignon in Paris; the Algonquin, Sardi's, and la Scala in New York; the White Tower, L'Étoile, the Ivy, and the Connaught in London; the Sacher in Vienna; the Excelsior in Rome; the Mamounia in Marrakesh; Spago and Chasen's in Los Angeles.

Plummer's range of film and TV roles has been nothing if not eclectic. His first major TV series was *Counterstrike*, a swashbuckling thriller. He has enjoyed playing such roles as General Chang in *Star Trek VI: The Undiscovered Country* (1991), bad Uncle Ralph in *Nicholas Nickleby* (2002), and Norman Thayer in a

Beginners with Ewan McGregor

TV version of *On Golden Pond* with Julie Andrews in 2001. An important film was *The Insider* (1999), in which he played the TV interviewer Mike Wallace, grilling Russell Crowe as Jeffrey Wigand, the man who blew the whistle on the cigarette companies. Also in the cast was Al Pacino, all under the direction of Michael Mann. The film was abandoned by its original producers but eventually had a considerable impact, and Plummer was touted for an Academy Award.

Plummer later played the title role in *The Imaginarium of Dr. Parnassus* (2009) for Terry Gilliam, and in the same year *The Last Station*, in which he was nominated for an Oscar as the aging Tolstoy, opposite Helen Mirren as his longsuffering countess. Both were important films and showed different aspects of Plummer's skills as a film actor. After being nominated for the Academy Award several times, he finally won for his performance as an older man who confesses to his son, played by Ewan McGregor, that he is gay, in the 2010 film *Beginners*. Although a touching portrait, it is hardly Plummer at his most remarkable, and he was obviously awarded the honour for his long and varied career in film. At the presentation ceremony he quipped, holding his Oscar, "You are only two years older than I am, darling. Where have you been all my life?"

Now in his 80s, Plummer seems to have abandoned his bad-boy antics. He and his wife are a sociable pair, she attractive and charming, he affable and easygoing. They spend a good deal of time with friends, both at home and abroad. In his rollicking, anecdotal memoir *In Spite of Myself* he recounts his exploits and adventures, his affairs and pranks, his professional failures and triumphs, all with a sort of amused nonchalance.

Plummer has worked for all the major film and stage directors, from John Huston to Mike Nichols, Peter Hall to Gene Saks, and played with the leading actors and actresses of the twentieth century, from Edith Evans to Natalie Wood, Bette Davis to Julie Andrews, John Gielgud to Al Pacino, Alec Guinness to Nathan Lane. Unlike many successful actors he has shown no interest in directing. Though an important part of his career has taken place in Canada and he enjoys visiting Montreal, he has shown no interest in Canadian scripts and has only once made a Canadian movie. Canada has recognized him with its highest honours and is justifiably proud of this native son who, in spite of changing fashions in contemporary theatre, is now recognized as the finest living classical actor in the English-speaking world.

AMAZON

Colleen Dewhurst

In the late 1970s I was teaching a class about theatre to undergraduates at the University of Toronto. One of my students was a tow-headed kid called Kevin Sullivan who looked a bit like a young Robert Redford. He showed a ready aptitude in the exercises I set for the class and produced a project, a tape of narration interwoven with musical themes that might have been the work of a professional. He acted for me in a couple of Hart House Theatre plays and showed considerable charm and humour. I thought he might want to become a professional actor and was not surprised when he came to me for advice.

But I was not prepared for the idea he presented to me. He wanted to make a film and asked me to collaborate with him. We wrote a screenplay based on a Hans Christian Andersen tale called *The Little Fir Tree*, talked several of my students and friends, as well as my wife, into performing in it, and persuaded Black Creek Pioneer Village to let us shoot there in early December when they were closed to the public. Kevin found a cameraman and edited the footage himself. We produced a half-hour film at a cost of about $7,000, which Kevin sold to the CBC for $5,000. As they showed it every Christmas for several years for a similar fee, he soon made a profit.

I worked with Kevin on a couple of other shorts films, including one about the painter Cornelius Krieghoff, for which he persuaded Ken Thompson to let him shoot his extensive collection of the artist's paintings. We disagreed about some of the details of the script, and as I was busy with other stage productions, I told Kevin he could use my work and revise it in any way he wished. I wonder whether I wouldn't have been smarter to throw over my university job and team up with Kevin in his next projects, which included two full-length movies, one of which starred Marilyn Lightstone and was backed and aired by her partner Moses Znaimer.

Having demonstrated his ability as a filmmaker, Kevin then secured the rights to *Anne of Green Gables.* He was determined to attract some big-name players and approached Katharine Hepburn to play Marilla, the spinster farm-woman who with her brother adopts Anne. Miss Hepburn turned him down but instead offered him her niece to play Anne. Kevin cast her as Anne's best friend, partly perhaps because he needed a

mainly Canadian cast to attract government funding. Instead he settled on Megan Follows as his heroine and chose Richard Farnsworth, the aging stuntman turned actor who had been highly effective in the Canadian film *The Grey Fox* with Jackie Burroughs, to play the gentle, easy-going farmer Matthew. But Kevin needed a forceful actor with TVQ—television acting experience—to play his strong-willed sister Marilla.

Barbara Hamilton had played the role in Don Harron's musical adaptation that was an annual feature of the Charlottetown Festival, but Kevin did not see the character as comic. Apparently Diane Buchan, his casting director, came up with the idea of Colleen Dewhurst for the role. Dewhurst was an established actor of the American stage and to a lesser extent film, and because she had been born in Montreal she qualified as a Canadian. She was to be a major factor in the success of Kevin's film adaptation of Lucy Maud Montgomery's classic, with her forceful presence and down-to-earth wisdom.

Colleen Dewhurst was born in 1924, the daughter of a strongly convinced Christian Scientist mother whose religious belief she adopted, and a father, Fred, who played football professionally for the Ottawa Rough Riders. From her father she inherited her statuesque

Kevin Sullivan as a student

212

Colleen Dewhurst

physique and her ability to be aggressive when needed. Before she reached school age the family moved to Wisconsin and then to New England, where Colleen would attend public and high schools. Naturally shy, she was taught by her father to defend herself against school bullies. She was something of a tomboy and captained the women's baseball team in high school. She decided she wanted to be an aviatrix like Amelia Earhart, but a visit to a performance of *The Glass Menagerie* kindled her interest in the stage.

Her parents separated and she enrolled in Wisconsin Downer Young Ladies College. She was determined to become an actress and played Olivia in *Twelfth Night*, where she garnered some unwanted laughs, but this only momentarily dampened her ambition. When she failed her sophomore year her mother agreed to let her enter the American Academy of Theatre Arts, where after a less than stellar audition she pleaded with Harold Clurman to admit her. She gained his approval as a student and also attracted the attention of Tyrone Guthrie. He cast her as a Turkish concubine in his production of *Tamburlaine the Great*, with Anthony Quayle and Canadians William Shatner and Robert Christie in the cast. Before graduating she married a fellow acting student James Vickery, in 1947.

"Tall, luminous and leonine," in the words of her biographer Gary Brumburgh, she was not an obvious ingénue. She performed with a number of small summer-stock companies and supported herself working as a reception-

213

The Queen of Off-Broadway

ist and an elevator operator. She invited her mother aboard to show off her prowess and was told that she had missed the floor requested going both up and down. Shy in real life, she would later be described by *People* magazine as "a madwoman on stage." She made the rounds often saying, "I guess you've got nothing for me," but because of her striking appearance she was often cast as an eccentric character in a variety of roles in small productions in New York. In her autobiography she wrote, "I had moved so quickly from one Off-Broadway production to the next that I was known, at one point, as the 'Queen of Off-Broadway.' This title was not due to my brilliance but rather because most of the plays I was in closed after a run of anywhere from one night to two weeks. I would then move immediately into another." This gave her a range of experience, however, which built up both her confidence and her acting skills. She landed her first professional role as a dancer in a production of Eugene O'Neill's *Desire Under the Elms.* It was something of an omen. She would go on to play many of O'Neill's women, including the lead Abbie Putnam a few years later in this drama of frustrated passions on a New England farm.

She attracted the attention of Joseph Papp, who offered her the role of Juliet. She asked him, "Have you seen me? I couldn't have played Juliet at the age of thirteen." Papp then cast her as Katharina in *The Taming of the Shrew* in Central Park. She was seen by *Times* journalist Arthur Gelb, who wrote a glowing review of Dewhurst in spite of the fact that the second half of the show was rained out. Business picked up immediately. Colleen would go on to play Lady Macbeth and Cleopatra for Papp at the Public Theater, as well as Camille in Dumas's *La dame aux camélias* and Mrs. Squeamish in Wycherley's *The Country Wife*, a comic role for once.

Colleen, now a recognized presence on the New York acting scene, began to be cast in TV movies and series. Her first major appearance was as the slat-

Katherina in The Taming of the Shrew *in Central Park*

214

ternly girl whom Don Quixote, played by Lee J. Cobb, idealizes as his lady fair Dulcinea on the DuPont Show of the Month. On the Play of the Week series she appeared with Judith Anderson in *Medea* and played the lesbian in love with Miriam Hopkins in Sartre's *No Exit*. She also appeared in an episode on the *Alfred Hitchcock Presents* series.

In 1958 she had played in *Children of Darkness*, directed by José Quintero, opposite a powerfully emotional actor, George C. Scott. Sparks flew between them onstage and off and they moved in together and married soon after, in 1960. Scott was a large personality in every sense, volatile and opinionated. He had served several years in the Marine Corps, much of it as an honour guard at Arlington National Cemetery. Perhaps as a result of this assignment he suffered from depression and began drinking heavily. He had written short stories as a teenager and studied journalism at college before becoming involved in theatre. Like most young actors he worked in summer stock, once in Leamington, Ontario, where he directed the young

215

With George C. Scott in Antony and Cleopatra

as Elizabeth with George C. Scott as John Proctor in The Crucible

216

Martha Henry. He came to prominence in New York working for Joseph Papp, for whom he played what one critic described as "the angriest Richard III I've ever seen." Dewhurst and Scott would work together during their marriage, particularly in television dramas, notably two plays by Arthur Miller, *The Crucible* and *The Price*, in both of which they played husband and wife. Their home life was stormy but never boring. They produced two sons, Campbell and Alexander, both of whom would grow up to become involved in the entertainment business.

Dewhurst and Scott each had burgeoning movie careers. Scott would play a number of lawyers and soldiers, most famously General Buck Turgidson in Stanley Kubrick's *Dr. Strangelove* (1964) and General George S. Patton in 1970, for which he won an Academy Award that he refused, saying the awards ceremony had turned into a "meat market." Dewhurst did two movies opposite John Wayne, *The Cowboys* (1972) and *McQ* (1974), played a psychiatrist who treats Sean Connery in *A Fine Madness* (1966), was cast as Diane Keaton's mother in Woody Allen's *Annie Hall* (1977), and had a small role in *The Nun's Story* (1959) with Audrey Hepburn. She played the strong-willed mother of Farrah Fawcett in *Between Two Women* (1986) and another controlling mother in David Cronenberg's *The Dead Zone* (1983). However, she never found a movie vehicle that would fully exploit her unique talent.

In fact, her most acclaimed work was on stage. In 1973 she played Josie Hogan in Eugene O'Neill's *A Moon for the Misbegotten*, which was directed by José Quintero and ran for over 300 performances. She showed outward reserve but inner strength and warmth, great simplicity but also singularity. She earned a rave review from Brooks Atkinson, who said it was one of the most magical theatrical events he had ever witnessed. The night I saw her in this play, a man died of a heart attack in the front row of the balcony. Colleen came downstage and told the audience to remain calm while the man's body was removed. She then went

back and resumed the action where she had left off. Curiously, while doing nothing she had remained in character throughout the break, and the incident somehow seemed to contribute to our understanding of the character. It was filmed with the original cast a year after it played on Broadway.

Perhaps her Irish ancestry was a factor that helped Dewhurst to become a supreme interpreter of O'Neill's women. She acted almost all of them. As well as Abbie in *Desire Under the Elms* she played Sara in *More Stately Mansions* with Ingrid Bergman; Christine Mannon, the murderous wife in *Mourning Becomes Electra*, O'Neill's rewriting of the *Oresteia*, opposite Canadian actor Donald Davis as her husband Ezra Mannon; Mary Tyrone in *Long Day's Journey into Night*, in which Jason Robards Jr. played James Tyrone and Colleen's son Campbell played Edmund; and Essie in O'Neill's only comedy, *Ah, Wilderness!*, again with Campbell in the cast. She also played O'Neill's second wife Carlotta in Barbara Gelb's *My Gene*.

She would portray many strong or eccentric women: Gertrude in *Hamlet*; Mary Follett in Tad Mosel's *All the Way Home*, based on James Agee's novel *A Death in the Family*; Shen Te, who spends half the play disguised as a man in Brecht's *The Good Woman of Setzuan*; and Argia, the deposed queen in Ugo Betti's *The Queen and the Rebels*. Her final appearance on Broadway was in *Love*

217

In Long Day's Journey Into Night
with her son Campbell Scott

Josie Hogan in Moon for the Misbegotten
with Jason Robards Jr.

Letters, the bittersweet comedy by A.R. Gurney in which she again played opposite Robards, one of her favourite acting partners. Perhaps because of her unconventional appearance and personality, she was a favourite actress of Edward Albee and played Miss Amelia Evans in his adaptation of Carson McCullers's *Ballad of the Sad Café*; Martha in *Who's Afraid of Virginia Woolf?* opposite Ben Gazzara, which Albee directed himself; and The Mistress in *All Over*.

The marriage between Dewhurst and Scott was stormy, whether they were working together or not. Scott was strong-willed and determined; Dewhurst was not exactly docile and had a fiery temper. They divorced in 1965 after five years of marriage but remarried in 1967 and remained together until 1972 when they divorced for a second time. Scott was married five times, had a total of three daughters with two of his other wives and a torrid affair with Ava Gardner. Colleen spent most of the remainder of her life after her second divorce with Ken Marsolais, whom she described as "the kindest man I have ever met." However, she remained on amicable terms with Scott and in her autobiography wrote, "I have a great love and affection for George. And admiration. He's brilliant. I always said we got on much better during the divorces. I'm very subjective; he's very objective. We

218

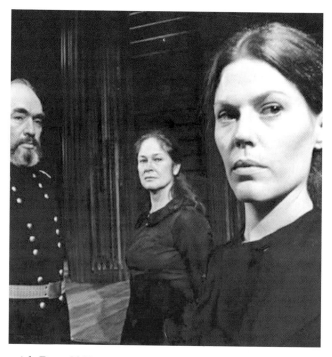

with Donald Davis and Pamela Peyton-Wright in Mourning Becomes Electra

make a much better brother and sister."

Colleen was active in working on behalf of her fellow actors. She was a presenter at several Tony Award ceremonies. (She won two Tonys herself as well as two Obies, two Geminis and four Emmys.) She was concerned about the deteriorating condition of the professional theatre in America but said, "I definitely believe the Broadway theatre will rise again." She became the president of Actors' Equity, a position she held until she died.

With Ken she shared a commodious 240-year old farmhouse in Westchester

County in New York state. They also summered at a smaller house on Prince Edward Island. "People come for the weekend, then they stay two or three years. When my boys were children, people would phone and they'd say, 'Do you know where your children are today?' and I'd say, 'Yes and I know where everyone else's children are too. They're here.'" Dewhurst was bashful and at the same time gregarious, and extremely generous with her family, friends, and colleagues. She and Ken also gave a home to a menagerie of animals: cats, dogs, and a parrot in the house; outside, two mules, a goat, a ram, chickens, and a peacock.

Given her home life, it wasn't much of a stretch for Colleen to assume the character of a hardworking farmwoman in *Anne of Green Gables*. The grit and backbone that were part of her nature provided a basis for her characterization. She was imposing and authoritative, just being herself. She balked at wearing a corset, although she eventually gave in, but she refused to wear make-up. She made friends with many of the cast, especially with Patricia Hamilton, who played the busybody Rachel Lynde. In their first day of shooting together, Patricia, who was very much in awe of Colleen, was required to give her a sharp-tongued dressing-down. She went home and told a friend that she was sure

Marilla in Anne of Green Gables

Miss Dewhurst would have her fired, but in fact they soon came to like each other.

Patricia is a formidable woman in her own right and was already an established actress with a great deal of experience. The two women enjoyed talking together in their trailers while they were waiting for the next set-up. They shared an edgy sense of humour and a love of gossip. Colleen confessed to Patricia that she had accepted the role of Marilla in large part because she

219

needed the money. Her manager had managed to abscond with the bulk of her savings, something that seems to have been a common occurrence with performers who entrusted their finances to others. But she was happy in her role and her work in *Anne*, and the follow-up series *Road to Avonlea* would be seen by millions when it was picked up by Disney and broadcast in the United States and eventually around the world.

I asked Kevin for an interview with Colleen, and she agreed. She greeted me in her trailer and offered me some tea. She said that she was impressed by the production values and that Martha Mann's costumes had given her the necessary support (her corset perhaps?) to find her character, but she couldn't discuss her internal acting process. Instead she had asked young Megan Follows to join us and she spent most of our time together praising Megan. She admired Megan's qualities of perkiness and independence that in many ways matched her own and that were also responsible for making the film both poignant and believable. She called Megan "a kindred spirit." She confessed she had read the *Anne* books as a young girl and was initially concerned that whoever played the character would not measure up to her childhood image, but Megan had completely won her over. I was struck by Colleen's generosity toward the young

220

Megan Follows as Anne and Marilla ride to town

actress, who was at that time almost completely unknown.

In between shooting seasons with Kevin, Colleen continued to make films in the United States. She had an ongoing role as Candace Bergen's outspoken and flamboyant mother in *Murphy Brown* and in 1991 made a film, *Dying Young*, with her son Campbell. When she showed up for the next season of *Avonlea*, Patricia noticed that she looked considerably thinner. They had both talked about losing weight, and Patricia wondered if she was on some sort of special regimen. In fact she was suffering from ovarian cancer. She told nobody about her condition and true to her Christian Science principles refused treatment. Before the season's shoot was over she died. There had been plans for her to continue in the series, but

Colleen Dewhurst

Kevin managed to put together a death scene for her character using outtakes from her previous work, and the plot of the rest of the series was rejigged so that Jackie Burroughs as Hetty King became one of the pivotal characters of the series.

Considered the finest tragedienne of the American stage, Dewhurst confessed that she wished she had done more comic work. But she had the career she wanted. At one point she likened her life

With Candace Bergen in Murphy Brown

221

Colleen and Patricia Hamilton share a laugh on set

to swimming in the sea, facing the oncoming waves of triumph and disappointment: "Forget whether it's the one that's going to break your shoulder, or the one that's going to carry you all the way to the beach. Maybe I'm lucky that I just move instinctively. Then, after having done something, my intellect comes forward and says, 'Wait a minute. What have we done here, Colleen? Let's go back.' But there is no going back. God knows I've made mistakes, some of them close to tragedies, but then I suppose I'm greedy. I wanted it all."

222

SHAPESHIFTER

John Colicos

I n the early 1950s, I was cast by Herbert Whittaker in a couple of leading roles in the annual shows he directed for my college. He decided that my real future should be as a producer. He normally directed two shows a year, one for Trinity College and the other for the University Women's Alumnae Drama Society, which was almost always entered in the Dominion Drama Festival competition, at the time one of the foremost showcases for emerging theatrical talent. Whittaker asked me to assist him on a production for the Alum Ladies of George Bernard Shaw's *In Good King Charles's Golden Days*, to be presented at Hart House Theatre. It turned out I was mainly expected to be a go-boy, unpaid and unconsulted.

However, the experience led me to observe and to some extent get to know some of the more experienced amateur actors. But the main personality I remember was the actor who played King Charles, John Colicos, imported from Montreal by Whittaker, who had told him

it would be a splendid opportunity to show off his talents in Toronto. Colicos was excellent casting as Charles. With his off-beat, rather Mediterranean looks, abundant sexual energy, sonorous baritone, and ready wit, he caught the essence of the character. He already possessed the stature of a professional actor and therefore easily dominated the other players in the cast, particularly the bevy of women who played Charles's various mistresses. Far from being temperamental and difficult, he was agreeable and therefore well-liked by all involved in the production.

223

I knew nothing of Colicos's background but discovered that although he had been born in Toronto he had grown up in Montreal. As part of a Greek family he had been exposed at an early age to large-scale emotions. He had made this theatrical debut playing Jesus in a church pageant. He would later say, "One of the first roles I ever played was the Son of God, and I've been going downhill ever since." Whittaker, who started his theatrical career in Montreal, had spotted him as one of a quartet of promising young actors that included Richard Easton, Richard Gilbert, and Christopher Plummer. He christened them "the Four Horsemen of the Apocalypse." Three of them would go on to have highly successful theatrical careers.

Like so many aspiring actors of his generation, Colicos worked for radio producer Andrew Allan in his *Stage* series, most notably in an adaptation of Joseph Conrad's *Heart of Darkness* with Lorne Greene, who would remain one of his closest friends throughout the rest of his life; the two actors would frequently work together in TV in the years ahead. In London, Colicos took on the role of King Lear at the age of 22 when the aging and alcoholic actor who had been engaged to play the role was unable to go on and Colicos, as understudy, stepped into his shoes. His rugged face and stocky build made him look older than his years, and his performance was a critical success.

In 1956 Colicos made his first appearance in New York playing Edmund, the bastard, in *King Lear*, and soon after Mortimer in Schiller's *Mary Stuart*. In the 1960s he would play leading roles in John Whiting's *The Devils* and John Arden's *Serjeant Musgrave's Dance*, both serious British dramas. These portrayals led to his being hired by the American Shakespeare Festival in Stratford, Connecticut, where his most successful role was Leontes, the volatile, jealous king in *The Winter's Tale*. This in turn led to his being invited by Michael Langham to appear at the Canadian Stratford Festival.

In 1956 Colicos married Mona McHenry, a beautiful woman who was not in the theatre business. They bought a house in Toronto, which would be John Colicos's home for the rest of his life. He built up a theatrical library of 4,000 books. John and Mona had two sons, Nicholas and Edmund, who went to school in Toronto. Edmund, who was named for John's favourite actor Edmund Keen, was a teenage friend of my son Ben, who remembers him as animated and amusing. However, it was Nicholas who would play in Gilbert and Sullivan musicals at North Toronto Collegiate, apprentice at the Stratford Festival, and move to England where he would have a

224

Young John Colicos

career as an actor, mainly in musicals, including *Wonderful Town*, *Joseph and the Amazing Technicolor Dreamcoat*, *The Producers* and the film *Superman IV: The Quest For Peace* (1987).

In his first season at Stratford in Canada in 1962, John played Tullus Aufidius to the Coriolanus of Paul Scofield with Eleanor Stuart as Volumnia, and Berowne in Langham's signature production of *Love's Labour's Lost*, opposite Zoe Caldwell as a spirited Rosaline and with Scofield as Don Armado. In the same year he played a highly emotional Caliban in *The Tempest*. Martha Henry, who played Miranda, remembers that even as he raged at William Hutt as Prospero, "his anger was filled with a sense of loss and

regret…. Even his 'lust' for [me] had a kind of 'Please love me. I'm your big brother.'" She recalls him warming up in the dressing room, booming out, "'This stage is MINE, MINE, MINE.' He sounded like a big trombone."

In one season Colicos had demonstrated his ability to hold his own with some of the finest actors in the profession, and also to tackle major roles in tragedy with passionate conviction and in comedy with ready wit and invention. In the next season he showed similar versatility with his rollicking interpretation of Petruchio opposite the headstrong Katharina of Kate Reid in *The Taming of the Shrew*, and the duplicitous Comte de Guiche in *Cyrano de Bergerac*, featuring Christopher Plummer in the title role.

The following year he would take over as Cyrano in a revival of this production, giving a more deeply emotional

225

Cyrano de Bergerac *at Stratford*

and, in the opinion of Robertson Davies, more poignant performance, though no less verbally dexterous or athletically supple. In the same season he was a bluntly forceful Hector destroyed by the vain and arrogant Achilles of Leo Ciceri in *Troilus and Cressida.* But it was as Timon that Colicos did his most powerful work that year. Michael Langham had boldly given the play a contemporary setting, evoking the highs and lows of a corrupt city, modelled on Havana before the revolution perhaps, or swinging London—banquets where wine flowed like blood, gaming tables where fortunes were frittered away in an hour, parties where women in chic gowns danced the night away to music provided by Duke Ellington.

The greatest challenge of *Timon of Athens* is its language: ornate, convoluted, studded with extreme images and bizarre epithets. Colicos delivered this complex text clearly and convincingly in his resonant baritone as he moved from the extravagant grandeur of the profligate philanthropist in the first half, to the rage and bitterness, the scatological ravings, of the misanthropist he turned into in the second. Colicos's journey through the two parts of the play—leading from careless grandiosity through contempt and loathing to ultimate self-knowledge—was both searing and deeply moving. The production went on to play

Timon of Athens

in Chichester for the centenary of Shakespeare's birth. It astonished the British critics, many of whom were not ready to accept this radical take on the work of their national dramatist. Some praised, some condemned, but none was indifferent. Never given to theorizing about his work, when asked for advice by younger actors Colicos would shrug and say, "When all else fails, be enigmatic." The quip, in fact, contains useful advice: don't give away too much too soon.

The year 1964 was to be Colicos's final season at Stratford. He was a

John Colicos

Horner in The Country Wife *with Mary Savidge as Lady Fidget*

charmingly lascivious Horner in pursuit of Helen Burns as a delightfully naïve Margery Pinchwife in Wycherley's Restoration romp *The Country Wife*. But it was in this year that he achieved the Festival's first and arguably most compelling interpretation of *King Lear*; at least until Peter Ustinov's very different take on the role fifteen years later. As the aging king, Colicos was relentless in his rigidity, a man no one could love, which made his daughters' unfilial treatment easy to comprehend and Martha Henry completely believable as her father's headstrong and uncompromising youngest daughter, Cordelia. Martha remembers that he had great strength in spite of his apparent fragility, and that his sudden recognition of her in their last meeting moved her

King Lear

228

with its quiet pathos. Once again Colicos underwent a desperate journey through rage and madness toward a final self-understanding that came tragically too late. It was his most powerful stage performance up to this point, and although he was still in his 30s he would never again quite rise to this height.

In the 1960s, the Stratford seasons were much shorter than they are today, which allowed actors to take on a variety of other work in the winter months. Colicos had already begun to appear in television dramas, playing a variety of characters, many of them in classical plays or adaptations of well-known novels. He played the Arab chieftain Sidi El Assif in Shaw's *Captain Brassbound's Conversion*, Rawdon Crawley in *Vanity Fair* opposite Diane Cilento, and Tom Pettigrew opposite Edna Best in a film based on the London hit *Berkeley Square*. These were all roles that would normally be cast with romantic leading men, but Colicos brought a welcome idiosyncratic twist to the characters. He also appeared as the foolish suitor Lucentio in *The Taming of the Shrew*, with Lilli Palmer and Maurice Evans, and reprised his role as De Guiche in *Cyrano* starring Christopher Plummer. In the Du Pont Show of the Month he had a variety of small character roles in *Treasure Island*, *Oliver Twist*, *The Count of Monte Cristo*, and *Wuthering Heights*.

In the same period he was cast in the United States Steel Hour seventh season, in which he played in *The Troubled Heart* with fellow Canadians Ted Follows and Toby Robbins, and in *The Case of the Missing Wife* with Red Buttons. Meanwhile he was appearing as three different characters—Chief of Internal Security Manuel Ferrar, Milos Kuro, and Commissioner Taal Jankowski, employing a variety of accents—in the ongoing spy series *Mission: Impossible*, alongside Martin Landau, Leonard Nimoy, and John Vernon. He also appeared in the

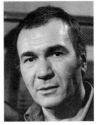

John Calicos

dark, moody American series *The Secret Storm*, about the seemingly endless tragedies of the Ames family. He was wracking up what in the trade was referred to as TVQ, a solid résumé of work in that rapidly expanding medium.

But he was not yet through with the stage. In 1968, Colicos took on the role of Winston Churchill in Rolf Hochhuth's play *Soldiers*, about the famous British

Winston Churchill in The Deputy

prime minister's complicity in the assassination of the Polish leader General Sikorski, carried out as part of a secret pact with Stalin. At the centre of the play is a debate about the saturation bombing by the British of German cities during the Second World War, in which Churchill is opposed by the Bishop of Chichester. The play was highly controversial and caused a sensation when it premiered as part of Theatre Toronto's winter season at the Royal Alex—so controversial that it soon transferred to New York and then to the New Theatre in London once the ban on its subject matter was lifted by the abolition of the Lord Chamberlain's office as censor. Another factor that helped publicity was the fact that the author had been sued and lost. The play was not that skillfully written, but Colicos's performance gained him a great deal of attention in both London and New York, where one critic wrote, "An uncannily believable and sustained portrayal of Winston Churchill by John Colicos was hypnotically interesting. The actor created not a replica, but a strong impression of the great man."

Partly as a result of his growing celebrity, Colicos won the part of Thomas Cromwell in the high-profile film *Anne of the Thousand Days* (1969), starring Richard Burton and Geneviève Bujold. The scheming political manipu-

229

lator was an excellent role for Colicos, not perhaps as complexly written as the same character in *Wolf Hall* but showy enough. And he was now playing in the big leagues. He followed it up with appearances in other films: as a commando once again with Richard Burton in *Raid on Rommel*, the neighbor of a Southern teenager in *Red Sky at Morning* with Richard Thomas and Claire Bloom, a jealous husband who kills his cheating wife in *Doctors' Wives* (all 1971), a scheming CIA boss in *Scorpio* with Burt Lancaster, Paul Scofield, and Alain Delon (1973), and a Mafioso in *Breaking Point* and a rather camp Southern doctor in *Drum* (both 1976). Though they displayed his versatility, none of these roles turned out to be particularly memorable, but he managed to establish himself as a film actor working with major stars. His finest film performance would be as the likeable Nick Papadakis, who is murdered by his wife played by Jessica Lange in the steamy drama *The Postman Always Rings Twice* (1981).

Colicos continued to work in television, appearing on *Mannix* as Dr. Myles Considine in several episodes, in the Canadian historical drama *The National Dream* as the railway tycoon Cornelius van Horne, and making guest appearances on other Canadian series such as *Seeing Things* and *Street Legal*, and on *Alfred Hitchcock Presents* as Moriarty, the arch-

Nick Papadakis in
The Postman Always Rings Twice

enemy of Sherlock Holmes. On *General Hospital* he played a mad scientist bent on freezing the world. Increasingly he would be cast as a villain, something he came to relish: "Villains, like blondes, have more fun." He would go on to explain, "When you get a really kooky, offbeat villain you can explore all kinds of devious twistings and turnings in the human mind...."

John Calicos

People tend to remember the villains more than the heroes.... It gives them a sense of superiority because they can feel, 'Well, at least I'm not as bad as he is.'

In fact, it was in science fiction films and series that he achieved his greatest notoriety, first as Kor the Klingon in *Star Trek* in 1967. Asked how he saw the character, Colicos suggested that he should look like Genghis Khan, and the make-up artists complied with his wishes. He would later say, "On *Star Trek* I just literally walked from set to set, following my make-up around." He would return to the character of Kor in 1999, playing him at the age of 140. He also played in *X-Men* and *War of the Worlds*. The other villain he created was the evil Count Baltar in the cultish *Battlestar Galactica*, who sold out the human race to the Cylons, the arch-enemy of Captain Adama, played by his old friend Lorne Greene. Colicos spent most of his screen time seated in a swivel chair on a high

Kor the Klingon in Star Trek

pedestal, barking out commands to his robotic henchman. Again he thoroughly enjoyed himself: "When you do science fiction, then the imagination can run wild. These films appeal to the childish imagination in everybody. *Battlestar* was like playing games again, with mad costumes and ridiculous lines. It was a ball."

During this period Colicos lived in Los Angeles. He and Mona divorced in 1981 after some stormy quarrels, which were not only verbal but physical; reportedly on one occasion she hit him over the head with a frozen turkey. He worked frequently and sometimes hung out with fellow Canadians Plummer, Greene, and William Shatner. But eventually he tired of his Hollywood life: "I finally got to the point where I thought if I talked to any more to bloody robots, I would go out of my mind…. I was homesick, typecast and bored doing the same role over and over again." He came back to Toronto, but he was no longer in demand as a stage actor. Richard Monette considered his technique "old-fashioned." I saw him sometimes at parties looking very much the stereotypical nineteenth-century actor, wearing a beret and a flamboyant scarf. He did do some radio work for CBC, and in the opinion of one casting agent, he was more effective in modern plays than classical pieces, but radio is a very intimate medium that requires underplaying, and that was not his style.

When John died in 2000, Herbert Whittaker enlisted me to produce a memorial for him at Hart House Theatre. I felt the wheel had come full circle. Late in life John confessed, "I've always remained a nineteenth-century, slightly hammy, overblown actor. I prefer gigantic parts with huge emotions to playing kitchen drama. I'm too big for television now. I'm too big for my house. I belong on another planet somewhere. I wish there were a space shuttle going to Mars. I would take my Shakespeare and start a new company … somewhere up there."

Back in Toronto 1999

232

EUTERPE

Teresa Stratas

When I was working as sales manager for my father's paper merchant company Buntin Reid, one of our major customers was Art Printing. Art Ginou, its founder, had come to my father's office with an idea but no money. A recent immigrant from Greece, he wanted to start a business printing menus and placemats for all the Greek restaurants in Toronto. He soon built up a successful business, and he would sometimes invite me to have dinner with him at the restaurants of his favourite customers. One of these was a small establishment on the edge of Cabbagetown long before it became gentrified. Like most Greek restaurants it was a family affair: the sons and daughters waited on table and the mother presided over the cash register. What was different about this particular place was that one of the waitresses sang popular songs in a high, clear soprano. Though not exactly a beauty, she had distinctive appearance and she sang with what I can only describe as passion. I went back to the restaurant a few times to hear her sing, and then she was gone.

Unbeknownst to me, she had auditioned at the insistence of her mother for the Royal Conservatory at College and University Avenue. She didn't know any classical music, so she sang "Smoke Gets in Your Eyes." She was accepted and studied for the next two years with Irene Jessner, who insisted she sing without resorting to artificial techniques. Anyone who has worked with young performers realizes that every so often someone comes along who is so talented that it is immediately recognizable. Although this person can benefit from instruction and training, they seem to know instinctively how to use their innate gifts. Irene Jessner understood that Teresa Stratas was a natural.

Anastasia Stratakis was born in 1938, the younger daughter of a Greek family. Her father had been a shepherd boy in the mountains of Crete who tended his flock in bare feet. He took the shoes of his dead brother and in them emigrated to Canada, where he stayed initially with one of his older siblings and his wife. In their house was a young woman whose family had arranged for her to marry a much older man. She met him and apparently cried all night. Moved by her plight, the young brother proposed and married her. They set up a small restaurant and lived in an apartment above it.

Their older daughter wanted to take dancing lessons, but when she practised, the neighbours in their building objected. They scraped together $75 and bought a piano so that she could have music lessons to compensate. Every week she was given a piece to learn. Her younger sister, aged two, immediately picked out the tunes by ear. Like most Greeks, Teresa's family had a great deal of music in their lives. They sang at home and attended community events where they danced the *sirtaki*. The

evening usually ended with high spirits and broken plates. Young Teresa was terrified that she would be asked to sing, but sing she did, and it was soon clear that she had a wonderful, natural voice. Still, her stage fright before a performance was something that never left her.

When she was sixteen, Teresa and her brother were given two tickets to a performance by the Metropolitan Opera of *La Traviata* at Maple Leaf Gardens. Teresa tried to bow out, but that night convinced her that this was what she wanted to do. As a teenager she sang not only in her in her father's restaurant but also in small night clubs and on radio. At the time I remember a CBC producer's assistant saying, "She has a good voice but she's just a bit vulgar." It was unclear whether she was referring to Teresa's innate sensuality or to the fact that she did not have the mid-Atlantic accent fashionable with actors at the time, but instead spoke with an American accent that she had probably picked up from watching television (her family spoke Greek at home).

Teresa's talent as a singing actress was quickly recognized by Arnold Walter, the head of the Conservatory, and Herman Geiger-Torel, the artistic director of the Canadian Opera. He cast her as Mimi in *La Bohème* in a production at the Royal Alexandra in Toronto. This was a perfect role for Teresa, small

234

and very young, fragile but determined. She had a natural feeling for the music of Puccini with its emotive lyricism, and she would go on to sing all the major Puccini heroines. Growing up, she experienced and overcame tuberculosis, which may have given her an understanding of the role, but Teresa would attribute her dramatic powers to her experience as a member of a Greek family where every day she was exposed to laughter and anxiety, rage and hilarity, the full spectrum of the emotions pushed to their most extreme. Anyone who has attended a Greek funeral and heard the women keening will have some understanding of what she meant.

In 1959, encouraged by her ambitious mother, Teresa auditioned for the Metropolitan Opera and was accepted. She has said that in her first few years in New York she was aware of her vast ignorance about music and expected at any moment to be exposed as a fraud. She was given small parts to sing. Then one night Lucine Amara was ill, and Teresa was asked to go on for her in the role of the slave-girl Liù in *Turandot*, with Birgit Nilsson and Franco Corelli. She gained enthusiastic reviews and was on her way. A year later she sang this role when the Met visited Toronto on tour. Once again she was in Maple Leaf Gardens, but this time on stage in a leading role. A year later she made her debut

at Covent Garden in *La Bohème*, and soon after at La Scala in Milan singing Isabella in Manuel de Falla's *Atlántida*.

Teresa would continue to sing Puccini heroines: Mimi, Liù, and Cio-Cio-San in *Madama Butterfly*. Her portrayals of these women, all of them attractive but victims of circumstance, were individual: her Mimi was inexperienced, bewildered, but brave; Liu accepting of her fate; Cio-Cio San trusting and proud. Teresa seemed to grow a different skin as she entered into each new role. She would say that when she looked in the mirror at herself every morning, she didn't really know who she was.

When she first arrived at the Met she was asked by Rudolf Bing to sing some Wagner for him; she admitted she didn't know any of his music. Bing asked for Mozart; Teresa said she didn't know anything by that composer either. She would not go on to sing Wagner, but she soon proved to have a distinct flair for the Austrian composer's characters, whom she interpreted with delicacy and a certain saucy spirit as she took on Cherubino, Despina, Susanna, and Zerlina. She was a quick study, and before long she had mastered more than a dozen roles.

Teresa did not confine her activity to New York. She was asked to interpret the leading role in *Nausicaa*, for the premiere of a new opera created by the

235

Australian composer Peggy Glanville-Hicks at the Herod Atticus Theatre in Athens in 1961. Engagements in London and Salzburg soon followed, as did more roles: Micaëla in *Carmen*, Marguerite in *Faust*, the heroines in *Pelléas et Mélisande* and *La Périchole*, roles that called for emotional intensity rather than the vocal gymnastics of coloraturas like Sutherland and Callas or the melo-

236

Mimi in La Boheme *with José Carreras*

dramatic heavy lifting of Nilsson and Caballé in *Aida*, *Tosca*, and *Turandot*. She would be heard in all the principal opera houses of Europe: Berlin, Munich, Paris, and Moscow. Already bilingual as a child, she mastered Italian, French, German, and Russian.

Perhaps because of her Greek origins and partly because of her short stature (she was only five feet tall), she was sometimes referred to as "the baby Callas." Like Callas she was stunningly exotic in appearance, less elegant, more openly sensual but equally alluring. Unlike Callas, she did not confine herself strictly to operatic works but extended her talents to operetta, particularly Offenbach and Franz Lehar, many of whose works she performed with Fritz Wunderlich. Later she would record *Show Boat*, singing such hit tunes as "Can't Help Lovin' Dat Man." This was the first full recording of this groundbreaking musical and is still considered the finest.

Although Teresa had made her reputation in established works of the late eighteenth and nineteenth centuries, she did create new roles in several new works, including Sardulla in Gian Carlo Menotti's *The Last Savage* and Marie Antoinette in John Corigliano's *The Ghosts of Versailles*. But perhaps her most vivid portrayals were in three master-works of the early twentieth century. In

Marie Antoinette in The Ghosts of Versailles

237

1974 she made a film of Richard Strauss's *Salome*, working with conductor Karl Böhm and the Vienna Philharmonic. As the disturbed adolescent sexually obsessed with the oracular prophet John the Baptist, she was lithe, sinuous, and completely erotic, a far cry from the delicately appealing women of Puccini.

In 1979 she was chosen by Pierre Boulez to sing the title role in the first completed version of Alban Berg's *Lulu* in Paris, directed by Patrice Chéreau.

Her complex characterization of this sexually desirable woman ranged from languid boredom to aggressive confrontation and predatory seduction. Asked about her interpretation, she said that she wanted to bring to Lulu the many colours and conflicting emotions that a woman would have in real life. Her performance won her high praise and led to one of her last roles, as Jenny Hill in Kurt Weill's *Rise and Fall of the City of Mahagonny* at the Met. Under the directions of John Dexter she was both outrageous and affecting as she taunted the soldiers with the mock ballad "O Moon of Alabama" or lamented her lover's betrayal in "Surabaya Johnny." Although she probably owed something to the influence of Marlene Dietrich, all of these portrayals were highly original, sexually charged, and riveting for audiences.

During the rehearsals of *Mahagonny*, Teresa saw an older, red-haired woman sitting in the stalls. She learned it was Lotte Lenya, Weill's widow, who had created the role of Jenny in the original German productions of the opera. The two became acquainted and soon hit it off. Teresa asked Lenya for pointers and was told to just keep on with what she was doing. Lenya later got in touch with her, and the two women spent a good deal of time together. Eventually Lenya entrusted Teresa with the manuscripts of

238

Jenny in Mahagonny at the Met

all of Weill's unpublished songs. Stratas made two recordings of Weill's music, including *The Unknown Weill*. She also interpreted Weill in a performance of his short work *The Seven Deadly Sins*.

Unlike her compatriot Jon Vickers, Teresa made a number of films, particularly with the Italian director Franco Zeffirelli. They had a good rapport; Zeffirelli obviously was attracted by her striking appearance and appreciated the subtlety but also the honesty of her portrayals. He filmed her as Nedda in *Pagliacci* (1982) and Violetta in *La Traviata* (1983), both opposite a young

239

Violetta in La Traviata *in Zeffirelli's film*

and handsome Plácido Domingo. This last film became a hit in the art houses of the world. Zeffirelli surrounded Teresa's impulsive, charming, and susceptible courtesan with the opulence of *troisième empire* Paris, colouring the film with the decadent splendour of high romanticism. Although some critics criticized her coloratura passages in the role, Teresa was totally convincing as the doomed Violetta—brave, extravagant, impulsive yet vulnerable.

Teresa made a very different film for the Canadian producer Kevin Sullivan, in which she played the neurotic mother of an autistic daughter. In this movie, *Under the Piano* (1996), acting with Megan Follows and Amanda Plummer, Teresa demonstrated that she was not afraid to be completely unsympathetic. She understood the need to scale down her work for the screen without losing the dynamic intensity that characterized her work onstage. With her skills and range as an actress, Teresa could probably have had an extended film career, but she chose to devote most of her efforts to her first love, opera.

It is tempting to think that Teresa would have had a highly colourful private life like Callas, but in fact she has always been very reserved. Her fellow students at the Conservatory in Toronto remember her as pleasant but not particularly outgoing. In Manhattan she kept

240

With Ashley Taylor in Under The Piano

an apartment that was comfortable but not extravagantly decorated. It contained mementoes including a number of clown dolls, one of which was in a cage. It was given to her by the poet Tony Harrison, who said he thought of her as "imprisoned by her music." She made her own clothes, rarely went to a hairdresser and almost never attended parties. She is known to have had extended relationships with the conductor Zuban Mehta and with Harrison.

Teresa sang opposite Vickers at the Met, notably in *Pagliacci*, where her animal spirits, easygoing flirtatiousness, and earthy practicality provided an effective counterbalance to his wounded pride and self-pity. She also displayed a talent for slapstick in the commedia scenes; her comic flair also coloured her interpretations of the Composer in Strauss's

Nedda in Zeffirelli's film of I Pagliacci

Ariadne auf Naxos and Antonia in Offenbach's *Les Contes d'Hoffman.* She was again paired with Vickers in Smetana's *The Bartered Bride,* one of his few comic performances. Again the contrast between his somewhat heavy-handed humour and her sprightly grace proved highly effective. As Vickers gradually withdrew from these operas, Teresa continued to play in them, usually opposite Domingo. He was also her leading man when she appeared in the three short operas of Puccini's *Il Trittico,* a *tour de force* contrasting the dreamy daughter

Lauretta in *Gianni Schicchi* with the blighted nun in *Suor Angelica* and the earthy peasant girl in *Il Tabarro*.

In the 1980s, Teresa decided to visit India. With only the minimal necessities in a backpack, she travelled throughout the country from the tropical south to the snowbound Himalayas, finally winding up in Calcutta where she went to see Mother Teresa. She asked to work in the hostel for the dying, but Mother Teresa sent her first to the orphanage, where she looked after young children before going on to the more agonizing experience of comforting people at the end of their lives. She wanted to be in Calcutta for an extended stay but realized that if she returned to singing and donated a substantial part of her fees to Mother Teresa's work she would be making a greater contribution. Somewhat later Teresa also went to work with refugees in the Balkans, doing menial tasks like scrubbing floors and washing and caring for sick orphans.

By the time she was ready to retire, Teresa had sung in forty-one different roles at the Met alone. She underwent surgery on her vocal cords, and this botched operation permanently destroyed her ability to sing. She seems to have accepted this without public complaint. She left New York and went to live quietly in Florida where, never one to seek the limelight, she has become something of a recluse. She had achieved the career she had set her heart on and has refused to spend the last part of her life in an atmosphere of acrimony and regret but instead enjoys the simple pleasures of retirement.

Lulu, the ultimate vamp, at the Paris Opera

WHERE IS LOVE?

Richard Monette

In 1963 I received an invitation from Joe McCulley, the Warden of Hart House, to a buffet supper before an evening of plays in the theatre. I would probably not have attended without this offer of a free meal, and neither would many of the Toronto actors who assembled in the Warden's apartment. Having eaten his food and drunk his wine, none of us were uncouth enough to skip the show, even though little was to be expected from the performing students, and so we were caught by surprise when a young actor burst on the stage with the charisma of a movie star. He was garbed in motley in a light-hearted piece called *An Unemployed Jester Is Nobody's Fool*, and he utterly charmed the audience and the adjudicator David Gardner, who gave him the best actor award. His name was Richard Monette.

The next year I saw him again at the Crest Theatre playing Hamlet opposite the Ophelia of my friend Jackie Burroughs, again the only reason I attended the performance. He did not manage to evoke all the colours and nuances of the most complex role in dramatic literature (he was only nineteen), but he was an electric presence who held the audience's attention throughout. He was panned in the press, but then so was Richard Burton, who was playing the role at the O'Keefe Centre at the same time. It was a bold move on the part of the Davis family who ran the Crest to give this unknown kid such an unparalleled opportunity, but they saw in him a unique quality, which might be defined as star power.

"What is star power?" I remember the

An Unemployed Jester is Nobody's Fool

244

question being argued by Andrew Allan, the CBC director one night when he was holding court, as was his wont, at the Chez Paree on Bloor Street. He vigorously defended his opinion that it was synonymous with sex appeal. But if this were so, Anita Ekberg and Dean Martin would have been major stars. Still, sex appeal was certainly a factor in the performances of Laurence Olivier and Vivien Leigh, Marlon Brando and

Marilyn Monroe. But there must have been more to it than that. Wit? Confidence? Intelligence? Valuable ingredients but not essential. Intensity? Closer to the mark, although I still don't know what is at the heart of the mysterious essence that radiates from a star actor. But I was convinced that Richard Monette possessed it, and from then on I would go to see him whenever and wherever I could catch his performances.

Richard Monette was born in Montreal in 1944, the first child of Maurice Monette, a smalltime businessman, and Florence Tondino, a beautiful, spirited, and erratic woman of Italian descent. He was close to his mother and she encouraged his creative instincts. In childhood his constant companion was his doll Pom Pom. When he turned six and had to go to school, his mother insisted he throw the doll down a chute into the furnace, saying, "You have to grow up now." He did want to grow up and so he obeyed. He would recall, "It was she who first inflicted on me the kind of pain that changes the way you look at the world."

When Richard was twelve, his father insisted he should go to Loyola College, an English-language institution run by Irish Jesuits. Richard remembered that until then he had spoken a mixture of *joual*, Abruzzi dialect, and "street English." His schooling would reinforce

his knowledge of English, and he read widely. He would later say that this was the most important thing his father had contributed to his life. His father worked for the Anglos, and Richard believes he wanted his son to be on the winning side.

At the age of fifteen, Richard made his first visit to Stratford and saw a production of *As You Like It*, starring Irene Worth and William Hutt. He recalled that on entering the theatre he automatically genuflected toward the stage. This veneration of the theatre, which was soon to replace the church as the centre of his spiritual aspirations, was apparently unconscious. His conscious decision at the end of the afternoon was that he wanted to play Shakespeare and appear at the Stratford Festival. Six years later his wish would be fulfilled.

As a result of this first experience of Stratford, Richard decided he would concentrate on completely mastering one language—English. This was the first major step in creating his adult persona. As a teenager he went to Eleanor Stuart, the Montreal actress who had coached Christopher Plummer and John Colicos. "I want to be an actor like Laurence Olivier," he told her. She took in the handsome face, the green pussy-cat eyes, the urgency underlying the Québécois accent. "Mr. Monette, we have a great deal of work to do." Under her guidance

Eleanor Stuart

245

he lost any trace of his former accent, though not a certain underlying cadence. She also taught him to seek the aesthetic sound and probe the layered meaning of words, and how these two elements could be used to reinforce each other.

At around the same time Richard began acting, playing Mark Anthony at school and Candy in *Of Mice and Men* with an amateur group, The Paupers. He also entered public-speaking contests and won an award sponsored by the Rotary Club. The fathers who taught at Loyola were worldly enough to be encouraging; they realized Richard had a gift and believed he should develop it, even giving him time off to act in shows and setting special exams for him. And one of them recommended him for a summer apprenticeship at a sister college in Vermont, where he helped build sets and run lights and played small roles.

This provided a welcome escape from a home life that had become more and more traumatic. Richard was delighted by the arrival of his brother Mark when he was eight, but upset when he realized that his parents' marriage was coming apart. His mother, who had always been high-strung, became increasingly unpredictable, pretending to attack his father with a carving knife and, on another occasion, after he had tried to strangle her with a telephone cord, running out into the winter street in her nightgown and lying down in front of his father's car screaming, while Richard stood on the balcony with his brother Mark saying, "Don't worry, I'll take care of you." Not surprisingly, Maurice Monette spent less and less time with his family and Florence started to drink heavily. Increasingly she suffered from delusions and was eventually institutionalized.

Richard internalized and covered his emotional distress and soon fled to Toronto and Stratford, but he would carry the pain inflicted by his parents

through the rest of his life. After playing small roles in *Falstaff (Henry IV, Part Two)* and *Julius Caesar* in 1965, in his second season at Stratford he was Eros, the personal slave of Mark Antony, played by Christopher Plummer. Richard idolized Plummer in spite of his bad-boy antics, even as his character, as the name Eros suggests, adored his master. The scene in which he kills himself in order to avoid obeying Antony's order that he hold the sword on which the Roman general plans to impale himself had an emotional resonance that can still be seen in photographs of the production.

The next year Richard played the title role in a new Canadian play, *The Drummer Boy*, set in Quebec before the British conquest, at the Royal Alexandra in Toronto. It was a gritty tale of a young recruit who is accused of raping an 11-year-old girl and featured a gruesome scene in which Richard's character is sodomized in a prison cell. He was performing with another powerful Canadian actor, John Colicos, in a role that was suited to his gifts. Boyish and beautiful, with his huge green eyes and his hair dyed blonde, Richard exhibited the vulnerability of a lost soul bravely combatting the forces of convention in a performance that presaged a much more celebrated later portrayal. In an era when a Canadian play was almost a synonym for commercial disaster, *The Drummer*

246

Richard Monette

Boy was a success with audiences and even some of Toronto's notoriously censorious critics.

The hit of the season was Rolf Hochhuth's drama *The Deputy*, in which John Colicos did a brilliant portrayal of Winston Churchill. The British director Clifford Williams arranged for the show to be transferred to New York and then to London, and Richard, who was playing a supporting role, went with the company. He would stay in England for the next four years, playing everything from Puck in Regent's Park to Solange in Jean Genet's *The Maids* on a Welsh tour, and a radically deconstructed *Hamlet* and *Othello* with the experimental director Charles Marowitz at London's Open Space. But his most significant experience was appearing as part of the original cast of the nude revue *Oh Calcutta!*

In his autobiography *This Rough Magic*, Richard describes in considerable detail the exercises he underwent preparing to be comfortable doing the nude performances in Kenneth Tynan's controversial *succès de scandale*. He undertook the project to rid himself of what he believed was his innate shyness and to open himself up both physically and emotionally. It seems to have succeeded. Up to this time Richard had experienced close relationships with a number of women: filmmaker Aviva Slesin, and actresses Diana Leblanc and Roberta

247

Puck in Regent's Park

Maxwell, some of whom were lovers and all of whom would remain friends, but during *Oh Calcutta!* he performed with the woman who would continue to have a central place in his life, Domini Blythe: "Shy, serious and absolutely silent … though when she did speak you could detect immediately… a well-trained voice, powerful, with a sexy modulation. She captured my heart immediately and has kept a part of it ever since."

Although Domini was initially involved with another cast member, that affair ended when he left the show. Richard was living on the ground floor of a house in Finsbury Park. One night when he was asleep she climbed in the window and remained with Richard for the next four years. Their relationship was often stormy, with spectacular fights featuring broken dishes and physical violence. Richard was possessive and "insanely jealous … it seemed to me that everyone in London—and beyond—was madly in love with her." They were no doubt reenacting to some extent the scenario played out by his parents.

In 1972, Leon Major invited Domini and Richard to be part of his season at the St. Lawrence Centre. Domini was the main attraction, playing Viola in *Twelfth Night* and, the following year, the heroine in Arthur Wing Pinero's *Trelawney of the Wells*. In this latter play Richard was the heartbroken playwright Tom Wrench, in a wryly nuanced performance that was in marked contrast to his usual bravado and probably reflected the breakdown of his relationship with Domini. They had both come to accept the fact that physically he was more attracted to his own sex.

This was only one factor in his pursuit of a role he had set his heart on. Bill

Richard and Domini Blythe

Tom Wrench with Domini Blythe as Rose in Trelawney of the Wells

Glassco, the co-founder of the Tarragon Theatre, had persuaded Michel Tremblay to allow his plays to be performed in English translation. *Forever Yours, Mary Lou* and *Les Belles-Sœurs* had been hits in Toronto, and Bill wanted to follow up with *Hosanna*, a play about a mouthy Québécois drag queen. Richard felt the part should be his; he pestered Glassco for months and finally got an audition. He wanted to read using the *joual* accent he had as a boy; Glassco said absolutely not, but eventually relented. Both men realized that the accent brought the character vividly to life and Monette was cast. Together they worked on the play. Richard would later say, "I had ideas, Bill had taste. One day I came into rehearsal with a huge salami that I wanted to use in one scene. Bill laughed so hard I thought he was going to have a heart attack, but he nixed the salami." Hosanna allowed Richard to use the full complement of his outrageous wit, his unabashed vulgarity, his liberated sexuality, and his emotional neediness.

The play, which opened in 1974, was an instant hit. A week or so into the run, Bill Glassco told Richard he was being too comic and asked him to tone down that aspect of his performance. Richard somewhat grudgingly assented. Thereafter he got fewer laughs, but every night he received a standing ovation at a time when this was an uncom-

Hosanna at the Tarragon Theatre

mon recognition of talent. *Hosanna* received rave reviews, sold out at the Tarragon, transferred to the Global Village, then to the Bijou Theatre in New York, and later toured the country. When Michel Tremblay visited from Montreal he praised the production though he thought Richard was too glamorous. William Hutt pronounced this the first truly star performance he had seen in Canada. Robin Phillips invited Richard to join the company he was assembling at Stratford, offering him the opportunity to play any role he wanted.

Hamlet

The Phillips years at Stratford would be the highpoint of Richard's acting career. He would play a corrosively sleazy Lucio in Robin's signature production of *Measure for Measure*. In 1976 he shared the role of Hamlet with his good friend Nicholas Pennell, in a performance that was intellectually clear and witty, emotionally raw and complex. His need for his mother's love was clear as he revisited old wounds from childhood.

His other memorable roles would include a painfully inarticulate Caliban in *The Tempest*, a suavely evil Edmund in

Henry V

Richard Monette

King Lear, a madcap Prince Hal in the Henry plays, a mellow, highly articulate Berowne in *Love's Labour's Lost*, and the gruelling reminiscences of the half-mad Russian officer Andrei Vukhov in the one-man show by Barry Collins, *Judgment*. Richard was directed in this piece by Phillips, whom he credited with teaching him more about acting than anyone else: "Robin was a superb coach. Although the performance was mine, he shaped it and made many of the key choices. Only one move was allowed me in the entire hour and 45 minutes: to go to a table and pour myself a glass of water. I did this in rehearsal and then Robin, in one of his flashes of inspiration, said, 'Don't drink it.' It was a brilliant choice, which created enormous dramatic tension. I could have done with the water, though."

Caliban in The Tempest

As an actor Richard benefitted from Robin's insistence on restraint and nuance, although as he has said, this was not his way; his taste prompted him toward the unabashedly theatrical. He also thanked Robin for the opportunity to play so many major Shakespearean roles. The two men respected each other but became more distant after Phillips's reign ended.

During this period Richard lived with a succession of lovers: Patrick Christopher, Stewart Arnott, Andrey Tarasiuk, Raymond O'Neill, Robert Lachance, Andrew Jackson. All were theatre artists but none were as talented or successful as Richard. Nor did he treat them as equals. He was generous and sometimes sentimental, but verbally bitchy as well as physically demanding. And they all knew that his career came first. "In spite of the fact that I'm lots of fun all of my lovers have left me," he once said. Most of them remained friends, and at his fiftieth birthday a chorus of his former lovers both male and female serenaded him with a revised version of a song from *Gigi*: "Ah Yes, I Remember It Well." It was a telling choice.

After Phillips's departure, Richard's star dimmed somewhat at Stratford. He was not a favourite of John Hirsch, who cast him in only minor roles: Doctor Caius, Boyet, Cinna the poet. He would

251

Sparkish with Rosemary Dunsmore in The Country Wife

252

also be cast as a series of fops: Sparkish in *The Country Wife*, Scandal in *Love for Love*, and, more happily, Benedick in *Much Ado About Nothing*. He would play in a number of CBC television dramas, but his acting style was often a bit overblown for the small screen. He had a promising role in Norman Jewison's film *Iceman* in 1984, but most of his work ended up on the cutting room floor. He continued to work at CentreStage and the Tarragon in Toronto and toured in the United States in Michael Frayn's *Noises Off.*

Chronically short of money, he began to do voice work. His distinctive burnished, coppery tones ("the product of twenty years of whiskey and cigarettes") were soon in high demand, and he eventually found himself with a six-figure income. But his manager absconded with most of his earnings, leaving him with an outstanding tax bill. Then came a severe attack of stage fright. He could no longer bring himself to go on stage. Instead he turned to directing.

Robin Phillips had given him his first assignment, Beckett's *Come and Go*, in 1978, and he had staged a one-man show, *Blake*, with Douglas Campbell in 1983. The same year he produced and directed *Stevie* with Roberta Maxwell and Kate Reid, sustaining a financial loss he could ill afford. He restaged *Hosanna* at

The Taming of the Shrew *with Colm Feore and Goldie Semple Scott A. Hurst, Geraint Wyn Davies, Keith Dinicol*

the Tarragon with Geordie Johnson, and then came his big break. In 1988 John Neville invited him to direct *The Taming of the Shrew* at the Festival, starring Colm Feore and Goldie Semple. It was a perfect vehicle for his sensibility. Drawing on the histrionics of his own dysfunctional family he staged the scenes between the principals with extravagant displays of temperament: a dismembered teddy bear, flying plates, sudden bursts of rage. He set the play in the 1950s, the era of his own youth, and even included an excerpt of a period song: "Chances Are." Goldie Semple was a haughty Katharina, unappreciated by her philistine family, who was gradually won over by Colm Feore's tough, tricky, but commonsensical Petruchio, who ultimately showed genuine affection toward his spirited bride. This production set the tone for the best work Richard would do as a director, demonstrating his sure touch for comedy with heart.

In the early 1990s, Richard followed up with a swift, swinging version of *The Comedy of Errors* and a hauntingly romantic *As You Like It*, starring a luminous, heartsick Lucy Peacock. On short notice John Neville asked him to direct a Restoration comedy, *The Relapse*, starring Brian Bedford. Richard agreed but commented, "Brian is undirectable." The next day in the Green Room, Brian accosted him. "I hear you told John I'm undirectable," to which Richard shot back, "I know you're undirectable, but don't worry. I'll put you centre stage and move everybody else around you." The two became frequent collaborators, with Richard directing Brian in *The School for Wives*, *Tartuffe*, *Much Ado About Nothing*, and *The School for Scandal*. Brian once said to Richard, "I can't direct comedy and you can't direct tragedy." He was proved wrong, however, when Richard directed William Hutt in *King Lear*, a production shot through with wit but deeply moving, while Brian directed a very funny if bittersweet *Waiting for Godot* with Tom McCamus and Stephen Ouimette.

In 1990, Richard mounted a vigorous *Saint Joan* for Theatre Plus in Toronto, featuring Seana McKenna, who was brusque, forthright, and challenging as the Maid of Orleans. An actress of incredible range, power, and wit, she would become one of the most valuable and versatile actors in the Stratford company. Both she and Richard won Dora awards. The next season Richard would direct the delightfully raucous Susan Wright in *Shirley Valentine*, and a moving *Romeo and Juliet* with Megan Follows and Antoni Cimolino playing the young lovers. Over a five-year period he had demonstrated an ability with "Tragedie, Comedie, Historie, Pastorall, Pastorall-Comicall-Historicall-Pastorall-Tragicall,

253

Comicall-Historicall-Pastorall." Small wonder that he was put on the short list to become the Festival's next artistic director.

Throughout 1993 Richard wrestled with the idea of this opportunity. He had found his stride as a director but was totally inexperienced as an administrator. His private financial affairs had been more or less disastrous. As an artist he had been outspoken, calling the presi-

254

Romeo and Juliet
Megan Follows and Antoni Cimolino

dent of the Stratford Board "you pig" when he announced the dismissal of the Gang of Four in 1980. He possessed charm but little tact, imaginative plans but no evidence of practicality. He spent the better part of one day discussing with Martha Henry whether they might share the artistic directorship; he concluded that the role could only successfully be carried by one person, a conclusion borne out by the fact that all the attempts to set up a multiple rule at Stratford had failed. I remember saying to him at this time, "Richard, your whole life has been leading up to this; if you don't do it, you will regret it." Not that my words were decisive in his choice, but in the end he accepted the Board's offer.

Richard's appointment was widely hailed by the arts community and the press. His early productions were popular and well attended. He was seen as bringing a new spirit and a more open sensibility to the Festival. In his first year he staged a low-key, moody *Hamlet* starring Stephen Ouimette. He eschewed obscure classics and rounded out his seasons with popular modern plays: *Amadeus, The Little Foxes, Who's Afraid of Virginia Woolf?* He programmed family shows to broaden his audience, especially among the young: *Alice Through the Looking-Glass, The Three Musketeers, The Scarlet Pimpernel, To Kill a Mockingbird.*

He handed shows to Canadian direc-

Richard Monette

tors and especially women: Martha Henry, Jeannette Lambermont, Diana Leblanc, Marti Maraden. He built a company of seasoned male actors: James Blendick, Peter Donaldson, Bernard Hopkins, Stephen Ouimette, Tom McCamus, Scott Wentworth; and attractive, vivacious women: Domini Blythe, Cynthia Dale, Sheila McCarthy, Seana McKenna, Lucy Peacock. And heading up the roster were his stars: Brian Bedford, Martha Henry, and William Hutt.

In his first season the Festival ended in the black for the first time in a good many years. Soon he was racking up large surpluses, and in the fourteen years of his artistic directorship the Festival never went into the red. During most of the 1990s his work was favourably reviewed by the critics. I remember saying to him, "Enjoy it now because sooner or later they'll turn on you." Sure enough, about halfway through his tenure, he began to be criticized for being too populist, too predictable, and even too vulgar, condemned by his former friend Urjo Kareda and the implacable Kate Taylor. In July 2000, Kareda wrote in an article in *Toronto Life* titled "Sold Out": "I cannot argue with Richard's success as artistic director…. His instincts for programming, though characterized by middlebrow predictability and unadventurous execution have nevertheless proven profitable…. What was once within living memory a visionary artistic enterprise has now been remade as a show palace with leadership that has greater affinities with P.T. Barnum than with Tyrone Guthrie…. Richard who began as a passionate, searching artist has now willed himself to serve as a huckster."

Certainly Richard favoured a broad style and had an unabashed desire to please audiences. In *The Comedy of Errors* in his last season, Richard indulged his propensity for sight gags, corny jokes, and yes, outright vulgarity to the full. It was his final snub of what he considered the effete sensibilities of his critics, and it must be stated that his audiences laughed heartily. In his memoir *This Rough Magic* he wrote, "Robin Phillips aimed to put a lid on the unrulier energies of the theatre…. I did everything I could, in the course of my own tenure as artistic director, to take it off again."

Richard had a natural taste for comedy but also for melodrama. This was evident in two of his finest Shakespearean productions, *King Lear* and *The Tempest*, as well as Molière's *The Miser*, all starring William Hutt. All three productions emphasized the comic dimensions in the texts but unleashed and heightened the exaggerated emotional elements. And then there were his grippingly dramatic stagings of *The Little Foxes* and *Inherit the*

255

Wind, featuring vigorous battles between his most accomplished actors. Interestingly, productions of both these "old warhorses" would be successfully remounted on Broadway shortly after Richard's revivals, a tribute to his instinct as a popular programmer.

Inherit the Wind owed much of its appeal to the insertion of large swathes of gospel music sung by a black choir. It may have been this that emboldened Richard to try his hand at directing a musical. Although he had no training in music, he was an avid listener with a taste for both classical and popular works, particularly the show business songs of the 1920s, 1930s, and 1940s: George Gershwin, Cole Porter, Rogers and Hart. (Indeed Richard, a deadly mimic, did a spot-on imitation of Ethel Merman; some of his other specialties included Maggie Smith, Pierre Trudeau, and his Italian grandmother.)

In 1997 he staged *Camelot* with a beautiful, flighty, impetuous Cynthia Dale as Guenevere, a thoughtful, vulnerable Tom McCamus as Arthur, and a bold, dashing Dan Chameroy as Lancelot, in a gorgeously colourful spectacle designed by Desmond Heeley. This was a perfect vehicle for Monette's talents, engaging his wit, his taste for opulence, and his nostalgia for an imagined past, a fairytale world so different from his own experience of childhood. He

Camelot *The Merry Month of May Cynthia Dale as Guinevere*

would go on to stage other musicals, but only *My Fair Lady* in 2002 would capture the same magic.

Camelot also introduced the young actor Michael Therriault to the Stratford stage. Slight and unprepossessing physically with a rather high voice, Michael might not have seemed destined for a successful stage career, but

256

Richard Monette

Gigi - *Jennifer Gould*
with Patricia Collins and Domini Blythe

Monette saw his promise and continued to cast him in a variety of roles, from the foolish Sir Andrew Aguecheek to the young lover Valère in *The Miser*, the timid tailor Motel in *Fiddler on the Roof*, and the vacillating young king in *Henry VI*. Other young actors that Richard discovered and showcased in leading roles were Graham Abbey, Donald Carrier,

Jonathan Goad, Adrienne Gould, Michelle Giroux, Claire Julien, Jordan Pettle, and Sara Topham. Though not all Richard's protégés were highly talented, with young actors, as with young directors, Richard took many chances. If they did not at first succeed, he would give them a chance to try, try again, though if they did not then deliver, he could ruthlessly eliminate them. He expected his actors to be physically attractive and vocally pleasing, and he certainly had an antipathy to certain actors who, though perhaps interesting and original, were neither. And he expected loyalty. While patient with genuine errors and misunderstandings, when crossed he was unforgiving. He was not half-Italian for nothing.

Gradually Richard perfected his last and most faceted role, that of the artistic director and impresario. He dressed the part, became an excellent and always entertaining public speaker, improved his French accent, and learned to move easily among the elite: board members and bureaucrats, bankers and bean-counters. He gathered around him a staff of shrewd and supportive assistants, particularly his early publicist Janice Price and his assistant director and later general manager Antoni Cimolino, who would prove himself to be not only a talented number-cruncher and fund-raiser but also an excellent sounding board when it

257

came to casting and programming. Antoni also proved to be a skilled director of both modern and classical texts. Hard-working, tough, and utterly committed to Richard, Antoni and his wife, actress Brigit Wilson, provided Richard with a surrogate family. He became godfather to their two children and spent many happy hours in their home.

Richard also had many non-theatrical friends and supporters: his longtime friend Bennett Solway, Otto and Evelyn Beyer, my wife Judith and I, various prominent board members, especially Rafe and Jane Bernstein, Julia and Robert Foster, Sandra and James Pitblado, and Joan Chalmers, all of whom generously provided him with opportunities to travel and see art and theatre in other countries. (When Richard and I travelled to Greece and Turkey, Joan took me aside and said in her throaty tones, "I want you to see that Richard gets laid.") And always there were his brother Mark and his wives, Christine and, after Christine died, Judy. With all of these people Richard enjoyed good food, good drink, and above all good conversation. He did not make his own wine, but he was an accomplished cook and an unparalleled raconteur.

Artistically and socially Richard was fulfilled. He had spent a lifetime serving his fickle mistress, the theatre. He was recognized with awards, honorary doc-

258

Filumena: *Richard as Domenico Soriano Michael Therriault as his putative son.*

Richard Monette

Antoni Cimolino: Richard's right hand man.

torates, and the Order of Canada. But emotionally he was starved. He continued to be attracted to young men. Various people would say, "Surely he can have the pick of the company," but this was not the case. Young actors did not

want to be labeled as the "director's boyfriend." And Richard's schedule left little time for romance. He would be in the theatre soon after he tumbled out of bed in the morning, returning home near midnight, often more or less drunk. In many ways his closest companion was his devoted assistant Elke Bidner.

Drink, cigarettes, and overwork eventually ruined his constitution. He talked about playing some of the mature roles he might still tackle: Prospero, Galileo, Falstaff. He had managed to play Domenico Soriano in De Filippo's *Filumena* in 1997 without a recurrence of his dreaded stage fright. In 2002, at the instigation of Cynthia Dale, he planned to take over the role of Higgins in *My Fair Lady*, but he could not summon the stamina and lost his voice after one performance. Shortly after his retirement he came to Toronto to audition for a substantial role in a film. "I wasn't right for it, but even if I had been cast, I couldn't have done it. I haven't the energy."

He was in almost constant physical pain. He put a brave face on the situation, but he often said that he regretted not having been able to share his theatrical insights and discoveries with a partner, some aspiring actor and director. My final image of him is sitting in his dressing gown, cigarette and vodka in hand listening to his favourite Italian aria "Nessun dorma," though perhaps more

259

Christmas dinner at Richard's house, Domini, Judy Monette, Richard, Ben Solway, Jean Beaudin, Pat Collins and William Hutt

appropriate might have been "Ridi, pagliaccio"—a fellow of infinite jest and generosity, but cruelly aware of the price he had paid. The little boy who had lost his treasured doll, sacrificing it to the need to move on, felt pain and a deep loneliness. He had achieved his theatrical ambitions, but at the end of the road he was on his own.

260

NATIVE ACTIVIST

Buffy Sainte-Marie

As Yorkville transformed itself in the 1960s from a not particularly upscale residential area into a hangout for hippies, I often went to coffee houses to hear folk singers: the Riverboat or the Purple Onion. I was already tuned into folk music, beginning with English songs like "The Foggy, Foggy Dew" or "The Water Is Wide" and sea shanties like "Shenendoah" or "Haul Away, Joe." I started out with Kathleen Ferrier but began to seek more authentic voices: Ewan MacColl for Scottish ballads, and Jean Ritchie, the Appalachian singer with her dulcimer. The more exotic the better. I started with some French-Canadian tunes and in time I would travel to faraway places in search of authentic musical experiences: Greece, Egypt, Peru, Kenya, and Indonesia. But the most exotic singer in Yorkville in that era was an Indian woman, Buffy Sainte-Marie.

I use the term "Indian" because at that time we had not yet learned to talk about "natives" or "First Nations." In Toronto we had virtually no first-hand experience or contact with the original inhabitants of our country. We sometimes bought beaded moccasins or woven baskets and we saw pictures of men wearing feather headdresses and squaws with papooses strapped to their backs, but the reality of their lives was as distant as the courts of old Cathay. That would change when my wife brought a young Aboriginal girl of nine home to spend a weekend and she stayed on to live with us for a number of years. Not that she taught us anything about her culture, but we became interested and gradually realized the shocking treatment the white man had meted out to her people.

Buffy Sainte-Marie was exotic in appearance; there was no mistaking her ethnicity, with her long, thick black hair, sparkling black eyes, and aquiline features. She dressed the part, with beaded vests and fringed outfits. Her voice was deep and vibrant, but her articulation was crisp, with no trace of an accent. She didn't come across as someone who had just left the "rez." In fact, she was born a Cree on the Piapot reserve in the Qu'Appelle valley of Saskatchewan. Orphaned as a baby, she was adopted at an early age by a couple in Massachusetts, Albert and Winifred Sainte-Marie, who had some Mi'kmaq ancestors. She finished high school and went to the University of Massachusetts, Amherst, studying oriental philosophy. She was a good student and went on to do a Ph.D. in fine arts.

As a teenager she taught herself piano and guitar and began composing songs with titles like "Now That the Buffalo's Gone." She spent her holidays with her family in Maine, where she identified with the simple life of farmers and woodsmen. At the age of 23 she attended a powwow at the Piapot Cree reserve in Saskatchewan, where she still had relations, and was "adopted" by Emile Piapot, the son of the chief. Growing up she knew little about native life, but Emile and his wife taught her a great deal about the traditions of their tribe.

She already had a career as a singer, touring alone in both Canada and the United States. As a native person she could cross the border freely, and she had both Canadian and American citizenship. Although she probably has spent more time in the United States, she told the *Ottawa Citizen* in 1993 that she considers herself a Canadian. As well as singing in Yorkville alongside Leonard Cohen, Joni Mitchell, and Neil Young, she continued to perform regularly in Greenwich Village in New York at the Gaslight and Gerdes Folk City, and at folk festivals. Not long afterwards, I heard her again at Mariposa.

In 1963, she contracted a throat infection and in the course of recovering became addicted to codeine. The song she wrote after her recovery, "Cod'ine," became popular and was covered by

Buffy singing in Greenwich Village

Buffy Sainte-Marie

Donovan, Janis Joplin, The Charlatans, and The Barracudas, and later by Courtney Love. At about this time she was in an airport in San Francisco where she saw wounded and bandaged soldiers being moved off a plane. She talked to them and found out they were returning from Vietnam at a time when military involvement in Asia was still not being openly acknowledged by the United States government. The song she wrote as a result of this experience, "Universal Soldier," inspired a lot of controversy. This song of protest asks who is sending these men to fight. Is it the generals or maybe the politicians? It concludes that it is ultimately all of us who send these men to war.

> He's fighting for democracy,
> He's fighting for the Reds,
> He says it's for the peace of all....
>
> His orders come from far away no more.
> They come from him and you and me,
> And brothers, can't you see
> This is not the way we put an end to war?

It was only one of many songs that Buffy would compose dealing with political and social issues.

During the 1960s and 1970s, Buffy's and Joni Mitchell's paths crossed frequently. They sang in the same Yorkville and Greenwich Village coffee houses, though as far as I know they never sang together. They would have made a stunning duo: Joni with her silky blonde hair, Buffy with her jet black tresses; Joni's clear high soprano, Buffy's dusky vocal tones with her resonant vibrato. They had much in common as songwriters: sharp and pointed observations, melodic vocal lines. Both singers made vivid use of contemporary idioms. But while many of Buffy's songs were focused on politics, Joni's were more concerned with personal relationships. However, Buffy wrote a number of love songs: "Until It's Time For You To Go," "Darling, Don't Cry," and "Dance Me Around." Joni's images were more unusual, with surprising juxtapositions of the poetic and the vernacular, but Buffy could come up with a sharply jagged line, usually with a satiric edge:

> If I had a way to reach the sky
> I'd grab that crescent moon,
> Wield it like a knife (from "The Big Ones Get Away")
>
> Laughter is the grease of growth
> Support your local clown. (from "Mongrel Pup")

Musically, Joni was more experimental, especially as time went on; her unconventional intervals and tunings were legendary. Buffy was less interested in musi-

263

cal exploration. Many of her recordings have fairly conventional rhythmical back-up, or even in the case of "Soldier Blue," the theme song she wrote for the 1970 film of the same name, a conventional film-score accompaniment. She introduced elements in some of her recordings that were taken from native traditional dances, with a strong rhythmic percussive backup and chants that echoed the vocal elements of powwows. She even included the barking of wolves on one track.

Buffy was more attuned to commercial media than Joni. She wrote a number of film scores, unlike Mitchell, who was told that her songs were so dramatic that they left no room for the narrative to play out. Besides "Soldier Blue," Buffy wrote a film score for *Spirit of the Wind* (1979), a docudrama about George Attla, the "winningest dog musher of all time," which was shown at Cannes in 1979. Her song "Up Where We Belong" was sung in the film *An Officer and a Gentleman* and received an Oscar for Best Song in 1982. Another song became the theme song of the CBC series *Spirit Bay*.

In 1985 she had a role in the film *Broken Rainbow*, about the ongoing land dispute between the Hopi and Navajo tribes. She appeared in the telefilm *The Broken Chain* in 1993 and provided the voice for the Cheyenne woman Kate Bighead in the 1991 TV movie *Voice of the Morning Star*, which was based on the Battle of Little Bighorn, often referred to as Custer's Last Stand.

Buffy signed a record deal with the Vanguard label, which specialized in folk music. Her initial album *It's My Way* was released in 1964. William Ruhlmann of the All Music Guide website called it "one of the most scathing topical folk albums ever made"; its subject matter ranged from incest to drug addiction. It included "Co'dine," "The Universal Soldier," and another of Buffy's trademark songs, "Now That the Buffalo's Gone." Her second album, *Many a Mile* (1965), mixed traditional songs with Buffy Sainte-Marie originals such as "Until It's Time for You to Go." This song was never well known in Buffy's own version, but it was covered by a long list of musicians that included Elvis Presley, Cher, Neil Diamond, Barbra

Joan Baez with Bob Dylan

264

Buffy Sainte-Marie

Streisand, British icon Vera Lynn, and jazz vocalist Carmen McRae. Presley's version became a major hit in Europe in 1972 and helped put Buffy on a firm financial footing.

Following these initial albums, Buffy went to Nashville, where she recorded *Little Wheel Spin and Spin* and *Fire & Fleet & Candlelight.* She had always enjoyed country music, and working with country musicians she would put out another album, *I'm Gonna Be a Country Girl Again.* These albums included love songs as well as "Piney Wood Hills," a lyrical evocation of the wooded countryside she had loved as a teenager in Maine. In her next album she experimented with electronic musical back-ups, although "He's an Indian Cowboy in the Rodeo" is a simple country-style tune that would gain her a big fan base among native Americans. The album *Native North American Child* contained the title satirical song, highlighting the invisibility of native Americans in the mass media:

Sing about your ebony African queen,
Sing about your lily-white Lily Marleen.
Beauty by the bushel, but the girl of the hour
Is your native North American prairie flower.

265

With Johnny Cash

Eventually Buffy would release some 20 albums, but there was a 16-year hiatus in the 1970s when she was considered by the American government of Richard Nixon to be subversive and was placed on a White House list of performers who "deserved to be suppressed."

Although she was known primarily as a singer, Buffy was active as an educator. She taught courses on a wide variety of subjects including song-writing, women's studies, digital technology, and art. She began using computers in the early 1980s, both for musical composition and for the creation of visual art. She has said that she began painting at the age of three, at the same time as she discovered the keys on the piano in her parents' home. She would continue to paint in a style that combined the figurative with the abstract, using bright colours and design elements derived from traditional native art, with its beadwork and geo-

metric patterns. Her works hang in the Winnipeg Art Gallery, the Glenbow Museum in Calgary, the Emily Carr Gallery in Vancouver, the American Indian Arts Museum in Sante Fe, New Mexico, and the G.O.C.A.I.A. Gallery in Tucson, Arizona. She wrote a children's book, *Nokomis and the Magic Hat*, and eventually collaborated on an autobiography with native historian Blair Stonechild, with the same title as her first album, *It's My Way*.

In late 1975 she had been approached by the producers of *Sesame Street* and invited to appear on the show. Instead of reciting the alphabet as she had been asked

266

One of Buffy's paintings

On Sesame Street *with Big Bird*

Buffy Sainte-Marie

to do, Buffy insisted she wanted to show children that "Indians still exist." She appeared regularly on the show for the next six years, sometimes accompanied by her son Dakota Starblanket Wolfchild, whose father was her second husband Sheldon Wolfchild, whom she had married in Minnesota in 1975. She made frequent guest appearances on television, including *Pete Seeger's Rainbow Quest*, *American Bandstand*, *Soul Train*, *The Johnny Cash Show*, and *The Tonight Show* with Johnny Carson.

In 1969 she had set up the Nihewan Foundation, designed among other things to support native Americans who wanted to study law. Using funds from her foundation she later instituted the Cradleboard Teaching Project, which offered resources to educators wishing to change the way Native American history was being taught in the schools, as exemplified by her son's textbooks, which she declared were "shallow, inaccurate and not interesting." Her interest in technology surprised observers, but she was quick to point out that the Internet can help to decentralize power in society generally and spread North American culture specifically. She told the London *Independent*, "It gives an image of Stone age to space age…. It's natural for any indigenous community to be online, because of our desire to remain in the local community, yet be part of the global community."

Buffy settled in Hawaii as her home base. Her first husband, Dewain Bugbee, had been a surfing instructor and introduced her to the Pacific island, where she found a place in the woods to renew and nourish her spirit when she was not performing. Here she would bring up her son and create both songs and visual images. In 1992 she recorded a new album, *Coincidence and Other Likely Stories*, which contained the song quoted earlier, "The Big Ones Get Away," with its blistering condemnation of commercial society:

> If the bad guys don't get you, baby,
> Then the good guys will.

It became a hit on the Canadian and British charts and brought her back into the musical limelight. She followed up with an album *Up Where We Belong*, which included many of her earlier hits, "Now That The Buffalo's Gone," "Bury My Heart at Wounded Knee," and "My Country 'Tis of Thy People You're Dying," with its musical echo of the anthem "My Country 'Tis of Thee." Lines such as these—

> Of the genocide basic to this country's birth

> The tribes were wiped out and the

267

history books censored

The white nation fattens while others grow lean

Surprise in your eyes that we're lacking in thanks

—are direct accusations about what happened when, as Buffy likes to put it, "America discovered Columbus." Two more albums followed: *Running for the Drum* in 2008 and *Power in the Blood* in 2015.

Buffy had appeared at the National Baha'i Youth Conference in Oklahoma in 1973, and she would continue to attend Baha'i events and conferences, singing at the prelude to the World Congress and appearing in a film, *Live Unity: The Sound of the World* directed by Douglas John Cameron in 1992. Although she does not consider herself a member of the Baha'i faith, she says, "I gave a lot of support to Baha'i people in the 80s and 90s. Baha'i people, as people of all religions, is something I'm attracted to. I don't belong to any religion. I have a huge religious faith, or spiritual faith, but I feel as though religion … is the first thing that the racketeers exploit…. But that doesn't turn me against religion."

Now in her 70s, Buffy continues her work on behalf of the North American native peoples. Her efforts have borne fruit, particularly in Canada, where the First Nations are receiving increasing media coverage and support. And many native artists are beginning to receive recognition. In our foundation in the last few years there have been at least one or two indigenous artists receiving awards every year. Buffy has been a trailblazer, and the paths she opened up will be followed by many of her people in the years to come.

She has continued to perform about 20 concerts annually, one of which was captured on her *Live at Carnegie Hall* album of 2004, and the size of the crowds she draws—a concert in Denmark was estimated at over 200,000 people—testifies to the lasting impact she has made on the musical world.

Buffy in concert

268

WILL YOU JOIN THE DANCE?

James Cunningham and David Earle

I first encountered Jamie Cunningham in the fall of 1947 when I was playing a small role in *The Pied Piper of Hamelin* with the Toronto Children Players. He was a mere sprite, thin and frail with huge blue eyes, but even at the age of eight he exuded confidence. He was playing a lame boy, and his reaction when he was left behind by the other children failed to convince our director Dorothy Goulding. "No, no," she said, "That's not it at all." Little Jamie burst into tears. "Yes, yes, that's it," cried Mrs. G. And he understood his first time out that he had to make a genuine emotional connection with his character.

A year or so later, another very engaging young actor joined the Toronto Children Players. Like Jamie, David Earle was small, but lithe and flexible physically. He also had enormous eyes and the look of a startled faun. Both boys were cast in a play called *Elidor and the Golden Ball*, about a magic kingdom under a mountain peopled by little men. I remember David, who claims he was

high on spirit gum when his crepe hair beard was stuck on his chin, watching with a combination of admiration and envy Jamie, who was playing the prince of the golden kingdom, in the Green Room while Mrs. Goulding sprinkled gold dust in his hair.

I soon learned that Jamie's abilities were backed up not only by the admiration of his fellow actors, which he took for granted, but also by his tightly knit and supportive family. I visited them in their Rosedale house, where his mother Jean, a diminutive and pretty woman with a welcoming smile, fed us cinnamon toast and milk after our shows and sometimes played for singsongs around the piano. She had a sweet, clear voice and an enthusiasm for the songs of Gershwin and Rodgers and Hart, which she played with rippling ease.

Jean Cunningham had studied with Dr. William Blatz before her marriage and had absorbed his theories of child development. She believed in encouraging children to express themselves rather than trying to mould their personalities. Jean's permissiveness was tempered by her husband Frank's sense of decorum. Like many lawyers he was highly confrontational, challenging every opinion anyone advanced, arguing now on one side of a question, now on the other, and laughing delightedly when his inconsistency was exposed. Jamie would later say he was terrified of his father's sudden outbursts of temper, though he admits Frank taught his children to question everything and to think for themselves.

David came from a similarly middle-class family. He has been known to say that he grew up in a war zone, because his parents were constantly at odds. He tried to make peace between them, and he believes that he is still playing the role of the "messenger." His mother was not at all maternal and suffered from various nervous ailments. His father was worldly and cosmopolitan. He inherited and operated a company that provided elaborate buttons and other ornamental accessories to manufacturers of women's clothing.

David remembers turning to the various housekeepers his parents employed as surrogate mothers. He would pick flowers from the neighbours' gardens to gain their affection, only to have his mother dismiss them as incompetent. He also recalls filching buttons from his father's warehouse on Adelaide Street, laying them out on a table and moving them around to make "button ballets." At the age of five he appeared in a dance concert. His father appears not to have objected to David's interest, unlike most parents of that era. He encouraged David to read Benvenuto Cellini's *Autobiography*, thus kindling his interest in Renaissance art. David would later say, "I was not allowed to be a child. That's why I am living out my childhood now in my old age."

Jamie went to nursery school at Blatz's Institute of Child Study. He remembers that "Fletch" (Margaret Fletcher), who ran the kindergarten, frequently told him, "You're a star." He believed her and proceeded to build a life on that assumption. In Grade 1 at Whitney Public School his teacher was in the habit of pasting gold stars in the exercise books of her students. Unsatisfied by the number of these stars she allotted to his work, Jamie went to Woolworth's, bought his own packet of gold stars and pasted them onto every page.

David began almost as soon as he

270

could write to keep a diary, something he would continue to do for the rest of his life. He later told me that the early entries were not of any great interest ("Got up, walked to school. Came home for lunch. Dinner: mashed potatoes again"). He gave me a peek at some of the later entries, which were more colourful, not to say salacious. The diaries now run to thousands of pages. An edited version might provide a valuable record of the world of dance in Toronto over a period of the last fifty years.

David began to study dancing, eventually taking classes from Mildred Wickson. But it was with the Toronto Children Players that he experienced the excitement of live performance. He made friends with Rodney Archer, a younger member of the troupe. His relationship with Rodney would continue and David would often stay at Rodney's eighteenth-century house in Spitalfields when he visited London. David was soon given more demanding roles by Dorothy Goulding: the title character in *Little Black Sambo*, a pantomime performed to Gershwin's Preludes before political correctness raised its ugly head; the Squirrel in the Indian legend *He Who Makes Music*; the young god Horus in the Egyptian fantasy *The Bird and the Princess*; the Faun in the Greek legend *Pomona*; Mole in *The Wind in the Willows*;

David Earle, age 8 at his grandmother's farm

271

and the Knave who stole the tarts in *The Queen of Hearts*.

David was a frequent visitor to his paternal grandmother's house near Peterborough, which had an extensive library. His aunt encouraged him to read Dickens. He discovered a copy of *Les enfants terribles* lying on a table, which prompted him to delve into French literature: all of Cocteau and Colette, Gide's journals. Later he would discover the eighteenth-century novels *Les liaisons dangereuses* and *La princesse de Clèves* with their descriptions of aristocratic intrigue. Their frank depiction of sexuality would make a strong impression on his adolescent mind.

With his sisters, Jamie studied music with Kitty Tattersall, a tiny, highly animated woman who concentrated on music appreciation more than pianistic technique, insisting that her students sing. She particularly emphasized the work of Bach but also had an enthusiasm for folk songs, sea shanties, and the tunes of Gilbert and Sullivan. Jamie would eventually play Buttercup and Ko-Ko in school productions of *H.M.S. Pinafore* and *The Mikado*.

Jamie attended the University of Toronto Schools. He got good marks and there was a certain respect for his independent outlook, but he found the games-dominated, macho atmosphere of the school intimidating. But he continued to play major roles for Dorothy Goulding. Her early attempts to cast him as a romantic figure in a play called *The Prince and the Puppet* fizzled; he was no Romeo. Small, skinny and angular, he instead relied on his sly, inventive sense of humour and exploited it in a string of comic roles: Puss in Boots; the Joker in *The Queen of Hearts*; a gaggle of witches, goblins, and dwarves; and a variety of animals—the Wolf in *Red Riding Hood*,

the Coyote in *He Who Makes Music*, and his deliciously self-inflated Mr. Toad in A.A. Milne's adaptation of *The Wind in the Willows*.

David became a student at the National Ballet School, which was run by Betty Oliphant. David recalled that she was a strict disciplinarian and given to playing favourites. However, David was not one of them. He found the gruelling schedule punishing;

James Cunningham with sister Alison in Runabout Royal

272

many of the other kids suffered nervous breakdowns. He formed a relationship with a young boy with a beautiful body and thick glasses: James Kudelka. Indeed, from an early age David was turned on by the other boys in the school. There was a certain amount of promiscuity there, both heterosexual and homosexual, which led David to experiment.

After graduation from UTS at the age of seventeen, Jamie studied English language and literature at Trinity College. He played character roles for Robert Gill at Hart House Theatre and became the centre of a group of bright young things with a lively interest in the arts. Jamie wrote short stories for the Trinity literary magazine. One in particular showed the influence of J.D. Salinger and Eudora Welty and evidenced a gift for lively, idiosyncratic dialogue. However, he never seems to have considered a literary career, and his major artistic outlet would be performance. Still, at the insistence of his father, Jamie stayed on after graduation to complete an M.A. in literature, writing a thesis on the work of Tennessee Williams, whom his supervisor, Norman Endicott, declared a fraud. In spite of this he was awarded a first-class degree and after his oral examination was asked what he would like pursue in his

David Earle in New York in te 1960s

273

Ph.D. program. "I'm not going to do a Ph.D.," he declared. "I'm going to work in the practical theatre."

"The practical theatre," echoed the astonished professor. "How extraordinary. And what a waste."

David left home and moved in with

Donald Himes, a handsome young man about six years his senior. Donald had studied the Dalcroze method of movement in Switzerland and set himself up as a teacher of piano. He drove a red convertible sports car, and on one occasion they were stopped by a policeman, who asked, "Do you realize that you have exceeded the speed limit by over twenty miles an hour?" Donald responded, "I didn't but do you realize you've never outgrown your chidish love of uniforms?" He received the maximum fine the law allowed.

During his M.A. year, Jamie lived in the residence of Wycliffe College, which allowed him to keep his own schedule and pursue his attraction to some of the young men he had met at university and in the theatre. Earlier he had consulted Blatz about his "abnormality" and been told that many of the greatest artists in history had been attracted to their own sex. He embarked on a number of *affaires*, including one with the young actor Timothy Findley.

In his graduate year Jamie directed T.S. Eliot's *Murder in the Cathedral* in the Trinity College chapel. It was a stunning visual production, with a chorus of a dozen women, moving in cleverly choreographed patterns and speaking Eliot's verse with precision and clarity. I was asked to step in and take over a small role when somebody else dropped out. I met Jackie Burroughs, with whom I spent half an hour holed up in the tiny vestry before the play began. It proved a splendid way to warm up for performance.

David realized he was not cut out to be a classical dancer. He moved to New York where he studied with Martha Graham, the acknowledged high priestess of modern dance. He mastered her technique and also absorbed the ambiance of her studio, which was a hotbed of rivalry and intrigue, gossip, invective, and innuendo. This overheated atmosphere would surface again in the future when he returned to Canada. While studying with Graham he encountered a handsome young Italian-Canadian dancer named Peter Randazzo. Peter was recovering from shock treatment, which had been administered to cure his supposed schizophrenia. They became lovers and would live together for the next fifteen years. After leaving Graham's studio, David danced for a season with the company of José Limón. He acquired a green card but was given notice that he was about to drafted. He and Peter made a rapid departure for England.

When Jamie completed his M.A., he persuaded his father to fund his training at one of the top theatre schools in London. He enrolled at the London Academy of Music and Dramatic Art

and roomed with his friend Powell Jones. Over the next few years they sampled the delights of British theatre in the heyday of such figures as Peggy Ashcroft, Edith Evans, John Gielgud, Vivien Leigh, Laurence Olivier, and Ralph Richardson. Theatre seats were cheap, and living could be managed on a very small income.

David was in England at roughly the same time as Jamie, but their paths do not appear to have crossed. David was asked by Robin Howard to become assistant to robert Cohan who was training a group of dancers who were to perform at the re-opening of Liverpool Cathedral, celebrating its restoration following German bombing. Howard was a member of the historic Howard family whose family seat was used as the setting for the film version of *Brideshead Revisited*. He offered David and Peter the use of the Moat Cottage in East Grinstead, where they spent a sort of honeymoon. Robin, who was confined to a wheelchair, was a pioneering patron of modern dance in Britain. He introduced David to the London Contemporary Dance Theatre, whose work he financed. The company was headquartered in a converted building known as The Place, and David also danced at the Sadler's Wells Theatre in London's east end. He choreographed for them *Witness of Innocence*, one of his earliest works.

Meanwhile, at LAMDA Jamie fell under the influence of the formidable Iris Warren, who taught him the fundamentals of voice production. Warren's approach was almost religious; she taught her students to "find their centre," which was more a matter of physical and emotional alignment than mere technical facility She insisted they find their own natural rhythm and vocal timbre. She would say to them, "I know that you think much of what I am doing is ridiculous, but if you continue in the profession, one day you will understand." Jamie mimicked her orotund tones, but later on he would acknowledge how much she had taught him. In his final year at drama school his major role was the old doctor Tchebutykin in a production of *The Three Sisters*. He saw clearly that his future was as a character actor and had no illusions about his prospects as a glamorous juvenile. But his boyish charm must have shone through the crepe hair and painted wrinkles, because he attracted the attention of Brian Way, a major producer of children's theatre, under whose direction Jamie toured the provinces as the title character in a production of *Huckleberry Finn*.

David and Peter returned to Canada and moved in with Donald Himes on Washington Avenue. They began to teach classes in a space provided by cultural innovator John Sime. Soon after-

275

wards they joined forces with Patricia Beatty, who provided them with studio space, and together they inaugurated the Toronto Dance Theatre. They performed initially at the Toronto Workshop Theatre, with all three members of the triumvirate choreographing.

In London Jamie's sister Alison joined him. She was pregnant with her first child, and Jamie's friends, particularly Powell, rallied around her. Powell was already deeply interested in high church Anglicanism. For him this would be a lifelong commitment, for Jamie and Alison a continuing influence tempered by later experiments with Buddhism and Quakers, psychics and astrologers, Jungians and practitioners of yoga. They would continue to explore the realm of the spiritual, forming their own eclectic synthesis of these elements.

Both Jamie and Alison became involved with modern dance, performing with a fringe company in London. They created several dance dramas, notably one based on *Othello*. Out of this seemingly marginal exposure Jamie received an invitation to audition for Martha Graham and was offered a year's scholarship in New York. Fed up with the cold and the snobbery, the bad food and the endless game-playing of London, he returned without regrets to the New World. He would revisit London with pleasure often over the years, but he was

never tempted to return on a permanent basis. His tastes in literature and art, his vocabulary, and his manners had been enriched by his stay in England, but his roots were in North America.

So in New York Jamie entered the world of the aging Martha Graham. She was still dancing, but her body could no longer follow the commands of her vision. She resented the physical dexterity of the young dancers and attacked them vigorously, not only lacerating them with her tongue, but often hitting them with her arthritic hands. She was regal, rigorous, and demanding, totally dedicated to her art, a sort of demonic sister of Dorothy Goulding. Jamie had had no conventional dance training, but he had worked in his youth with an acrobatic dance teacher in Toronto, Fanny Birdsall, and consequently was limber and flexible. He also had an innate sense of rhythm, reinforced by his work in TCP pantomimes and his exposure to Kitty Tattersall. Jamie survived for a year with Graham and absorbed the rudiments of her technique.

At the end of his year in New York, Jamie landed a job as movement coach at Canada's Stratford Festival, working under the guidance of Kristin Linklater, who was bringing the vocal gospel according to Iris Warren to North America. He arrived in Stratford with his New York lover, Richard Silverman, a

276

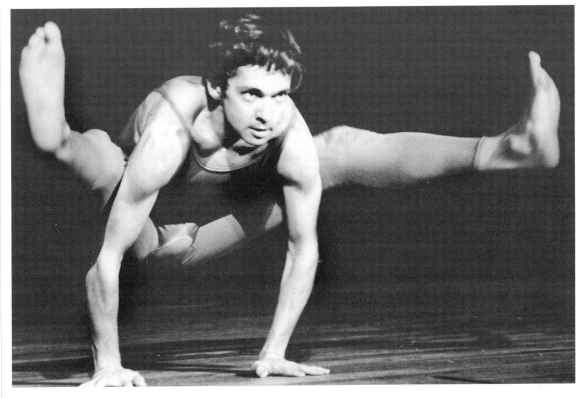

James Cunningham as a young dancer

small, dark, savagely intense would-be actor with an outrageously extravagant manner. Although he kept Jamie under his spell for over a year, his highly destructive personality was apparent to everyone else.

Back in Toronto at the end of the Stratford season, Jamie's father Frank was not about to accept Jamie into the family home with Richard in tow. Richard and Frank sized each other up immediately and the battle lines were drawn. So Jamie and Richard also moved into Donald Himes's house on Washington Avenue. I remember visiting them there: Donald reclining in his drawing room on a Louis XVI chaise longue, analyzing the various young men who passed through as David and Peter began auditions. This *ménage à cinq* played recordings of Billie Holiday, Carmen McRae, and Blossom Dearie, blew dope, and cruised Queen's Park after dark.

Within a few months Jamie and Richard moved in with us. We found them stimulating, perhaps a bit over-stimulating. It was not unusual for us to arrive home from a party at two in the morning to find Jamie locked out of the house and Richard throwing his clothes out of an upstairs window. Some days Richard would come home at noon, disheveled and exhausted, and sleep till dinnertime, before heading off again into the night. But he introduced us to Bob Dylan and Joni Mitchell, and to expressions like "groovy" and "cool," moving us a bit belatedly into the swinging 60s, which really didn't arrive in Toronto till the 70s.

During that winter of 1967, Jamie directed three productions in Toronto; the first was a version of Hans Christian Andersen's *Snow Queen*, for which I provided the script and lyrics and Donald Himes wrote the music, with David as a reindeer and a saucy sunflower, a young Irish female dancer Kevin McGarrigle as Gerda, the heroine, and Richard as her boy companion Kay and a witchy old lady. This was followed by Euripides' *The Bacchae*, with Richard playing Dionysus as a perverse and mocking imp. Then came John Coulter's *A Capful of Pennies*, in which Sean Mulcahy played a temperamental and very Irish Edmund Kean. All three productions made inventive use of music, movement, sudden transformations, and the juxtaposition of seemingly incongruous elements. The style was imagistic, prefiguring the work of direc-

tors like Robert Lepage and Gilles Maheu. It was not dissimilar to the work that David and Peter were beginning to do with their burgeoning dance company. But Toronto audiences were not yet ready for this, and the reviewers were either hostile or indifferent.

Richard decreed that Toronto was a Philistine wasteland and returned to Manhattan. Jamie followed him there and they lived together until one night Richard threatened him with a knife and the pair separated. Jamie went into analysis with a therapist and began a healing process, which would continue for thirty years. He also began a serious study of yoga and the eastern religions from which it sprang.

David had started the school of Toronto Dance Theatre in 1968 and continued to train young dancers. Trish Beatty's family provided some of the early financing. Friends and dance enthusiasts also came up with contributions and formed a board on which both Trish's and David's brothers served at different times. The company went on tour in Europe and was very well received. TDT was beginning to make a strong impact by the middle of its first decade. Modern dance was new to Toronto, but dance wasn't. Many young people were attracted to this medium during the 1960s, with the explosion of rock and roll and the hippy culture that accompa-

A typical James Cunningham fairy tale piece

nied it. Young people saw modern dance as a freeform means of expression that did not require the years of rigorous training demanded by ballet.

The founders of TDT were all in their different ways eccentric. Their work suggested a world of fantasy, with bright costumes and dramatic lighting, and involved close physical contact, which was sexually stimulating for both performers and audience. The visit of Lindsay Kemp to Toronto made a particularly strong impression on David, as it did on many in the Toronto theatre community. The vivid visual imagery, the unashamed sexuality, and the witty juxtaposing of classical and contemporary elements into a sort of high camp mythology would influence David's work in the 1970s.

The over thirty dance pieces David created in the this period were marked by a strong sense of drama, not surprising for someone on whom the influence of Dorothy Goulding continued to be strong and ongoing. By this time she was frail and ailing; David went to see her frequently until she died. His dances often contained mime, which had been one of the strongest ingredients in her work. He also picked up on her interest in various periods of history and incorporated this into his creations, which embodied aspects not just of the European Renaissance, one of his favourite epochs, but also primitive rituals: Egyptian, Aztec, Japanese. His pieces were less about storytelling than the evocation of atmosphere.

For the next forty years David would travel extensively, particularly in France and Italy. He learned to speak fluent French and conversed readily with the people he met. I once went on a holiday with him in Normandy, where I manned the wheel because David did not drive. As we toured through the countryside David would quietly but firmly insist we stop at a number of abbeys and châteaux, not just the obvious tourist spots like Bayeux and Mont St. Michel, but obscure places that tourists never visited. One afternoon we stopped to see a beautiful garden. There were two elderly people in large straw hats working away on the flowerbeds. David chatted them up, and it turned out they were the titled owners. They laid aside their trowels and opened a bottle of champagne for us.

After his split with Richard, Jamie regrouped. He found a new boyfriend, Bill Florio, who worked as an interior decorator at Bloomingdale's. They lived in a fourth-floor walk-up on Second Avenue that had primitive amenities but was furnished with an eclectic mix of antiques. They slept in a Napoleonic sleigh bed under a crystal chandelier and set their table with Georgian silver and Wedgwood china. As neither of them cooked, they ordered in take-out from local pizza joints. Jamie found a teaching gig at the Pratt Institute in Brooklyn. Marcia Lerner, a friend he had made at the Graham school, introduced him to three young gay choreographers who ran Dance Theatre Workshop on West 19th St. Before long he was performing there and soon founded his own company, working with a group of young dancers led by Lauren Persichetti and Ted Striggles, an American-Greek lawyer. They christened their new enterprise The Acme Dance Company, but Jamie's name appeared above the title. Over the next

James Cunningham as Le Spectre de la Rose

decade, dancers came and went but the company continued under Jamie's artistic direction throughout the 1970s.

The Acme Dance Company's work was both hippy and poppy, combining a dance vocabulary derived from Graham with yoga exercises and steps borrowed from popular dances from the twist to the bunny hop. The dancers often wore masks and were clothed in bright, eclectic costumes. They impersonated a wide variety of characters, from the White Rabbit to Wonder Woman in comic juxtaposition: Diaghilev meets Disney, Debussy dished up by The Doors.

One of Acme's earliest pieces, *Lauren's Dream*, was a lyrical duet in which Jamie and Lauren danced together naked, their conjoining bodies at once evoking the sacred and the erotic. Inspired by an actual dream, it involved bits of spoken dialogue and snatches of song. The two performers worked together in an intuitive fashion with little or no analytical or technical discussion. They performed this piece for several years, during which time it changed, sometimes subtly, sometimes radically. On one occasion Jamie recalls they decided to give it a new twist by covering their bodies with oil, which caused them to slip and slide around the floor, achieving an effect that was no longer lyrical but rather hysterically funny.

281

David Earle With Kathryn Brown in Boat, River, Moon

David Earle in Time in a Dark Room *with René Highway and Susan MacPherson*

282

Although Peter and Trish both devised new works on a regular basis, David gradually emerged as the leader of the group. As with his parents, he played the mediator in ongoing altercations between Trish and Peter. The company worked with many interesting dancers: Kate Alton, Bill Coleman, Danny Grossman, Grace Jones, Allen Kaeja, Laurence Lemieux, Michael Sean Marye, Susan Macpherson, Grace Miyagawa, and Robert Desrosiers, among others. A few of these dancers choreographed work for TDT; many would later set up their own companies.

In 1979, TDT acquired an abandoned church on Winchester Street in Cabbagetown and with the help of arts council and private funding refurbished it. There was a small lobby, a performance space with a good sprung floor and seating accommodation for about a hundred people; it was equipped with lighting and sound equipment, administrative offices and a sizable studio for rehearsal as well as dressing rooms and showers in the basement. The school expanded to include classes for children, for older people who had no professional aspirations but just wanted to dance, and an intensive summer program that attracted many foreign students as well as young people from across Canada. David gave classes in various Canadian cities across

the country, especially in Victoria and Quebec City, where he stayed with Bill Glassco and taught in French. David had met Bill when they were both working in Guelph for a festival that Nicholas Goldschmidt had initiated. David choreographed movement for Britten's *Rape of Lucretia*. He discovered he possessed a skill for dealing with large groups of people forming original and striking patterns. This ability was demonstrated in *Realm*, a piece he choreographed for the National Ballet at the invitation of Erik Bruhn.

David's large-scale masterpiece, which he created in collaboration with James Kudelka, was *Court of Miracles*, set in medieval Paris in the teeming area around the cathedral vividly described in Victor Hugo's *Hunchback of Notre Dame*. The piece brought together a large company of David's favourite dancers and included a section depicting the Seven Deadly Sins, in which Sloth was played by Donald Himes. Veronica Tennant, a friend from the National Ballet School days, danced in the piece as the Gypsy Princess.

Soon after its inception, Jamie's company was invited to visit such campuses as Bennington and Sarah Lawrence, where he was asked to give classes to dance students. They began touring across the country under the auspices of the Dance Touring Program of the National Endowment for the Arts, not only to universities, but as part of the Artists in the Schools Program also to public and high schools. Their horizons widened. They usually spent a week

283

Court of Miracles

284

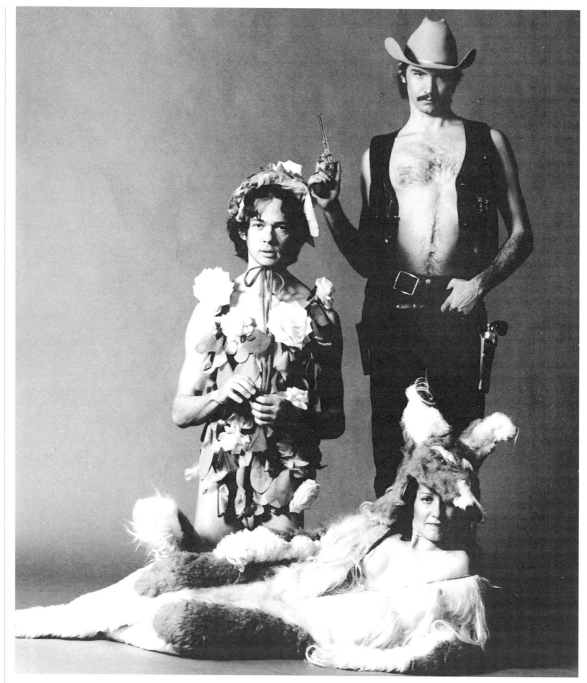

James Cunningham with Bill Holcombe and Barbara Ellman in Dancing with Maisie Paradocks.

doing workshops and then staged one or two performances in which the students participated.

Jamie proved to be a dynamic teacher, relaxed, funny, and highly articulate. He seemed to be able to galvanize a class of any size from six to sixty. He could also work with any age group: six-year-olds, teenagers, college students, middle-aged housewives, even seniors. Jamie trained the other members of his company to take their own workshops. Before long Acme was on tour several months a year. The company all pitched in to pack up props and costumes and load them off and on buses and planes. They traveled to the Midwest, Florida, the west coast, Alaska, and the American Virgin Islands. Inevitably liaisons developed and reconfigured within the company. Jamie and his second-in-command after Lauren left the company, Barbara Ellman, roomed together and spent their mornings sitting up in bed together, hearing the confessions and complaints of company members who felt in need of counselling, or perhaps absolution, before they went off to teach their classes.

Many of Acme's pieces were simple and direct, easily apprehended by school kids. *The Fox and the Grapes* was a good example. This simple retelling of Aesop's fable involves a voluptuous purple-clad woman sitting on an arbour draped with vine leaves and being wooed by a male dancer in a football outfit with a fox mask and bushy tail. Any six-year-old could follow the story. In contrast, other pieces were more sophisticated. In *Cheek to Cheek*, Jamie in tweed hat and raincoat appears as a professor and begins to lecture the audience on the importance of the size of the *thyrsos* in ancient Greek drama. He is interrupted by the appearance of a Nijinksy-like faun who offers to dance with him and eventually seduces him into a wild Dionysian waltz as echoes of Professor Endicott, Dorothy Goulding's pantomimes, and Euripides' *The Bacchae* collide in a hilarious parody.

Early on, one of the board members of Dance Theatre Workshop said Acme's work was "an outrage" and shouldn't be allowed on the stage. Artistic director Jeff Duncan countered, saying, "I think it's good to have something controversial. It brings in an audience." Later in Alaska, Jamie was confronted by a tight-lipped matron who told him, "You have turned this high school gym into the House of Satan." The phrase was picked up by a local journalist and resulted in a ruling that students had to have written permission to attend Jamie's dance classes. As for the critics, they seemed confused. "Is this dance?" they wondered. "Is it even Art?"

But there was never any doubt that David's dance pieces were art. Indeed, they were sometimes criticized for being

285

286

David Earle's Sacra Conversazione

too "arty." Although David, like Jamie, possessed a lively sense of humour, it did not often appear in his work. An exception was a piece in which his dancers were kids at a high-school dance, awkward, uncertain, the boys competing for the attention of the girls who flaunted their charms in a caricature of female sexiness. Some of us thought it was a pity that David did not compose more pieces in this vein. More often his work was inspired by his innate feeling for the otherworldly. This was based not on a specific religious affinity but rather on his belief in the universal human connection with the world of the spirit. In his own words, "Dance connects you to the most vital sense of yourself—not only of your life force within—but of your identity, the goal, I believe, of every art form."

One of his signature pieces was set to Allegri's *Miserere*. The dancers elevate each other and reach heavenward as the music soars. In another the dancers lie on the floor with interlocked arms and bodies suggesting a Grecian frieze. Many of his pieces loosely based on biblical texts were originally commissioned by religious groups and performed in churches. Other pieces were based in

David Earle with Grace Miyagawa in **Elsewhere**

288

James Cunningham and Lauren Persechetti in Lauren's Dream

struggle and combat, such as *Sunrise*, a piece that the company often danced on tour, and *Maelstrom*; both works are protests against the horrors of war. Much of David's work is set to medieval, baroque or modern music. He has little use for the romanticism of nineteenth-century composers or for contemporary popular tunes. Bach has provided the score for more of his pieces than any other composer. An early work, *Baroque Suite*, has entered the repertoire of dance groups across Canada, as has *Sacra Conversazione*, set to Mozart's *Requiem*. In both of these works the dancers aspire to create forms that evoke the celestial and the transcendental. David would continue to rework these images in new and unexpected patterns.

As well as the inspiration provided by ancient master painters, David has been strongly influenced by German Expressionism: the work of Käthe Kollwitz, Ernst Ludwig Kirchner, Franz Marc, Otto Dix, Georg Grosz, and some of their predecessors, Egon Schiele, Edvard Munch, and James Ensor. Musically David is drawn to the work of Britten and Shostakovich as much as to early composers such as Johannes Ciconia, Claudio Monteverdi, and Josquin Des Prez. He has also worked with music written by Canadian composers such as Milton Barnes and Ann Southam.

While David was absorbed in exploring the spiritual, Jamie was busy inventing new pieces for the company based in pop culture. *First Family* featured Linda Tarnay, a tall striking Texan blonde, as Isadora Duncan in a *pas de deux* with Donald Duck. In another piece a belligerent general gave up practising army drill long enough to dance with *le Spectre de la Rose*. *The Dying Duck* evoked Pavlova, and *Junior Birdsmen* involved a parody of *Swan Lake* in which the prince makes a pass at the evil enchanter. Ballet was saluted and at the same time lampooned, as were the comics, the movies, academe, the military, and the bourgeois family.

In *Dancing with Maisie Paradocks*, a six-foot Playboy Bunny (Linda Tarnay again) was propositioned by a handsome young sheriff wearing only a jockstrap and two six-shooters. "I have my principles," she states, "and I'm not giving them up for anyone but the man I marry." Whereupon Wonder Woman, who comes to the rescue, tells her, "You've been mind-fucked, honey." School trustees found these pieces hard to condone, while some critics declared, "James Cunningham is not really part of the dance world at all."

Jamie, however, saw what he was doing less as modern dance than as "total theatre." As he put it, "if you're a free spirit, you can do anything." He cited as

289

his motto the words E.M. Forster penned at the beginning of *Howard's End*: "Only connect." At a time when much modern dance was becoming increasingly abstract, he emphasized the human; his dancers had recognizable personalities. And of course there was always a sexual element, as there always had been in the work of Martha Graham. Jamie remembered her saying, "I want you to walk across the room and sit in that chair, and then I will know everything about your sex life."

290   Jamie, in some ways more intellectual than David, has always been fascinated by systems: the yoga exercises involving the seven chakras centred in different parts of the human body, the twelve signs of the Zodiac with their accompanying depictions of human personality, the eight "efforts" that defined and classified the Laban system of movement, the seven colours of the spectrum. He used this rainbow image to provide a structure for his one-man show *B.B.B.*, in which he assumed a variety of characters from the White Rabbit to Queen Elizabeth II. "I see the company as a little U.N. in orbit," he once declared. "Either we find ways to interact, or else ...." He is also fond of invoking the motto painted on the wall of the 14th Street Yoga Centre: "One Truth; Many Paths."

By the end of the 1970s, TDT's offerings came to be seen as lacking novelty and its appeal started to dissipate. A second European tour garnered some negative reviews, and the arts councils no longer automatically approved their grants. The Winchester Street facility proved a mixed blessing as costs mounted for salaries and upkeep. The triumvirate began to feel that their individual works were not getting the attention they believed was merited. There was recognition that perhaps outside help was needed.

Kenny Pearl, a dancer who had participated in *The Snow Queen* and then gone on to the United States, was therefore brought in to run the company. His tenure was brief, however, and after little more than a year David picked up the reins as sole artistic director. Eventually the stress of choreographing, teaching, and administration proved too much for him. He stepped down in 1994 in favour of Christopher House, who had been one of his protégés. David stayed on as resident choreographer, but he and Christopher soon disagreed about programming. David left, not without acrimony, and from then on TDT would show largely Christopher's work. David retreated to the small Ontario town of Elora and took a much-needed break.

Both Jamie and David still hark back to the influence of Dorothy Goulding. Jamie would say, "I realized early on

that women knew how to live. For me Mrs. Goulding was like a house where all the lights were on. She was the most fully alive person I knew. But also I remember my mother saying, 'Have the courage to be yourself and speak in your own voice.'" In his early 20s he had faced up to his sexuality. "Being gay in Toronto in the 50s seemed to lead to alcohol, self-loathing and suicide. I didn't want that. I fled to England but after I toured as Huck Finn my agent said, 'You must never be seen going into a gay bar.' That was when I thought, 'If I'm a dancer everyone will think I'm gay anyway, so why not go for it?'"

David had come to terms with his sexuality at a much earlier age. He would tell me later that having older boys apply body make-up to his nearly nude body when he was eight years old excited him physically. He had sex with a number of lovers after he and Peter's relationship had begun to fade, at least physically.

Both Jamie and David wanted the freedom dance offered to invent their own worlds, juxtaposing the everyday with the mythic and passing through space from the ordinary into the dream world. They would bring together the spiritual and the sensual, being at once in the world of magic, "swimming in the water, dealing with the death or rebirth

James Cunningham with Lauren Persichetti as Lassie

291

of the individual, and also watching from the shore from an observer's perspective, recording the survival of the race."

By the late 1970s Jamie had become a real New Yorker, living in a studio apartment on the edge of the Village, travelling on the subway, going to the Met for special exhibitions or to visit the Egyptian and Aboriginal galleries, eating in a few small inexpensive restaurants with a small circle of friends. With them he went to movies, anything by Disney or featuring his favourite actors: John Gielgud, Vanessa Redgrave, Mel Gibson, Jeanne Moreau, Jeff Bridges, Maggie Smith. He read enthusiastically but was drawn more to P.G. Wodehouse and Agatha Christie than to Auden or Yeats, though he remained faithful to his childhood favourites Lewis Carroll and Beatrix Potter.

David never completely settled into Toronto, although he had been born there. He thought the city ugly and the people cold and unreceptive. He longed for the elegance and grace of Fontainebleau or Florence. But although his life was governed by an ongoing search for beauty, he maintained a quizzical and often mocking attitude toward it. One day in the Uffizi as we contemplated a Caravaggio he turned to me and said, "What are we all doing? The world already has enough art."

By the early 1980s Jamie was weary of being on the road eight months a year: waiting in airports, checking in and out of motels, teaching in smelly college gyms, going to faculty cocktail parties, sorting out the erotic entanglements of his company. He remembers seeing Duke Ellington in his 80s playing in a bar in St. Louis and thinking, "Is this what I have to look forward to?" Funding was being drastically cut back. He landed a full-time job at the

David Earle in New York

University of Delaware, where he would teach voice and acting and direct student shows.

Although David was a keen student of visual art, he did not wish to paint himself but instead took up photography. He became an avid shutterbug, shooting his dancers and friends, often naked. He photographed buildings and statuary

that caught his fancy. He would return home from one of his many European outings with literally hundreds of photographs, full of not only decorative architectural detail but also candid shots of passersby or vendors in an outdoor market, all as beautifully composed as the pictures he contrived to make onstage with performers.

David has never been a militant gay activist, but Jamie embraced the political movement that grew up following Stonewall, attending demonstrations and the Gay Pride parade. He spoke out in defence of his sexual preferences and became increasingly identified with other gay men. Though he was not an obvious drunk, he decided he was an alcoholic and gave up liquor, attending AA meetings and then becoming active in Al-Anon, where he made new friends. As a companion he could be critical and opinionated, teasing or encouraging, unhesitatingly voicing immediate likes and dislikes. As he puts it, "In bed and out, I just love to talk."

After leaving TDT, David set up shop in the small Ontario city of Guelph as Dancetheatre David Earle. He found a studio on Quebec Street and began to give classes. And he continued to invent new dance pieces, some thirty in the last fifteen years. He worked with a range of dancers, many of whom he had trained in Toronto: Danielle Baskerville,

Michael English, D.A. Hoskins, and Suzette Sherman, as well as newcomers Julia Garlisi, Anh Nguyen, Georgia Simms. They perform regularly at the River Run Centre in Guelph and by invitation in Toronto, Niagara-on-the-Lake, and St. Jacob's, often accompanied by live musicians: the Penderecki String Quartet, the Elora Singers, the Art of Time Ensemble. Their circle is smaller but the work goes on.

In the early 1990s Jamie seemed to have left the dance world behind, but in 1998 he joined forces with Tina Croll and began working on a project to showcase modern dancers of various ages and persuasions. Bringing a dozen dance personalities onstage to demonstrate their skills, he got them to come downstage centre and deliver brief monologues about pivotal moments in their careers. The project was called *From the Horse's Mouth* and premiered at Joyce/SoHo. It featured such legendary dance personalities as Carmen de Lavallade and Viola Farber. The first performances were hailed in the press as an important contribution to dance history in America as well as one of the most entertaining dance events of the year. Using the same format they staged shows in Los Angeles, San Francisco, Philadelphia, and Chicago and eventually even Toronto, using local dancers.

Jamie was back in the news in the dance world and obviously happy to be so. In

February 2004, *From the Horse's Mouth* came to Broadway playing five nights at Duke Theatre on 42nd Street in a celebration designed to commemorate the work done over seventy years at the 92nd Street YMHA. The show featured ballerinas and Broadway hoofers, native Americans and strippers, hip hop and tap, classical Indian and flamenco.

Returning to his native Toronto he mounted *From The Horse's Mouth* at the newly renovated Fleck Dance Theatre at Harbourfront and then as part of the World Pride celebration in 2014 at the Buddies in Bad Times Theatre. Among the participants was David Earle. He no longer resembled a young faun but had a more mature aspect, half sage, half satyr. When it came his turn to speak he said, "For thirty years I tried to make love to Toronto but most nights she had a headache." Jamie

performed in the show. As usual he exuded confidence and charm. He told his audience that when he was thirteen he remembered waiting in the wings of Eaton Auditorium wearing an animal mask; one of his fellow actors put a hand under his loincloth and gave him a friendly feel and he thought, "Hey, I could really get into this."

These two, both brilliant performers with very different sensibilities appeared together onstage at these two events for the first time in over forty years. They have each made their own distinctive mark in the world of dance. They have understood the importance of connection and communication and followed their own convictions. David has written, "Dance is the oldest of all the arts. It is a metaphor for Life. It allows the artist to explore his identity and express it to the world at large, to connect with the rest of humanity."

294

After a performance of From The Horse's Mouth *with Jamie's nephew Ben Stein, Jamie, his niece Sarah Hunter and Tina Croll*

TWENTIETH-CENTURY TROUBADOURS

Joni Mitchell and Leonard Cohen

In the early to mid-1960s I began to hang out with some of my students in Yorkville, which had transformed itself from a conservative residential area to a centre for the burgeoning number of hippies that had suddenly sprung up in Toronto. We visited a number of coffee houses; my favourite was The Purple Onion. One night we heard a young woman who sang folk songs, accompanying herself on the guitar. She had a high clear voice and an intense manner that immediately caught my attention. I went back and caught her act several times, and then she disappeared.

My friend John Uren had encountered Joni Anderson, as she then was, a few years earlier in Calgary, where he was running a coffee house called The Depression. She made a cold call and auditioned for him, accompanying herself on the ukulele. John, who always had an eye for the fillies on and off the race-track, was impressed by her waif-like appearance: long silky blonde hair, high cheekbones, and a generous mouth with prominent front teeth. He was also impressed by her clear soprano voice and her skill as an accompanist. He would later crack, "Joni did more for the ukulele than even Tiny Tim." But more seriously he commented, "She was radiant, poised, confident. When Joni began singing the audience knew who was in charge. She owned the audience from the beginning."

At the time Joni was a student at the art college in Calgary. She had been born in 1943 in Fort McLeod, Alberta, where her father trained pilots for the Royal Canadian Air Force. After World War II her family moved to the town of Maidstone in Saskatchewan, where her father set up as a grocer. It was a small primitive place on the main railway line. A major event was waiting at the window every morning to watch a train that ran outside her bedroom window. She loved the outdoors and played with the other local kids, many of whom were Aboriginals or the children of Ukrainian immigrants. At the age of eight she contracted polio, which interrupted her schooling, and she was bedridden for several months. To while away the time she sang loudly in the hospital and eventually recovered, though she would experience a recurrence of some of the symptoms many years later.

She has said that she knew in Grade 2 that she wanted to be an artist. She was not a keen student, rebelling against the conformity of the curriculum, but in that grade she excelled in a project proposed by her teacher: "I drew the best doghouse. I knew there was something I was better at than the others," she would later report in the book *Joni Mitchell: In her Own Words*, based on interviews recorded by Malka Marom. Joni took piano lessons for two years and acquired a love of Chopin, Debussy, Ravel, and Stravinsky, but rather than reading music she played by ear, which her teacher disparaged. "Why would you want to play like that when you can play the work of the masters." She whacked Joni on her left hand with a ruler, so she stopped taking lessons. Her mother accused her of

Young Joni Anderson leaning on her guitarcase

being a "quitter," an accusation that seems to still rankle.

She developed an interest in rock and roll and listened to Elvis Presley, Chuck Berry, and the Everly Brothers. In order

to hear their music she hung out in cafés that had jukeboxes. At age nine she started to smoke, which would become a life-long habit. Many of her friends were juvenile delinquents. She would later say, "Crime is very attractive when you're a teenager." Much of this early experience would be reflected in the lyrics of the songs she would later write.

When Joni was eleven, the family moved to Saskatoon. She still found school boring, although she came under the influence of one teacher who encouraged her to write, even though she had no interest in grammatical structure and her juvenile poems were full of slang. She was a sociable teenager and loved to dance. She loved to dress up and made her own clothes. Her early interest in rock and roll waned: "It went through a really dumb vanilla period … folk music came in to fill the hole." She began singing at parties and campfires. One of her early classmates, David Moe, remembers, "She couldn't really play the guitar but she had this amazing voice." She picked up on tunes sung by the Kingston Trio, which she sang in coffee houses and on local TV.

Her primary focus was visual art, and she would later sometimes describe herself as a "derailed painter." At art school she was an honour student. Her teachers were impressed by her skills as a draughtsman, but the current vogue was for abstraction whereas Joni persisted in being a figurative painter. She was impressed by the work of Gauguin, Van Gogh, and Picasso in his blue period. To support herself and "buy smokes and pizzas," she sang in coffee houses in Calgary and Edmonton on the weekends, often returning late and tired to her Monday classes, for which she was chastised, in her opinion unfairly. She eventually left the college because she differed with her teachers and felt she was not getting the quality of instruction she had hoped for.

"I was the only virgin in art college, but then one weekend I was Banffed." On a holiday in the mountains she slept with a local boy, and soon after she discovered she was pregnant. In this era before the Pill and accessible abortion, she saw no solution but to have the baby. In order to keep her condition a secret from her parents and friends she moved to Toronto, where she sang in the streets and in various dives. Penniless and alone, she remorsefully gave up the baby for adoption.

She began working in the women's clothing department of Simpsons/Sears to pay the rent and continued to sing at The Purple Onion, where I had first heard her. She could not afford to pay union dues, but "It was a scab house. I was the best scab. When I couldn't sing there anymore, it closed." She later sang

297

298

Joni singing in a coffeehouse

at The HalfBeat and The Riverboat. While singing in Toronto she met the American singer Chuck Mitchell, who told her he could get her work at various clubs in the United States. He proposed and they married. "I made my own wedding dress and came down the aisle in it clutching my daisies." They moved to his home city of Detroit and began to sing together in local clubs. Joni had hoped that Chuck might adopt her baby but he made it clear that he had no intention of

bringing up another man's child. Joni would later say, "It was a bad marriage. We had got together for all the wrong reasons. I felt betrayed." But they stayed together for two years, during which they performed at various local hotels and night spots.

In Toronto Joni had begun to write her own songs because she discovered that many of the tunes she was used to singing were "owned" by other singers who had a very proprietary air toward the material they performed. "Before that I had no idea I had the gift." She interspersed some of her own compositions into the sets she sang with Chuck, and she also performed for TV on the program *Let's Sing Out.*

In 1967 Joni left Chuck and moved to New York, where she began to sing in various small venues. She travelled to Boston and Philadelphia and Florida. In Toronto the American folksinger Tom Rush had heard Joni and was impressed by her appeal as a performer. He helped her meet other singers, notably Judy Collins. Soon afterward, Collins added Joni's song "Both Sides Now," to her repertoire; it became her first big hit record. Earlier Joni had met the Aboriginal Canadian folksinger Buffy Sainte-Marie at the Mariposa Festival on her first trip east. Buffy got her a gig at Mariposa and began to cover some of her songs. Joni was gradually becoming

known. Judy Collins then covered another Joni tune, "Chelsea Morning." This song, written in New York, is like so many of Joni's songs about love; it is positive and romantic, full of sunshine and optimism and contains some of the vivid images that would become one of the hallmarks of Joni's highly original lyrics: "the sun poured in like butterscotch and stuck to all my senses."

It was no doubt inevitable that Joni would meet up with another Canadian songwriter, Leonard Cohen. Cohen was the son of reasonably affluent Jews and grew up in Westmount, an upscale Anglo neighbourhood in Montreal. One of his grandfathers was a rabbi and the other founded the Canadian Jewish Congress. His name Cohen is a variation on Kohan, the name given to the men who were traditionally cantors in the synagogue and who claimed descent from the high priest Aaron. "I had a very Messianic childhood," he has said. Not surprisingly his poems and lyrics would turn out to be full of religious images, not just Jewish but Christian and even Catholic: "twenty-seven angels from the great beyond," "there's a mighty Judgment coming," "the mountain's going to shout amen," "Jesus was a sailor when He walked upon the water," "take one last look at this Sacred Heart."

As a teenager, Cohen studied the piano and played the clarinet. He taught

299

himself to strum the ukulele and then the guitar and formed a musical group with friends Terry Davis and Mike Doddman. At the age of 15 he discovered the poet Federico García Lorca; it was, he said, like coming upon a landscape that you thought you alone walked on. At 16, he and his friend Mort Rosengarten began driving around the city and hanging out in the dives on "la Main," Saint-Laurent Boulevard, which divided the Anglo section of Montreal from the French quarter that was populated by the "whores, pimps, gangsters and wrestlers" that the early plays of Michel Tremblay celebrated. There he sometimes read his adolescent poetry.

He attended McGill University, where he came under the influence of poets Louis Dudek and Irving Layton, who encouraged his interest in W.B. Yeats, Walt Whitman, and Henry Miller. Before long he published his first collection of poems, *Let Us Compare Mythologies.* He did graduate work at McGill and Columbia but found it unsatisfying: "passion without flesh, love without climax." He had begun to take acid, which started to affect his health. In order to recover and write, he went to the Greek island of Hydra with his lover Marianne Ihlen. He would later describe his process of composition by saying he was "like a bear stumbling into a beehive or a honey cache. I'm stumbling right

The Buckskin Boys (1952) Terry Davis, Mike Doddman, Leonard Cohen

into it and getting stuck, and it's delicious and it's horrible, and I'm in it and it's not very graceful and it's very awkward and it's very painful and yet there's

something inevitable about it." He wrote a novel, *The Favourite Game*, and then another, *Beautiful Losers*, which he described as "a disagreeable epic of incomparable beauty." In 1967, disappointed by his lack of success, he moved to New York and began to sing some of the songs he had composed as a teenager and in Greece in small clubs. Judy Collins covered his song "Suzanne," which helped him gain acceptance among folk singers.

Leonard as a teenager

Joni was also beginning to sing in various venues, travelling to Boston and Philadelphia and Florida. One night when she was singing at the Gaslight South club in Coconut Grove, Dave Crosby walked in and was immediately impressed by her performance. He persuaded her to go with him to California where he lived and sang with his partners in the group Crosby, Stills, Nash and Young. He had sufficient clout to persuade a record company to record a first album for Joni, which was released as *Songs for a Seagull.* Joni also entered into a two-year relationship with Graham Nash, the first of many liaisons she would pursue in the next two decades. A second album, *Clouds,* was released in 1969. Joni produced the artwork for the covers of both albums, something she would continue to do for her future recordings.

Joni has explained that she usually begins with a melody that reflects the influence of popular songs but also of the classical composers she identified with in her youth: Chopin, Ravel, and Debussy; they often contain unusual intervals and unconventional chords. As a result of polio her left hand lost some of its strength and she developed her own system of open tuning on the guitar, something that would make some of her tunes difficult for other musicians to cover. Her new album included

302

Joni, the lifelong smoker

several songs that had already become familiar in other artists' renditions, including "Woodstock" and "The Circle Game." It introduced "Big Yellow Taxi" with its famous opening line: "They paved paradise to put up a parking lot," apparently written in Hawaii when she was on tour and stayed in a hotel that overlooked an expanse of asphalt where there once had been palm and frangipani trees.

The most striking feature of Joni's songs was the lyrics, which combined startling images often juxtaposed with quite ordinary objects and common expressions of the day: "ice cream cas-tles in the air," "the bed's too big, the frying pan's too wide," "songs are like tattoos." She employed many of the traditional devices of poetry: rhyme, alliteration, and assonance. In some ways her lyrics recalled the startling combinations of images favoured by the metaphysical poets Donne and Marvell, as well as the more recent verse of T.S. Eliot. The two other songwriters among Joni's contemporaries who produced similarly original and poetic lyrics were Bob Dylan and Leonard Cohen, but neither of them had much of a voice, whereas Joni ranged over three octaves, from a high clear soprano to deep husky

chest tones, sometimes jumping from one extreme to another, as at the end of "Big Yellow Taxi."

Joni had met Leonard Cohen at the Newport Jazz Festival. She looked up to him, thinking he was sophisticated, whereas she told him she hadn't read anything. "Maybe you shouldn't read anything," he commented, but he gave her a list of books that included Camus, the *I Ching*, Hermann Hesse, and Lorca. Reading Camus she discovered that he had lifted one of his lines from the French author, which inspired her to use one of Cohen's lines in a song she wrote. He was annoyed and confronted her, saying "I'm glad I wrote that." At the time he was suffering from chronic depression and was often very abrasive. She found him hard to talk to and distant: "There wasn't much relationship other than the boudoir." He could be deliberately enigmatic: "He'd say to me, 'Joni, they'll never get us.'"

Cohen's lyrics, like Joni's, were studded with startling images. He juxtaposed everyday expressions like "that's how it goes," "take me for a ride," and "isn't worth a dime" with original images: "the moon is swimming naked," "love's the only engine of survival," "freshly cut tears," "dead as heaven on a Saturday night," "piece that was torn from the morning," and "crimes against the moonlight." His

rhymes were original and striking—"do ya" and "knew ya" matched with "Hallelujah"—or inexact, involving assonance:

> I will step into the ring for you, ...
> I'll examine every inch of you
> or
> I'm aching for you, baby ...
> I need to see you naked
> or
> Everybody knows the fight was fixed
> The poor stay poor, the rich get rich.

303

Cohen began touring in the 1970s in the United States, Europe, and Israel. Joni was touring in America and she found it a grind: second-rate motels, bad food, endless driving through bad

Leonard and Suzanne Elrod

weather, sleep snatched whenever it was possible. It earned her extensive radio play and her first Grammy award for best folk performance, but the strain of touring told on her temper. Spider Robinson, the mystery writer, tells of a concert he attended where Joni sang the first set, followed by Tim Hardin. As soon as Joni was finished most of the crowd headed for the exits. They made no attempt to keep silent but laughed, shouted, and lit up as Hardin began his first song. He followed with another number, and then gave up halfway through and left the stage. Joni came out and lambasted the audience: "She cursed the crowd. We were barbarians, pigs, reptile excrement…. She maligned us and our relatives and ancestors until she ran out of breath and stormed off-stage, leaving behind hundreds of baffled people … and a handful like me, cheering even louder than we had for her songs." Joni has often spoken proudly of her Irish blood, which no doubt fuelled her invective.

After touring in America, Joni travelled to Europe, and the songs she wrote reflected her experiences there, as in this example from "California":

> Went to a party down a red dirt road
> There were lots of pretty people there
> Reading Rolling Stone, reading Vogue.

In the same song she expresses her homesickness, asking:

> Will you take me as I am
> Strung out on another man?

These songs are contained in her next album *Blue*. This collection of songs voices Joni's most intense personal feelings, her sense of loss and loneliness, but also the joy of a deeply personal relationship. She would later say, "at

California, will you take me as I am?

304

that time I had no personal defences. I felt like the cellophane wrapper on a pack of cigarettes." The openness of this album caused some of her male colleagues, particularly Kris Kristofferson, to criticize her songs for exposing herself too much. Joni's response was that films were dealing with this kind of intimacy, so why not songs? In "Little Green" she sings in veiled words about the sadness of giving up her child. But "A Case of You," the most upbeat song on the album, affirms a positive emotion:

> Oh, you're in my blood like holy wine,
> You taste so bitter and so sweet.
> Oh, I could drink a case of you, darling
> And I would still be on my feet.

In 1974 Joni released the album *Court and Spark*, working with a back-up group called The L.A. Express playing a mixture of folk/pop/jazz fusion. Joni toured with this band across the United States and Canada. The album contained the song "A Free Man in Paris," which included lines about "stoking the star-maker machinery behind the popular song," written about David Geffen, the entrepreneur who controlled Joni's record label. He apparently didn't like the song, but it proved to be a hit. Another song on that album, "Help Me," which

begins "Help me, I think I'm falling in love again. When I get that crazy feeling I know I'm in trouble again," peaked at number seven on the charts. Most of the other songs dealt with the frustration and disillusion of love affairs, although "Raised on Robbery" is a comic satire on singles bars.

In the second half of the 1970s Joni released a number of albums, including *Miles of Aisles*, *The Hissing of Summer Lawns*, *Hejira*, and *Don Juan's Reckless Daughter*. Although her career as a pop singer had peaked, her albums continued to sell. She had begun experimenting with jazz rhythms and jazz musicians: Jaco Pastorius, Don Alias, Wayne Shorter, and later Pat Metheny and the bassist Larry Klein, whom she married in

305

For the Roses

1982, a union that lasted twelve years. She toured with Bob Dylan and Joan Baez and sang in *The Last Waltz* with The Band. She was approached by jazz great Charles Mingus and they recorded an album together, which appeared only after Mingus's death. The critics' reviews were mainly negative, but nevertheless Joni continued to experiment with jazz and started to work with synthesizers. The various managers who tried to steer her career wanted her to continue in the style of her earlier hit records, but Joni was determined to break new ground, to "try for something fresh."

In 1983 she embarked on a world tour, visiting Japan, Australia, several European countries, and ending up in the United States. She had continued to paint throughout the years, landscapes in California and British Columbia, where she had bought a property near the coast, and portraits of friends, relatives, and herself. She rarely showed her artwork in public, but she did mount a show in Japan where she sold a number of paintings. More albums followed: *Dog Eat Dog, Chalk Mark in a Rain Storm,* and *Night Ride Home.* She performed with Willie Nelson, Billy Idol, and especially Peter Gabriel, with whom she recorded "My Secret Place" as a duet. After 1990 she rarely performed live, although she did sing "Goodbye Blue Sky" in Roger Water's *The Wall* concert in Berlin along with Cyndi Lauper, Bryan Adams, and Van Morrison.

In her early years as a singer Joni was not involved in political protests as much as Joan Baez and Judy Collins, but her later recordings contain a good deal of social commentary as she became increasingly disgusted with the greed and environmental degradation that took place in the 1990s. She visited the Pine Ridge Indian Reservation, marched with Aboriginal leaders in protest, and wrote the song "Lakota" based on this experience, which Peter Gabriel added to his repertoire. She had always shown contempt for the bourgeois life, as seen in these lyrics from "The Last Time I Saw Richard"—

Richard got married to a figure skater
He bought her a dishwasher and a coffee percolator.

—but now her scorn became lacerating. She attacked televangelists in the song "Tax Free." As always she stood up to criticism and rather enjoyed the controversy: "The churches came after me; they attacked me, though the Episcopalian Church, which I've described as the only church in America which actually uses its head, wrote me a letter of congratulation."

Cohen is one of the very few Canadian performers whose dominant

image is that of a Don Juan. The recurrence of love and sex in his songs suggests obsession. In appearance Cohen was a beautiful teenager like many Jewish boys, but as an adult he has the rather tough, hardened visage also typical of many men of his heritage. He has said he was "born in a suit"; he always appears in public well-groomed, usually wearing a tie and a hat—not for him the jeans and plaid shirts of most folk singers nor the spangled costumes and exposed flesh of many rock-and-rollers. Though a consummate performer, Cohen is not really an actor. In spite of the macho bravado of *I'm Your Man* and the dogged insistence of the refrain of "there ain't no cure for love," he is often self-deprecating, as he tells us: "it don't matter how it all went wrong," "I'm crazy for love but I'm not coming on," "I was never any good at loving you," "I was just a tourist

I'm Your Man – Leonard with his ladies: Rebecca De Mornay, daughter Lorca, manager Perla Batalla

in your bed."

Often Cohen projects an image of himself as the streetwise cynic, as in the lyrics of in "Everybody Knows":

> Everybody knows that the dice are loaded
> Everybody rolls with their fingers crossed
> Everybody knows that the war is over
> Everybody knows the good guys lost
> ...
> That's how it goes
> Everybody knows

In "The Future" and "First We Take Manhattan" he adopts a persona that borders on the psychopathic, even to interpolating into the lyrics a demonic laugh, though at least he offers some a vestige of hope with the line from "The Future," "Love's the only engine of survival." Cohen sings in a baritone that is sometimes husky, sometimes resonant, but with very little range, often using the *Sprechstimme* technique borrowed from the original singers of Brecht and Weill songs. His tunes are simpler melodically than those of Mitchell. Often he is backed up by one female voice or sometimes several singing in harmony, which adds variety and texture. The arrangements are simple, with a strong rhythmic bass, sometimes overlaid by a variety of instruments: violins, piano arpeggios,

307

guitars, a zither or a mouthorgan, punctuated by snare drums and cymbals and more recently synthesizers. Like Mitchell, Cohen often disagreed with his producers about the back-up for his tunes, but once his work became accepted by a wider public he could insist on minimal instrumentation that enhances but does not overpower the lyrics. Different songs show the influence of different musical traditions: country, martial, klezmer, honky-tonk, flamenco, rhythm and blues. "Take This Waltz" references the Vienna of Strauss; "Democracy" evokes a parade to the strains of Sousa.

Cohen's view of the world is much less optimistic than Joni Mitchell's. They share an awareness of the seamier realities and injustices of contemporary life, but where Joni connects with and finds solace in nature, Cohen's landscape contains only the symbolic: rivers, deserts, and towers. He sees the world as fatally flawed, though not completely doomed:

> There is a crack in everything.
> That's how the light gets in.

But there is another side to Cohen's songs that depicts a nostalgia for times past, a desperate loneliness and a longing for lost love. This is evident in songs like "Take This Waltz," "In My Secret Life," "A Thousand Kisses Deep," and "Dance Me to the End of Love":

> Dance me to the children
> Who are waiting to be born
> Dance me through the curtains
> That our kisses have outworn.

Throughout her career the birth of Joni's daughter remained a secret, though it was alluded to in some of her songs: "And my child's a stranger, / I bore her / But I could not raise her." These lyrics from the song "Chinese Café" did not attract much attention when they appeared, but in 1993 one of her former classmates spilled the beans in an article she sold to a tabloid. Joni's daughter Kilauren Gibb had already begun a search for her birth mother, and in 1997 they finally met. Although there were some initial conflicts, mother and daughter remain in touch and Joni enjoys being a grandmother. After the reunion Joni said she had no further interest in writing songs, although she would continue to paint. She divided her time between California and her property near Sechelt in British Columbia, where she discovered that John Uren was a neighbour. "L.A. is my workplace; B.C. is my heartbeat."

Cohen has continued to be an observant Jew, which he does not see as inconsistent with his absorption of Buddhist beliefs: "Well, for one thing, in the tradi-

308

tion of Zen that I've practiced, there is no prayerful worship and there is no affirmation of a deity. So theologically there is no challenge to any Jewish belief." Unlike Bob Dylan, who renounced both his Jewish name and faith, Cohen observes the Sabbath even when on tour and in Israel has recited Hebrew prayers during his concerts.

Cohen left the concert stage to take up residence at the Buddhist monastery at Mount Baldy in California, where studied under a Zen master Roshi and was eventually initiated as a monk. While he was there Cohen's daughter Lorca became suspicious that Kelley Lynch, who was handling his financial affairs, might be cheating him. Investigation proved that she had indeed been selling rights to his songs without his permission and had absconded with most of his savings. A number of lawsuits resulted in her being convicted and sent to prison.

Partly for financial reasons, Cohen decided to return to the concert stage and throughout the early years of the new century he toured extensively and released a number of albums, including *Ten New Songs*. It was evident that many of his preoccupation were the same as they had always been: love, sex, nostalgia, and the pleasures of the flesh ("a sip of wine, a cigarette"). But his depression had lifted and he faced the world with

renewed vigour and determination. He continues to tour the world: Europe, North America, New Zealand, Australia, and Israel.

His songs have been covered by many artists and bands from around the world, initially Judy Collins and James Taylor, more recently his fellow Canadians k.d.

Cohen, performing on tour

309

lang, Martha and Rufus Wainwright (the latter who, although a professed homosexual, fathered Lorca Cohen's daughter Chloe), and the Barenaked Ladies. His songs have also been used by filmmakers from Robert Altman to Atom Egoyan and have inspired everything from a musical revue to a work by Philip Glass. Ultimately Cohen offers a vision that celebrates "the majesty of creation." It permeates the lyric of a piece, "Hallelujah," that has been covered by more singers than almost any other contemporary song, with its bleak picture of lost love and disillusion:

My friends are gone and my hair is grey

> I did my best, it wasn't much
> I couldn't feel, so I tried to touch
> I've told the truth, I didn't come to fool you
> Even though it all went wrong
> I'll stand before the Lord of Song
> With nothing on my tongue but Hallelujah.

In "Tower of Song," he faces up to old age with a sort of wry acceptance:

> Well my friends are gone
> And my hair is grey.
> I ache in the places where I used to play.

Throughout the early 2000s, Joni's health deteriorated and she was diagnosed with a mysterious disease known as Morgellons Syndrome, which may be an after-effect of polio. But she continued to work on various projects. She became involved in working on a ballet mounted by the Alberta Ballet Company titled *The Fiddle and the Drum*, which choreographer Jean Grand-Maître set to her songs. She also performed at the Saskatchewan Centennial Concert attended by Queen Elizabeth II. In 2013 she attended a special gala staged by the Luminato Festival in Toronto in honour of her seventieth birthday, during which her music was covered by Rufus Wainwright and Herbie Hancock, among others. She sat and listened, and then she stood up, her hair piled high on her head and her face set in the same

310

fierce determination that led her to pen such lyrics as "Songs to aging children come / Aging children, I am one." Unexpectedly she kicked off her shoes and sang. Her voice was low and husky but it was clear she could still put a song across. She returned to the stage to recover her shoes and received an enormous ovation.

Much has been written about Joni's originality as a musician. She has influenced singers from Madonna to Prince, Annie Lennox to Courtney Love, Janet Jackson to Björk, fellow Canadians Sarah McLachlan and Alanis Morissette. She has won eight Grammy Awards and been

Joni at Luminato

made a Companion of the Order of Canada. Although not in any sense academic, she has been influenced by many artists and thinkers, from Nietzsche to Billie Holiday, W.B. Yeats to Picasso, Buddha to Miles Davis.

For me Joni's great achievement is the creation of a unique world. A world of illusion and disillusion, of images of beauty and innocence where "the painted ponies go up and down" and "we're captive on the carousel of time." A world of stars and feathers, midways and bars and dance-halls, low dives where jukeboxes play, where men drink and women dance, newspapers blow along the sidewalks and people walk by, ignoring musicians playing on a street corner. It is a world laced with humour and hurt: "thin skin, thick jokes." A world where women fall in love and are bruised or deserted by gamblers and dreamers who make them happy for a moment but can't settle down, leaving them with memories

vividly captured in images. In one of her earliest songs Joni sings "I really don't know life at all," a claim negated by the all the words she has written since.

Joni with John Uren in B.C.

312

ACTIVIST

R.H. Thomson

Back in the 1950s, the most innovative amateur theatre group in Toronto was the Women's Alumnae Dramatic Society. Every year in June after their season was finished they held their annual meeting at the Thornhill country house of Cicely Thomson. The ladies assembled in the early afternoon bringing with them casseroles, salads, jellied aspic, devilled eggs, and other delicacies fashionable at the time. They reviewed their financial situation, voted in officers for the coming year, and discussed a possible repertoire for the following season. Then at 5:00 the men who had participated in their shows in the past year were invited for a sort of picnic supper. Beer was provided by Woody, Cicely's husband, and an evening of conviviality followed, featuring skits and songs. One I remember:

> Here's to good old Harold.
> How loyal can you get?
> Four shows this season,
> Honorary Alumnette.

Many of the "Alum Ladies" had children, but they were not invited to this festivity. But I remember a lanky redheaded sixteen-year-old peering through the bushes. He was Cicely's son and obviously would have liked to join the party, but Cicely had brought him up to be mannerly and to know his place.

Two years later in 1967, a play I had written was chosen as one of four to take place in the annual Dominion Drama Festival for the region of Central Ontario. Cicely had agreed to be producer and selected Ron Hartmann to direct. He called for actors, and Cicely's

313

son Robert auditioned for the juvenile lead, playing opposite Terry Tweed, the daughter of a well-known radio actor at the time. The play won the regional festival, and both Terry and Robert won acting awards. We then took the play to the national finals in St. John's, Newfoundland, where we didn't win best play, but again Terry and Robert won awards and one of their scenes was televised for the CBC. They were an effective duo: she cross and uncompromising, he a bit shy but determined. They were both on their way to acting careers.

314

The fact that in the play they met at a party and spent a night together was considered rather shocking at the time. Terry confessed to me that although Robert had a girlfriend, he was pretty inexperienced and she had to teach him a thing or two. She managed to do this under Cicely's watchful eye. Or perhaps Cicely was tacitly pleased. She did say to me that she was relieved that Robert was not cast as the gay brother. She need not have worried.

Robert was still at high school. Probably by choice rather than parental fiat he did not go to a private school but to Richmond Hill Collegiate, where he was a good student, popular with his peer group, played cello in the school orchestra and guitar at home, and began to dabble in amateur theatricals. He acquired a pretty girlfriend. He would go

Aspiring young actor up a ladder

on to study maths, physics, and chemistry at the University of Toronto, graduating with good grades from a course that many flunked in first year. He was not a party animal but had the ability to hold his own in social situations.

The year Robert turned up at the University of Toronto, I had just been appointed playwright-in-residence. On the strength of his performance in my

R.H. Thomson

315

In Young Hunting *with Clare Coulter and Meg Hogarth*

earlier play I cast him in another play of mine, a four-hander whose cast included Annette Cohen, a very young Clare Coulter, and my friend Meg Hogarth. The play was not a rousing success, but Robert gave a sensitive performance as a volatile teenager who played the guitar, which he did rather skillfully, sang songs that were more or less inspired by Simon and Garfunkel, and was by turns rude, funny, and pathetic.

The next year we opened a studio theatre on Glenmorris Street, and I chose as the initial show *The Just Assassins* by Albert Camus, in which Robert played a young Russian revolutionary. This time he was fiery and intellectual and a bit mad. He was part of a strong cast, and the production was favourably reviewed by Herbert Whittaker, the drama critic of *The Globe and Mail* at the time. Herbert apparently took young Robert out for a drink and suggested a completely different performance. When I saw him the next night he performed as a sort of surrogate Christ. Afterwards I told Robert that it was one thing for an actor to pay attention to critics but quite another to let them override the work of the director without even discussing it with him. He reverted to his earlier interpretation for the following performances. Herbert continued to take a particular interest in Robert, and they remained friends until the critic's death

some forty years later. Robert eulogized Herbert at his memorial.

The following summer I directed Bertolt Brecht's *The Caucasian Chalk Circle* at the Studio Theatre. I asked Robert to play Simon Shashava, the young soldier lover of the heroine. He told me that he had planned a trip to London and would not return to Toronto until ten days before we opened. I told him that didn't worry me. I gave him a script and set to work with the large cast in his absence. He came to his first rehearsal with his lines learned. He had worked before with Mary Mulholland and they had a certain rapport. Their scenes were emotionally moving and gave the play real heart. He was stubborn and persistent but at the same time quick-witted, particularly in the exchange of proverbs with the wily judge Azdak in the final scene.

The production was a great success, earning a rare positive review from Nathan Cohen, the *Toronto Star*'s critic, and played to packed houses. Soon afterwards Robert came to our house for dinner. Before he left he told me I had seen qualities in him that he didn't know he possessed and asked me if I thought he should be an actor. I gave him my standard reply, which was, if you have to ask that question, no. But if you are serious you should get out of here and go somewhere you can get

With Mary Mulholland in The Caucasian Chalk Circle

proper training. He finished his degree and told his father, "I have a present for you," handing him his diploma.

Robert then went to the National Theatre School in Montreal, mainly because he had been turned down by the most important British drama schools. In Montreal he came under the influence of Bill Davis, who introduced his students to the "touchie-feelie" improvisational techniques fashionable at the time. Thomson concedes that this may have had some value in opening him up emotionally, but he also felt that Davis did not have the skills to deal with the havoc his work wreaked with many of his students.

Thomson left the NTS at the end of his second year to be with his girlfriend Kate Nelligan. Once in London he realized she was actually living with another guy, and so they broke up. But he was accepted into the London Academy of Music and Dramatic Art. There he came under the influence of Tina Packer, and after he finished a year's study she invited him to join a company of young actors from the United States, Australia, and South Africa who would be based in Stratford-upon-Avon and put together Shakespearean productions to tour in England. They worked intensely with a number of instructors, most importantly the vocal coach Kristin Linklater. Thomson remembers, "I had a chip on each shoulder. One feeling superior to the Americans, the other feeling inferior to the British. In the course of that year, I got rid of both."

He decided to return to North America, did a few gigs in Canada, and then went to New York, where he managed to get work in off-off-Broadway productions and attracted the attention of a powerful agent, who interviewed him and said, "I am prepared to represent you but let me ask you a question. What do you want to be? A good actor or a rich actor?"

"I want to be a good actor."

"Then my advice is go back to Canada. Your chances of being a good actor are greater there."

Thomson took his advice. He went to see productions at the alternative theatres in Toronto. He remembers Carol Bolt's *Red Emma* at the Berkeley Street Theatre: "It was not a great play but I remember the excitement of seeing an emerging theatrical community who were doing work they believed in. I thought, I want to be part of that." And so the die was cast.

"It is not enough to have talent. One must have a talent for having talent," wrote Timothy Findley, though I don't believe he originated the observation. What I take this to mean is that you have to figure out what you can do and what you can't, your strengths and shortcomings, how to capitalize on your strongest qualities and how to market them. Robert Thomson set out to figure out what kind of actor he could be. He projected from the beginning qualities of sincerity and integrity. He had a distinctive appearance. From his mother he inherited his red hair and somewhat aristocratic bearing, and perhaps some of her charm. As the *grande dame* of Richmond Hill and a World Commissioner of the Girl Guides, Cicely possessed a certain gracious hauteur that she passed on to her son, though he had a more down-to-earth personality. From his father Woody, a naval officer and economist, he inherited intelligence, a

318

passion for independence, and an enthusiasm for the outdoors. His sense of humour was very much his own.

Back in Toronto he rapidly became involved in the burgeoning alternative theatre scene centred at Tarragon, Toronto Free, and Passe Muraille. He played in the original production of Michael Ondaatje's *Billy the Kid* alongside Nick Mancuso. He would also appear in Denise Coffey's production of a Feydeau farce, *Hand to Hand*, in which he did a hilarious impersonation of Joe Clark, the federal politician, which brought the house down. He had established himself as a formidable comic. He followed up with Henry in *The Real Thing*, directed by Guy Sprung at the Royal Alex, where his quick wit and easy insouciance were perfectly suited to Tom Stoppard's nimble manipulation of complex language and outrageous wordplay.

In this period Thomson identified with a clutch of young actors working in these up-and-coming venues: David Ferry, Jerry Franken, Michael Hogan, Stephen Markle, Neil Munro, Miles Potter, Booth Savage, Albert Schultz. He remembers that these young Turks did not identify with what they regarded as the Old Guard, the generation of actors who had worked at the Crest and the early years at Stratford: William Hutt, the Davises, Kate Reid, and John Colicos, although Thomson had greatly admired Colicos's performance as King Lear. Thomson played in the alternative venues in Toronto but also in regional theatres in Fredericton, Lennoxville, Victoria, and particularly Winnipeg, where he worked for John Hirsch and Brian Rintoul, who directed him in *Cyrano de Bergerac*. He not only got to play a spirited Romantic but also got to show off his considerable skills as a swordsman. He has been fight director for at least a dozen productions.

Thomson also played at Toronto Theatre Workshop in *The Mac-Paps*, a show about the Canadian regiment who went to Spain to fight against Franco in the late 1930s. This show was a group effort led by George Luscombe, who had picked up on the idea of collective creation from Joan Littlewood in England. The idea of a theatre piece in which everybody contributed caught on for a while in Toronto, where one of its foremost exponents was Paul Thompson, who followed up his groundbreaking *Farm Show* with a series of projects created in this fashion for Theatre Passe Muraille. The idea was picked up by James Reaney, when he worked with John Hirsch on *Colours in the Dark* for Stratford. It was widely copied in schools too, where the idea of improvisation, introduced by John and Juliana Saxton, became popular with drama teachers. Today Thomson deplores the decline of this brand of theatre and indeed the atrophy of the collaborative spirit in many spheres, from the business world to government.

In the early years of his career, Thomson was picked out by director Malcolm Black as a highly original talent. Black remembers him as "committed, hardworking and highly physical in his approach. He spent hours working out a routine where he fell down a staircase." Black gave Thomson a chance to hone his talent as a comedian in *Black Comedy* and Robertson Davies's *Hunting Stuart.* "Malcolm took a chance on me and gave me some terrific opportunities," Thomson recalls. He played in both *Waltz of the Toreadors* and *Waiting for Godot* with Gerard Parkes. Black recalled, "They had an extraordinary rapport. They were both funny and pathetic as Vladimir and Estragon. Later I offered Robert roles in Philadelphia but he turned me down, I think because he didn't want to work in the United States." Thomson refutes this notion, saying he'd have been happy to work with Black anywhere.

Somewhere about this time I mounted a production of Chekhov's *The Cherry Orchard* with a mixed cast of graduate students and professionals who had worked at Hart House Theatre in the past, including David Gardner, Meg Hogarth, Eric House, Robert Joy, Rex

320

Trofimov with Dorothy Kelleher in The Cherry Orchard

Southgate, and Terry Tweed. Robert agreed to play Trofimov and he was splendid in the role: romantic, idealistic, and bumbling. It was a difficult production because some of the players not only acted but acted up, but Robert was supportive and kept his sense of humour throughout. Robert Joy also gave a wonderful performance as the rejected lover Yepikhodov. He and Thomson enjoyed working together and would do so again, when Eric Till cast them in a German-

Canadian co-production, *Bonhoeffer: Agent of Grace* (2000), about a German Lutheran pastor who defied Hitler. The film was shot in Prague, and although it was in English the other actors were Europeans. The two Roberts looked at each other and then simultaneously decided to put on German accents to match the rest of the cast.

Born in 1947, young Robert grew up with the movies and, by the time he was five or so, television. It was only natural when he decided to become an actor that he would want to work in those media. But he waited for the film people to come to him. His first venture was with CBC in David French's *Of the Fields Lately*. In those days television drama was broadcast live from a studio with three or four cameras, the director editing as the actors played out the scenes. Thomson remembers. "I had no idea what I was doing but Mike Newell, the director, taught me on the fly. He told me, 'The important relationship is between your eye and the eye of the camera.'"

Thomson's first feature was an eminently forgettable Canadian film called *Tyler* (1978), followed soon after by a version of Margaret Atwood's *Surfacing* (1981): "It was a horrible experience and almost made me turn my back on the whole world of film." But actors must eat, and film and television offer much better money than stage work. A few

years later, Thomson would have a much more satisfying experience playing a bereaved farmer whose wife dies in childbirth in Margaret Atwood and Peter Pearson's *Heaven on Earth* (1989) about the settlement of British orphan children with Canadian families in the early years of the twentieth century. Thomson's farmer is by turns angry, strict, and practical. He marries the girl who comes to live with him and his young children, and accepts her younger brother as part of his family.

Thomson would appear in a film or TV series in large roles or small from then on, sometimes as many as four appearances a year, for a total of eighty-eight titles. He would play everything from a gay shoe salesman to a wisecracking sidekick of Julianne Moore in the marital drama *Chloe* (2009). He has played a number of real-life figures as well: Charlie Grant, Edsel Ford, Duncan Campbell Scott, Mitchell Sharp, James Cross. Many of these were brief cameos, played with authority and occasionally humour. But in *Glory Enough for All* (1988) as Frederick Banting, the discoverer of insulin, the drug that would control diabetes, he turned in a complex portrait of a man who was proud, sensitive, persistent, and highly demanding of himself and others but also bad-tempered, foul-mouthed, awkward, and inarticulate in public. He was admirable believable in all his varied roles. He is in fact a natural TV actor. Richard Monette opined that he was primarily a film actor, not a stage actor at all. Certainly Thomson had none of Monette's flamboyant theatricality, just as Monette never mastered Thomson's easy-going naturalness. Being with Richard, one had a sense he was always giving a performance. Having lunch or a beer with Robert, one can tell he is relaxed and a good listener, occasionally shooting off a quick-witted riposte.

Anne Tait remembers that Kevin Sullivan cast Thomson for his ongoing role in *Road to Avonlea* without an audition after seeing him in *Hand to Hand*. This was probably just as well, because Thomson is not good at auditioning. He gave a memorable performance as the awkwardly innocent inventor Jasper

322

As Frederick Banting in Glory Enough for All *with John Woodvine and Robert Wisden*

rather than likeable, determined more than insightful. The performance won Thomson a Gemini Award in 1989.

His low-key style helps to make him

Jasper Dales in Road to Avonlea

Dales that was both funny and endearing. Anne remembers at that time he insisted on negotiating his own contracts without going through an agent, typical of his hands-on approach to many things. Unlike most of the actors in the show he did not want as many episodes as possible but restricted his appearances to a few episodes each season in order to allow time for stage work. Eventually he signed with the agent Perry Zimel, first at Great North, and when Zimel moved to Oscars and Abrams, Thomson stayed with him. They have had a happy working relationship over the years.

When Hollywood came calling, Thomson decided to give it a whirl. He landed a role in the popular TV series *Moonlighting*, starring Cybill Shepherd, where he played her gynecologist. The gossip magazines speculated that they were an item off-screen, even though they only saw each other on set, when Cybill was almost invariably accompanied by her mother. In fact he briefly became emotionally entangled with another actress, but he remained loyal to his wife Laurie. The producers of *Moonlighting* agreed to write him into the next season. On the final day of shooting they finished all the shots of Cybill before they broke for lunch. They told Thomson they would finish his reaction shots right after the break. He waited in his trailer until 6:30 when he was finally

called. He went to the studio to find the set had been struck and the rest of the actors sent home. They did his close-ups in a small studio against a blank wall. "I was humiliated. It made me think about going home."

But it was another incident that cemented his decision. He was called in by the head of NBC casting. He sat waiting while another actor completed his audition. When the other actor left, the casting chief said to her assistant. "No good. Too subtle."

"Excuse me, I couldn't help overhearing what you said," Thomson commented. "I liked what he was doing."

"Subtle is no good for television. We don't want fine acting. It's lost on people who are only half paying attention. They want broad and simple." That clinched it for Thomson. He headed back to Toronto.

Thomson has worked with many of the major Canadian film directors: Donald Brittain, Jerry Ciccoritti, Atom Egoyan, Ken Finkleman, Guy Madden, and Kevin Sullivan, among others. He has worked extensively with the director Eric Till, who recalls that he always did his homework and came to rehearsal with lots of ideas: "He was never dull and never lazy. Initially he brought too much energy to the screen. He had to learn that the close-up was what made a film performance and that sometimes the best strategy was to do nothing. But he always approached his work with both sensitivity and humour. I remember once running into him when he told me he was going to do a voice-over audition for the role of a giraffe. I saw him later and he told me he didn't get the role. 'I guess my neck wasn't long enough.'"

Three films made as a mature actor show the range of his talent. In *The Lotus Eaters* (1993) he plays Hal, an uptight school principal on an island off the coast of British Columbia. Strict

324

Chaim in The Quarrel *with Saul Rubinek*

With Sheila McCarthy in The Lotus Eaters

with his daughters and fond of a wife he more or less takes for granted, he seems sure of himself until he falls for a new schoolteacher, a hippy girl from Montreal, who breaks through his starchy exterior and persuades him they should sail away together to Mexico. In the scene when his family tells him during Christmas dinner that they know about his escapade, Thomson is truly

R.H. Thomson

hilarious. The word gets around the community, the students turn against the girl, and his wounded wife literally burns his boat. His return to his old life is painful, and we feel for him in spite of his momentary folly.

In *The Quarrel* (1991), Thomson plays a Holocaust survivor who unexpectedly meets up with a man he knew as a young Jew in Europe. Thomson's character Chaim is an embittered agnostic, unable to believe in a God who would permit the destruction of his wife and sons; his

Tom Hardwick in The Englishman's Boy

friend Hersh has become a rabbi and is running a yeshiva, where he preaches to his young acolytes about the necessity for all Jews to believe passionately in their religion as a way of overcoming the stigma of shame at the persecution meted out by the Nazis. Thomson is stingingly intellectual and unbending in his arguments. We feel his pain as we come to understand the rigour of his thought processes. The film is relentless in its concentration on the conflict between these two men who meet and argue, only to part as friends, even though neither of them will abandon his faith in his own convictions.

A third film, the TV miniseries *The Englishman's Boy* (2008), shows us Thomson as Tom Hardwick, a ruthless game hunter. Rough, mean, blasphemous, and proud of it, he treats his accomplices with contempt and leads them through the uncharted forests in search of an Indian band, whose members he believes stole some horses. When they find their camp he incites his followers to destroy it, setting fire to their houses and gang-raping one of their women. It is a brutal portrayal of a man filled with self-disgust but utterly unable to bend his will to any act of compassion or decency toward his fellow humans. In these three films we see different aspects of Thomson's own complex nature. Like another fine film

325

actor who played a wide range of characters, Alec Guinness, Thomson is never the same twice—and yet he is always unmistakably R.H. Thomson.

Although he has continued to appear in television series like *The Republic of Doyle* and *Human Cargo*, Thomson's comments on the quality of most TV scripts are derogatory: "Most of the stuff I'm sent is completely disposable, like so much bumwad. There are exceptions, but they are rare. Of course most of these scripts are written by committees, who are more concerned by what reaction they will receive from teenage girls rather than whether they have believable characters or tell a good story."

Like most serious actors, Thomson has a great attraction to the work of Shakespeare and a desire to play major roles in the great plays. Early in his career he spent a season at the Stratford Festival, but in a children's show and not on the main stage. Then in 1982, artistic director John Hirsch offered him Hamlet in his first season, but Thomson didn't feel he was ready to play this role on the main stage. In the next season he agreed to play Mark Antony in *Julius Caesar*, under the direction of Derek Goldby. The production was not a resounding success and Thomson was miscast as the scheming Roman. As Rod Beattie put it, "Deceit is not Robert's thing." The same season he played Mortimer in *Mary Stuart*, directed by John Hirsch. By his own account he was terrible: "When Hirsch gave me notes he said, 'Robert, when I see you up there on that stage it makes me want to shit my pants.'" He did not return for the next season, although he has since had a couple of offers from the Festival that he could not manage to fit into his crowded schedule.

At about this time he played the corrupt de Flores in *The Changeling*, and he did play Hamlet in a very uneven production directed by Guy Sprung. Although the cast contained strong actors like Sheila McCarthy and Albert

326

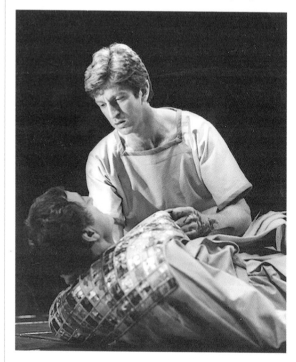

Antony with Jack Medley as Julius Caesar at Stratford

R.H. Thomson

Schultz, it was under-rehearsed. I remember asking Robert how long he had prepared for the role, and he admitted that he had only started working on it three weeks before opening. His performance did not give evidence of the subtlety and detail of his best work. He caught the intellect of the Danish prince but not his inner confusion and torment. And his resonant, dusky, sometimes cloudy baritone lacked the musicality and subtle vocal shadings of the finest Hamlets I had experienced: Gielgud, Plummer, Monette. But then all of them worked on the text over a period of years.

Thomson would go on to direct Shakespeare's *A Midsummer Night's Dream* in High Park and some years later *Romeo and Juliet* for ShakespeareWorks, a company he founded in conjunction with Marvin Karon, which staged outdoor productions for young audiences. Neither production was an unqualified success. He and Karon managed to attract significant corporate sponsorship, and the cast featured a few promising young actors backed up by some old standbys. But the result was disappointing, perhaps partly because Robert's love of Shakespeare was not grounded in a deep experience with the Bard's work. Also he was acting as producer, fundraiser, and promoter all at once. Thomson and Karon's venture, though its aims were commendable, failed after two seasons.

Thomson remains a Shakespeare enthusiast, but I believe he has come to realize he is not primarily a classical actor. Nor is he a matinee idol. There have been no charismatically handsome leading men in the tradition of Laurence Olivier, Leslie Howard, John Barrymore or Marlon Brando in English Canada (with the possible exception of Paul Gross). Rather, we have produced character actors like Thomson, Brent Carver, Colm Feore, Eric Peterson, and Albert Schultz, who when they play leading men come across as quirky and idiosyncratic rather than glamorous.

Thomson has worked with all the country's major theatre directors too: Bill Glassco, George Luscombe, Miles Potter, and Richard Rose, to name a few. Derek Goldby and Guy Sprung were two demanding and often badly behaved directors for whom Thomson has performed. He readily concedes their abilities but learned to stand up to their bullying and rudeness not only on his own behalf but in defence of fellow actors: "A director is like a dance partner. You learn how to waltz together. Or boogie, or whatever." Nowadays Thomson meets with the director when he is offered a role, and if their ideas are compatible he accepts; otherwise he turns the offer down.

327

Richard Rose, who has directed Thomson in a number of plays, comments, "Robert is a thoroughbred. And when he nails it, a champion. You need to point him in the right direction and then get out of the way. He runs a race that is a little different every night. If I think he is going off track, I call him on it but basically he finds his own internal image and then externalizes it. Often his image pushes my image. He has tremendous focus and is both demanding and challenging of himself, his director and his fellow actors. When he is playing with a powerful partner like David Fox, it is like handling two lions." One of the first roles Rose offered Thomson was the Puritan in *Glenn*, one of four portraits of the artist in David Young's intricate and highly cerebral portrait of the legendary Canadian pianist Glenn Gould. Indeed, music has always been important in Thomson's life. Although as a teen he played both the cello and the guitar, he had no ambition to be a musician, but when Rose approached him with the role in *Glenn*, he accepted immediately. It is one of the shows he talks about as a highlight of his career, even though he did not play in it when it moved to Stratford.

He has also had an active association with several music companies, especially Tafelmusik, for whom he has narrated a number of programs and is currently

Doc with Jane Spidell at Soulpepper

preparing a script about classical music from the point of view of an obscure oboist. He has also worked on several productions for Opera Atelier: "It was Marshall Pynkoski who made me realize that what we consider naturalistic acting is a style just the same as baroque acting or Victorian melodrama is a style. We think we have discovered 'true acting,' but we are kidding ourselves. Fifty years from now people will look at what we are doing and consider it dated and probably precious."

In recent times Thomson has chosen to do a number roles in plays grounded in social or political issues: David Mamet's *Oleanna*, Ariel Dorfman's *Death*

and the Maiden, Wajdi Mouawad's *Forests*, Sharon Pollock's *Doc*, Alistair MacLeod's *No Great Mischief*. But he has also played in revivals of classic modern comedy. He is strongly attracted to good writing. He usually learns his lines before he goes into rehearsal and is very conscious of the musical structure of a script. "*Oleanna* is like a piece of music. It must be played with the precision of a Mozart sonata. Albee is the same, although we didn't find the music when I played in *Sylvia*." Unlike some artists, Thomson doesn't believe everything he does is terrific. He can be highly critical both of himself and others.

"He can be prickly," says David Ferry, who has recently worked in several shows with Thomson. "He is opinionated, but you know that it coming from his convictions, his beliefs as a left-leaning Protestant with strong principles and beliefs. He is certainly not afraid to speak

his mind. When he was presented with the Barbara Hamilton Award at the Doras ceremony a couple of years ago he castigated the Toronto community for its lack of proper theatre facilities compared to many American cities or even Montreal. He really let them have it." Similarly, Diana Leblanc, who recently directed Thomson in *Doc*, *Harvey*, and *Same Time, Next Year* reports, "He's always a gentleman but not afraid to speak out. He knows what he wants and goes for it. He's generous with other actors but often develops inventive business for himself. In *Same Time* he devised a mini-pantomime where he put a foot from under the sheet where he is lying naked next to his partner and slowly retrieved his shirt and trousers. It must

329

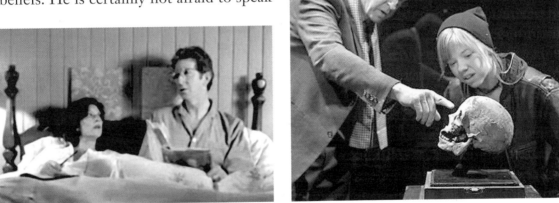

With Michelle Giroux in Same Time, Next Year *— le Centre Segal in Montreal In* The Forest *with Vivian Endicott Douglas at the Tarragon Theatre*

have lasted two minutes and brought down the house."

As a boy, Thomson read some letters written by uncles on his father's side, who had died in World War I. He revisited the letters many years later and decided to use them as a basis for a one-man show, which he wrote, directed, and acted in first at Berkeley Street and then at the Bluma Appel Theatre. It was a *tour de force*, drawing on many aspects of his skill as an actor: humour, intellect, emotion, and a very personal nostalgia.

This show in turn led to a major project to acknowledge and memorialize the fallen in the Great War. On the hundredth anniversary of the Battle of Vimy Ridge he arranged to project the names of all the Canadians who died in that conflict on the Vimy Memorial. A year later he repeated the exercise on Remembrance Day on the War Memorial in Ottawa, and a year after that on the façade of Canada House in Trafalgar Square in London. He is currently working on an extension of this project, which will include the names of all the war dead in the capitals of all the countries who participated on both sides in the war. He has currently enlisted the support of major players—France, Belgium, Germany, the United Kingdom, and Italy, among others—and is working to bring on board smaller countries like Serbia and

Montenegro. This project, now called *The World Remembers/Le monde se souvient*, is moving ahead, and the first manifestation of it took place in the autumn of 2014 in Ottawa and London, with more countries to follow up over the next two years.

In spite of often appearing in three or four stage productions and sometimes the same number of films every year, Thomson has found time for a variety of other activities. He has taught at the National Theatre School and several other academic institutions, chaired the Artists' Leadership Council, functioned as Artistic Producer of the Harbourfront World Stage Festival, sat on a number of boards including the War Museum, Opera Atelier, Equity Showcase, and the Ontario Film Development Commission, among others. In recent years he has also recorded interviews with many of Canada's leading actors for Theatre Museum Canada, some of whom, such as Douglas Campbell, William Hutt, and Michael Langham, have since died, while others like Martha Henry, Christopher Newton, and Christopher Plummer are still active. These interviews are available online. He is a skilled interviewer with a low-key style who is able to put his subjects at ease and draw them out. He has also served as host on CBC's *As It Happens* and *Man Alive*.

Now in his 60s, Thomson can be

alternately acerbic or self-deprecating, mischievous or commanding. He has enthusiasms and dislikes and is not reticent about giving expression to either. I once gave him a script I had written in what I thought was a Brechtian style; he returned it to me, saying he didn't believe a word of it. Never a pretty boy, although many audience members of both sexes find him attractive, his face now has a sort of rugged grandeur, sometimes bearded, sometimes clean-shaven, quickly lit up by his quirky grin and the playful sparkle of his piercing light blue eyes, vivid even behind glasses. His dress is almost invariably casual, blue jeans and an open-necked shirt, usually blue or green, the colours that set off his darkening russet hair beginning to be streaked with grey. Tall and rangy, he keeps fit by bicycling everywhere and playing hockey: "I've finally managed to overcome the fear I had of contact sports as a young and awkward kid. I guess I've finally gained some physical confidence."

Although he is often away for months at a time acting in theatres across the country or shooting films abroad, Thomson is at heart a home body and very much a family man. He and his wife Laurie Matheson have lived for three decades in a semi-detached house in the Annex with their two sons Macintosh and Andrew, now in their 20s. His favourite room is the kitchen, where the family customarily meets for dinner. It features a wood stove where Thomson sometimes cooks. His specialties are scones and porridge, not surprising for a Scot.

Thomson is proud of his skills as a carpenter, too. He laid the hardwood flooring in his house himself, using wood salvaged from trees that blew down at the family cottage in Muskoka. He finished the third floor where he has a study. Once when he was visiting us he made stilts for my daughter and taught her how to walk on them. When his mother died he made her coffin himself. Looking at her before the funeral he thought he saw in her face not only the lineaments of her Scottish ancestors but a trace of the Aboriginal woman that one of her forbears had married back in the fur-trading era. It confirmed his pride in his Canadian heritage.

Robert and Laurie are green enthusiasts and have a sizeable garden. Laurie is an activist in the field of education. They love their neighbourhood, which is an eclectic mix of intellectuals and artists alongside working-class people, some of them recent immigrants from all over the world. There is a strong sense of community and an active environmental group. Jane Jacobs was a neighbour and her influence persists. However, Thomson wishes the city would repair the streets in the Annex, so that he

331

wouldn't experience so many potholes when he rides his bike.

Thomson is also an activist on a much larger scale, championing the cause of Canadian culture. During the Free Trade negotiations with the United States in the 1980s he campaigned to keep culture off the bargaining table, with the result that the Canadians managed to get some valuable concessions. Then came NAFTA. He and his colleagues tried to get the Mexicans to come on board to again keep culture out of the negotiations. The Mexicans said in effect, "We're not worried about protecting our culture. We make thirty films a year." The next year they made only six films. "We see what you mean," they conceded. "The Americans have gobbled up our industry." Since then Thomson has worked to convince other nations that they need to protect their cultural identities, with some success. He is proud of the fact that Canadians have demonstrated to other countries the skills to combat American cultural domination.

332

Thomson has won a number of nominations and awards for his work in theatre and film—Doras, Genies, and Geminis—attesting to the high regard in which he stands with his fellow actors. Then in 2010 his phone rang and a voice said, "I'm calling to tell you that you have just been awarded the Order of Canada." After a brief silence Thomson replied, "You must be joking."

The Activist

LA SIRÈNE

Geneviéve Bujold

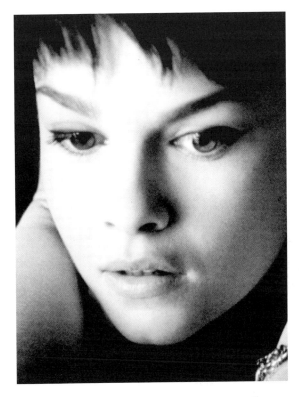

In the mid-1950s I went for several months to work at the mill of the Rolland Paper Company in St-Jérôme, Quebec. I boarded with a working-class family that lived in four rooms and a kitchen. They rented one room to me while the parents and four children lived in the other three. The wife cooked and scrubbed and shopped and washed and mended. Every day she fed her younger children at 5:00 and her husband and older sons and me at 6. She never sat down to eat with us but waited on table and cleaned up afterward. The first night I offered to help with the dishes. She roared with laughter. A man washing dishes. *Quelle drôle idée.*

After dinner the family watched television: *la lutte* (wrestling) and of course, on Saturday night, hockey: *les Canadiens* in their glory days. And also a *téléroman*: *Les belles histoires du pays d'en haut*. I had studied so-called Parisian French in high school, but the *patois* spoken in St-Jérôme was something else: I quickly recognized that "ben ouai" signified agreement, "icitte" translated as "here" and a dollar was a "piastre," a throwback to the French coinage of the seventeenth century. In order to improve my comprehension of the language I heard all around me (the inhabitants of St-Jérôme spoke no English), I often watched television with my hosts.

Les pays d'en haut was set in the village of Ste-Adèle in the Laurentians and centred around Jean-Pierre Masson as the mayor, Séraphin Poudrier, and Andrée Champagne as Donalda Laloge-Poudrier, the young woman who becomes the mayor's wife. The series, which ran from 1956 to 1970, had a huge cast. One of the characters was a beautiful and willful young girl named Julie Fourchu. I didn't know her name, but her distinctive face lodged in my memory. It was only later I realized that this was the soon-to-be famous actress Geneviève Bujold.

Geneviève was born in 1942, the daughter of a Québécois bus-driver father and a mother of Irish ancestry who both came from the village of St-Siméon-de-Bonaventure in the Gaspé. Like most girls in her generation whose parents had middle-class aspirations for their daughters, Geneviève was sent to study with the nuns. She disliked the rigorous discipline of the Hochelaga Convent. As a child she felt "as if I were in a long dark tunnel trying to convince myself that if I could ever get out there was light ahead." After twelve years she managed to get herself expelled by ostentatiously reading books on the Index, the list proscribed by the Vatican. She enrolled in the free Conservatoire d'art dramatique in Montreal and made her stage debut as Rosine in Beaumarchais's *Le Barbier de Séville*. Almost immediately she began acting in Canadian films and was soon playing leading roles in *Amanita Pestilens* (1963), directed by René Bonnière, and *La terre à boire* (1964), directed by Jean-Paul Bernier.

In 1966 she went on tour to France with the Montreal company *Le Rideau Vert* and was seen by the mother of the French film director Alain Resnais, who recommended her to her son. In 1966 Resnais cast her as a Leninist revolutionary involved in Spanish politics in *La guerre est finie*, opposite the suavely disillusioned Yves Montand. In the next two years she played opposite the naïve but resourceful British soldier Alan Bates, who goes AWOL in Phillipe de Broca's satiric anti-war fantasy *Le roi des coeurs*, and in Louis Malle's *Le voleur* opposite a young and smouldering Jean-Paul Belmondo. While still in her 20s she got to perform with three of the hottest male stars in the European film industry.

Most of Bujold's work up to this point was in French, which she spoke with more or less classical purity thanks to her training at the Conservatoire. She looked younger than her twenty-five years and had an exotic quality, with her abundant chestnut hair, almond-shaped eyes, retroussé nose, and small, pouty mouth. She came across as at once innocent and sensuous. In the words of the American critic Rex Reed, "Packed into her five-foot, four-inch doll's frame is an intriguing mixture of purloined innocence, succulent sexuality, and guerrilla warfare." In *La guerre est finie* she is a knowing sex kitten who falls for Montand. Playing opposite Bates in *Le roi des coeurs* she has more of a *gamine* quality as she dances around in her somewhat bedraggled tutu,

334

Coquelicot in King of Hearts

provocative, slightly mad, and naively curious as she approaches sexual initiation. With Belmondo in *Le voleur*, her appeal is more teasingly overt.

After her success in France, Bujold returned to Canada, where she made a picture with rising Québécois director Michel Brault, *Entre la mer et l'eau douce* (1967), about a folk singer played by Claude Gauthier, a sort of French-Canadian Jacques Brel, who comes to the big city to achieve fame and fortune and discovers the price that must be paid to achieve it. The script was a collaboration between Denys Arcand, Claude Jutra,

Marcel Dubé, and Gérald Godin, all of whom would soon make their mark as the foremost francophone writers and directors in Canada. The film contrasts rural and urban Quebec, focusing on ordinary people in everyday settings with meticulous attention to detail, providing an early example of the realistic style that was to prevail in early Québécois films before the Quiet Revolution. Already there is one scene in which a separatist airs his views. The dialogue is coloured with a liberal use of the religious expletives and crude jokes common among ordinary guys, with lyrical counterpoint provided by Gauthier's romantic chansons. Bujold plays a seemingly simple girl, a waitress in a diner who teaches ballroom dancing at night, discontented, hoping to find love and a better future. She is opaque, but she suggests depths of feeling beneath her calm demeanour. When she is abandoned by her lover she doesn't flare up in rage but instead expresses her pain with bleak, understated intensity.

At around the same time she had teamed up with Paul Almond, the son of a prominent Anglo Montreal family who had been educated at Bishop's College, McGill, and Balliol College, Oxford. While in England in 1964 he began a documentary, *Seven Up!*, in which he interviewed a carefully selected group of seven-year-old English boys of different classes and backgrounds. They would be

335

interviewed again every seven years by Almond's associate Michael Apted to find out what had happened to them, their career choices, marital status, and whatever other adventures came their way. The most recent installment, *56 Up*, was released in 2012.

Almond returned to Canada and began making films. He soon became a busy television producer, directing individual dramas and episodes for series. He directed Bujold in *Romeo and Jeannette* (1965), *A Doll's House*, and an adaptation of *Crime and Punishment* (both 1966), introducing her to English-speaking audiences. They married and he took time off from the CBC to complete a trilogy starring Bujold: *Isabel* (1968), *Act of the Heart* (1970), and *Journey* (1972), which were critically acclaimed though not very successful commercially. During this period some very ambitious and original films were made in Canada, but the English-speaking public did not support the work of their artists, perhaps partly because the producers lacked the financial resources to promote their products effectively, and also because distribution was largely controlled by American interests.

All three of these films centre on women who have otherworldly experiences. They are not thrillers but deal with psychological states that suggest a perception of reality that lies beyond the everyday world. In *Act of the Heart*, Bujold plays a simple country girl who comes to the city, moves in with an older woman played by a somewhat jaded Monique Leyrac, and falls in love with a priest, played by a young and rather gauche Donald Sutherland, who exerts a sort of puppy-dog charm. The film knits together in somewhat disjointed fashion various elements of Canadian life in that period: snowy winter landscapes, religion, hockey, and music. Bujold holds the film together with her ingenuous freshness and emotional spontaneity

Paul had already been married to ballerina Angela Leigh, but they divorced in 1964. He married Geneviève in 1967 at the tiny Hart House chapel in order to escape media attention. Their union lasted six years and produced a son Matthew, who would become an actor. Although they seemed to have a sympathetic bond that allowed them to work together, Almond would later comment, "It isn't so easy to live with an actress. I married Geneviève—not Isabel or St. Joan or Anne Boleyn—but I live with them all.... There is a curious internal process going on in her that begins the moment she signs to do a picture. At the first 'Action!' she has become the character, and it never leaves her until long after the last 'Cut!'"

This is not an uncommon phenomenon with some actors. In preparing for

336

Geneviéve Bujold

their work they take on the characteristics of the character they are about to play, not only physically, but also mentally. Some of this is conscious, but not necessarily all of it. If you meet one of these actors for lunch or dinner you become aware that you are sitting opposite not Colm Feore, for example, but Henry Higgins. Even the comments and responses that come out of their mouths are couched in the style of the imagined person they have temporarily become.

In 1967 Bujold starred in an American television version of *Saint Joan*, based on the play by George Bernard Shaw. The cast included Maurice Evans as Cauchon, Leo Genn as the Archbishop, Roddy McDowall as the Dauphin, and Raymond Massey as the Inquisitor. Bujold was highly praised for her realization of the Maid of Orleans and gave a performance both sturdy and spirited, but her version was somewhat sidelined by the films starring Ingrid Bergman and Jean Seberg as Joan of Arc from roughly the same period.

As a result of her work in *Isabel*, Bujold attracted the attention of American producer Hal Wallis. In 1969, Bujold went to England to play Anne Boleyn in Wallis's *Anne of the Thousand Days*, opposite Richard Burton as Henry VIII. The fact that Boleyn was educated in France may have had something to do with the casting choice, and it proved a splendid showcase

for Bujold's talents. The film is a highly intelligent and historically sensitive depiction of the historical facts and features accurate costumes and settings. There is a fine supporting cast of mainly British actors, including Anthony Quayle as Cardinal Wolsey, Michael Hordern as Anne's father, and Canadian John Colicos as Cromwell. Burton is a totally convincing Henry. Unlike Charles Laughton and Jonathan Rhys Meyers, Burton looks the part and is the right age. He is smart, handsome and stylish, quick-tempered,

Anne Boleyn with Richard Burton as Henry VIII in Anne of the Thousand Days

arrogant, and impetuous. Playing opposite him, Bujold is flirtatious but cool and calculating, keeping him at bay until he promises to divorce his wife Katherine of Aragon, played with proud disdain by Irene Papas.

Ironically, Anne falls in love with Henry only as he is beginning to lose interest in her, but she never submits to his tyranny and holds out for the legitimacy of her daughter Elizabeth, who will of course become one of England's greatest monarchs. Bujold invests Anne with intelligence and a full range of emotions, from driving ambition to sexual pleasure to the discovery of the pain of rejection and finally resignation. It is a performance that used all her physical grace and sensuality but also a keen and watchful mind. According to Burton's memoirs they had had an affair during the shooting of the film, something Bujold categorically denies.

Bujold had been signed to a three-picture contract and was slated to make a film about Mary, Queen of Scots. This would have been a logical role for her—again a woman brought up in France, spoiled, flirtatious, and arrogant, who eventually finds consolation in her devotion to the Catholic Church. However, Bujold felt she was being typecast and refused the part. ("It would be the same producer, the same director, the same costumes, the same me," she declared.)

This led to her being sued by Universal Studios for $750, 000. To avoid paying she fled to Europe, where she appeared in *The Trojan Women* (1971), directed by Michael Cacoyannis, with Katharine Hepburn, Vanessa Redgrave, and Papas again. As the mad prophetess Cassandra, daughter of King Priam, who after the fall of Troy is promised to the victorious Greek general Agamemnon, she is possessed by a wild, uncontrolled passion and an extravagant physicality, in marked contrast to the restraint and control she had exercised in most of her previous film work; her outsized frenzy and abandoned gestures match the material. In the opening scene Bujold sets the tone for the whole film, which has a stark, uncompromising grandeur; the large-scale performances of all these remarkable actresses are set against and accentuated by the bleak landscape and the weathered, strongly individualistic faces of the chorus of women. It is one of the few films that actually manages to achieve the tragic power of this ancient text.

In order to settle with Universal, Bujold then made two Hollywood movies: the disaster epic *Earthquake* (1974), with Charlton Heston, and the adventure film *Swashbuckler* (1976), with Robert Shaw. Neither film drew from her remarkable performances, but she was now playing in the big leagues, although this did not seem to particularly

Cassandra in The Trojan Women

impress her. Bujold possessed a practical, hard-nosed side when it came to choosing films and approaching her work: "I don't like to intellectualize about my acting. I don't sit around and study the pages of a script over and over again. I don't worry whether the period is contemporary or three hundred years ago. Human beings are all alike. The main thing in acting is honesty, to feel the humanity and get to the essence of the character. You can't put anything into a

character that you haven't got within you," she stated in 1969. But she also admitted, "I confess it, I love the camera. When it's not on me, I'm not quite alive." Somewhat later, speaking to *Revue de Cinéma*, she sounded more intuitive: "Un rôle m'apprend quelque chose quand j'arrive à trouver le courage de faire ce qui me fait peur, à surmonter des craintes terribles. J'en ressors plus forte." (A role grabs me when I find the courage to do something that scares me and to surmount that terrible fear. Then I become stronger.)

339

Her work in Hollywood gave her experience, but she didn't abandon the Canadian movie scene. In 1973 for Claude Jutra she made *Kamouraska*, based on a novel by Anne Hébert. It is a dark piece, set in rural Quebec in the 1830s. In it Bujold plays Élisabeth, a young woman who makes what is considered an advantageous marriage to a handsome young man, the seigneur of Kamouraska. But he is a sadist, and his brutal conduct disgusts his young wife and eventually makes her ill. He introduces her to a friend, an American doctor, and he and Élisabeth fall in love. Eventually the doctor kills the husband and Élisabeth is tried for murder. She is acquitted, but the doctor must flee back to the United States. To save face she marries a second time, a man she does not love.

Elisabeth in Kamouraska

340

Jutras lovingly recreates the life of that era in a series of beautifully composed shots full of shadows, lit in the manner of the painters Caravaggio and de la Tour. Bujold is a powerful presence. Almost never off-camera, she holds the film together as it proceeds irrevocably toward its violent climax. Her performance is austere, shot through with sudden unexpected flashes of spirited temper. She and her lover speak mostly in whispers; even their laughter is muffled. The film was slow-paced and contained none of the humour of Jutras's previous success, *Mon oncle Antoine.* It was not a commercial hit, but it gained Bujold both the respect of the Canadian acting profession and a Genie award.

In the 1970s, Bujold continued to make movies playing opposite major stars. One of her most affecting performances was as another Greek heroine, Antigone, in the 1974 TV film of version of Jean Anouilh's adaptation of Sophocles' tragedy. Seated at a long table as if in a modern totalitarian state, she confronts the King Creon, played by Fritz Weaver, who has refused burial to her brother. Her performance marries clarity with passion. Vulnerable but determined, she cleaves to her implacable belief that there is a higher moral authority than that wielded by the state and faces her inevitable doom with clear-eyed conviction.

Soon after she completed this intense political drama, she was portraying Charlotte, a clever French parole officer who tracks down the charming but elusive conman Victor Vauthier played by Jean-Paul Belmondo in *Incorrigible* (1975), Then she became a seductive young Cleopatra opposite the austere but captivated Caesar of Alec Guinness (1976), and in the same year a Romany girl, Maritza, who captures the heart of Jack Lemmon in *Alex and the Gypsy*. In *Coma* (1978) with Michael Douglas, Elizabeth Ashley, Rip Torn, and Richard Widmark, she is a young doctor who picks up on the unusual number of patients who are suffering from comas and uncovers a weird conspiracy. In *Monsignor* (1982) she plays a postulant who falls in love with an American soldier played by Christopher Reeve. She is the one sincere person in the corrupt

world of the Vatican. Her scorching anger when she discovers her lover is really a priest is the emotional highlight of the movie. In *Tightrope* (1984) she is a strong-minded, savvy rape counsellor who becomes personally involved with a detective, played by Clint Eastwood, who is trying to track down a serial killer who rapes and then murders young women. The film is very much dominated by Eastwood, but she provides emotional ballast. It was a commercial hit, which enhanced Bujold's status in the film capital. The sheer range of her work in this period is a testament to her virtuosity.

In the mid-1980s Bujold veered away from commercial Hollywood and became involved with Alan Rudolph, a young writer/director who made intelligent ensemble films somewhat in the manner of his mentor Robert Altman, featuring witty dialogue and cleverly detailed settings. Bujold appeared in *Choose Me* (1984), a comedy about interpersonal relationships and the choices they involve, with a cast that included Keith Carradine, Lesley Ann Warren, and Rae Dawn Chong. She plays Dr. Nancy Love, who gives advice to romantically confused or damaged callers to her radio show in a cool but sympathetic manner, while in real life she has an affair with a handsome drifter. It is a complex characterization of a woman who is at the same time knowing and yet curiously naïve, who finds she can't resist the charm of a man she meets only casually but who instantly arouses her erotic curiosity.

This was followed by *Trouble in Mind* (1985), again with Carradine and Kris Kristofferson, in which she plays Wanda, a young woman who wants to get rich quick in the fictional Rain City. Then came *The Moderns* (1988), with Carradine, Linda Fiorentino, Wallace Shawn, and Geraldine Chaplin, set in Paris in the 1920s and about a young American painter (Carradine) who hopes that a gallery owner (Bujold) will help him become famous. These films contain some of Bujold's most mature performances. She became romantically involved with Alan Rudolph, and although they did not marry they lived together for some time. During this period she had a son Emmanuel, who took his mother's surname.

Bujold continued to make films in Canada in both English and French. She participated in another film with Paul Almond, *The Dance Goes On* (1992), in which she played the mother of her real-life son Matthew, but it lacks the subtlety and intelligence of their earlier collaborations. In the same year she made *Oh, What a Night*, written by Richard Nielsen and directed by CBC director Eric Till, in which she plays an older woman who gets involved with a much

341

younger man, played by Corey Haim. She also made two other films with her longtime artistic partner Michel Brault. In *Les noces de papier* (1989) she plays a woman who makes a marriage of convenience with a refugee immigrant, giving a nuanced and poignant performance marked by the sensitivity and restraint that had by now become her trademark. In *Mon Amie Max* (1994), she plays a woman who had a brilliant career as a young pianist but stopped playing when she became pregnant. Forced to give her baby up for adoption, she searches to reconnect with her lost son.

In 1998, she had a small part in Don McKellar's end-of-the-world fantasy *Last Night*. The cast was a virtual who's who of Canadian acting talent, including Jackie Burroughs, Robin Gammell, Arsinée Khanjian, Charmion King, Sandra Oh, Roberta Maxwell, Tom

342

Claire Niveau with Jeremy Irons in Dead Ringers

McCamus, Sarah Polley, Tracy Wright, and directors Bruce McDonald and David Cronenberg. Probably Bujold's best-known Canadian film was made ten years earlier, Cronenberg's erotic masterpiece *Dead Ringers*. In it she is the woman that the twin doctors, both played by Jeremy Irons, battle over. This is Bujold at her most vibrantly enticing, playing a famous actress with a gynecological problem. She is temperamental, sophisticated, worldly, drug-addicted, a "cougar" still wracked by unquenchable desire yet quite capable of looking out for herself. She nevertheless becomes involved with both of the twins as she submits to their manipulative charm, and then chooses one of them before eventually moving on. Cronenberg has said that he cast Bujold because he wanted an actress who had both charisma and complexity, which she certainly provides. Her performance garnered strong critical attention and gave a new impetus to her career.

As she grew older, Bujold began playing mothers, nuns, successful lawyers, and the aging Canadian author Gabrielle

343

Denise Archambault in The Trotsky

Irene Morrison with James Cromwell in Still Mine

Roy in a series of films, most of which were either murder mysteries or horror flicks. She would work with American actors Ellen Burstyn, James Caan, and Stacey Keach, and with Canadians Robert Joy, Linda Kash, and Saul Rubinek, among many others. Sadly most of these films are not particularly memorable. In Canada she was often used by producers to gain funding, lending credibility to projects of dubious value that soon vanished into oblivion.

In 2012, however, she made a film with American actor James Cromwell, *Still Mine*. Seventy, with the fine bone structure of her face radiating a mature beauty, she plays a loving wife who, after fifty years of happy marriage, is slowly sinking into dementia, yet retains her warmth and humour. The film is about two decent people threatened by interfering bureaucracy and makes a strong statement about contemporary society without being didactic or preachy. Cromwell said about it, "Age is an abstraction, not a straitjacket." Bujold stated, "I liked the script because it doesn't treat old people like they're all the same or tell them what to do: be impeccable, remain the same, and never die. I picked the film because it has a quiet way of growing on you, of slowly, gently becoming implanted in your heart."

Appearing at a Toronto International Film Festival awards gala soon after, Bujold looked like the character in the movie, her greying hair pulled back in a ponytail, wearing no make-up and what one viewer described as an old house-dress. But another commented, "The liquid brown eyes are as alert, the jawline as defined, the smile as winning and the mind as sharp as they were thirty or more years ago when Bujold was a Hollywood marquee player."

Bujold now lives in a small house in Malibu, not far from where her ex-husband Paul Almond, with whom she often went on walks along the beach, lived until his death in 2015. She is still working, having recently completed a film in French, *Chorus*, with Québécois director François Delisle, and an American film, *Northern Borders*, in which she plays the feisty wife of Bruce Dern, a New England farmer with whom she has been locked into what their family refers to as "the Forty Year War." She recently declared, "At this age I am incapable of doing things I don't want to do. I live modestly, so that I'm never forced to do a job to pay a mortgage, and I don't own anything. I simply do not do what's not essential. This is because I have realized the secret of life: all the external decorations are less important than giving yourself the gift of time."

RURAL WIT AND WISDOM

Rod Beattie

In my first year as Artistic Director of Hart House Theatre I decided we should produce well-known plays and proposed to direct *Hamlet* myself. I was a bit nervous, as this would be my first Shakespearean production. I was approached even before I held auditions by a deep-voiced, bearded young student who told me he wanted to play the title role. After two or three meetings I realized he was highly intelligent, had some previous experience of Shakespeare, and possessed a ready wit. This gave me the confidence to proceed, and I was able to assemble a strong student cast.

Rod Beattie had grown up, as I had, in North Toronto, in some respects a typical upper-middle-class kid. His high-school years were spent at the University of Toronto Schools, which had a longstanding tradition of producing Shakespearean productions. Young Rod's interest in acting was sparked by his younger brother Douglas, who became friendly with Reed Needles at Allenby Public School and began

attending classes given by Jack Medhurst, a protégé of Dorothy Goulding, Reed's grandmother, who had directed the Toronto Children Players in the 1940s and 1950s. Initially Rod was not interested in Medhurst's classes, preferring to devote his leisure time to hockey, but soon after puberty struck he came to realize that drama classes offered opportunities to meet and hang out with girls, something not available in an all-boys school. This led to him trying out for school productions, where his innate ability was recognized

Hamlet's antic disposition

346

characterization that was sharp, watchful, mercurial, posturing, possessed of a wicked sense of humour, and quite possibly a bit mad.

He played the scenes where he assumes his "antic disposition" in a sort of jester's outfit with a foolshead, to which he addressed some of his quips. His scenes with Rosencrantz and Guildenstern were particularly original; in the scene where he says "You would play upon my pipe," he produced a flute and improvised a brief tune, a motif that recurred in the chase scene after the murder of Polonius, when the court is trying to track him down. In another scene he engaged Rosencrantz and Guildenstern in an imaginary game of shuttlecock, leading them into whatever mockery he chose to impose upon them. His final duel with Reed Needles as Laertes was a splendid display of swordsmanship, and one realized he might well have beaten his opponent had he not been brought down by treachery.

The cast included a young actor, Robert Joy, who would go on to have an impressive theatrical career, and Arlene Perly, who would later marry the politician Bob Rae. It also included not only Reed Needles but also his brother Dan, who played Horatio as a sort of humorous sidekick to Hamlet. Rod's brother Douglas was a member of the court. So the principal players of what would later

when he played Brutus and Macbeth in his senior years.

Rod was not a conventional Hamlet in the tradition of British matinee idols like the sensitive and mellifluous John Gielgud or the handsome glamour-boy Laurence Olivier, but rather came up with a highly idiosyncratic performance. He offered to shave his beard but I thought it accentuated his position as an outsider at the court. He developed a

become the Wingfield enterprise were all together for the first (and last) time in this production, although of course the realization of that project lay well into the future.

At the same time Rod was involved with the Trinity College Dramatic Society, which mounted an ambitious and moving production of *The Winter's Tale* and also an original poetic play by a student, Richard Reoch, titled *Phaeton's Birthday*. The Beattie brothers were convinced that Reoch had the makings of a major playwright, though in fact he ended up becoming deeply involved with the international organization Amnesty International.

The next year I directed *Troilus and Cressida* at Hart House Theatre, again with a highly talented cast. Rod was the

Troilus and Cressida Ulysses with Graham Harley as Nestor

wily Ulysses, a role that gave him ample scope to play the devious schemer, and he made sense of some of Shakespeare's most convoluted and complex verse. His handling of the "Time hath, my lord, a wallet at his back" speech was a model of persuasiveness, and his lecherous appraisal of Cressida when she is handed over to the Greeks was much more vivid than the rough physicality of some of the other actors in the scene.

Robin Phillips, then newly designated Artistic Director of the Stratford Festival, came to see this production, and he later told me that it showed him what both Rod and Barbara Stewart, who played Cressida, were capable of. Rod had already been hired by Jean Gascon at Stratford and was fingered to understudy Edward Atienza as King John. On opening night Atienza was indisposed, and Rod thought he would have to go on in his place, even though he had not had a proper rehearsal. William Needles, who was also in the cast, said, "Don't worry, kid. Teddy will turn up, even if he has to play it in a wheelchair." Needles was right, and Rod lost his chance to be catapulted to instant stardom.

Two years later Rod came back to the university to work on a graduate degree. One of the requirements was participation in a production, but Rod was now a member of Actors' Equity, who decreed he could not appear onstage unless he was paid. "Couldn't he be an usher?" they asked, to which I replied, "Yes, but he's an actor. If you were a young actor, wouldn't you rather have an opportunity to pursue your craft by playing a leading Shakespearean role?" Reluctantly Equity agreed, and Rod appeared as Parolles in *All's Well That Ends Well*, a role that displayed his talent as a comic: a vain, pretentious, smart-talking coward who in the course of the play is unmasked but remains unrepentant to the end. By this time Rod and I had become good friends and would remain so, our paths crossing again in the future. He also formed a warm and long-lasting relationship with Barbara Stewart, who played Helena.

During his first few seasons at Stratford, Rod was cast mainly as waiting gentlemen. He was deeply influenced by Robin Phillips, who dramatically raised the bar when he took over the reins of the Festival in 1975. Phillips swept away the fustian and exaggerated theatricality that had often characterized the work of some of his predecessors and insisted on absolute clarity and honesty of interpretation. He set up a series of exercises that challenged his actors, making greater demands on them physically, vocally, and emotionally. He was blunt and unforgiving of indulgence but also elegant and highly articulate. Rod responded to his demands with enthusiasm and entered on a period of training

and development more rigorous than he had previously experienced.

Phillips cast him primarily in comic roles: as the frustrated and fussy stage manager Quince in the rustics' presentation of Pyramus and Thisbe in *A Midsummer Night's Dream*, and as the loquacious braggart Pistol in *Henry IV* and *Henry V*. He also played a variety of small parts: the Friar in *Much Ado About Nothing*, a priest in *The Devils*, the sinister Ratcliff in *Richard III*, and Lucius in *Titus Andronicus*. Then in 1979 he got his chance to play a lead as one of two Bolingbrokes in Zoe Caldwell's production of *Richard II*. He followed it up with a scheming Richard Crookback in *Henry VI*.

Rod never faltered in his admiration for Phillips. Like many other members of the company he credited Phillips with teaching him what acting was. Although he can be highly critical of many of his peers, Rod is extremely loyal to those he admires, though he can also be standoffish with those he doesn't know. When I asked Martha Henry to comment on the experience of directing him, she responded, "The essential thing is to gain his trust." Rod's commitment to the Festival is also ongoing, even though he doesn't always see eye to eye with management.

During this period Rod's brother Douglas was emerging as a director/pro-

349

In The Woman *at Stratford With Clare Coulter*

ducer, staging a number of works in Toronto, most notably a production of *You Can't Take It With You* at the Bayview Playhouse , in which Rod played a Russian ballet master. This was a major undertaking with a large cast, and Douglas remembers that he began looking around for a smaller play, possibly a one-man show. It was at this point that Douglas reconnected with Dan Needles.

Dan was the son of long-time Stratford actor William Needles and his wife Dorothy-Jane, who wrote and acted in plays for her mother Dorothy

Goulding at Eaton Auditorium before creating and performing Kindergarten of the Air for CBC radio. "Dorf," as she is known to long-time friends, maintained a house in North Toronto and also a farm in Mono township, where she took Dan and his four siblings to live for six months every summer. Thus Dan acquired a knowledge of both city and country life. He also developed a humorous outlook on life in general, which Rod remembers was already in place by the time he was ten, when the two met playing ball hockey on the streets of Toronto. Both Rod and Doug visited the Needles farm in the summer, where they stooked hay and did various other chores.

Dan began and ended his professional theatrical career playing Macduff's son at the Crest Theatre in Toronto. This led to an offer from Stratford for him to play Moth in *Love's Labour's Lost* during Stratford's tour to Chichester. Hearing of the offer, Dan ran away from home to avoid it. His mother managed to corral him and bring him back, while his father told Jean Gascon, "I have another son." Reed joined the Festival company for the overseas tour. I did not realize that Dan's appearance in *Hamlet* would be almost his only stage appearance as an adult, undoubtedly motivated by his friendship with Rod.

After graduation, Dan worked as the editor of *The Shelburne Free Press and Economist*, a weekly rural newspaper. Before long he was writing a column supposedly penned by Walt Wingfield, a stockbroker who had bought a local property and proceeded to farm it using the agricultural methods of 1905. Dan left Shelburne to work in Toronto, first as an assistant to a cabinet minister in Bill Davis's Conservative government. He commented, "I went up to Queen's Park as a Conservative and left as an anarchist." He then took a job as a public-relations executive for Canada Life. He was well paid, enjoyed the work, and made friends in the city, but the pull of country life was strong. When he married his pretty wife Heath, a country girl from Mulmur, he decided to retire to a property he had bought near Collingwood, a forty-acre farm where they were soon tending "six sheep, two goats, two geese, two cows, thirty chickens and a horse," aided in time by the efforts of their four children.

Dan hoped to preserve a style of life that had all but disappeared in Rosemont, the community he had known as a child. Developers had moved in and the local farmers were for the most part only too glad to break up their farms and sell the land to commuters from the city. When he moved to Collingwood it was still a typical rural community, but the lifestyle there too would gradually be

The editor of the Larkspur weekly newspaper

eroded as city people built ski chalets around the lake. Dan was determined that if he could not counter the destruction of rural life, he would at least create some record of the characters he remem-bered. It was this that provided the inspiration for the Wingfield plays.

Although he is not a serious student of literature, Dan is aware that his work is part of a tradition that stretches back to

Mark Twain and Will Rogers and includes such Canadian practitioners as W.O. Mitchell and Don Harron, who created and more or less metamorphosed into Charlie Farquharson. Dan's characters do not indulge in the far-fetched malapropisms that characterize Charlie's speech, but they do reflect the vocal tics and vocabulary of the rural inhabitants of central Ontario. It is not surprising that Dan has been awarded the Leacock Medal for Humour for his mythical history of Persephone Township, *With Axe and Flask*.

Douglas and Dan met, and the idea for a one-man show based on the letters he had written a decade earlier for the paper in Shelburne began to take shape. There was a try-out of an early script acted by Dan's brother Reed at the Palmerston Library in Toronto. But Reed had a commitment as a teacher in London, and Doug suggested an expanded Wingfield script would be a good vehicle for his brother Rod. They opened the show in Orangeville, where it was thoroughly enjoyed by the locals, who opined that you couldn't do it in the city because they wouldn't get it. This was followed shortly thereafter by an engagement at the Arts and Letters Club in Toronto, whose members were highly amused but said it couldn't be done in the country, because the farmers would be insulted.

A typical exchange between Walt and one of his neighbours giving him directions goes like this: "You go down the town line until you get to the old brick church ... the one that burned down last summer ... only you don't turn there. You keep right on goin' and when you get to the bridge at the fifth sideroad, well it's about half a mile before that. So, when you reach the bridge, you've gone too far." This brand of humour proved to be immediately accessible to audiences everywhere.

Doug Beattie's conviction that Rod was the ideal performer for the piece was proven in those early performances. Rod's easy grasp of the eccentricities of the various characters, his highly mobile face and exceptional vocal range, and his ability to shift on a dime from one character to another displayed the timing of a virtuoso. Although the initial performances were greeted with enthusiasm, they did not immediately attract large audiences. When they rented a downtown theatre in August in Toronto, they often played to tiny houses. But they persevered.

At about this time I was writing and narrating short pieces for a CBC program called *State of the Arts*, produced by Geraldine Sherman. I covered the return of Robin Phillips and Brian Macdonald to Stratford, pieces on Lindsay Kemp and Alan Ayckbourn that I recorded in

England, and a variety of other profiles. I begged Geraldine to let me do a piece on Wingfield, but she was contemptuous of what she considered "some truck about farmers." She stalled but eventually capitulated. The show went on the air and the response from the listening public was immediate and enormous. Before long it reached the attention of Peter Gzowski, and soon episodes were being broadcast regularly on his daily *Morningside* program. Gzowski became a fan of such exchanges as this:

"What does a century farm sign mean?"

"A hundred years without a single decent offer on your land."

Walt Wingfield in dismissive mode

353

A cheerier Walt

With Doug directing his brother, they shaped and tightened the script. Rod visited some of the farmers on whom the characters were based, studying their speech patterns, including Freddy, the stuttering mixed farmer (livestock, auctioneering, and auto parts); the octogenarian Irishman Jimmy, his dour hired hand; and the Squire, a retired remittance man with an interest in rural politics: "There's one fellow lost in the last election because his wife's grandmother was born south of highway 2." Then there is Don, who practices capital-intensive dairy farming with all the latest equipment, and Freddy's two young nephews, the "genial maniacs" Willy and Dave, who observe the scene: "It was a pretty good year for us. But up there on lot 36 Walt had his own little depression."

Walt himself, the ex-urbanite, is enthusiastic if feckless, plunging into one ill-conceived scheme after another. He is to some extent the straight man, but his wry outlook matches well with Rod's own sardonic style. And then there is Maggie, Freddy's sister, who provides a love interest for and eventually marries Walt. Apparently Doug and Dan had doubts about Rod playing a female character, but by the third play they were prepared to chance it and she is now a firmly established personality. Doug is especially proud of the way Rod has grown into the various characters and of his growing skill at maintaining freshness and believability as he takes to the stage night after night.

The initial script, *Letter from Wingfield Farm*, was quickly followed by two sequels, *Wingfields's Progress* and *Wingfield's Folly*. The trilogy seemed self-contained, concluding as it did with Walt's courtship and marriage to Maggie. Although they are hilarious, the plays also contain emotional resonance, as characters die, fall in love or connect with family members they haven't spoken to for decades. And the episodes deal with real events: a fire, an ice storm, a shortage of drinking water.

The shows have toured all over Canada and also played south of the border, notably in Ohio and Florida, where Rod won one of the several acting awards he has garnered. The shows frequently play to sold-out houses and have provided a good income to both the Beatties and Dan. Dan would continue to write about the rural community: another play, *The Perils of Persephone*, which was presented at the Blyth Festival and aired on CBC radio; a novel, *Wingfield's World*, based on the plays; and *With Axe and Flask*, a supposed history of the fictional Persephone Township, which also won him an award.

Rod managed to find time to appear in other shows, including a role in *Glenn*, about the legendary Canadian pianist, presented at the Stratford Festival. Rod has a keen interest in music and has compared the plays to a Beethoven quartet, a Bach fugue, or Aaron Copland's *Appalachian Spring*. Other roles included an Anglo politician in *Johnny Bananas*, a play about Italian immigrants in pre–World War II Toronto, and a very unconventional Macbeth at Stratford, directed by Diana Leblanc with Martha Henry as the Lady. At one point in the production they sang together George Gershwin's "Our Love is Here to Stay."

In the next decade, four more Wingfield plays surfaced: *Wingfield Unbound*, *Wingfield on Ice*, *Wingfield's Inferno*, and *Wingfield Lost and Found*.

354

Rod continued to tour the country, performing in large theatres at Stratford and in Toronto, at regional theatres in Victoria, Vancouver, Hamilton, Winnipeg, Moncton, and Halifax, as well as many smaller venues. He won awards in three cities and has racked up over 4,000 performances.

The Wingfield story was televised for CBC with a multiple cast, winning a Gemini award in 1991, and 30 episodes produced by Norflicks can currently be viewed on *Bravo! Canada*. Recently I asked Douglas Beattie whether there was another script in the works, and he told me that they had decided against any further Wingfield plays. Dan says that although the audience would be happy for the series to continue indefinitely, theatre managers are less enthusiastic; they apparently consider the series to be "old hat." CBC also decided against continuing the TV series, even though surveys showed it to be one of the most popular shows they had ever broadcast. It is true that when *Wingfield Lost and Found* played at the Panasonic in Toronto in 2011 it did respectable business but did not sell out. The contract drawn up by the Mirvish organization was, in Dan's words, "particularly Byzantine; Rod discovered that he was more or less working for scale." When the run finished, David Mirvish summoned the trio to his office and told them the run had been profitable for him. He tore up the contract they had signed and presented them with a generous cheque.

Sometime during the Phillips years at the Festival, Rod, fed up with commuting from Toronto, bought a small but elegant Victorian cottage in Stratford, which he has gradually renovated. Rod claims he was led into theatre in search of girls, and he has remained something of a ladies' man—that is, a man who likes the company of women, starting with his mother. Eleanor Beattie was a warm, intelligent, and charming woman who remained close to her three sons during her long life. Often when I would have lunch with Rod he would bring his mother along and she would have no trouble keeping up with the largely theatrical conversation, and it was clear that both Rod and his mother had an informed interest in music, literature, and politics.

Although Rod is not conventionally handsome, but rather has the face of a bemused clown, he has always been attractive to women. My assistant director on *Hamlet* had a crush on him, and they went out together during the run. As he crisscrossed the country with the Wingfield plays he often enjoyed female companionship. For many years he had a dog named Chowkidor who travelled with him. Not surprisingly she was a female.

355

When I was directing *Johnny Bananas*, I was surprised one night during rehearsal to discover that Martha Henry was sitting quietly at the back of the house. I soon came to understand that Rod was courting her. They would eventually be married and live together in Rod's Mornington Street house. One of the Stratford staff quipped, "I always thought Rod wanted to marry his mother. And now he has." This shrewd observation contains more than a little truth. Like his mother Martha is attractive, intelligent, and possessed of considerable charm.

The marriage was not just one of true minds but also turned into a theatrical partnership. Martha would direct Rod as the overly aggressive professor in David Mamet's *Oleanna*, opposite the young

With Michael Macina in Johnny Bananas

Korean-Canadian actress Sandra Oh before she became a TV star. Rod and Martha would appear together on tour in A.R. Gurney's bittersweet two-handed comedy *Love Letters*, in which two long-time friends correspond, just missing romance but keeping in touch through middle and into old age. Martha's brave vulnerability is offset by Rod's rueful acceptance of the circumstances life brings. Although they no longer live together, Rod and Martha have remained close friends and often dine or attend theatre performances together. Rod cryptically refers to her as "my date."

As a mature actor Rod has come into his own playing leading roles in major contemporary plays at various regional theatres across Canada: Felix in Neil Simon's *The Odd Couple* in Montreal, Johnnypateenmike in Martin McDonagh's *The Cripple of Inishmaan* in Calgary, John Proctor in Arthur Miller's *The Crucible* and Father Gustave in Douglas Beattie's *Blessings in Disguise* in Winnipeg, and Greg in Edward Albee's *Sylvia* in Victoria. From Simon's eccentric bachelor to Miller's conflicted but upright Puritan to Albee's perverse lover, the range and variety of these roles speak to his breadth and flexibility.

Although Rod will continue to perform the seven plays that have provided the spine of his acting career for the past three decades, it will be interesting to see

As one of the four Glenns

every line, every joke. Dan says any script that is presented to a manager is handed back with the comment, "It needs more work." He recognizes that theatre is a collaborative art but believes that there has to be an initial vision conceived by a single writer. "A play starts with an idea in one man's brain." On the other hand he concedes. "I am not always the best judge of my own work."

Unlike Rod and Doug, Dan does not consider himself primarily a man of the theatre. Although he does a lot of public speaking he rarely goes to see plays and does not hang out with actors. He believes that he can only write about "real people" if he remains one of them, a belief he shares with the British playwright Alan Ayckbourn. Hence his decision to live on his forty-acre property, milk his cows, and grow his own produce. He has found that a farmer can be pretty self-sufficient if he accepts the limitations of rural life, but he deplores the intrusive meddling of government officials with their food-inspection programs, which he believes will quickly kill off the production of beef in Ontario.

He alternates the performance of regular chores on the farm with "periods of intense literary activity." His most recent play, *Ed's Garage*, premiered at the Grand Theatre in London in 2013. In it Rod plays Ed, a farmer who fixes things in his garage and before long starts "fix-

what projects he will tackle next. The collaboration seems to remain intact, and there is an understanding of a process that has evolved over the years. It is not just a question of Needles delivering a script that is then performed as written; Dan, Rod, and Doug work over it intensely until they are satisfied with

ing people," adding therapy to the range of skills he offers his neighbours. He hangs out his shingle only to find he is in competition with a trained professional from the big city. The successful premiere of this play suggests it will also tour the country. Dan also has another play, *The Team on the Hill*, which does not involve the Beatties. The fact that Rod acts in other productions and that Doug directs his own theatre productions in Guelph, as well as handling the marketing of DVDs of the series, means that all three collaborators continue to bring a variety of skills to the mix.

Dan has no intention of moving from Nottawasaga, but even if he lives as long as his 95-year-old father he needn't worry. As one of his characters observes, "Farmers are the only people who can lose money thirty years in a row and then move into a big house in town for their retirement." Doug has carved out an enviable career as a director whose work is welcomed in theatres across the land. And Rod will no doubt continue to exhibit his versatility and comic gifts in major roles of the modern repertoire. He is a consummate actor, and when all is said and done the theatre is first and foremost about actors. He is also capable of sharp and pithy comebacks in interviews. As he recently quipped, "I'm

not overly concerned about what the future holds because it is evident to me that the market for intelligent wit is still out there."

A skeptical Walt listens to the neighbourhood gossip

358

FREE SPIRIT

Jackie Burroughs

In Lancashire at the outbreak of World War II, two children were born within a little more than a year of each other. Both would become celebrated performers. The younger, John Lennon, would turn out to be one of the greatest songwriters of the twentieth century; the other, Jackie Burroughs, would become a highly idiosyncratic and widely admired actress on stage and screen. Though they came from different backgrounds—Lennon a working-class boy, Jackie the daughter of an upper-middle-class businessman—they would both plunge headlong into the social and cultural revolution that started in the "swinging sixties," not just as participants but as leaders of the parade.

Jackie moved with her family to Toronto at the age of thirteen. They had a substantial house on Rosedale's Chestnut Park Drive and a summer cottage in Muskoka. Jackie's mother Edna would eventually take up residence in Niagara-on-the-Lake, where she bought and refurbished an old hotel that became the centre of social life for the livelier spirits as this colonial town reinvented itself as a theatrical Mecca devoted to productions of George Bernard Shaw and his contemporaries. New Year's Eve or Canada Day at her Oban Inn were like private parties, where all the guests knew each other and gave themselves over to imbibing and lustily singing popular songs from the 1930s and 1940s, with Edna's friend Judy Finch pounding the ivories, punctuated at regular intervals by her throaty growl, "The piano player needs a drink."

Even before she became mistress of the Oban Inn, Edna was a formidable hostess. She sent her daughter to a nearby girls' private school, Branksome Hall. Jackie got good grades and flourished on the sports field. She was popular with her schoolmates and dated a variety of boys. She has described herself in this period of her life: "I was the jolliest girl. I was very straight. I was a prefect and reported on the smokers. I was awful." In fact, she was already playing a role and doing it so convincingly that she became Head Girl. But she failed to impress Edna.

After graduation, Jackie attended Trinity College and immediately dived into the pool of talent at the Drama Society, which included Rodney Archer, Jamie Cunningham, Ramsay Derry, Garrick Hagon, and Vals Echlin. In 1960, Jamie Cunningham directed a production of T.S. Eliot's *Murder in the Cathedral*. One of his cast dropped out a few days before opening, and I was parachuted in at the last moment. Jackie was one of the leading figures in the chorus of the women of Canterbury, and she stood out with her fluid movement, crisp diction, and resonant voice.

Because we both had to make our entrance from the chapel vestry, which had no outside access, Jackie and I found ourselves alone together there for fifteen minutes every night while the audience filed in. We became friends. She was sharp-witted and talkative with a ready laugh, a girl not so much pretty as striking with her huge brown eyes, auburn curls and strongly defined, rather aristocratic profile. Not surprisingly, I soon learned that she had an active social life, dating a number of fraternity boys including my brother, who recalls, in a favourite expression of the period, "Jackie was a piece of work."

In her time at Trinity, Jackie played St. Joan opposite the Dauphin of Rodney Archer to considerable acclaim, but it was as Middie Paradock in N.F. Simpson's absurdist comedy *A Resounding Tinkle* that she found full scope to exploit her wit and burgeoning eccentricity. She easily dominated the stage at Hart House Theatre, to the delight of her director Herbert Whittaker, then the critic of *The Globe and Mail* and a highly influential figure in Toronto theatre. He became a fan and booster of Jackie's talent, and the two would remain friends to the end of Herbie's long life.

At that time, college shows were seriously reviewed in the daily newspapers, and the recently established professional theatre companies looked to Hart House Theatre, which had first showcased the acting ability of Donald Davis, William Hutt, Charmion King, and Kate Reid, to discover new talent. Not surprisingly, Jackie was asked to join the 1958 summer stock company of the re-organized

Jackie Burroughs

Rainia in Arms and the Man *with Bill Brydon at the Crest Theatre*

Straw Hat Players, which was now led by Bill Davis, a cousin of Donald's and an aspiring director, and Karl Jaffary, a young law student. The company included Timothy Findley and James Mainprize. Plays were directed by Bill Davis, Brenda Davies, Robert Gill, and Herbert Whittaker, among others, and included such recent Broadway and West End hits as Gore Vidal's *Visit to a Small Planet* and William Douglas-Home's *The Reluctant Debutante*, in which Jackie played the title role that had originally been created in London by Anna Massey. Jamie Mainprize recalls that it was a very sociable company. They frequently partied at the Burroughses' cottage on Lake Rosseau on Sundays, often arriving for dress rehearsal that evening in a state of considerable inebriation.

The Straw Hat summer soon led to an offer from the Crest Theatre, where Jackie played Ophelia opposite the nineteen-year-old Hamlet of Richard Monette. The production coincided with another Hamlet at the O'Keefe Centre starring Richard Burton. The two versions were compared by critics, both professional and amateur, and both were widely panned. Nevertheless, the two young Canadians received widespread notice that in the end would work to their advantage. Monette remembers that Jackie cried a lot in rehearsals; when they worked together some twenty years later on a radio script I had written about John Glassco, Monette greeted her with, "Are you going to have a good cry before we begin?" "Maybe that's just what I need," said Jackie and headed to the washroom. When she reappeared, she turned to me: "Tell me about this woman I'm playing. Not that what you say will make any difference." The remark was typical of her combination of a deep inner insecurity and a pose of outward bravado. Throughout her career she would continue to have periods when she ran away, sometimes to the dressing-room for a good cry, sometimes to another city.

A few years earlier I had offered her the role of Ranevskaya in *The Cherry Orchard*, in a production whose cast included Eric House, Robert Joy, R. H. Thomson, and Terry Tweed. She accepted, but then at the last moment she dropped out go to an obscure workshop somewhere in the States, pleading that she needed further study before she could tackle such a major role. John Van Burek, who would direct her in *Madame Stass* some years later, remembers that she once called him at three in the morning and he rushed out to find her sobbing in an alley behind the theatre.

Jackie has said, "After university I just sort of fell into acting." In fact, after her breakthrough with *A Resounding Tinkle*, she ran away to London for a year, where she shared the ground floor of a house in Kensington with her friend Vals Echlin and hung out with other Canadians, including the young Donald Sutherland. She took a break from acting. Vals remembered, "She was in denial that year and not for the last time in her career." She worked for a time as a waitress in a seedy restaurant until Bill Davis approached her to act in his rep company in Chesterfield. She was cast opposite Donald Sutherland in *Two for the Seesaw* and as Beatie in *Roots*, a part originally played by Joan Plowright. Jackie was apparently splendid in both plays, mastering the country dialect of Arnold

Wesker's lower-class heroine, and the experience rekindled her interest in acting. She also slept with both Sutherland and Davis, adding their scalps to the considerable collection already hanging from her belt.

In spite of persistent misgivings, Jackie rapidly developed a highly disciplined professionalism that she would maintain in the future. She was punctual, learned her lines, and came to rehearsal with lots of ideas about what she wanted to do. Her early directors have described her as both "tense" and "intense." One of them, René Bonnière, recalls, "She was insistent on her own vision of the character. I often had to approach her on tiptoe. But her instinct was right. She was playing a down-and-out woman who was living in the streets on a bitterly cold night. She arrived at rehearsals wrapped in newspapers. It was a brilliant image for which I was later given credit, but it was entirely Jackie's idea." Bonnière learned to accept her ideas and work by suggestion and experiment rather than insisting on his own views. "She forced me to be a better director."

Her fellow actor R. H. Thomson has said, "You never knew what Jackie would do next. This was challenging; it could throw you for a loop." But it did give her work a strong sense of immediacy, a quality she shared with many of the greatest actresses of the twentieth century, from Ruth Draper to Judi Dench, in

Jackie as Gail with Michèle Chicoine as Donna in the film Notes for a Film about Donna and Gail

contrast to the carefully planned effects of Lynn Fontanne, Katharine Cornell or Martha Henry. "She was committed to truth," Van Burek has said. "Not objective truth but the truth of the character. And this meant sparks flying between her and other actors."

Back in Toronto, Jackie was quickly accepted by Toronto's small and rather cliquey theatre community. She learned by taking on a variety of roles and playing them to the hilt, but she was ambitious for fresh worlds to conquer. I remember Herbert Whittaker saying, "Somebody should take Jackie and put her in front of a movie camera." That

somebody soon appeared in the person of Don Owen, an aspiring filmmaker a few years older than Jackie, who cast her in two films in the 1960s, *Notes for a Film about Donna and Gail* (1966) and *The Ernie Game* (1967).

The first of these films was Jackie's first feature role and shows the extent of her already highly developed onscreen presence and expressiveness. Fresh-faced, brave, and full of curiosity about life, Gail is a lower-class rebel who takes on anyone who threatens her—bosses, landladies or randy boyfriends—but remains loyal to her scatterbrained and impractical friend Donna, played by Michèle

Chicoine. The details of Jackie's performance, her working-girl accent, gum-chewing and nervous fiddling with her hair, perfectly express her inner insecurity as she confronts and defies authority. Don Owen remembers, "She was the ultimate perfectionist. I can still see her banging her head against a wall because she couldn't get a scene to play the way she wanted it."

This short film, shot in black and white and cut into small titled segments, recalls the early films of Jean-Luc Godard and is a small masterpiece. *The Ernie Game* is more ambitious and reflects the CBC's and the National Film Board's willingness to collaborate to create a Canadian film industry, an ambition that would remain largely unfulfilled. The film calls up the sweet naïveté of the late 1960s: the vivid psychedelic colours, the lyricism of Leonard Cohen, who appears briefly, the self-conscious bohemianism. The whimsical plot and sometimes arch dialogue have a certain charm, and the handling of sexual politics is bold for the time even though it now seems something of a period piece.

Jackie appears again as a character called Gail, who may or may not be the girl of the earlier film at a later stage of development. Here Jackie is more like her off-screen self at the time, a bit kooky but basically good-natured and rather sensible. Her tie-dyed dresses and

sleek short coiffure give her an exotic air that set off her distinctive face, with its prominent cheekbones that prompt comparison with the young Katharine Hepburn. By the end of the 1960s Jackie had become as unconventional as Hepburn was in the 1930s. She would turn up at parties wearing chandelier earrings and a monkey-fur jacket, carrying her treasured Babar books and puffing on Gauloise cigarettes.

By now Jackie had dived into the heady libertarian whirlpool of artistic, political, and sexual revolution that in Toronto was centred in the Yorkville area. Here Leonard Cohen and Joni Mitchell sang their early songs at The Purple Onion or The Penny Farthing, Scott Symons flaunted his newly discovered homosexuality, while painters Graham Coughtry, Greg Curnoe, and Gordon Rayner theorized over beers at the old Pilot Tavern and a young poet named Margaret Atwood recited at the nearby Bohemian Embassy. Jackie hung out with many of these people. She lived in Yorkville in a building that housed a number of aspiring artists, including writer John Frizzell and actor Stephen Ouimette, with both of whom she would collaborate in the future. She maintained this tiny, bare-walled apartment as her Toronto base until her death.

This was the era that took as its motto "sex, drugs, and rock and roll," and

Jackie bought into all three. She danced till dawn, had a succession of affairs, and took a great deal of speed. By the mid-1970s she had changed from the fresh-faced schoolgirl with a curvaceous figure to a slender wraith with a figure like Twiggy and a face that seemed to have endured the ravages of time. Her school friend Martha Butterfield said, "I think Jackie changed more than anyone else I ever knew. But I loved her in both incarnations. We provided comfort for each other and when we meet we still do." Although Jackie would say, "I'm consumed with vanity," in fact she would accommodate herself to this new look and turn it to her advantage, beginning to play women much older than her real age. A few years later Herbert Whittaker would refer in a review to her "delicate and haggard beauty."

Jackie was aware that she had little or no formal training for her chosen profession, but she was not about to go to a conventional theatre school. She would devise her own methods and curriculum. She adopted the habit of starting to learn her lines at the end of a script and working backwards, realizing that many directors spent most of the early rehearsals on the first scenes and skimped on the later ones. At different times she tried to work with Jacques Lecoq and Peter Brook in Paris and various teachers in New York, including the legendary Uta Hagen. She hung out at the Factory with Andy Warhol and his disciples, hoping to work with filmmaker Paul Morrissey.

Somewhere along the line she hooked up with Canadian rock star Zal Yanovsky, who along with John Sebastian was a founding member of the vocal group The Lovin' Spoonful. She says, "I never got any work in New York, but then Zalman became rich and we had to spend all the money and that took at least four years." Their liaison produced a daughter, Zoe. Zal and Jackie returned to Toronto and decided to divorce soon after. Jackie was too much of a free spirit to be tied down by domesticity. It was Zal who sought a conventional life.

"I was no good at marriage," Jackie would say later. "But our break-up was amicable." Zal started a restaurant in Kingston, Ontario, called *Chez Piggy*, and he and his new wife Rose brought up Zoe, but Jackie was a frequent visitor. Since Zal's death in 2002, Zoe has presided over the eatery he established. Jackie was a regular visitor to her daughter and grandsons, a colourful presence in one of Canada's more staid and conservative small cities.

In the late 1960s, modern dance came to Toronto, spearheaded by the triumvirate of Patricia Beatty, David Earle, and Peter Randazzo, who established the Toronto Dance Theatre and began giving concerts at Hart House Theatre and in various public venues. Jackie not only was an enthusiastic supporter but also appeared with the company in *The Recitation*, a piece that David Earle choreographed in 1968. She began attending dance classes, a practice she would continue for forty years. She did not master the Martha Graham technique but rather invented her own idiosyncratic style, which would carry over into

366

In David Earle's dance drama The Recitation

her stage work. She could be seen at the back of dance classes, moving to the rhythms of the music, completely and unashamedly out of sync with the rest of the dancers, creating her own world of fantastic movement.

Through the 1970s Jackie continued to work on stage and in film, experimenting with a variety of styles. She had already made her debut at Stratford playing the young Queen Isabella to William Hutt's Richard II in a company that included Bruno Gerussi, Eric House, and Heath Lamberts. She gave a lacerating portrayal of a highly neurotic Miss Julie in the famous Strindberg play at Toronto Workshop Productions. She appeared in the CBC comedy television series created by Lorne Michaels and Hart Pomerantz before they went on to create *Saturday Night Live*. She made an experimental film about a night in the life of a bunch of misfits, with Louis Del Grande, Victor Garber, and Jim Henshaw, called *Monkeys in the Attic*, which has been described as "weird even by the standards of marginal Canadian filmmaking," and a gritty social drama, *Twelve and a Half Cents*, directed by René Bonnière, about desperate down-and-outs. In the latter, she played a mentally disturbed woman, and at the end of several days' shooting at 999 Queen Street, Bonnière recalls that she was "a total wreck but she was wonderful."

Jackie Burroughs

Then came a shot at the big time. The mercurial Irish actor Peter O'Toole, fresh from his film triumphs in *The Lion in Winter* and *The Ruling Class*, decided in 1975 to mount two productions, Chekhov's *Uncle Vanya* and Noël Coward's *Present Laughter*, and tour them in North America. He decided to rehearse and open in Toronto and chose Jackie to play two *femmes fatales* opposite him. Jackie and O'Toole hit it off. Apparently rehearsals were chaotic but hilarious, and O'Toole's reputation for outrageous high-jinks onstage and off guaranteed a good deal of media coverage, especially when he decided to switch roles in *Vanya* in the middle of the run at the Royal Alexandra. The company went on to play in Washington and Chicago, and Jackie gained recognition as a highly stylish comedienne. She returned to Toronto and immediately received an offer to join Robin Phillips's company at Stratford.

Robin Phillips had a greater impact on English-Canadian theatre than anyone since Tyrone Guthrie in the 1950s. His combination of elegance, sexual energy, and emotional honesty transformed the work of the company. As Jackie stated, "The Edwardian era was a perfect fit for Robin; everyone in whalebone and starched shirtfronts but underneath they've all got a hard-on." But she also loved Robin's unconventionality and unpredictability: "Robin is the only

Yelana with Peter O'Toole in Uncle Vanya

director I've met who understands that if you're playing a queen or the beautiful Sylvia, you don't have to be noble or beautiful. You can be the slouch you normally are, and everyone around you makes you what you are."

Jackie played leading roles in the two productions of Robin's Young Company that toured Ontario before opening at Stratford. The company included Mia Anderson, Graeme Campbell, Douglas Chamberlain, Eric Donkin, Gale Garnett, Bernard Hopkins, Barry MacGregor, and Nicholas Pennell and went into rehearsal with Robin telling the actors, "This is a beginning and we all have much to learn." He led them in a series of theatre games and improvisations that melded them into an intimate ensemble and resulted in two saucy productions that provided a foretaste of Robin's inventive and energetic handling of Shakespearean comedy. Robin's con-

367

With Nicholas Pennell in The Comedy of Errors *at Stratford*

368

stant challenge played into Jackie's low boredom threshold and resulted in spontaneity and inventiveness.

As Julia in *The Two Gentlemen of Verona*, Jackie gave an athletic and spirited performance that began with a cartwheel, which revealed that she was not wearing any underwear. Jackie would later say, "Robin was naughty, but then I've always had a weakness for naughty boys." Jackie also played Victoria, the young heroine, in Brecht's *Trumpets and Drums*, a reworking of the eighteenth-century comedy *The Recruiting Officer* by George Farquhar, demonstrating that she could bring both charm and edge to the playing of classical comedy.

In Robin's second season, Jackie would play Mariana in Robin's trademark production of *Measure for Measure* that set the standard for much of his subsequent work and established the pre-eminence of Martha Henry as one of Canada's leading actresses. The cast also included

Maggie Smith, with whom Jackie would often be compared in the future. Certainly the two actresses had in common the command of a deliciously mannered style, a certain gaunt elegance, and an innate instinct for comic inflection and gesture.

Jackie's other role that season was as Portia in *The Merchant of Venice*, in a cast that included Hume Cronyn as Shylock and Nick Mancuso as Bassanio. It was the first (and only) production on the Festival stage directed by Bill Glassco and was fraught with conflict. Cronyn denounced Glassco as an amateur; Mancuso was a handsome lad with no classical acting experience; Jackie overcompensated for Glassco's inexperience by an excessively aggressive performance. The production was a critical disaster and sparked a controversy about Stratford's use of domestic as opposed to imported directors that continued for years to come. Jackie would not appear again on Stratford's stages during Robin's tenure as artistic director, but they would remain good friends and her admiration for his work was ongoing.

At about this time Jackie began working on a project with her Yorkville neighbour John Frizzell to adapt a book by Maryse Holder, *Give Sorrow Words*, the story of a middle-aged woman seeking love and fulfillment in Mexico, into a screenplay. Over the next five years they

With her Mexican lover in A Winter Tan

369

would raise the necessary funds, put together a production crew led by four directors including Jackie and John, assemble a cast of mainly unknown Mexican performers, shoot the script in segments, edit it, and obtain distribution.

In the film, *A Winter Tan* (1988), Jackie gave one of the most compelling performances of her career as a woman desperate and obsessed, masochistic but brave, who destroys herself in her quest for fulfillment and affection. It is almost a one-woman film, emotionally raw, unabashedly self-indulgent, and sometimes over the top. We watch Jackie as Maryse with her elegant long legs and provocatively abbreviated costumes on the beach, in bars and dancehalls and crumby hotel rooms, as she chases after men who are obviously only interested in using her. Meanwhile she drinks and smokes and writes and talks. It is painful yet funny and fully embodies the experimentation and excess that Jackie experienced in the 1960s and early 1970s and parallels the experience Joni Mitchell was simultaneously evoking in her lyrics. Commenting on the film much later, Jackie said, "We thought of it as a comedy. She talks and talks. It should have been called *Shut Up*." The film would receive both rave notices and complete pans from the critics. It was released in 1978 and won Jackie a Genie. She considered the picture her finest achievement, even though it did not gain her wide recognition.

In 1982, Jackie appeared in *The Grey Fox*, Peter O'Brian's film about the legendary stagecoach and train robber Bill Miner. In it Jackie plays Kate Lynch, an independent woman of intelligence and sensibility who has an autumnal affair with the crafty but charming criminal played by the longtime wrangler and stuntman Richard Farnsworth, who blossomed into a first-rate film actor in late middle age. His easy-going charm is perfectly complemented by Jackie's mixture of flighty eccentricity and carefully concealed vulnerability, and both characters emerge as warm and complex human beings out of step with the society they are caught in yet manage to transcend. This was the film that first showcased Jackie as a mature and charismatic film artist. It also mined the territory of Canadian history, not for its political content or pedagogical value but as a source of entertaining human stories. It set an example that would be much emulated in the next decade.

From here on Jackie would be in constant demand as a film actress. She made an appearance in Robin Phillips's adaptation of Timothy Findley's *The Wars*, but in spite of her sharply etched portrayal of a family retainer and the wonderfully detailed performances of William Hutt and Martha Henry, they could not save this story of a sensitive but essentially passive young man from coming across as a somewhat moribund period piece.

Meanwhile her co-star from *The Grey Fox* was cast as the sweet-tempered old farmer Matthew alongside Colleen Dewhurst in the enormously successful version of *Anne of Green Gable*s made by the ambitious young director/producer Kevin Sullivan. Jackie was cast in a smaller role, and her appeal was such that Sullivan cast her as a principal character in the spin-off television series *Road to Avonlea* that he produced in collaboration with Disney. This would prove to be an enormously popular family entertain-

ment that ran for seven seasons and was seen by millions, not only in Canada but in the United States and ultimately around the world when it went into syndication.

I was briefly involved in the casting of this series and I knew many of the actors. About ten years later I was seated in a small trattoria in Italy and entered into conversation with an American family sitting at a neighbouring table. They inquired what I did, and when I replied that I had been involved in radio and television they asked if I had ever done anything they would know about. I mentioned *Road to Avonlea* and their eyes lit up. They had seen every episode. Did I know any of the actors? I mentioned Jackie. "You actually *know* Jackie Burroughs?" they said, moving to my table. I had some difficulty escaping from them two hours later.

With Richard Farnsworth in The Grey Fox

Hetty King, the opinionated spinster schoolteacher that Jackie played, could have been a stereotype, but in Jackie's skillful hands she had a three-dimensional reality that was rooted in her instinctive grasp of the character's inner insecurity and aggressively defensive posture. Her reactions were immediate and emotional, bolstered by later rationalization. Jackie's unpredictability was what gave Hetty instant believability. It is somewhat ironic that Jackie, the bold experimenter of the 1960s, should find her most famous role as a nit-picking, buttoned-up old maid of the pre–World War I era.

Kevin Sullivan recalled that in the first day's shooting Jackie was "acting up a storm in the background of a scene that was dominated by Colleen Dewhurst." The director stopped to ask what she was doing. "I'm establishing my character," said Jackie. "She owned her character so completely that it was easy to write for her." Sullivan stated. "It got so we stretched the character further and further, just to see what she would do with it. Whatever we put into the script we got it back in spades." Sullivan also discovered that both Jackie and Mag Ruffman, with whom she played many of her scenes, were very mischievous and sparked each other on. "Although she could be bossy and often tried to get the other actors to march to her tune, more often than not her instinct was right. It was always a wonderful ride with Jackie."

In the course of making *A Winter Tan*, Jackie had fallen in love with Mexico. She took some of her Avonlea earnings and built herself a house on the outskirts of the old colonial town of Oaxaca. This is Mayan country, with a strong native presence and towering ruins but also some splendid Spanish colonial architecture. Her house was comfortable, decorated in a highly individual style and surrounded by a garden full of exotic plants. She became fluent in Spanish, made many local friends and spent about half of the year there leading a life that had nothing to do with the theatre. An avid reader and enthusiastic walker, she practiced Tai Chi, read novels, and worked in her garden. "I can take out all my fascistic tendencies on my plants," she would say with a mischievous grin.

Although in her last years she devoted much of her working time to film, she did not abandon the theatre, often appearing in small houses for low salaries. In 1984 she made a remarkable appearance in Judith Thompson's second play *White Biting Dog*, a savage depiction of a dysfunctional family in which she played the controlling mother of the heroine and was partnered by her longtime friend Stephen Ouimette. Unlike Thompson's first piece *The Crackwalker*, which dealt with the disadvantaged, this

372

As Hetty King with Sarah Polley in The Road to Avonlea

play's characters were from the upper middle class, and it shocked the Tarragon's liberal but respectable audience. Jackie drew on her own background in this role. She once admitted that a good deal of her work had been fuelled by her antagonism toward her own mother, a woman as strong-willed as she was herself.

Jackie continued to play women of strong and distinctive character: Mme. Stass in the French play of that name at Toronto Workshop Productions, and the American painter Georgia O'Keeffe in John Murrell's *The Faraway Nearby* at the Saidye Bronfman Theatre in Montreal. She had a particular affinity for such iconic figures, not only the strong-willed O'Keeffe but also the masochistic Canadian writer Elizabeth Smart and the promiscuous French novelist Colette. Tellingly, all three women had incredible psychological strength and unconventional sexual liaisons.

Jackie would continue to work in film, playing small as well as larger roles.

In 1983, Jackie had gained considerable attention in the United States when she appeared in *The Dead Zone* with Christopher Walken, Colleen Dewhurst, and Martin Sheen, whom she particularly admired. Thereafter she would work frequently in American pictures, such as the offbeat comedy *Willard* (2003), although she continued to be seen in Canadian films.

Her second film for Peter O'Brian was Gordon Pinsent's *John and the Missus*, released in 1987. Again she was paired with a strong actor, Pinsent, who por-

374

With Gordon Pinsent in John and the Missus

trayed the bullet-headed patriarch John who refuses to leave the cove where he was born when its only industry, a used-up copper mine, is closed. Pinsent is sardonic, quick-tempered, and stubborn; Jackie is sympathetic, unsentimental, controlled, but inwardly fanciful. Pinsent as a native Newfoundlander perfectly catches the local accent; Jackie matches him with seeming ease. And once again her performance is crafted with attention to detail: the deft way she handles a nee-dle while mending a shirt or shuffles and deals cards while she has a serious conversation with her son, or sings a few lines from a familiar song with an old family friend played with delightful oddi-ty by Roland Hewgill. The film is both realistic and lyrical, a heartfelt tribute by Pinsent to his native province and a human story that is deeply emotional without being spiked with meretricious dollops of violence or sexuality.

She would also appear among a stel-

Mother Mucca in Further Tales of the City *with Olympia Dukakis*

lar constellation of Canadian actors in Don McKellar's *Last Night* (1998), as a very liberal-minded headmistress in Judith Thompson's *Lost and Delerious* (2001), and as Betty, the loving mother of the confused perfectionist Fay on Deepa Mehta's adaptation of Carol Shields's *The Republic of Love* (2003). She obviously appealed to directors who delight in the unconventional. She averaged from three to five film roles in a year, and the total number of her film appearances was rapidly approaching 100 when she died in 2010.

One of her most interesting late appearances was in Armistead Maupin's *Further Tales of the City* (2001), where she played Mother Mucca, a curmudgeonly and foul-mouthed octogenarian, the retired madam of a brothel, and the mother of Olympia Dukakis, who in real life was eight years her senior. Jackie obviously relished this role, and her enjoyment was contagious. She attacked it with the same gusto as Aunt Hetty, and it is, as it were, the flip side of the coin. When I told Jackie I was working on this profile she seemed pleased but said, "I never give interviews. I'm very confessional and I've learned that I'm sure to say something I'll regret. I really don't want to hurt anyone dead or alive. And

in any case, I don't really have a social life." However, she continued to delight in one-on-one meetings with friends, visited old colleagues, especially those who were disabled, and devoted several years to helping her troubled teenaged daughter work through her problems. When we met near her Yorkville apartment for a coffee, we spent two full hours talking about theatre, politics, and where to get the best fried wontons. As always, Jackie talked a blue streak, smoked incessantly, and laughed a good deal. She had to be the hippest grandmother in Canada.

A few weeks after our last conversation Jackie was diagnosed with stomach cancer and told she only had a few weeks to live. She sold her Mexican property and planned her funeral, which was held at St. James Cathedral. There was a fairly large crowd, including a group from a nearby Salvation Army hostel, where she had worked as a volunteer, but not a lot of theatre people. She had told the priest that on no account were any actors to be allowed to speak. The service was simple and brief. She had recorded the twenty-third psalm, and her clear musical contralto filled the space with its sound. It was a more fitting monument to her life than any eulogy.

376

IRISH ROVER

Colm Feore

In 1988 Richard Monette moved back to his house on Douglas Drive in Stratford. Always sociable, he filled it with friends, mainly actors. I was a frequent guest. Another regular was Colm Feore, then in his late twenties and already on his way to being a star at the Festival. We gossiped and cracked wise. Both Richard and Colm were great talkers, and their conversation was studded with Shakespearean quotes, deadly accurate imitations and quick rejoinders, witty though not particularly profound. Colm in particular came across as a bit of a smart alec.

That year Colm would play in Richard's production of *The Taming of the Shrew* opposite the beautiful Goldie Semple as his fiery Kate. The show was gloriously funny, set in the 1950s and featuring a dysfunctional family based on Richard's own relatives. Sort of Fellini meets *I Love Lucy*. More than anything he had done up to this time, this production put Richard on the map as a director and displayed his talent for comedy with

heart. Colm at the centre of this mayhem downplayed the provocative and flamboyant qualities usually associated with Petruchio and instead provided a portrait of a commonsensical and straightforward wooer. His winning of Kate came across as a triumph of reason in a mad world. His genuine affection was sufficiently evident for Kate's ironically inflected speech of submission in the final act to

378

Petruchio with Goldie Semple in The Taming of the Shrew

be interpreted as an acknowledgement of his fundamental good will.

Colm would stick around when Richard took over the reins as Artistic Director of the Festival, in his first season playing a biting, extravagant Cyrano and a rollicking Pirate King, proving that he could carry the lead in a musical as handily as he could manage the lyrical verse of a Romeo or the witty badinage of a Restoration gallant. It was a gesture of loyalty to Richard before Colm took off to conquer the silver screen. In slightly less than a decade at the Festival he had played an extravagant Mercutio, a deliciously calculating Iago, a sour Cassius, a quick-tempered Leontes, a twisted and malevolent Richard III, and a commanding, vigorous Oberon, as well as the two greatest Shakespearean roles for young actors, Romeo and Hamlet. He had proved to be that rare animal, a leading actor who is lucid, energetic, sharp-witted, and sexy. His loss to the Festival, though temporary, was serious.

At the time he said, "Richard has offered me a short season, but there's no such thing. You have to rehearse three months and perform for three months. During this period you start at ten in the morning and often finish at eleven at night, six days a week. It's exhilarating but it eats up everything you've got. If it doesn't, you're not doing the job. It's not just that at this stage in my career I can't afford to be available for that long. It's also that being there for half the season is like being half pregnant. If you can't be totally involved, it's better to make way for someone who is. Anyway Richard realizes that no one is indispensable. People will come here to see good shows no matter who's in them. This has given Richard freedom and it's given him power." This speech not only reflects Colm's frequent flippancy but also his serious commitment to both his profession and the theatre that has become his life.

Colm Feore was born in 1958, the son

379

Cyrano de Bergerac *at Stratford*

Student at the National Theatre School with Ann-Marie MacDonald

380

of Irish parents. His name Colm is the Gaelic version of Columba, the saint who left Ireland to establish the religious community of Iona in Scotland and converted the pagan Picts to Christianity; his surname Feore denotes descent from the Spanish sailors who were washed ashore in Ireland after the defeat of the Armada. His parents emigrated to Canada and settled in Windsor where his father was a radiologist. Colm remembers his family life: "We were Irish, so there would be music, jokes, stories, tall tales and a musicality in it. We all tried to outdo each other, and my parents seemed to be reasonably amused by this. I don't think they thought anybody would make a career out of it. They worried that acting would be a very disap-

pointing and hard life. To this day they're not convinced."

He attended Ridley College, a private boys' school in St. Catharines, where he was the valedictorian, and decided to skip university and go straight to the National Theatre School in Montreal. While there he became fluent in French and met his first wife, Sidonie Boll. In his first year Tim Bond, a director who was teaching at the school, took him aside and said, "You'll never make it as an actor, Colm. Why don't you consider stage management?" So much for the theory that an experienced director can instantly recognize talent.

After graduation he auditioned and so impressed Anne Tait, a casting director, that she tried to get him an audition at Stratford, only to be told that all the audition slots were filled. When she was

Iago with Howard Rollins in Othello

hired as a casting director at the Festival, she told Colm to show up one morning before the sessions began. She sneaked him in to see John Hirsch, who was impressed by his soliloquy and asked him to do it again as if he were a dog, a typical Hirsch ploy. Colm rose to the challenge and was hired to play walk-ons. Because the Festival was in disarray after the departure of Robin Phillips, many of the actors they gave offers to turned them down. Colm landed the role of Tranio in *The Taming of the Shrew*, giving him an opportunity to show off his comic talents.

The next year he had roles in *Julius Caesar*, *The Merry Wives of Windsor*, and *Mary Stuart*, and the year following he played Claudio, the juvenile lead in *Much Ado About Nothing*, directed by Michael Langham. In 1984 he played Romeo and then Orsino in *Twelfth Night* and Marlow in *She Stoops to Conquer*. He had established himself as a *jeune premier*, handsome, charming, with an undertone of unpredictability. In 1986 he played Antipholus of Ephesus in *The Boys from Syracuse*, with Geraint Wyn Davies as his twin brother. The two would become fast friends. By way of contrast, that year Colm also played Leontes, the jealous, unstable king in *The Winter's Tale*, and the deceptive Iachimo in *Cymbeline*, his first experience working with Robin Phillips.

These last two roles proved that Colm could play roles with emotional weight and more than a dash of malevolence.

In 1987, his Joseph Surface was smooth and hypocritical, his Iago scheming and cynical, and this paved the way for his warped Richard III, exulting in his devious plots and relishing his own duplicity. In the same year his Petruchio was a straightforward good guy whose shaming of the haughty Katherina was motivated by genuine attraction. After a year away from the Festival, Colm returned to play two comic roles: Ford in *The Merry Wives of Windsor* and Valentine in *Love for Love*, as well as the sly conspirator Cassius in

381

Joseph Surface with Sheila McCarthy in
The School for Scandal

Julius Caesar and an intense, troubled Hippolytus to Patricia Conolly's Phaedra, a season that showcased the actor's extraordinary range and scope. He had worked with all the major directors at Stratford: Hirsch, Langham, Phillips, Campbell, as well as visiting English directors David Giles and Peter Dews. When I talked with him in 1988 it was clear he felt it was time to move on; he did not dismiss the possibility of returning to Stratford, but he felt he had honed his craft and now he wanted to make his mark in film and television.

When he was a young actor, some casting directors found Colm "full of himself." Now, as he approached the age of forty, he was still confident but he had overlaid his earlier brashness with an air of good-humoured bonhomie. He was slim, athletic, charming, and witty. Some attributed this mellower persona to the influence of his second wife, Donna. However that might be, he still had a fierce desire to work; unlike some actors who have established themselves he was not lazy but rather "bright-eyed and bushy-tailed." Early on, in 1990, he played a small part in the Canadian movie *Bethune*. Its star Donald Sutherland told Colm, "the important thing is to show up whenever you're asked. Actors like Jane [Fonda] and Goldie [Hawn] worry about finding just the right part for them. While they're worrying over one role, I've done ten. If you take on whatever you're offered, you'll work all the time and you can't help but get better and better." Sutherland knew whereof he spoke; when he couldn't get anything better he played a minor role in *Animal House*; the next thing he knew he was playing the lead in *M*A*S*H*.

Colm already had a presence in Canadian film and television. His Stratford performances as Mercutio, Petruchio, and Antipholus had been televised for CBC. He fairly quickly landed guest appearances on such CBC dramas as *The Great Detective*, *Street Legal*, and *Due South*. Then came a breakthrough. Rhombus, the most prestigious Canadian producer of the day, gave him the lead in *Thirty-Two Short Films About Glenn Gould* (1993). The film showcased Colm's versatility as he played various aspects of the Canadian musician who by then was a cultural icon—his fiercely articulate intelligence, his physical eccentricity, his utter self-absorption. It was an evocation of Gould the man, not an impersonation, though the physical resemblance was strong enough to be acceptable. The film received widespread critical praise and, for a Canadian film, extensive exposure. Colm would continue to work for Rhombus, playing a voluble auctioneer in *The Red Violin* (1998) and a loopy Indian promoter in their greatest success, *Slings and Arrows*.

382

But Colm was ambitious to break into the American scene. This involved spending time in California, where he hung out with his longtime friend Geraint Wyn Davies, who was living in Santa Barbara, and Mark Monette, Richard's brother, who worked as a sound engineer in Los Angeles. He went after small parts in big movies: *Pearl Harbour* (2001) and *Chicago* (2002), though not so small that he wasn't noticed. And he managed to get work in New York, playing Claudius in *Hamlet* at the Public and Cassius in *Julius Caesar* to Denzell Washington's Brutus on Broadway. His classical chops had also landed him a sizeable role in Julie Taymor's film *Titus* (1999).

Back in Canada, Colm was cast as Pierre Trudeau in a biopic in 2002. It was a perfect role for Colm. He perfectly captured the charisma, the arrogance, the slight accent, and the idiosyncratic behavior of the prime minister who charmed and infuriated the Canadian public by turns. Colm would continue to slip into this impersonation in interviews as easily as Monette would suddenly assume the accent and mannerisms of his signature role, Hosanna. It is arguable that Colm learned a good deal about how to present himself publicly through his association with Monette. It also gave Colm one of his best interview lines: "I do dead Canadians. If he's dead and he's Canadian and he's famous, I'll be playing

383

With Patrick Huard and Sylvain Marcel in Bon Cop, Bad Cop

him at some point. I joke, but I have played about five or six famous Canadians so there's a certain amount of 'Wait a minute, he's ours.'"

In 2006 Colm made his most famous Canadian movie, *Bon Cop, Bad Cop*. A hilarious bilingual comedy, it begins when a corpse of a well-known hockey player is found perched atop the billboard between Ontario and Quebec. Two police officers are called in to investigate: Patrick Huard from Montreal and Colm from Toronto. Inevitably they squabble as they try to track down the killer. The escalating plot involves an affair between Huard and Colm's sister, a hockey game in which the killer appears disguised in the costume of the Habitants' mascot, and a final sequence in which Colm dismantles a bomb seconds before it will explode. As police officer Martin Ward, Colm is calm and rather superior in contrast to the more explosive personality of the Québécois policeman. Working with a largely French-Canadian cast, Colm was perfectly at ease but was able to exploit his clipped tones and cool exterior in contrast to the more excitable francophones. The film was one of the highest-grossing Canadian films ever made.

By this time Colm had appeared in approximately a hundred films. He had made guest appearances on major American TV series: *Law and Order*, *The West Wing*, and *Battlestar Galactica*. He had played Caesar and Alexander Hamilton and starred in films with Joely Richardson, Laura Linney, and Judi Dench. He was ready for the big time. But he took a year off to return to Stratford. In 2002 he had returned for part of a season to play Henry Higgins in *My Fair Lady*. The orig-

Higgins with Cynthia Dale in My Fair Lady

inal plan was to split the run, with Colm playing the first third, Geraint Wyn Davies the middle section, and Richard Monette the final part of the run. Ill health and exhaustion prevented Monette from completing his part of the run, however, so Colm returned to finish the season. Once again Colm had a role that suited his talents down to the ground: an articulate man whose cool demeanour and apparent indifference to romance made him irresistible.

Colm's return to Stratford for a full season was motivated at least in part by a desire to further the career of his wife Donna. Colm's second marriage was a success. He took custody of Jack, his son by his first marriage, and settled into a large Victorian house two blocks away from the Festival Theatre in Stratford. He and Donna had two more children, Tom and Anna. Donna began to choreograph musicals for Stratford but was ambitious to direct. Colm agreed to a season that included *Coriolanus*, *Don Juan*, and *Oliver!*, on the understanding that Donna should direct him in this latter production. Coriolanus is one of Shakespeare's least attractive characters: stubborn, overbearing, unyielding. He lacks the delight in his evil schemes of Iago or Richard III. Colm's performance made no concessions to try to win sympathy for his character. His patrician Roman was a monster of self-absorption.

The production boasted a fine cast that included Martha Henry as his imperious mother, and it consolidated his relationship with Antoni Cimolino as director.

Molière's Don Juan, in contrast, was a thorough-going bad boy but had a conniving charm and plenty of sex appeal. Colm played the role in both English and French, with a supporting cast of bilingual actors, recalling Langham's

385

O, it is a glorious thing to be a Pirate King

386

Got to Pick a Pocket or Two: Fagin in Oliver!

1956 production that first introduced a band of Quebec's finest *comédiens* to the Stratford stage. After the Stratford run the production transferred to *Le théâtre du nouveau monde* in Montreal. But it was as Fagan that Colm managed to dominate the season. Fagan is one of the great characters of English literature, and Colm perfectly encapsulated his delight in his ingenious rascality. Skipping and twirling with gleeful energy and verve, Colm had a thoroughly good time in this role, and his audience picked up on his enjoyment. Colm is fond of saying in interviews that much of his work is fun. He instinctively realizes that if he as an actor is having a good time, the audience will have a good time along with him. Unlike many lead-

Cardinal della Rovere in The Borgias

387

The Lord Marshall in the Chronicles of Riddick

ing actors, Colm shows no interest in directing, having stated that "one director in the family is enough."

Then it was back to the silver screen. Colm was getting increasingly better roles in increasingly important TV series: ongoing roles in *The Listener*, and *24* with Kiefer Sutherland, and then the plum part of Cardinal Giuliano della Rovere in *The Borgias*. His unrelenting cardinal has the necessary weight and menace to provide a genuine threat to the wily pope of Jeremy Irons. Colm's experience playing Shakespeare would stand him in good stead playing in period pieces, something for which many good film and television actors have no feel. This was evident again in *Thor* (2011), in which he underwent five hours in the make-up department to play King Laufey in this prehistoric epic alongside Anthony Hopkins and Natalie Portman. Colm was now working with the major stars in the industry and being directed by such legendary figures as Kenneth Branagh and Clint Eastwood. He had established himself as an actor with presence and edge, and not surprisingly he was often cast as a villain. This specialty earned him the role of Donald Menken, the manipulative schemer in *The Amazing Spiderman 2* (2014), a turn balanced by Roger in *Sensitive Skin*, a new romantic comedy series starring Canadian actors Kim Cattrall and Don McKellar.

To reinforce his status as a major actor of both screen and stage, *Spiderman* opened in theatres across the continent in the same week that Colm made his triumphant return to Stratford as King Lear. His aging monarch was convincing and terrifying; he had completely mastered and absorbed the text and still had the energy to scale the physical and vocal heights demanded of the role, even if he lacked the sheer humanity of William Hutt's final interpretation. (Admittedly Hutt played Lear four times, an opportunity almost never granted to Canadian actors, unlike their British counterparts.)

Colm's dual openings were preceded by a battery of media attention rarely according to a Canadian performer. Slim as a whippet, now balding and lantern-jawed, Colm in TV interviews radiated good humour and continued to crack wise. Colm would go on to play Martin Ward again in a sequel to *Bon Cop, Bad Cop*, and his *King Lear* would be filmed and given a wide theatrical release in 2015, garnering excellent reviews.

In a conversation with *Toronto Star* critic Richard Ouzounian, Colm confessed that Lear was the most complex and difficult role he had ever taken on: "I should have done it when I was thirty-five, but I wouldn't have known enough then to do it properly. But I would have had the energy. Now I understand it, but what I failed horribly to address is what it would cost me, and that is everything."

King Lear *at Stratford*

PRIMA BALLERINA

Veronica Tennant

I remember going to the opening performance of *The Sleeping Beauty* at the O'Keefe Centre primarily to see Rudolf Nureyev, who had only recently defected from the Soviet Union and had made a sensation in London dancing with Margot Fonteyn. To the delighted astonishment of Torontonians, Nureyev had agreed to stage and star in a new production of Tchaikovsky's masterpiece for the National Ballet of Canada. He proved, as expected, to be charismatic, and his staging was extravagantly opulent, but the real star of the evening turned out to be the dancer who appeared opposite him as Princess Aurora. During the Rose Adagio in the first act she was magical as she slowly revolved on point while four cavaliers circled around her. I had seen Veronica Tennant before as an impassioned Juliet, but this ballet demonstrated a completely different aspect of her balletic skills: classical poise, elegance, and a radiant aura of expectation.

When Veronica Tennant was sixteen, her mother Doris, a script assistant for CBC's daytime magazine show *Take Thirty*, was auditioning a young Adrienne Clarkson to be an interviewer. She arranged for her daughter to be interviewed, and the two hit it off. Adrienne was impressed by this poised, serious, articulate girl; Veronica by the sympathetic intelligence of her interviewer. Adrienne was hired and Veronica went back to classes at the National Ballet School. They would stay in touch over the years, and the relationship would lead eventually to Adrienne, as Governor

General, making Veronica a Companion of the Order of Canada, the country's highest honour.

Veronica had arrived in Toronto at the age of eight with her parents and sister. Up until that time the Tennants had lived in Hampstead in north London. At an early age Veronica had begun to dance around the drawing-room whenever her mother turned on the radio. Doris was a cultivated woman with an interest in the arts, and she enrolled Veronica in the Arts Educational School where she began to get classical ballet training. The move to Canada was inspired by her father Harry's need to find more profitable work. Even before Britain's disastrous military adventure in Suez, many English families decided to emigrate to one of the dominions.

Doris remembered being shocked by the lack of a vibrant cultural life in Toronto in comparison with what she had experienced in London. Nevertheless, she immediately set about finding dance classes for Veronica. That summer, ballet classes had just begun, led by Betty Oliphant, the British ballet mistress who had recently joined Celia Franca's National Ballet of Canada. Veronica remembers, "As soon as the family arrived in the city, I was in class. We didn't even have any furniture but I was at the *barre* doing *pliés*." She quickly made friends with one of her classmates,

Victoria Bertram. The two women would study together, dance together, and remain firm friends after both stopped dancing. Victoria was impressed by Veronica's total dedication: "I would go home to my normal middle-class family and play baseball. But Veronica had no interest in that. She was either dancing or studying. However I did teach her how to make a snowman."

The summer classes ended, and for the first year full-time classes were being offered by the new ballet school, which had found a home in a renovated church on Maitland Street. Veronica recalled that as summer classes ended there was a buzz among the young dancers as one after another learned she would be admitted to the school. Finally she went to Miss Oliphant and asked if she could attend the school. "You? I think not. But you can continue to come to evening classes if you wish." A year later Miss Oliphant relented: "I suppose if you're that determined you might as well come to the school."

Betty Oliphant was initially not a strong supporter of Veronica. But by the time the girl was ten she had caught the eye of Celia Franca, who was her first examiner at the school. Mary McDonald, the rehearsal pianist, remembers, "She was such a determined little thing. Celia liked that. She didn't have an ideal body for classical dance. Her feet were not even

the right shape." With unswerving dedication, Veronica worked on her body and her feet. Her efforts were rewarded by a herniated disk. She was put in a body cast for several months and her training was suspended while her back healed.

"The first doctor I talked to said, 'You're perfectly normal.' I said. 'But I can't do backbends.' He said. 'You're not supposed to bend your body like that. Why would anybody want to?' Then there was a nurse who said, 'You must be realistic and accept that are never going to be a dancer.'" Veronica refused to accept. It took nearly a year for her injury to mend, but she went back to work. This was the time when she really resolved that dance would be her life. Asked a few years later if she regretted the long slog of perfecting her technique, she replied, "No." And would she do it again? "No."

Veronica would later confess to a period of self-conscious anxiety when she was in her middle teens. She was conscious that she was being closely watched in class, at the same time wanting and fearing this attention. But she never stopped working. She was by now completely committed to becoming a dancer. Part of her anxiety was concerned with her physical appearance, so she began to wear elaborate make-up that emphasized her large dark eyes. She would almost never appear without make-up, neither

in class nor when she was exercising in a swimming pool. As her confidence grew she wore exotic earrings and colourful printed outfits that complemented her exotic features—bright prints, edgy fashions. The black mane of her hair was twisted into elaborate styles, often set off with bright blossoms or elaborate combs, suggesting a Spanish princess or an Eastern goddess. She did not have the prettiness of a Karen Kain, but her appearance was striking and eminently photogenic.

During her teenage years, life in her family was complicated by her father's steady disintegration. Unsuccessful in building a career in real estate, he became a heavy drinker, then an alcoholic. Doris did not leave him, but the strain was all too apparent. Veronica had few outside friends or interests, though at one point she did go to live briefly with the family of her friend Victoria. Mostly she hid her feelings. Dance was an escape and a release. And perhaps she sensed that Celia Franca had her eye on her.

When she was just eighteen, Veronica had a telephone call from Celia. "Are you sitting down, darling, because I have a surprise for you." It was an offer to join the National and to play the role of Juliet. Veronica would not only be the youngest dancer to be invited into Celia's company, but she would begin by playing a leading role. Celia had persuaded British chore-

391

ographer John Cranko to let her add his version of *Romeo and Juliet* to the repertoire the year before. Juliet had been played by the visiting Russian ballerina Galina Samtsova, whom Veronica had decided to model herself on, in spite of their differences in body type. She sat in on rehearsals daily and so she had already mastered many of the steps. Celia may have known this, but even so she was taking an enormous gamble. But she believed that Veronica had the necessary qualities: "youth, passion, intensity. There was fire in her eyes."

Veronica lived up to Celia's expectations. Her performance was indeed intense, passionate, and fiery. Her diminutive figure lent credibility to the fact that she was young and inexperienced. Her dark Mediterranean appearance was perfect for an Italian adolescent. She was innocent but impulsive, shy but determined. And her mother, Lady Capulet, was played by Celia, who was noted for the dramatic quality of her dancing. Now this dramatic flair was being matched by Veronica. "I have always thought of myself as an actress who dances. Ever since I saw Margot Fonteyn at the age of six," Veronica recently told me. It is what sets her apart from some other dancers whose main appeal is their technical virtuosity rather than emotional immediacy.

Veronica's debut gained her instant

Veronica as Juliet with Earl Kraul as Romeo

recognition. As a principal dancer she was offered other leading roles, and she set about learning the steps and exploring the unique characters of Kitri, Odette/Odile, and Cinderella. She used her sharp intelligence to analyze these characters but also drew on the reservoir of turmoil and pain that she had repressed during her teenage years as part of an increasingly dysfunctional family.

Veronica had always had the strong support of her mother Doris, but she had virtually no social life, until one night she went to a dance with some friends at Hart House, where she sat in a corner for over an hour, watching the others. Then she was approached by a young medical student, John Wright, who swept her out onto the floor and into his life. It was the year she first danced Juliet, and here at a university ball she met her Romeo.

Dancers are often thought to be promiscuous; the close physical relationship that is inevitable in the work sometimes leads to offstage couplings and recouplings. But Raymond Smith, Veronica's main partner for over a decade, recalls that Veronica was always reserved about her private life: "In spite of the emotional heat of her performances, she kept her private life to herself. She was a true professional." Paradoxically, Veronica onstage was increasingly open and vulnerable. In her various roles she found a new freedom: "Dance allows you to express what cannot be said." Interviewed for a CBC film at the age of twenty-five, she spoke of the drudgery of endless classes compared to the excitement of dancing for an audience, the magical immediacy of sensing their response. "I am confident as a dancer but I am still striving to grow as an artist." With success came a new assurance. At the same time as she sought pre-cision she found a freshness and spontaneity by experimenting from performance to performance. Raymond Smith has said this was what made it exciting to work with her as a partner: "She was almost always dancing in the moment."

She would ultimately dance all the great classical roles, but perhaps her finest portrayal other than Juliet was Giselle. Her innocence and hurt as she descended into madness had a haunting simplicity. "French romanticism, darling. You've mastered it," said Celia Franca, but it was more than the mastery of a specific style. Veronica's probing of her own inner pain gave her interpretation individuality and pathos. Veronica has spoken of the difference between such classical roles as Princess Aurora in *The Sleeping Beauty*, which demand technical perfection and charm but no real characterization, and Giselle, which calls for a dramatic interpretation that compels belief from the audience in the reality of the character's psychological journey. It was this emotional honesty that made Veronica's dancing unique.

In order to provide work for her dancers, Celia Franca took them on tour in these works throughout Canada and to some of the smaller American cities. By 1972 she decided they were ready for major international exposure. The National Ballet played at Covent Garden in London, as well as various European

393

394

Veronica with Rudolph Nureyev in The Sleeping Beauty

cities, to considerable critical acclaim. The next year Franca confessed, "I may have made a horrible mistake. I've sold the company." She had made a deal with the American impresario Sol Hurok to open a season at the Metropolitan Opera in New York and tour the major cities of the United States. The company would be led by the young Russian dancer

Rudolf Nureyev, who had recently defected to the West and had been seen in Europe but not North America. The leading attraction would be a lavish new production of *The Sleeping Beauty*, which Nureyev would choreograph.

Veronica remembers her first meeting with Nureyev. There was an immediate connection, which she described as "fire

Veronica rehearsing with Nureyev looking on

meeting fire." As prima ballerina of the company she would dance the lead opposite him at the premiere in Toronto, New York, and during the American tour. Hurok had wanted to bring in leading international ballerinas, but Franca insisted that it should be the National company with only Nureyev as the visiting star. Nureyev respected Veronica's technical virtuosity in a piece that was fiendishly difficult to perform, and he was also pleased with her diminutive stature, partly because he was not particularly tall. Veronica had come to realize that her compact, well-coordinated body was an asset. She had learned what she could do and to stop worrying about what she lacked. When Nureyev asked her to do something she felt she could not execute perfectly, she stood up to him and he enjoyed that. Dancing with the Russian virtuoso, she experienced a heightened elation: "Never again would this moment happen."

famous Russian dancer, Mikhail Baryshnikov, defected when the Bolshoi were playing in Toronto. Four days later, Veronica found herself in class with the handsome Russian and soon they were dancing together in Erik Bruhn's version of *La Sylphide*, which would be performed on stage and filmed for the CBC.

Celia Franca has said that her time at the National Ballet was "one long fight." When she decided to give up her title as artistic director, her position was filled first by the English dancer Alexander Grant and then by the Danish *danseur noble* Erik Bruhn. Bruhn was an enthusiastic supporter of Veronica, and she continued to be the company's prima ballerina, although many of her roles would now be shared with Karen Kain. The two would become friends; Veronica had no feelings of jealousy. When Veronica was injured and Karen took over one of her roles, Veronica went to Karen's dressing room and helped her fix her hair. Karen has always had enormous respect for Veronica's drive and energy. Discussing a dance project recently, Karen said to me, "If you can get Veronica involved, it will happen."

In 1976, Veronica's life suddenly changed. Dancing in *The Nutcracker* on tour with Nureyev, she heard an audible snap as her left knee buckled. She couldn't walk but husband John phoned and said, "As long as it isn't your ante-

In La Sylphide *with Mikhail Baryshnikov*

Her performance was greeted with enthusiasm in New York and other major cities. Finally she was receiving international exposure and acclaim. This led to offers to be a guest with several prominent companies, which she accepted, but she remained loyal to the National and to Toronto. Then in 1974 another

rior cruciate ligament ...." But of course that is what it was. She underwent radical surgery, and it took her four months to learn to walk again. Veronica didn't dance again for well over a year, but during her recovery period she wrote a children's book, *On Stage, Please*, utilizing her own experience as an aspiring dancer, including the pain, uncertainty, and tedium involved in acquiring a solid technique, as well as the joy of performance.

She also became a mother. Her daughter Jessica Robin Wright was born in October 1977. Veronica took to motherhood with the thoroughness that had characterized her passion for dance: "It made me realize that life is not all about me. I stopped taking myself so seriously. It freed me up to experience greater joy and especially greater humour." This carried over into her work when she returned to dancing. Although her injured knee never fully straightened, she danced with a newfound sense of lightness and exuberance.

Interviewed by Ramsay Cook on CBC television after the National's first American tour, she was asked what she felt the National Ballet's greatest challenge was. She replied that they needed to do more original work, work with more contemporary relevance. Celia had used her influence to obtain works by Roland Petit and Frederick Ashton, but

where was the choreographer who would be resident with the company and set new roles on its principal dancers? As it happened, he was already at the National Ballet School and would soon enter the company as a dancer. His name was James Kudelka.

Kudelka remembers that when he was fourteen and still at the school, Veronica came to see a short work that he had choreographed in a workshop with two other students, Lynda Strong and Robert Desrosiers. She was very encouraging, and when he joined the company four years later she asked him to choreograph a piece especially for her. "I was perhaps eighteen and she was the headliner.... She was easy to work with and liked trying things. ... When I did an ending she didn't think was good enough for what had come before, she took me to task and pushed me to redo it."

Kudelka went on to create *Apples* and *The Party* with Veronica. "She was not a technical ballet animal and demanded some kind of emotional throughline for her artistry to excel." Kudelka was encouraged by Alexander Grant to keep working on story ballets. Veronica's first performance after her injury was in *The Party*. In a *pas de deux*, Veronica danced with Kudelka for CBC television. He courted her, made love to her, and then abandoned her. *The Party* explored very modern emotions: attraction, desire,

397

rejection. It not only used contemporary body language; it was sexy.

Kudelka went on to make other ballets for Veronica, with emotional roles that exploited both her vulnerability and her strength of character, most notably *Washington Square*, based on Henry James's novel, and *Hedda*, in which she played Thea, the other woman. Other Canadian choreographers would also create new works for her: Constantin Patsalas's *Paranda Criolla, Liebestod*, and *Canciones*, Anne Ditchburn's *Mad Shadows*, and David Allen's *Etc!*, *Villanella, Capriccio, Masada*, and *Botticelli*

Pictures. Veronica had always been willing to be part of any experiment. I remember attending a rehearsal of David Earle's *Realm*, a group piece with no leading roles. Veronica was in it dancing along with members of the corps. She often danced with other companies, including Toronto Dance Theatre in which she performed in David Earle's signature work *Court of Miracles.*

Veronica was also keen to bring ballet to a wider audience. She pointed to the fact that when she danced at Ontario Place the spectators were the most enthusiastic she had ever experienced.

Veronica centre stage in David Earle's Realm

Her most celebrated roles in *Romeo and Juliet*, *The Sleeping Beauty*, and *La Sylphide* were televised and played to a wide audience as well as winning awards. This was an era when dance enjoyed great popularity, thanks in part to the Russian stars and the 1977 film *The Turning Point*. And the CBC was still interested in examining and profiling the arts, before the programmers decided their audiences weren't interested in "elitist culture."

Veronica would lead an active social life throughout her dancing career and long after. Her inquisitive mind and natural curiosity prompted her to investigate many areas that she did not have time to pursue when she was training for her profession. She knew that her time as a dancer would eventually come to an end. Margot Fonteyn continued to dance into her fifties, but most dancers would be through at the age of forty; their bodies simply could no longer do what they had once been able to. Increasingly Veronica experienced considerable physical pain, and her private life had become more turbulent. Kudelka believes that this contributed to a tendency for her to internalize her interpretations and made her less flexible in her approach to new work. "I remember seeing her at Artpark after a performance of *Washington Square* with her leg up on the dressing room counter, drinking brandy for the pain....

Veronica's farewell performance as Juliet

I thought, why should life hurt so much?"

Her decision to leave the National Ballet came in 1989. She wanted to stop when she was still at her peak and "go out in a blaze of glory." Her performance of Juliet on February 14 of that year would be her last. She gave a performance that was emotional, moving, and magical. She was assured and determined yet utterly convincing as a girl discovering herself and her feelings for the first time, even though she was forty-three years old. Her dramatic powers had grown since her first performance exactly twenty-five years before. Kudelka has spoken of her "intensity, her need for love ... poignancy, vulnerability, inner

399

400

With Michael Sean Marye in Stardust

strength, courage and resourcefulness.... She was wonderful, to the last second." She would continue to be devoted to the art of dance, but she would look for new ways to express it.

She did some teaching, but she wanted to explore other outlets and taught a number of master classes in which she emphasized dramatic expression rather than technique. She became active in a number of organizations, especially UNICEF, serving as Canada's ambassador for several years. She would also appear at the Shaw Festival, playing the leading role of Ivy Smith in the musical *On The Town*, act as assistant director to Derek Goldby in Tarragon Theatre's production of *The Cherry Orchard*, and appear with Sylvia Tyson and Joe Sealy in a 22-city tour of her longtime friend Timothy Findley's *The Piano Man's Daughter*. In 1999 she participated in a Banff Festival program, Women in the Director's Chair.

Veronica had begun to think about her future some time before she retired. She had always been a good communicator, and she was an intelligent interviewee. Why could she not ask the questions as well as answer them? Her television appearances had become more frequent, and her assurance in front of the camera had grown. Her early connection with Adrienne Clarkson may have influenced her, since Adrienne had become one of CBC's stars. But she had left television to take a diplomatic job in Paris and there was no one appearing on the network who had her cultural savvy.

As a teenager Veronica had known Michael Levine. They both lived in Forest Hill, but whereas Michael even as a teenager was an accomplished networker, Veronica was more isolated. Levine remembers she had few financial resources to fall back on; she had an English accent, which gradually disappeared, and a highly limited wardrobe. She was shy and serious and he remembers seeing her at a swimming pool and wondering why she had such calloused feet. Nevertheless he was intrigued by her dark intensity and the two remained in touch.

By the time Veronica retired, Michael had become the foremost entertainment lawyer in Toronto. He had guided or brokered the careers of Patrick Watson, Brian Linehan, and Adrienne Clarkson, acted for Mordecai Richler and Moses Znaimer, and had a stake in the foremost literary agency in Toronto headed by Bruce Westwood. He put together deals in film and publishing, often acting for several parties at once. And he was more than willing to help his old friend Veronica make the transition to a new career.

Veronica was no stranger to television. Her interview at sixteen identified her as a "young person who is going places." In 1966, when she was only nineteen, she

401

had starred in Norman Campbell's televised version of *Romeo and Juliet*, and the
following year in his film of *Cinderella*
for CBC. In 1976 she was filmed with
Frank Augustyn in the *pas de deux* from
Le Corsaire, and she had also been filmed
dancing with Roland Petit in his ballet
Le Loup. Before long she began to appear
as herself, reviewing the film *The Turning
Point* in 1977 and doing book reviews
soon after. She was interviewed for *The
Journal* when she danced *La Sylphide* at
Canada Place and *Napoli*, *Masada*, and
The Nutcracker, and with Toller Cranston
when she published a book of *The
Nutcracker* that he illustrated.

402

Then came her first gig as a television
host in 1983, introducing Norman
Campbell's film of Stratford's *The Taming
of the Shrew*, starring Len Cariou and
Sharry Flett. She would host a number
of TV specials from 1983 to 2003 for a
Variety Club special, the Toronto Arts
Awards, Sunday Arts Entertainment, and
the Canada Day Celebrations in Ottawa.
She would interview actors Peter
Ustinov and R.H. Thomson, dancers
Margie Gillis, Evelyn Hart, and Danny
Grossman, and introduce the work of
Canadian native and traditional Thai
dance companies. She would direct seg-
ments for *Adrienne Clarkson Presents* and
host the Governor General's Awards,
instituted by Ramon Hnatyshyn, at the
National Arts Centre in Ottawa. By 1996

A dancer's dancer

she had become interested in making her own films, first as a writer on the special *Dancers for Life*, which involved performances and interviews with many prominent members of the Canadian dance and theatre community, including Brent Carver, Robert Desrosiers, Édouard Lock, Margie Gillis, Rex Harrington, Evelyn Hart, Tomson Highway, Karen Kain, and Monique Trudelle.

The day after her retirement gala in 1999, she reported to CBC to work as host, creative consultant, and continuity writer for Sunday Arts Entertainment. She has said, "I loved exploring every aspect of Canada's vibrant artistic life. Our motto was 'art is any human endeavour that combines Imagination and skill.'" This was followed in 2000 by the first of several documentary biographies of dancers, *Margie Gillis: Wild Hearts in Strange Times*, which involved the participation of fiddler Ashley MacIsaac, actress Seana McKenna, and poet/songwriter Leonard Cohen. Throughout her career Veronica would consistently work with the most gifted people in Canadian entertainment. Astrid Janson has said that one of Veronica's most significant gifts is her ability to talk almost anyone into doing almost anything. She would go on to make two more vivid biographies of female dancers with whom she had been intimately involved: *Karen Kain: Dancing in the Moment* and *Celia Franca: Tour de Force*. These portraits are both an invaluable record of the most memorable dance artists of our time and a heartfelt tribute from one of their own. In these projects she was mentored by George Anthony and Joan Tosoni, who taught her much about television and film production.

Making these films, Veronica discovered she had a talent for finding vivid and compelling images and an intuitive feel for editing. Unlike Norman Campbell, she was not content to go for the big picture and then cut away for close-ups; instead she moved the camera in close to the dancers so that it could capture their subtle shifts of mood, the delicate nuances of their performances. She would choreograph for the camera, planning her shooting angles carefully, but experimenting on the spot, taking risks, following her instincts, exploring the possibilities of the moment. She would find cameramen willing to follow her ideas of how to shoot, dancers who were willing to cooperate with her improvisatory method, editors who shared in her vision. And she was fortunate enough to find two important collaborators: producer Peter Gentile and designer Astrid Janson.

Two early short films are thematically tied together by the colour red and original music by Ron Sexsmith. In one, a young woman wearing red shoes saunters along a downtown street past some musi-

403

*Celia Franca as Lady Capulet
in* Romeo and Juliet

404

Karen Kain and Frank Augustyn

cians. She picks up on their rhythm and starts to dance. They follow her along the street and eventually into a bus station, where she encounters an older woman in a red hat and a younger woman with a red purse. She eventually acquires both hat and purse and dances off with them. The other film involves three middle-aged women (Victoria Bertram, Nora McLellan, and Lorna Geddes) who have a crush on a handsome young singer (Rex Harrington). They decide to go the big city, where they discover that their hero is a waiter in a restaurant. Each has a moment of fantasy about the boy before they head

for home. Shot in real locations, the films are simple, light-hearted, upbeat, and whimsical.

These films were made on a small budget for broadcast by Bravo/FACT. Michael Levine brokered the deal through his connection with Moses Znaimer and arranged for financing in collaboration with his legal partner Eddie Goodman. Bravo would become a major sponsor and outlet for Veronica's films as the CBC moved away from arts coverage in its search for higher ratings. Veronica would lead the protest against this change of attitude and other cuts to the funding of the arts alongside such outspoken advocates as Margaret Atwood and Adrienne Clarkson.

Veronica Tennant

Though not a militant feminist, all her work has reflected her strong feelings about the place of women in the arts. All her biographical films are about women, and much of her choreography is set on them. In 2007 she devised dance interludes for the staging of Margaret Atwood's *The Penelopiad*. The cast was made up entirely of women who did everything from a sailors' hornpipe to a sexy mermaids' shimmy. Dance critic Paula Citron described her choreography as "kick-ass." It certainly was well matched to Atwood's knife-edged wit.

Veronica's first major film was the poetic fantasy *Northern Light: Vision and Dreams*. Dancer Robert Glumbek sets out on an imaginative quest across cultures and centuries to penetrate the mystery of the Northern Lights. This involves visual and musical elements juxtaposing Inuit throat singers with medieval plainchant, the music of twelfth-century composer Hildegard von Bingen with modern Canadian composer Christos Hatzis. The dancers include Margie Gillis moving against a background of brilliantly coloured stained glass, Sarah Laakkuluk Williamson performing an erotic Greenland masked dance, and Ronda Nychka, who leads Glumbek into the spirit world to meet the "ancient and not so old souls" who inhabit the Northern Lights. This bold merging of disparate

worlds and talents has truly evocative moments but doesn't quite come together as a unified whole. Filmed in Iqaluit and broadcast by CBC, it nevertheless established Veronica as an accomplished filmmaker with a distinctive vision.

There soon followed *Shadow Pleasures*, also broadcast by the CBC in 2004. It is based on sections of the prose and poetry of writer Michael Ondaatje, who reads passages from various works: *In the Skin of a Lion*, *Running in the Family*, *Anil's Ghost*, *The Nine Sentiments*, and *The Cinnamon Peeler*. The choreography is angular, jagged, and erotic without being explicitly sexual. The movement is strong, simple, and evocative, as Astrid Janson's design conjures up the sensual, tropical world of Ondaatje's native Sri Lanka. Rhythms that combine Hindu music of tabla and sitar with natural sounds of dripping water, ukulele riffs, cheering crowds, railway trains, and temple bells evoke the rich texture of an exotic Eastern world. The dancers enact a drama of male and female conflict: sexual intimacy, male to male confrontation, female solidarity. The choreography is fluid, the visual context abstract, imagistic.

By 2005, not only the CBC but also Bravo were cutting down on their cultural programming to the point of virtual elimination. Undeterred, Veronica proceeded to make films. Playwright Judith Thompson

405

developed a work, *Finding Body and Soul*, improvising with a group of middle-aged Canadian women telling their stories. Her sponsor Dove Soap wanted a film, and Veronica was brought in midway through the process. Thompson was impressed by Veronica's "fierce intelligence and instant ability to take charge. But her true genius is in editing a vast welter of material into a fluid narrative."

Shortly after working with Thompson, Veronica went to Cuba to catch the vivid dancing of Lizt Alfonso and her all-female dance company, who had performed an original creation *Vida!* at Toronto's Royal Alexandra Theatre as part of the initial Luminato Festival in 2006. As in *Northern Lights* with the Arctic and *Shadow Pleasures* with Sri Lanka, *Vida y Danza* brilliantly evokes the atmosphere of Cuba, its intense sunlight and deep shadow, its poverty, sensuality, and pulsing vitality. Financed in part by philanthropists Gretchen and Donald Ross, Veronica used some of her own money to complete the film.

In spite of financial pressures she continues to forge ahead. Her latest project, *NIÁGARA ~ A Pan-American Story*, was shown as part of the Pan Am Games in Toronto in the summer of 2015. Her head is still full of future projects. Peter Gentile reported that he often receives e-mails from her at one in the morning outlining some new idea. Backed up by her mother Doris, vigorous in her eighties, and in constant touch with her daughter Jessica, who is doing graduate work in New York, she has surrounded herself with a network of loyal friends and associates, many of whom have said, "Veronica is a truly good person." She still has abundant energy and a crackling imagination. She fully deserves the title bestowed on her in the biographical film of her life made by Peter Gentile for CBC: *Renaissance Woman*.

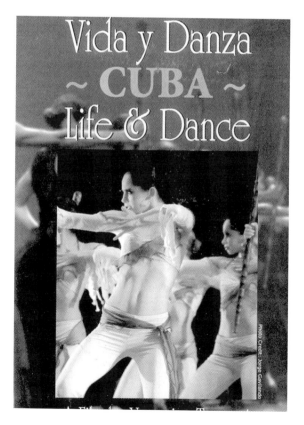

Veronica's Cuban dance film Vida y Danza

SEND IN
THE CLOWNS

Stephen Ouimette and Tom McCamus

Sometime in the early 1980s I held auditions for a piece I had written called *Power Play*. A young actor turned up to read who immediately came across as both comical and sexy. He looked about twenty. I had heard of Stephen Ouimette and even seen him onstage, but this was our first meeting. He read for the part of a young Brazilian hustler, and it was immediately obvious that he was perfect for the role. I asked him if he was willing to play this disreputable rascal and he replied, "Sure, I think he's a hoot." But that production never got off the ground and the play was not presented until several years later. By then he was no longer available.

At that time I was writing plays and documentaries for radio, and Stephen was working a lot in that medium. We sometimes ran across each other in the new CBC building on Front Street and we began to hang out together, meeting for coffee, and then going out to dinner or to a movie. He was excellent company, sharp and funny, hip to a lot of things besides theatre. I learned that he had grown up in the southwestern Ontario town of St. Thomas, one of six children of a postman. Like many working-class families, they made their own fun. Stephen recalled that one of the happiest days of his childhood involved tumbling down a mudslide with some other kids and returning home covered with mud. His mother just laughed as she scrubbed him in the tub.

408

Tom as Peter Pan fights Christopher Newton as Captain Hook
with Marti Maraden as Wendy and Herb Foster as Smee

Thirty years later,
Tom as Captain Hook with Brian Tree

Stephen had gone to the local high school where he was less than a brilliant student. By his own admission he began running around with a bunch of wild kids; they smoked, drank, and partied till all hours. He had a girlfriend who wanted to get married right away and have kids. But he had had a taste of performing in school plays, and he knew he wanted to try to be an actor. He broke up with his girl and headed off to theatre school at the University of Windsor.

In Windsor Stephen made friends with two other young guys, Robert Lachance and Tom McCamus, and a Greek-Canadian girl, Maria Vacratsis. These last two would remain friends for life and they would continue to act together whenever possible. Tom in particular shared with Stephen an irrepress-

ibly goofy sense of humour. Soon after graduation they were hired by William Hutt, who was then the artistic director of Theatre London, Tom's hometown when he was growing up. They enjoyed working for Hutt, who took a particular interest in giving opportunities to young players. In *Equus*, Stephen played Alan, the psychologically challenged youth who has blinded horses, while Hutt played the psychiatrist Dr. Martin Dysart. It was Stephen's first major professional role and revealed him as an actor both charismatic and complex.

Tom McCamus joined the Shaw company at Niagara-on-the-Lake, where he soon became a favourite of director Christopher Newton. He performed the title role in *Peter Pan*, traditionally played by a young woman, and gave a rousingly athletic performance, looping the loop high above the stage when he flew out into the night sky at the end of the first act. Two decades later he would play the villainous Captain Hook in the same play at Stratford with equal verve.

Stephen also spent a season at Shaw, but Newton apparently did not take to him, nor he to Newton. He soon decamped to Toronto, where he began to appear at the small alternative houses that had sprung up to enliven the theatre scene. An early success was the alienated and delinquent son of Jackie Burroughs in Judith Thompson's *White Biting Dog* at the Tarragon, which involved a scene in which he was totally naked. He has never shied away from this, although he can be very shy when off stage. Another early success was playing opposite Maria Vacratsis as the two young lovers in John Patrick Shanley's *Danny and the Deep Blue Sea*, for which he won a Dora award.

He rented a small apartment in Yorkville in the same building as Jackie Burroughs and screenwriter John Frizzell. They partied together. Stephen enjoyed good food and drink but lived simply, rid-

Stephen is the voice of Beetlejuice

ing a bicycle because he didn't drive. His theatre work did not pay high fees, but he started to make good money doing voice work, especially for animated films, most notably for Tim Burton's *Beetlejuice*. This led to voicing other children's films: *Babar*, *Care Bears*, *A.L.F.*, *Richard Scarry*, *Anne of Green Gables*, and *Alligator Pie*. At some point in the early 1980s he decided to take a year off and went to live in Vancouver, where he worked as a baker. He later commented, "I thought it would be a good thing to get away from the theatre and find out something about how ordinary people live."

Tom married actress Chick Reid, and they also moved to Toronto. He soon began taking small roles in TV series, including *Street Legal*, *Beyond Reality*, and *Friday's Curse*. Then he was cast as Henry Adler, an actor who gets to play a cop on a TV show. In the film the role takes over the man and he becomes more and more like the tough character he is playing. This film, *A Man in Uniform* (1993), written and directed by David Wellington for Rhombus Media, in which he moved from a sweet and rather nerdy character at the outset to a brash and violent tough guy, quickly became a hit and established Tom as a formidable movie actor. Before long he would go on to play leading roles for Atom Egoyan in *The Sweet Hereafter* (1997) and Robert Lepage in *Possible Worlds* (2000).

Tom in I Love a Man in Uniform

Tom did not abandon the stage, however, appearing as Hamlet in Neil Munro's eccentric deconstruction of the play at Canadian Stage, which featured Tom giving one of his soliloquies buck naked. He took on the leading figure in Morris

Panych's 7 *Stories* at the Tarragon, for which Stephen shaved his head and donned a series of wigs to portray three comic cameos. He described his performance at the time as "hair acting."

Stephen had already outshone his friend and fellow actor Tom Wood in *B Movie: the Play*, which convulsed audiences in the old Toronto Workshop Productions space on Alexander Street. Stephen played a waiter who did a hilarious turn thanking a diner for a five-dollar tip, smelling it, tasting it, and finally wiping his ass with it. It played to sold-out houses and went to the Edinburgh Festival, where it did not get quite such a favourable reception. This was Stephen's first trip to Britain, and he enjoyed sight-seeing and picked up a few English expressions, but he would not return for two decades and has never been much of a traveller.

Stephen was invited by Robin Phillips to join the Stratford company, along with his friend Robert Lachance. They played small roles, although they both made an impression in Pam Brighton's production of *Henry VI*. Stephen was slated to play Hamlet the next year, but Phillips's regime collapsed and Stratford was taken over by John Hirsch, who promptly vetoed that plan. Stephen returned to Toronto and rented an apartment in the Annex. He gave a brilliantly funny performance as Erwin Trowbridge in a

411

Stephen and Tom in Seven Stories *with Tanya Jacobs*

412

revival of the 1930s comedy *Three Men on a Horse* at the Royal Alexandra. He played a richly comic Sir Wilfred Laurier in one of Michael Hollingsworth's historical series *The Village of Small Huts*. More serious roles were in translations of Michel Tremblay's *Bonjour, là, Bonjour* and Jeanne-Mance Delisle's *A Live Bird in Its Jaws*, which he played opposite his good friend Tanya Jacobs. It would often be assumed because of his surname that Stephen was Québécois. He did nothing to discourage this idea, but in fact his

paternal grandfather had come directly from France to settle in Ontario, and his family spoke no French.

In the 1980s and 1990s, Stephen appeared in several TV series and also played the lead in a thriller, *The Top of His Head* (1989) for Rhombus Media and a smaller role in *The Adjuster* (1991) for Atom Egoyan, neither of which was particularly successful, but the TV movie *Conspiracy of Silence* (1991), in which he played Steve Frishbilski, a cop who tracks down the killer of a native girl in a

northern Ontario town, showed evidence of an increasingly strong presence as a film actor.

When Richard Monette began to direct at Stratford, he persuaded both Ouimette and McCamus to join his company. In his first season as artistic director he offered Ouimette the role of Hamlet, to compensate for the opportunity that had been promised him a decade earlier. In a low-key production Ouimette proved an intelligent, troubled, introspective prince, supported by a sym-

413

Stephen and Tom with Yorick's skull

pathetic McCamus as Horatio. It was the first time the two had worked together for some time. In the same season, Ouimette played a foolish Sir Andrew Aguecheek, a role he would revisit several times in the years ahead. In that season McCamus was a vulnerable, tough-minded young Edmund Tyrone in Diana Leblanc's brilliantly realized evocation of Eugene O'Neill's *Long Day's Journey into Night*, which featured William Hutt and Martha Henry as the parents and Peter Donaldson as the older brother Jamie. The production

Stephen as Hamlet

was remounted in the next season and then made into an acclaimed film directed by David Wellington.

During the fourteen years of his tenure, Monette found good roles for both actors. He was careful to include Chick Reid in these seasons, playing a variety of smaller parts to which she brought a strong sense of humour and a distinctive personal style. Ouimette would play most of Shakespeare's clowns. One of his finest creations was Touchstone in *As You Like It*, in which he first appeared as a foppish courtier with dyed blonde hair; after several months in the forest of Arden, the dark roots began to show ever more obviously. ("Hair acting" indeed.) His intricate routine when

414

Stephen as Sir Andrew Aguecheek in Twelfth Night *with his dog Taxi*

Stephen as Touchstone in As You Like It *with Sara Topham as Rosalind*

he dismisses the youth William, who is his rival for the country wench, Audrey was worthy of Harpo Marx (he referred to it as "forty ways to kill your rival.") It echoed the similarly inventive piece of shtick he had earlier devised that had brought the house down in *B Movie*.

But for sustained comic invention Ouimette and McCamus outdid themselves as the two tramps Vladimir and Estragon in *Waiting for Godot*, which they played at the Tom Patterson Theatre in 1996. Their performances were rooted in

Stephen Ouimette and Tom McCamus

415

Vladimir and Estragon in Waiting for Godot

416

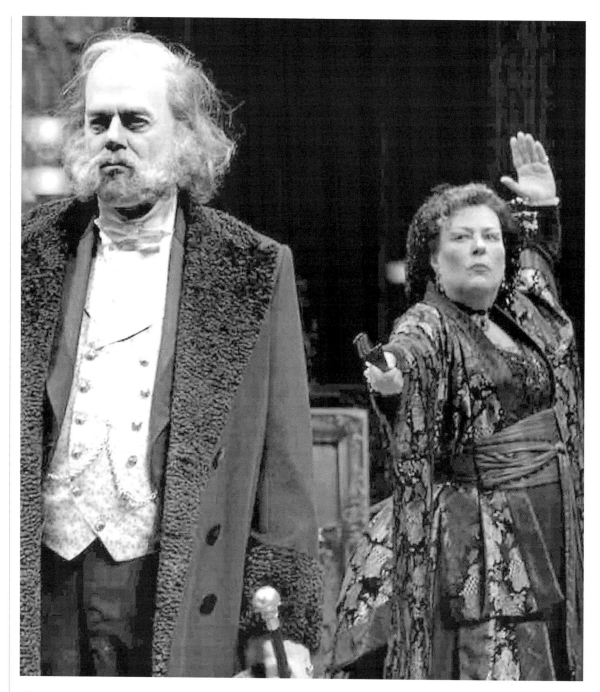

Tom as Horace Vandergelder in The Matchmaker *with Nora McLellan*

Tom as Vershinin in The Three Sisters

the pervasive and freewheeling sense of fun they shared and referenced the world of the English music hall, which Samuel Beckett had cited as an influence. Their interlocking characters were in sharp contrast: McCamus's Vladimir was provocative and challenging, while Ouimette's Estragon alternated between self-pity and a sudden acerbity as he hit out with a quick, stinging retort.

*Stephen as Mozart
with Brian Bedford as Salieri*

*Stephen as the slave Hysterium with Bruce Dow in
A Funny Thing Happened on the Way to the Forum*

418

During Monette's tenure and the years that followed under Des McAnuff and Antoni Cimolino, McCamus and Ouimette would become major players and two of the most versatile members of the company. McCamus would take on a number of roles that emphasized his romantic appeal. His slightly offbeat good looks, inherent sensuality, and laid-back charm made him an effective partner for Seana McKenna as the scheming aristocratic libertine Valmont in *Liaisons dangéreuses*, the seducer Iachimo in

Cymbeline, and the lovelorn but predatory Colonel Vershinin who wins the heart of Lucy Peacock's Masha in *The Three Sisters*. His first entrance as he looks around at the three women to see which of them might be available sets the tone for his performance. He is the only actor I have seen who avoided turning Vershinin into a bore, and the seduction scene in which he and Peacock demonstrate their passion by merely removing their shoes was masterly. In contrast, McCamus was a pompously bewhiskered

Horace Vandergelder succumbing to the charms of the scheming Dolly Levi of Seana McKenna in Wilder's *The Matchmaker*, straightforward and affecting as a bewildered King Arthur opposite Cynthia Dale in *Camelot*, which proved he could put a song across, as he would do again singing an edgy version of "Mack the Knife" as the philandering libertine Macheath in *The Threepenny Opera*.

Ouimette would play a silly and scatological Mozart in *Amadeus*, a rattled Dr. Molineux in Feydeau's farce *A Fitting Confusion*, a cynical Lucio in *Measure for Measure*, and also two of Shakespeare's royal tyrants, Richard III and King John. But his most memorable stab at Shakespearean tragedy was the production he directed of *Timon of Athens*, eliciting perhaps Peter Donaldson's finest performance as the embittered millionaire who loses everything. McCamus played the cynic Apemantus with a light touch, and the early scenes featured rock music. Ouimette has followed popular music since his teenage years, and it has been an important factor in his acute understanding of contemporary culture.

After seeing *Timon*, Monette remarked, "Finally we have an actor who can direct Shakespearean tragedy." The next year he offered Ouimette a chance to direct *The Threepenny Opera*, with somewhat less successful results. The production brought out the darkness of the Brecht/Weill collaboration, but the characters somehow lacked the dimension they achieved in some other productions I had seen. Ouimette then undertook to direct *Much Ado About Nothing* on the main stage. Suffering from stress, he abandoned this project early in rehearsal and retired to his country house for an extended period of complete seclusion.

Once settled in Stratford, Stephen had learned to drive and settled on a property with his two small dogs, one of whom sometimes made an appearance with him on stage. He realized that he would not likely find a suitable partner and settled for a very private and mostly solitary life. At about the same time, Tom and Chick Reid acquired a country property near Warkworth north of Port Hope, where they bred retrievers and spent their time between seasons, although Tom continued to do film and TV on a regular basis, most notably in the science-fiction series *Mutant X*, in which he played a leading character, the evil Mason Eckhardt, sometimes wearing an improbable blond wig.

Although he had not played major roles for him at Stratford, Ouimette had connected with Robin Phillips during his early years with the Festival, and the two continued to have an ongoing relationship. Phillips introduced Ouimette to the role of the foppish seventeenth-century would-be actor Valere in David Hirson's

419

La Bête. He played it in Edmonton and would later join the British company of Mark Rylance that presented the piece in London and then New York. He also appeared as the hard-drinking Harry Hope in Eugene O'Neill's *The Iceman Cometh* at the Goodman Theatre in Chicago. Soon after, Phillips would direct Ouimette in Doug Wright's *I Am My Own Wife* at CanStage in Toronto, a one-man show about the transgendered German antiquarian Charlotte von Mahlsdorf, who killed her father as a teenager and went on to survive the Nazi and Communist regimes in Berlin.

In 2003, Rhombus media produced *Slings and Arrows*, a TV series about a theatre company quite transparently based on Stratford. It had an intelligent, literate, and witty script, largely the invention of producer Tecca Crosby, actress Susan Coyne, and Kids in the Hall comedian Mark McKinney. The show was so successful it ran for three seasons, each one centring on the production of a major Shakespeare play: *Hamlet, Macbeth,* and finally *King Lear.* It would involve the cream of the Canadian acting community: Martha Burns, Susan Coyne, Colm Feore, Paul Gross, William Hutt, Rachel McAdams, Mark McKinney, Don McKellar, and Geraint Wyn Davies, with a host of other actors, well-known or more marginal, in supporting roles.

Ouimette appears as Oliver Welles, the aging artistic director of the theatre who at the end of the first episode, crossing the street in a drunken stupor, is run down by a truck carrying a load of cured ham. He subsequently appears in every episode as a ghost, often manipulating the cast through a series of threatening or farcical situations. It was widely thought at the time that Stephen had based his character on Richard Monette, and certainly there were unmistakable similarities, though there may have also

Tom as Mason Eckhart in Mutant X

Stephen as Oliver Welles in
Slings and Arrows *with Paul Gross*

been some sly references to the personality of Robin Phillips. I thought the series hilarious and urged both Monette and Phillips to see it, but they resolutely refused. Though both had a sense of humour, it apparently did not extend to seeing either themselves or their beloved Festival lampooned.

The series was hugely successful, not only in Canada but later when it was widely shown in the United States. It no doubt had the effect of providing the Stratford Festival with free publicity and catapulted Rachel McAdams toward Hollywood stardom, but it also preserved for posterity two remarkable performances: Paul Gross as Hamlet and the aging William Hutt as King Lear, shortly before his death. And it provided Ouimette with his best film role to date.

McCamus appeared briefly in one episode in *Slings and Arrows*. He continued to make films, including *Waking up*

Stephen as Harry Hope
in The Iceman Cometh *in Chicago*

Wally (2005), about the father of hockey great Wayne Gretzky, and a number of films in which he would play with international stars: Samuel L. Jackson, Lindsay Lohan, and Tilda Swinton. Unlike his contemporary Colm Feore, most of this film work was in Canada, where he appeared with many of his compatriots: Martha Burns, Roy Dupuis,

Megan Follows, Martha Henry, Stuart Hughes, and Waneta Storms.

Now both around the age of sixty, Ouimette and McCamus are firmly ensconced as headliners at Stratford. Stephen played the Fool to Colm Feore's Lear, wry, pathetic in his loyalty, and disappointed at the effect of his unheeded jibes. He also tackled the greatest of Shakespeare's clowns, Bottom the Weaver, in Chris Abraham's pop-inspired, updated production of *A Midsummer Night's Dream*. His performance was, as might have been predicted, hilarious, but also notable for its warmth and sense of wonder. Tom did a turn as a bluff March Hare in *Alice Through the Looking-Glass*, and a forthright and plain-spoken Enobarbus in *Antony and Cleopatra*, but it was his performance as King John as a slippery, unpredictable knave in a surprisingly amusing interpretation that contrasted effectively with the more emotional characters in the piece. In 2015, Tom has taken a year off from the Festival to appear in the TV series *Orphan Black*, while Stephen is appearing in only one show, *The Alchemist*, as the outrageously conniving and utterly fraudulent Subtle. However both actors are at the height of their comical powers, and their many fans will be anxious to see what they take on next.

422

Tom's King John, Stephen's Bottom at Stratford

LADY CHAMELEON

Seana McKenna

When Richard Monette asked me to direct *Yeats in Love* for the CBC/Stratford radio series, he informed me that the actors who had played in the stage version, Donald Carrier and Anaya Farrell, were not available. He asked me who I wanted. I immediately thought of Seana McKenna to play Maude Gonne, the Irish beauty and revolutionary who was the love of Yeats's young life, and opted for Rod Beattie to play the young poet. I did not know McKenna personally but had seen her onstage a number of times, most memorably as Saint Joan in Shaw's play, and I thought she would be a perfect fit for Maude: intense, passionate, and highly articulate. She delivered all these qualities in spades.

She was already a celebrated actress, and I was a bit intimidated, especially when she arrived early for rehearsal with a sheaf of questions. As Anne Tait, the author of the play, and I had worked on the show over several months, we were able to provide answers to most of her queries. And I had a strategy. I had worked with Rod on a number of occasions and felt I had his confidence. I therefore gave him one or two directions to which he responded favourably. Catching sight of Seana out of the corner of my eye, I could see her relax as she listened. I hoped that she was thinking to herself, I guess this guy knows what he's doing. When I gave her a suggestion, she accepted and absorbed it. I didn't give either of these actors many instructions, which was probably just as well. Miles Potter, Seana's husband, who has directed her in many shows, confirmed that she is not difficult, but she can detect and deflate pretence in a moment.

Seana McKenna grew up in Etobicoke and Port Credit, the daughter of an Irish entrepreneur who came to Canada from Dublin in 1930 and a woman of Polish extraction who was an accomplished singer. She went to a Roman Catholic school, where at the age of eight she played her first part. "Brian Bedford and I started out playing the same role: the Virgin Mary," she announces with a twinkle in her eye. "No wonder we are compatible; we have the same background experience." At an early age she came under the influence of an actress, Ellie Walsh, who directed her in a number of children's plays such as *Pandora* and *Ali Baba* and something called *Tomm, the Time Traveler.*

She was often cast in "britches" parts, playing a boy. In high school she met other would-be actors like Steve Yorke and Jeremy Rank. They were directed by Brigit Haines in more adult plays: Seana was cast as the octogenarian Rebecca Nurse in *The Crucible*, as well as various roles in everything from *The Trojan Women* to the Feydeau farce *Hotel Paradiso*. She did workshops with Dorothy-Jane Needles and was in a Youtheatre company run by Ron Hartmann, before winning a scholarship to study English literature at Trinity

An early "britches" role Viola in Twelfth Night

College, where she played Cosimo de Medici in Brecht's *Galileo*. Obviously, even at an early age she had a considerable range.

Seana was offered a scholarship for her second year at Trinity, but she was also accepted by the National Theatre School. She decided to go to the NTS, thinking she would return to finish her

424

college degree, but she never did. In Montreal she fell under the influence of Douglas Rain, a stern taskmaster who gave her a thorough training in the analysis of text. She responded to the rigour and discipline that Rain imposed on his students; he recognized her intelligence and commitment.

She played various classical roles, notably Isabella in Thomas Middleton's Jacobean tragedy *Women Beware Women*. She remembers preparing an audition for John Hirsch with a speech by Queen Margaret in *Henry VI*. He handed her a wooden coat hanger and commanded her to beat the back of a chair with it as she spoke the lines. When she had worked up such a head of steam that the coat hanger splintered into a dozen shards, Hirsch told her, "Now, that's where you start." She received an offer to join Robin Phillips's company at Stratford after her second year, but she opted to stay and finish her training.

Soon after graduating she was working at the Blyth Festival. Miles Potter was directing a play there called *Saint Sam* by Ted Johns, and two weeks into rehearsal he lost his leading lady. Janet Amos, the artistic director, suggested a girl who was a very quick study, and Seana joined the cast. Miles and Seana were billeted in separate farmhouses. They visited back and forth and before long they were dating. Soon afterwards they married and formed what would not only be a love match but an ongoing professional partnership. They felt they needed a home base and bought an old farmhouse in the village of Harrington, a few miles west of Stratford. Miles explains that it was not a huge investment but it gave them a sense of security. Over time they would add to it and turn it into a very comfortable and livable residence.

In the late 1970s Seana caught the attention of Neil Munro, the innovative director who worked mainly at the Shaw Festival at Niagara-on the-Lake, where he usually directed one or more plays a season. At the Shaw, Seana played Eliza Doolittle, the sharp-tongued Cockney flower girl in *Pygmalion*, and the assured and sympathetic Candida, who must choose between the upright clergyman who is her husband and an impetuous young poet who has fallen in love with her. Seana brought her edgy intelligence to both roles. During her time at the Shaw she received an offer from Stratford, initially to play Desdemona, but when the offer was changed to Emilia, she turned it down, believing that there would be opportunities in the future for her to tackle this more mature role.

Once John Hirsch took over as artistic director at the Festival, perhaps remembering her prowess with the coat hanger, he invited Seana to join the Stratford Company. She would play major youth-

Cordelia and Juliet at Stratford

426

ful roles in the next four years: a spirited Helena in *A Midsummer Night's Dream*, a slyly seductive Diana in *All's Well That Ends Well*, a passionate Juliet opposite Colm Feore, an impetuous Jessica in *The Merchant of Venice*, a quick-witted and vulnerable Viola in *Twelfth Night*, an honest, outspoken Cordelia in *King Lear*, as well as a smart and saucy Kate Hardcastle in *She Stoops to Conquer*. Her directors would include Peter Dews, David Giles, Mark Lamos, and David William, as well as Hirsch himself, and her acting companions were Benedict Campbell, Douglas Campbell, Patricia Collins, Colm Feore, Mary Haney, Richard MacMillan, Richard Monette, John Neville, Nicholas Pennell, and Joseph Ziegler, among many others. If Malcolm Gladwell is right in stating that the road to excellence in any field is a long and concentrated hands-on experience, then this opportunity of playing major roles in great plays alongside some of the finest actors in the country made a major contribution toward Seana becom-

ing one of the most accomplished theatre artists in the land.

Judith Thompson, who was a classmate of Seana's at the NTS, says that Seana could command space on stage even in those early days. This innate quality, which causes the audience to focus on a performer, used to be called "star power" and is easily recognized. It can't be taught or learned. As Mama Rose sings in *Gypsy*, "Either you've got it, or you've had it." There are many good actors who don't have it, but it is what allows an actor like Seana to dominate a scene. Miles Potter says he has often warned actors working with Seana to brace themselves for her first live performance. In rehearsal she can be tentative, trying things out, testing her options, deliberating on her choices. But in performance she can be so powerful that she blows both her audience and her fellow actors away, sometimes with the strength of her passion, sometimes with the dead-on perfection of her comic timing.

Michael Shamata, whom she met when she was an apprentice and he a young stage manager at Stratford, would go on to direct her in a number of shows. He emphasized that she always brings an arsenal of ideas into rehearsal but is very collaborative, using the time to get to a place where neither the director nor the other actors would have reached on their own. She is serious and loves to explore, but at the same time she is fun to work with. "We always laugh a lot."

Many actors, particularly in large companies like Shaw and Stratford, more or less stop going to watch theatre. Seana, in contrast, is an avid theatregoer. "She sees everything and stores up all the tricks, all the innovations, all the nuances, so she can call on them if she needs to," says Tom McCamus, who in recent years has frequently played opposite her. When I met for a drink with her after a matinee, she insisted I should go with her to see a performance of three short Brian Friel plays in an abandoned warehouse, so she could check out the work of a young actor, Tyrone Savage. She loved his energy but was not uncritical of some of the other actors.

In spite of her obvious ability, Seana's work did not appeal to John Neville. She took a break from Stratford during his years as artistic director and worked in various theatres across the country. She and Miles had developed a particularly warm relationship with Steven Schipper at Manitoba Theatre Centre in Winnipeg, where she would play a definitive Blanche DuBois in *A Streetcar Named Desire*, perfectly capturing both the desperation and fragility of Tennessee Williams's doomed heroine. She also infused her portrayal with comedy, as she would later do in her portray-

427

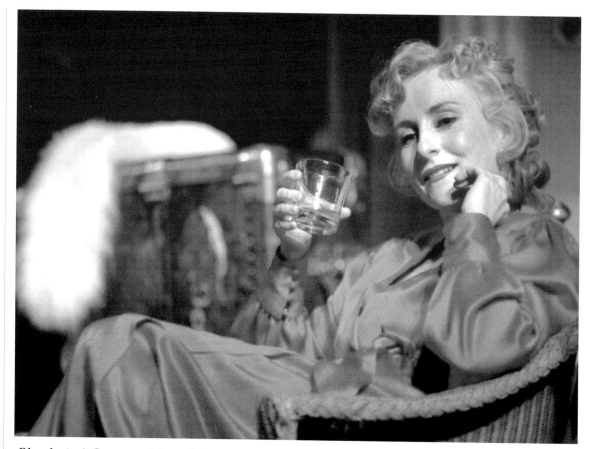

Blanche in A Streetcar Named Desire *in Winnipeg*

al of Amanda in *The Glass Menagerie* when she returned to Stratford. She has sometimes been criticized for "playing Williams for laughs," but Miles believes her instincts are impeccable. Williams himself saw much of his work as having comic reverberations and frequently laughed during performances, to the irritation of the management and often the audience. Seana has played all the major Williams heroines: Stella, also in *Streetcar*,

Maggie in *Cat on a Hot Tin Roof*, Hannah Jelkes in *Night of the Iguana*, and Lady Torrance in *Orpheus Descending*, which won her a third Dora award.

Her first Dora was for *Saint Joan*, directed by Richard Monette at Theatre Plus in Toronto. Seana and Richard connected first when she went to see him in *Hosanna* at the Tarragon. Their collaboration on the Shaw play was a turning point in both their careers, giving Seana her

first major exposure in Toronto and Richard his first success directing a large-scale production. (He also won a Dora.)

Seana had returned to the Stratford company by the time Richard became artistic director, and he would regard her as one of his leading ladies throughout the fourteen years of his reign. "She isn't beautiful; her nose is too big and her neck too short but she is the most versatile actress in Canada," I recall him commenting. Every year he would build his season around the five major players in his company: Brian Bedford, Martha Henry, William Hutt, Lucy Peacock, and Seana.

During her years away from Stratford, Seana had worked continuously, playing everything from Cleopatra at the Centaur in Montreal to Iris, the estranged mother in the maritime-Gothic film *The Hanging Garden* (1997), for which she won a Gemini. She has occasionally played cameo roles in other films, such as *Glory Enough for All* (1988) and *Save the Last Dance* (2001), and in series including *Road to Avonlea*, *Street Legal*, *Flashpoint*, and *Rookie Blue*, but she prefers live theatre. Perhaps for this reason she doesn't even have an agent.

For two summers during this period Seana and her friend Goldie Semple led a small troupe of actors in readings and songs at the Art Gallery in Stratford. As a teenager she had done some public speaking, and this was a natural exten-

Antony and Cleopatra at the Centaur *with Scott Wentworth*

429

sion of that experience. During one of these summers both women produced children. Seana's son Callan would spend a happy childhood in Harrington, mentored by one of his parents if the other one was away working, or by his devoted nanny, Martha Henry's daughter Emma.

Seana returned to the Stratford company under the aegis of David William, playing Portia in *The Merchant of Venice* (yet another "britches" role, but not her last), directed by Michael Langham and with Brian Bedford playing Shylock. Seana and Brian easily formed a strong rapport. They would work together frequently in the years to come: in a rather

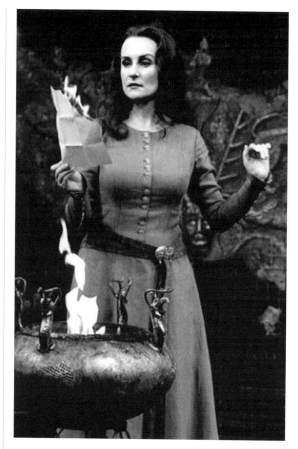

Lady Macbeth

Private Lives and *Present Laughter* and the nineteenth-century romp *London Assurance*, in which Seana's galloping interpretation of the horsey aristocrat Lady Gay Spanker stole the show, despite Bedford's hilarious impersonation of an aging but still amorous fop.

As artistic director at the Festival, Monette recognized that Seana and Miles formed a potent team. Their productions usually involved Peter Hartwell as designer and Marc Desmarais providing music. They led ill-fated *Macbeth* (in a season redeemed for Seana by her wickedly randy performance as Lady Fidget in *The Country Wife)*, and much more happily in *Tartuffe*, in which Seana played the pert and knowing maid Dorine, who sees through the hypocrisy of the conniving religious fanatic of the title, portrayed with comic duplicity by Bedford. These two would become master interpreters of a series of comedies, including Noël Coward's

Katherine of Aragon

Seana McKenna

off with a Wild West production of *The Taming of the Shrew*, with Seana offering a rowdy, temperamental Katherina. Seana's comic turns in *Fallen Angels* and *Noises Off* alternated with vivid performances in more serious roles: an angry and ultimately malevolent Margaret in *Henry VI*, a dignified and wounded Katherine of Aragon in *Henry VIII*, a defeated Andromache pleading for the life of her son in *The Trojan Women*, and her triumphant portrayal of the betrayed Medea, bent on inhumanly destructive revenge.

As has often been the case, it was Miles who first had the idea of Seana playing Medea. He proposed the idea to Steven Schipper in Winnipeg that Seana might play Medea and Hedda Gabbler in repertoire: an exploration of two angry women, one modern, one ancient, who act out their rage and frustration, the one by ultimately shooting herself, the other by taking a bloody revenge on her enemies.

Seana's Hedda was proud but inhibited by the society she lived in. Her Medea was towering, magnificent in her passionate determination to get back at the man who had wronged her. Her bitter humour, her vacillation between her love for her children and her consuming hatred of the man who had betrayed her, was gripping for the audience as they watched her battle with herself until she finally commits the horrific act of killing

431

A vengeful Medea

her children. Seana's love of language prompted her great respect for the spare but lyrical translation of the text by Robinson Jeffers, which added some nuances not found in the original Greek. The force of her delivery and the intensity of her passion took Seana into a new realm of emotional truth and ferocity. This would become one of her signature roles. She would play it three times over a sixteen-year period in Winnipeg, at Stratford, and in Toronto.

Asked if she digs down into herself to find the feelings she is portraying or actually becomes the character on stage, she responds by saying it is a mixture of both so-called "methods." While she identifies with the character and follows her journey into darkness, she is also aware that she is taking the audience with her on that journey. This, for her, is part of the joy of working in the live theatre, knowing that spectators are absorbed in what she is doing onstage. She is not concerned with whether the members of the audience like her, but rather that they should understand her and experience what she is thinking and feeling, whether she is playing in a frivolous comedy or a disturbing drama involving ethical decisions and desperate actions.

In the words of Judith Thompson, Seana has always been a "girl's girl." She has said, "I guess that means I wore heels and make-up. But being Angelina Jolie or Jennifer Aniston is not my dream." As the scheming Marquise de Merteuil in *Dangerous Liaisons* who challenges her former lover to seduce a young wife for her amusement, she was utterly unsympathetic. As Dolly Levi in *The Matchmaker* she had both charm and smarts but again she was playing a manipulative woman who couldn't resist interfering in other people's lives, sometimes for their own good but always to further her own interests.

Not surprisingly, Seana has inspired young playwrights to write vehicles for her, two of which have been presented at Stratford. In *Good Mother* by Damien Atkins, she played a middle-aged woman who had suffered a stroke. Although she could not speak comprehensibly, except in brief flashback scenes before she became impaired, she held the stage as she struggled to be understood by the members of her family. In *Shakespeare's Will* by Vern Thiessen, she took on the role of Anne Hathaway, reviewing her life with and without the master dramatist over the years, only to discover at the end that he has left her nothing when he dies but his "second-best bed." Alone on stage for a whole evening Seana galloped through a range of emotions, from romantic attraction to grief at the loss of her son, to final anger and then acceptance.

432

Two scheming women:
The Marquise de Merteil; in Dangerous Liaisons *Dolly Levi in* The Matchmaker

Seana has also taken on two other one-woman shows. The first was *The Search for Signs of Intelligent Life in the Universe*, which Jane Wagner originally wrote for Lily Tomlin, a text that involves a range of extreme characters, from a bag lady to an extraterrestrial. The show requires split-second comic timing and the ability to change rapidly from one character to another. Soon afterwards, Seana took on *The Year of Magical Thinking*, which she played at the Tarragon Theatre directed by Michael Shamata, an account of the battle experienced by Joan Didion in her efforts to cope with the grief she felt when she lost both her husband and her daughter in the course of a year. Shamata remembers her performance as being

Good Mother *by Damien Atkins*

"extremely moving because it was open, honest and at the same time very simple."

Seana is also in demand by a variety of regional theatres across the country to play contemporary characters in plays that have been recent successes on Broadway, notably *Wit* by Margaret Edison, in which she played an English professor stricken by cancer, and *Doubt*

by John Patrick Shanley, in which she played a straight-laced nun who suspects a local priest of having had sexual relations with a young altar boy. Though neither play is a one-hander, they call for an actor who can dominate the stage. Seana attributes her success in these roles in part to the fact that as a young woman she knew many strong-minded women who were role models for her, women who were not afraid to speak their minds. And neither is she. In conversation she is direct and opinionated and ever ready to puncture pomposity or insincerity. Once when rehearsing with Brian Bedford, he said to her plaintively, "I'm not sure where I'm supposed to be," to which she quickly retorted, "How about downstage centre, Brian. You know where it is."

At Miles's suggestion, in 2012 Seana played Richard III. This early Shakespeare play contains perhaps the first great role the master dramatist created. It is an actor's dream, but although it has been programmed half a dozen times at Stratford, including the initial production directed by Tyrone Guthrie starring Alec Guinness, few have managed to bring it off completely convincingly. Perhaps the most successful interpretation of the villainous monarch was offered by Brian Bedford in Robin Phillips's production of 1977. Undaunted, Seana donned a balding wig

434

and hump on her back and adopted a halting limp. Her Richard was mean, conniving, ruthlessly ambitious, totally without moral scruple, the embodiment of evil. She attacked the part with reptilian glee. The audience soon forgot it was a woman playing a man. They followed her progress to the throne, enjoying her sharing with them her outrageous plans for advancement. Her performance was hailed in the reviews, though like many actors she claims she never reads them.

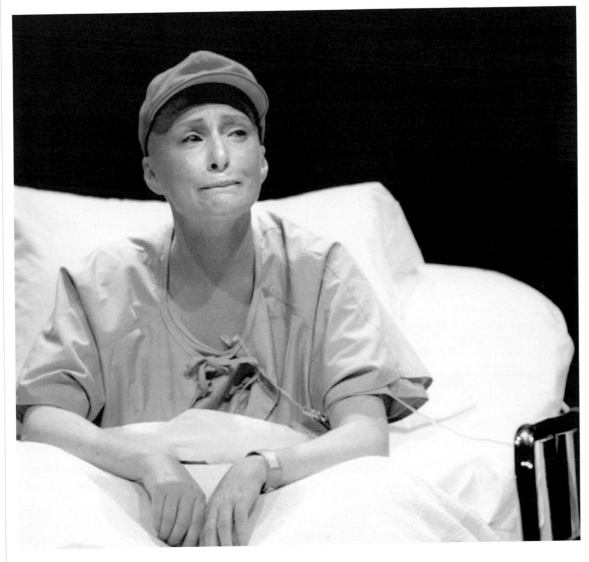

Wit by Margaret Edson in Vancouver

Richard III plotting for the crown

Asked what other male roles she was interested in playing she hesitated, but only for a moment. She has already

436

turned down an offer to play Hamlet, a role undertaken by several actresses in the past, starting with Sarah Bernhardt. She did not warm to the idea of King Lear but toyed with the notion of Timon of Athens and thought it might be fun to play Prospero, though probably as a woman. Seana has no compunction about turning down projects she thinks she is unsuited for. At this stage in her career she can afford to be choosy. But there are many roles that interest her: Martha in *Who's Afraid of Virginia Woolf?*, Mary Tyrone in *Long Day's Journey Into Night*, the Princess in *Sweet Bird of Youth*, and possibly another Cleopatra—all fairly heavy dramatic roles.

There is also a wealth of comic roles she could tackle: Judith Bliss in *Hay Fever*, Lady Wishfort in Congreve's *The Way of the World*, Mrs. Malaprop in Sheridan's *The Rivals*, and she might reclaim the role of Lady Bracknell from the male actors who have played her recently at Stratford. And then there are the great roles for mature women in the European repertoire: Claire Zachanassian in Dürrenmatt's *The Visit*, The Countess in Giradoux's *The Madwoman of Chaillot*, Mme. Desmortes in Fry's *Ring Round the Moon*, and Mme. Alexandra in Anouilh's *Colombe*. It is often said that it is hard for women actors after the age of forty, but Seana is able to look ahead with confidence and

Seana McKenna

Elizabeth I *with Lucy Peacock as Mary Stuart and Geraint Wyn Davies*

anticipation. In the 2014 season she took on Mother Courage, dominating the space at the Tom Patterson Theatre in rubber boots and a second-hand military jacket, covering her emotions with an assumed bravado, and singing Brecht's cynical lyrics with acerbic relish. In contrast, her Constance of Brittany in *King John* revealed passionate fury and a descent into a restrained and touching madness.

Although she prefers to act, Seana is interested in the prospect of directing. Her one foray into the area, a production of *Valley Song* at the New Globe, won her a Jessie. She is a committed teacher, having taught classes at the National Theatre School and the Birmingham Conservatory at Stratford, Equity Showcase, and the now defunct Maggie Bassett Studio at Tarragon. She is respected as a mentor of younger actors, never brushing them aside but taking the time to discuss process with them. She is noted for her generosity both to the other actors in productions and to the aspiring young performers who approach her seeking advice.

437

She has established good relationships with a number of theatres across the country, notably the Belfry in Victoria, the Manitoba Theatre Centre, the Grand in London, and the Tarragon in Toronto, and has played in Racine's *Phèdre*, Eduardo di Filippo's *Napoli!*, and Colm Tóibín's *The Testament of Mary* at the American Conservatory Theatre in San Francisco (thus revisiting her very first role). She will no doubt continue to be offered opportunities by Antoni Cimolino, the present artistic director at the Festival.

She still manages to spend time with Miles and her son Callan. A few seasons ago they took off in the middle of the summer for Disney World. Asked how she was able to arrange that, she replied,

"I took a huge pay cut, for starters." But for a good part of her time she chooses to be acting. "When I'm onstage, I'm enjoying myself. I sometimes think that good acting is just about the actors up there having a good time. I love what I do."

438

Seana in Mother Courage, *with Geraint Wyn Davies as the Cook*

CHARMER

Albert Schultz

My first assignment for Geraldine Sherman, the producer of the CBC radio program *State of the Arts*, was to report on the young company that Robin Phillips had assembled at the Tom Patterson Theatre in 1987 during the second year of John Neville's tenure as Artistic Director at Stratford. His opening production was *Romeo and Juliet*. The staging was simple, suggesting not the medieval pomp of tradition but rather the cool elegance of an Antonioni film: light and shadow, hot afternoons under spreading white awnings, steamy nights when the sirocco stirs the gauzy draperies of the bridal bed. The casting was equally unconventional: the lovers were emotional outsiders within their privileged society, innocent but hot-headed, drawn together by irresistible attraction, in over their heads and chancing everything on a sudden throw of the emotional dice. The actors were Susan Coyne and Albert Schultz, new to Stratford but destined to play a major if brief role there before making their mark elsewhere.

I recognized that Albert was the little boy I had seen when I visited his father Peter at the family estate, Penryn, on the outskirts of Port Hope two decades earlier. I met Peter through my friends the Ketchum family, whose father was the headmaster of Trinity College School. Peter was an American who in his childhood spent summers in Canada and then settled in as the editor of the *Port Hope Evening Guide* with his wife

Virginia and their three children, Albert being the youngest.

Peter and his wife were hospitable and easy-going. Peter loved the countryside, the woods, and the lakeshore, and particularly the local birds. I recall that I impressed him when I told him I had actually heard a hermit thrush. Inevitably we talked of theatre; Peter's wife was an amateur actress. I would later learn that Albert's introduction to theatre was watching his mother play Nancy in *Oliver!* at the age of four. He was apparently not horrified by her violent death but rather relished the chance to mingle with theatre folk.

Two years later Peter died of leukemia. Albert remained in Canada with his mother, though he did attend a private boys' school in New Hampshire, where he played Sherlock Holmes in the school play. He later went to school in Alberta when his mother remarried. His education was financed by a wealthy American aunt in New Jersey. By the time he finished high school he was determined to be an actor. He was turned down by the University of Alberta's drama program and enrolled at York University in Toronto. There he met two actors who would play ongoing roles in his life: Stuart Hughes and Oliver Dennis. Already Albert showed a talent for friendship and for keeping in touch.

Wanting more classical theatre training, Albert left York after two years to study in England at the LAMDA, then generally regarded as the school offering the best training in classical theatre. As Albert explains, "My real training was London. I not only went to all the galleries and monuments. I must have gone to forty shows that year. The great actors of that era were still playing and I saw them all."

He returned to Canada and got his first professional job at Young Peoples' Theatre, playing in Mordecai Richler's *Jacob Two-Two*, and then landed the roles of Mercutio and Laertes in productions directed by Guy Sprung at Toronto Free Theatre. His Hamlet was R.H. Thomson, who would become a strong influence. They had already performed together on tour in Tom Stoppard's *The Real Thing*, and Thomson apparently insisted that Sprung hire Albert. Thomson also persuaded Albert that he should not go to the United States but stay in Canada. Thomson, who was getting good roles both on stage and in television, convinced Albert that Canada was indeed a land of opportunity for young actors.

Robin Phillips invited Albert to join his Young Company. Albert would work with Phillips over the next two years, playing Romeo and Touchstone, one of Shakespeare's least funny clowns, with a

440

 Albert Schultz

sort of gauche charm, and the wiser but more melancholy fool Feste. But his most important role in the second year of Phillips's brief tenure was Edgar in *King Lear*, a young man who feigns madness in an attempt to try to protect the demented monarch and then rescues his blinded father. At the play's end he is the last sane survivor of the play's violent carnage. It is a role that demands both warmth and craftiness, technical

441

Edgar in King Lear
with William Hutt – "Poor Tom's a cold"

Albert Schultz as Romeo

agility but also a broad emotional range. Albert delivered all of this.

For Albert the highlight of this production was the chance to perform alongside William Hutt, whom Albert still regards as the greatest actor he has ever worked with. Their paths would cross repeatedly in the years that followed, including memorable productions of Pinter's *No Man's Land* and Beckett's *Waiting for Godot* at the Young Centre in Toronto, in which Hutt gave a definitive protrayal of Beckett's tramp Vladimir, but it was in *King Lear* that he and Albert formed a bond that would last until Hutt's death. When Hutt died a few years later, Albert called Phillips, to whom he had not spoken for several years. He found Phillips's response to the news perfect, "Albie, darling, didn't we laugh?"

Albert's stage romance with Susan Coyne sparked an off-stage courtship and, before long, marriage. They settled in Toronto, quickly made friends, and had an active social life. I remember we entertained them to dinner along with some of the Ketchums. Albert more or less dominated the conversation, and I seem to remember that some of his sallies ruffled the feathers of our other guests who had rather serious moral views. But because of his amusing delivery, they went along with it.

Albert and Susan had two children, a boy and a girl, whom Albert sometimes jokingly referred to as "Montague and Capulette." Before Albert settled down in Toronto he would work again with Robin Phillips, this time in Edmonton, where he played in Arthur Miller's *The Crucible*, Oliver Goldsmith's *She Stoops to Conquer* and *The Music Man*: a serious drama, a Restoration comedy, and a musical, illustrating his range as a performer. The role of Harold Hill, the conman who charms the inhabitants of River City, Iowa, by pretending to be a bandleader, called on Albert's saucy assurance and nimble-witted dash. It was a role that might have been written for him, and he brought it off with aplomb, as well as convincingly wooing the play's heroine Marian the Librarian. Like his near contemporaries Brent Carver and Colm Feore, he proved to be just as effective in a musical as in a more serious dramatic drama.

Although Albert considered himself primarily a stage actor, he soon became involved in the burgeoning television industry in programs that were being shot in Toronto in the late 1980s and 1990s, beginning with small roles in such shows as *Alfred Hitchcock Presents*, *American Playhouse*, and *Beautiful Dreamers*. In 1994 he became a regular on the popular Canadian show *Street Legal*, playing an aggressive and sexy young lawyer, Rob Diamond. Here he formed a strong connection with actor

Albert Schultz

443

Touchstone in As You Like It *with Marion Adler as Audrey*

Eric Peterson, with whom he would have an ongoing professional relationship.

The same year Albert landed a continuing role in *Side Effects*, playing Dr. Noah Knelman. Then came *The Red Green Show*, a zany comedy in which he played hoser Arnie Dogan for three seasons. He would be justifiably proud of his more recent impersonation of Canada's most controversial tycoon in *Shades of Black*. He studied everything he could find about the intelligent, arrogant, and crafty financier and was delighted when some of Conrad's closest associates complimented him on the accuracy of his portrayal. In his early 30s he had become a recognized TV presence. He made enough money to buy a house and enjoy a relatively affluent upper-middle-class lifestyle, something both he and Susan had been used to when growing up. (She was the daughter of a Governor of the Bank of Canada.) Albert dreamed of being able to return to Penryn on vacations and had a plan to convert it into a retreat for artists, but in 1988 it was sold by the family.

Albert also dreamed of founding his own theatre company, and in 1988 a group of twelve actors banded together to do just that. They wanted to present classics, and they turned to Robin Phillips to direct them. Robin was still a potent name in Canadian theatre. He had a reputation for being difficult, but his best work at Stratford, in London,

and then in Edmonton had revolutionized theatrical practice in Canada, and he was renowned for working with young actors. In their first season at Harbourfront they mounted two productions: Schiller's *Don Carlos* and Molière's *The Misanthrope*. The leading actors, Brent Carver and Albert, were both stars; the other actors were not hungry kids but established players. *Don Carlos* received rave reviews from the Toronto critics, and both plays became must-see shows. The new company immediately established itself as a vital contributor to the Toronto theatre scene. The distinctive name Soulpepper was apparently contributed by Susan and Albert's daughter Julia, when she overheard her father searching for a catchy phrase, something that combined spice and depth. It proved to be both evocative and memorable.

The new company would play eight seasons at Harbourfront. Initially, Phillips continued to direct, but it became obvious that he was not the leader they needed. His production of *The Mill on the Floss* was not ready on opening night, and it proved to be a turgid evening. The company established a directorate of four, but it soon become apparent that Albert was their natural leader, and he assumed the title of Founding Artistic Director.

Was this like Napoleon crowning himself Emperor of the French? Maybe a

bit, but Albert possessed not only passionate commitment but also a quick intelligence and a charismatic charm that would enable him not only to dominate actors but also to convince people with money to support his dream. As someone who grew up in a privileged environment he is at ease with people who have power and influence. As one of his most ardent admirers in the business community, Roger Garland, expressed it, "Albert could have been anything… he could have been the CEO of a large corporation…. Cost structure, ticket sales, marketing, the logistics of scheduling, employee relationships—he absorbs everything. He runs an amazingly complex theatre company, while he's acting, while he's directing, and while he's dreaming up what's going to happen next season. He's amazing."

For two years Albert took no salary, living off his TV earnings. The season expanded, and administering it became ever more complicated. The Harbourfront space was intimate and challenging but had some real limitations. Albert began to think about finding a permanent home for the company. Then inspiration hit. The buildings that once housed the distillery of Gooderham and Worts when they manufactured Canadian whisky and shipped it all over the world, a maze of Victorian brick buildings in a miniature village with cob-

blestone streets that had stood empty for decades, was to be restored and turned into an arts centre, complete with shops, galleries, and restaurants. A perfect place for a theatre.

Albert understood the problem of selling seats in big theatres like the Stratford and Shaw Festival theatres and the St. Lawrence Centre: great if you have a hit and can fill the place, but not every show can be a hit, unless like David Mirvish you import Broadway and London hits. He therefore opted for two theatres of approximately 200 seats each, opening onto a large central atrium where people could buy food and drink, talk to their friends during intermissions, and mingle with the actors after the shows, a sort of theatrical community centre. Albert's sense of community is a very strong element of his vision; it not only harks back to his early days in Port Hope, where Penryn was the centre of a family and intellectual community, but has also built on his ability to connect with and maintain relationships with actors.

Albert set out to raise the money needed to refurbish the building in Tank House Lane that would become the Young Centre. It was named for a family foundation whose president, David Young, met with Albert at Upper Canada College and was so convinced by Alfred's pitch that he sat bolt upright in bed that night and said to his wife, "We have to

445

The Stage Manager in Our Town

446

Flecks, the Pitblados. He haunted the building site, checking to make sure that the work proceeded according to his specifications. He was consumed by the project and as a consequence his home life suffered, but the Centre opened in 2005 and the company began performing a season of plays in repertory all year round. The Centre also housed the drama department of George Brown College, some of whose graduates would participate in Soulpepper productions, sometimes proceeding through a post-graduate program offered by the newly formed Soulpepper Academy.

In time some of the original twelve founders would drop out. Other actors would become regulars: Dan Chameroy, Oliver Dennis, Raquel Duffy, Jeff Lillico, and Michelle Monteith. Distinguished Canadian actors would join the company for individual shows: Brent Carver, David Fox, Charmian King, Dawn Greenhalgh, Eric Peterson, Fiona Reid, and R.H. Thomson, among others. Albert controlled the choice of repertoire and casting and as General Director of the Young Centre oversaw everything else. As founding member William Webster puts it, "Let's call a spade a spade. Who is the creator of Soulpepper as it exists now? Let's not kid ourselves. It's Albert."

Over time, four of the founding members would develop their skills as direc-

back this guy." He would later explain, "We had no input. Zero. We were investing in Albert's vision."

Charles Baillie, former Chairman and CEO of TD Bank, was buttonholed by Albert in the Rosedale subway station and asked for a cool million to fund Soulpepper's rehearsal space and prop shops. Albert was on his way to Roger Garland's house, and after a ten-minute walk he arrived to be greeted by Roger saying, "Charlie Baillie just called. He said they'll put up the million." Albert went on to canvas other money men: Donald Ross, the financier and his father's friend, other philanthropists interested in theatre: Ivan Fecan, the

tors: Ted Dykstra, Diana Leblanc, Joe Ziegler, and Albert himself. They were influenced heavily in their earliest years by the visiting Hungarian László Marton, who had directed several of the founding members in a highly praised production of Chekhov's *The Three Sisters* for a no longer functioning company called Masterclass. Albert invited Marton to direct for Soulpepper, and for several years he would do at least one annual production of a European work: Chekhov's *Platonov* and *Uncle Vanya*,

Ibsen's *The Wild Duck*, Molnár's *The Guardsman* and *The Play's The Thing* (adapted by P.G. Wodehouse), Feydeau's *A Flea in Her Ear*. His productions, particularly of Chekhov and Ibsen, have presented these dramatists' work in a more robustly emotional interpretation than the rather restrained, nostalgic, English-inflected versions often mounted in Canada. They have also inspired some of Albert's most original performances as Platonov and Astrov, two energetic dreamers frustrated by the society in which they find themselves.

Albert would continue to head the company not only as producer and frequent director, but as one of its leading actors as well. The range of his characterizations has been extraordinary. Having played almost all of the major Shakespearean roles for young actors, it is not surprising that he wanted to play

447

Platanov with Nancy Palk

Platanov with Susan Coyne

Hamlet, first in Chekhov's reinterpretation of the character as Platonov and then in the canonical text itself. But it was in modern comedies that he would do his most successful work: the wryly philosophical Stage Manager in Thornton Wilder's *Our Town*, the wise-cracking, ruthless real-estate agent in David Mamet's *Glengarry Glen Ross*, two smart-talking duplicitous urban Londoners in Harold Pinter's *Betrayal* and *The Real Thing*, the charming, irresponsible seducer in Alan Ayckbourn's *The Norman Conquests*, and the needy, frustrated bachelor in Neil Simon's *The Odd Couple*.

These roles displayed facets of Albert's personality: his charm, his quick intelligence, his cunning, his innate sexiness, his knowingness, his apparent air of authority covering an underlying wariness, his ability to turn on a dime from affability to anger or disbelief and back again. Physically he is impressive: tall and bulky, a bit shaggy with his curly hair and beard, and yet with a trace of the cheeky schoolboy he must have been, a broad open face dominated by a welcoming smile. Ready to take on all comers.

The list of plays that Albert has starred in demonstrates a definite tilt toward comedy, particularly the American brand. Critics have deplored what they see as the abandonment of Soulpepper's original "mandate": the

448

As Ricky Roma in Glengarry Glen Ross *with Eric Peterson*

production of little-known classical plays. Yet what is a theatre's mandate? Something imposed upon it by an academic theorist. It's a bit like the concept of "tradition," which one university president defined as "something one or two students think they remember doing last year." But an essential element of theatre is attracting and pleasing an audience and evolving along with that audience, and this Soulpepper has done extremely successfully.

Their Shakespeare productions of *Hamlet* and *King Lear* have not matched the best work of the Stratford Festival, but they have given resoundingly effective productions of Chekhov and Ibsen, as well as rarely produced classical works such as Lessing's *Nathan the Wise*, Goldoni's *The Mistress of the Inn*, Miklós László's *Parfumerie*, Molière's *Tartuffe*, and Bulgakov's *The Royal Comedians*, as well as such almost forgotten American

The Odd Couple *with Diego Matamoros*

comedies as Clifford Odets's *Awake and Sing!*, William Saroyan's *The Time of Your Life*, and Robert Sherwood's *Idiot's Delight*. And as Richard Ouzounian pointed out, Neil Simon's *The Odd Couple* is a modern comedy that is destined to enter the theatrical canon alongside the works of Sheridan, Wilde and Coward.

Albert has been fortunate in the calibre of talented people who founded the company. Foremost among them is Diego Matamoros, who was one of the original four directors and was responsible for taking over the mantle and acquiring the charitable status of the now-defunct Masterclass company. Like Albert he worked as a young actor at Stratford, and also like Albert he was somewhat miffed when he was not asked back. (Diana Leblanc, who has had a long association with both Albert and Richard Monette, once commented, "Those two egos could never be compatible.") Diego has shown himself to be an actor of power and yet subtlety, bringing depth and humour and idiosyncrasy to characterizations as varied as the bombastic and hypocritical Roy Cohen in *Angels in America*, the beleaguered and disillusioned Molière in *The Royal Comedians*, the frustrated and infatuated Vanya in *Uncle Vanya*, the punctilious Felix in *The Odd Couple*, and the cuckolded husband Robert in *Betrayal*. Both

449

actors play comedy with finesse and antic grace. Diego evinces a kind of skewed rapport in his work with Albert. He has described his colleague's directorial method as "improvisationally dictatorial." Albert accepts this comment but has declared, "The age of the autocratic director is over."

Other stalwarts among the founding members are Nancy Palk, who has displayed her idiosyncratic verve as the foul-mouthed Martha in *Who's Afraid of Virginia Woolf?* and the drug-addled Mary Tyrone in *Long Day's Journey into Night*, as well as various embattled mothers and wives in *Awake and Sing!, You Can't Take It With You*, and *Death of a Salesman*; Stuart Hughes, who has offered ruggedly virile performances in *The Glass Menagerie, True West*, and *The Crucible* and displayed comic invention in *Entertaining Mr. Sloane* and *The Time of Your Life*; Ted Dykstra, who has brought mercurial wit to *Rosencrantz and Guildenstern are Dead* and *The Government Inspector*; and Diana Leblanc, who still acts occasionally in shows such as *The Road To Mecca*. All four have proved to be effective directors. Other members of the company who have taken on a great variety of roles are Derek Boyes, Oliver Dennis, Michael Hanrahan, Jeff Lillico, and William Webster. In the early years Susan Coyne and Martha Burns gave a number of

vivid performances. More recently Raquel Duffy and Fiona Reid have appeared regularly. All of these artists also work at other Canadian theatres and in television.

Diego is Albert's only serious acting rival at Soulpepper, and the two seem to coexist harmoniously enough. Albert sees his company as a community, almost a family, an image that was also used by Tyrone Guthrie when speaking of his Stratford company in the early 1950s. Guthrie characterized himself as Nanny; Albert is much more a paterfamilias, genial but capable of threatening punishment when his plans are thwarted, as they were when visiting actor Ben Carlson bolted from a production of *The Importance of Being Earnest* to play Hamlet in Chicago. The cohesive fabric of the company was further disrupted when Albert and Susan split and subsequently divorced. Martha Burns, a close friend of Susan's, has not worked with the company since. Martha's loss had an impact, not only because she is one of the most accomplished actors of her generation but also because she was the guiding light of Soulpepper's outreach program to inner-city youth. Recently Soulpepper lost the counsel and administrative skills of their longtime producer Claire Sakaki, but Albert's current partner Leslie Lester has made a valuable contribution as Executive Director, a

450

position she has held since 2001.

It is not clear to what extent Leslie influences Albert's choice of repertoire. But what is clear is that Albert has shown great skill in finding plays that fit the skills of his company and the interests of his audience, mixing modern and occasionally older classics with more innovative work such as the highly successful original play *Kim's Convenience* by Ins Choi, which after a very successful run at Soulpepper is touring Canada, or the improvised children's play *Alligator Pie*, based on the poems of Dennis Lee, which has sold out for two seasons, or Vern Thiessen's new adaptation of Somerset Maugham's *Of Human Bondage*. There are collaborations with playwright Judith Thompson and the company of Michael Hollingsworth's Video Cabaret. And there are musical salon evenings often organized by Mike Ross and Tom Allen that feature guest artists from Brent Carver and Murray Maclauchlan to Jackie Richardson but also members of the Soulpepper company. Albert is highly respectful of both authors and actors who have paid their dues and proven their worth. He is not afraid to take chances but has little use for what he refers to as "weird-ass shit."

As a director, Albert has proven himself to be one of the most original and sensitive talents in the land. The influence of Phillips and Marton are evident, but Albert's skill in staging elaborate epic pieces like *Angels in America* and *Of Human Bondage* goes well beyond imitation. Both productions use a great deal of open space and a few simple props and set pieces to evoke many different locations, so that the action moves in an almost filmic way from indoors and outdoors to realms of fantasy locations and the world of dreams. The action is fluid, inventive, and comic and combines all the important elements of theatre: music, imagery, and psychological depth. Albert attributes part of the success of these productions to the improvisational training and experimentation that have been major elements in the training of young actors at the Academy. What he has provided is his unique vision.

451

Albert as director

He was enormously pleased when recently László Marton told him, "You should no longer have to be in any doubt that you are the primary instigator and director of this theatre."

Though not exactly an intellectual, Albert has thought long and hard about the actor's craft. He theorizes that to be a great actor you must make four basic connections: first, with the text, which must be studied and absorbed; second, with the actor's self, his emotions and intelligence and imagination—his heart and mind; third, with the other actors with whom he interacts and shares the stage; and fourth, with the audience, of whom he must be aware as with a third eye. In Albert's view the only Canadian actor who had all four attributes in an almost perfect balance was William Hutt.

At just over fifty, Albert has obviously found his place in the world. "His blend of qualities comes along in a hundred years. There's a public showman there but there's also a mind behind the showman," asserts Diego Matamoros. Running Soulpepper has become his biggest, most demanding role. In this respect he resembles Richard Monette, another formidable actor who eventually stopped taking parts in order to concentrate his entire energy on becoming the Artistic Director of Stratford. But Albert is still acting. No longer a juvenile lead, he can choose to play many possible parts: Pierre Bezuhov, Galileo, Archie Rice, Volpone, M. Jourdain, Henry Higgins, Trigorin, Falstaff, and, in time, following the footsteps of his revered mentor William Hutt, King Lear and Prospero. Would he be tempted now if he were offered the leadership of Stratford or the National Theatre of Great Britain? It seems unlikely. He is the master of a theatrical world he has created, a community of artists growing and evolving but still small enough to allow for exciting and unforeseen developments in the future.

The Norman Conquests *Albert with Laura Condlin and Fiona Reid*

SONGBIRDS

Louise Pitre and Brent Carver

On one of my frequent visits to Montreal I was introduced by my friends Gerald Budner and Eric McLean to a recording of a Québécois singer called La Bolduc. She had been enormously popular, wrote her own distinctive patter songs, and travelled all over French-speaking North America, which at the time included New Brunswick, Northern Ontario, Maine, Windsor, Manitoba, and upper New York state, in her heyday in the 1920s and 1930s. She is still fondly remembered in Quebec but completely unknown in English-speaking Canada.

I promoted the idea of telling her story on Peter Gzowski's program *Morningside*. It was to be developed for broadcast by a young, up-and-coming producer, Gregory Sinclair. He quickly saw that the music would be crucial. I suggested we approach my friend John Roby. John agreed to arrange La Bolduc's tunes to the English lyrics I had devised and to assemble a small band. Greg insisted we needed someone with experience in musical theatre and suggested we approach Louise Pitre. I had never heard of her, but Greg had seen her playing in *Les Misérables* and was sure she could deliver what was required. I persuaded Greg we should cast the show using all French-Canadian actors, of whom there were a considerable number in Toronto. They wouldn't be concerned with *acting* French; they would simply *be* French.

The day for the first read-through arrived. I was nervous as the studio started to fill up with actors I didn't know, all speaking French. At two minutes before the appointed start time, an elegant woman with snow-white hair appeared. "Who wrote this script?" she asked.

"I did."

"It's my mother, my aunts, my grandmother. How did you know about this?"

"Because it's my mother and my aunts. They were farmers on the Ontario side of the Ottawa River. I guess farmers are pretty much the same everywhere."

"I think it's terrific." I adored her from that moment on.

Louise Pitre gave a wonderful performance: dynamic, vital and at the same time earthy. Not only did she have a rich and powerful voice, but she brought a ready sense of humour and a down-to-earth practicality to the role that was perfect for Bolduc. She had learned all the songs and easily got her tongue around the "turlutages," the rapid-fire nonsense syllables with which Bolduc embellished all her choruses. John Roby had expected to work on the songs with her for two days, but she mastered them in an afternoon. The show was popular with Gzowski's audience, who wrote some thirty complimentary letters (including one from one of Bolduc's granddaughters), an almost unprecedented response to a morning drama.

I learned that Louise had been born in Smooth Rock Falls in northern Ontario in 1957 but spent her childhood on Montreal. Although the family moved frequently, she quickly made friends with the other kids in the neighbourhood. "We were like an extended family. We played games in the street and in each other's houses. I had an older sister and a young brother. I was the mediator but also the wild one." She loved riding her CCM Gold Stripe bicycle in the streets of the Plateau, and when it was built, riding on the subway. In 1967 she visited Expo almost every day. On weekends the family would climb into their convertible and visit her grandmother and her aunts in small towns along the Ottawa River in Quebec and Ontario.

During the FLQ crisis in 1970, her mother was terrified of the events in

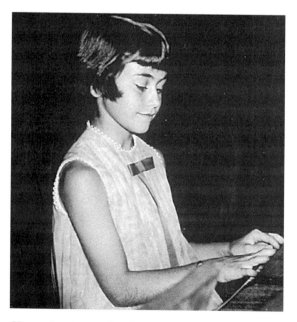

Young Louise at the piano

454

Montreal, and at her insistence the family moved to Welland, Ontario, where Louise attended high school. It was a French-speaking school but the kids spoke English among themselves. Louise had no English but learned rapidly. She also played popular songs on an old piano in the gym at noon-hour. This quickly broke the ice.

Although there was no drama program there were music classes. Louise sang in the choir and played trumpet in the band. She played other instruments in music class and became very close to her music teacher, Cheryl David. She soon became accepted by the other kids in the school, and in Grade 13 she was president of the student council. "That was huge for me. I sang at the piano at a couple at a couple of high school assemblies in the gym. I loved it."

She continued to take music lessons and entered the University of Western Ontario as a major in piano, expecting to become a high-school music teacher. In her fourth year she did her first show: *Flicks*, a revue with skits and songs, devised by Jim Saar and David Warrack. Although she had no training as a singer or actor this experience made her decide not to go to teachers' college but rather to look for work in musical theatre. Her energy, enthusiasm, and big voice won her roles in *Blood Brothers* in High Park and *Rock and Roll* at Canadian Stage.

She acquired an agent, who sent her out on auditions. She was cast in "industrials" and proceeded to climb into a bunny suit at a department store, where she sang jingles advertising everything from candy to toilet paper. "Is this really what I want?" she asked herself as she sat in the cafeteria at lunchtime. But then she was cast in *Beehive* at the Imperial Room at the Royal York and *Jacques Brel is Alive and Well and Living in Paris* at Massey Hall. Curiously enough, this show also helped launch the career of Brent Carver.

I was first aware of Brent Carver in a production of *The Beggar's Opera*, which Robin Phillips directed at Stratford in 1980. Carver was playing a character called Henry Paddington, whose name cannot be found in the original cast list. Suddenly in the second act he did a sort

455

a young Brent Carver

of jazz riff, a surprise turn that seemed out of key with the original music of the show, but all the more welcome for that. Brent had been discovered at the age of 29 by Phillips, who no doubt had plans for Carver: he appeared the same year in Carlo Goldoni's *The Servant of Two Masters*, one of the least successful productions of Phillips's regime, and as Edmund, the younger son in Eugene O'Neill's *Long Day's Journey Into Night*, with William Hutt and Jessica Tandy as his parents. Brent gave a sensitive performance, but this end-of-season production ran for only 16 performances. Phillips was running out of steam, and at the end of that season he would be gone. But he and Carver had formed a bond that would continue far into the future.

Brent Carver grew up in the small British Columbia town of Cranbrook, one of eight siblings. His parents were Lois and Kenneth Carver, who worked in the lumber trade. He claims he sang before he could talk, and he continued to sing in church choirs and perform in school plays. Convinced that his future lay in the theatre, at 17 he flew to Vancouver to attend the University of British Columbia. He threw himself into a student acting program that included Eric Peterson, John Gray, and Goldie Semple. "We all needed to be in theatre, needed to express ourselves. When you saw these people you loved and respect-

ed, you just had to be part of it." He left the university after three years to be part of a children's theatre company and was soon singing in a production of *Jacques Brel is Alive and Well and Living in Paris.* Soon afterwards, he was playing Claudio in *Much Ado About Nothing* for John Neville at the Citadel in Edmonton.

At the age of 23 he played the lead in Cliff Jones's musical *Kronborg: 1582*, based on Shakespeare's *Hamlet*, which originated at the Charlottetown Festival in Prince Edward Island and toured the country in 1974–75. He would later play Shakespeare's original text at the Stratford Festival in 1986 under the direction of John Neville, with Lucy Peacock as his Ophelia and Elizabeth Shepherd as Gertrude. His Hamlet had a heart-breaking vulnerability, a man too sensitive for this or any world. His exchange with the Gravedigger, played by Eric House, opened up a sudden understanding of mortal frailty that lies at the heart of the play. Speaking recently at a Festival seminar about the experience of playing Hamlet, Carver said the character had taken over and possessed him: "But I never felt I captured the whole role. He's such a complicated character you could play him all of your life."

Meanwhile, it was Louise's performance in *Blood Brothers* that established her on the Toronto scene. She received wonderful reviews in the press, which influenced David Mirvish to cast her as

456

Louise Pitre and Brent Carver

As Hamlet duelling with Scott Wentworth as Laertes

458

Fantine in Les Misérables

Louise Pitre and Brent Carver

Fantine in *Les Misérables* at the Royal Alexandra. "It was the first time I could show Toronto that I was an actress and not just a singer." She would go on to sing the role in French in Montreal and then in Paris. She later commented, "I would have to say that the Montreal production was my favourite. Grittier, truer, more emotional, more raw. Surprise! Surprise! A bunch of French Canadians, what do you expect!" Louise's ability to connect with an audience on an emotional level is instinctive and immediate. More than anything it is the foundation on which her whole career has been built.

During the next few years, Louise and I would continue to work together on CBC radio shows, particularly a biography of Sir Wilfrid Laurier, in which she played the woman who was probably his mistress with a sort of flirtatious tact. During this period I wrote a stage show in which she was to play Bolduc, but the script never quite gelled. In any case, slim, elegant Louise with her platinum hair and expressive gestures looked nothing like Bolduc, who had been a big heavy-set habitant *maman*. Louise also admitted that she would have been bored singing Bolduc's songs night after night for a stage run. She felt she needed greater variety to spark her creativity.

After Phillips left Stratford, he cast Brent Carver as the emotionally confused young soldier Robert Ross in his film version of Timothy Findlay's *The Wars* (1983). The cast included Martha Henry and William Hutt as his parents and Domini Blythe as his aristocratic English lover. It was a brilliant realization of a vanished Torontonian and English upper-class world. Unfortunately, the production company changed hands in mid-shoot and the new owners insisted that any homosexual content be cut from the film, thus eviscerating its emotional heart. The film received only limited distribution

Robert Ross in The Wars

and was not a critical success.

Carver would continue to work in film, however. In 1978 he had already given a complex and charismatic performance as Rafe, the nightclub singer that Chapelle Jaffe's Daisy picks up and brings home in the film of Carol Bolt's play *One Night Stand*. As a charming liar and possibly a psychopathic killer, Carver plays the role he originated onstage with a kind of enigmatic fluidity. He would also appear in the premieres of a number of other original Canadian plays, notably Lee MacDougall's *High Life* and Brad Fraser's *Unidentified Human Remains and the True Nature of Love*. Another outsider role was that of Horst, detained in a Nazi prison camp in Martin Sherman's *Bent*. He would also appear in leading roles in a range of classical plays: the title roles in Molière's *Tartuffe*, in a highly controversial S&M production by Derek Goldby in Edmonton and Toronto; in *Cyrano de Bergerac* for Robin Phillips in Edmonton; in *Don Carlos*, the initial production of the Soulpepper company, again directed by Phillips in Toronto; and later as Gregers Werle in Ibsen's *The Wild Duck* in Soulpepper's new home in Toronto's Distillery District. In all these plays, the characters he portrayed were outsiders at odds with the world. But Carver's interpretations were highly individual: Donnie, the drug-addicted thief in *High Life*, seemed almost retarded;

Cyrano de Bergerac *in Edmonton*

David in *Human Remains* was cynical and wise-cracking about the possibility of love; Tartuffe was devious, lustful, and sadistic; Don Carlos was passionately principled and heartbroken when his father married the woman he loved; Cyrano was wittily romantic and lyrical; and Werle was high-minded and driven by his wrong-headed search for truth at any cost. In these productions Carver offered an impressive range of vividly realized portrayals.

Soon after she left the cast of *Les Mis* in Toronto, Louise's and Brent's paths intersected when she was cast as Dorine, the pert and knowing maid in Molière's

Tartuffe, in Derek Goldby's production at Theatre Calgary. Louise was somewhat intimidated by the idea of acting in this classical play, but she ended up feeling very much at home with the material, and has said she loved watching Brent night after night. It is unfortunate that these two gifted musical actors have not had an opportunity to work together more often, although when Stratford invited Louise to do *Jacques Brel* with Brent she turned it down, unsatisfied with the songs she was assigned.

Louise is notable for her frank, forthright approach to work and to life. She has none of the airs and caprices of the traditional diva but speaks her mind in no uncertain terms and has a very low tolerance for bullshit. Perhaps this is why she was unfazed by Goldby, a notoriously demanding and acerbic director. Her colleagues report that she is always cooperative and sunny, "an absolute sweetheart."

Tartuffe emboldened Louise to do other non-musical roles, including Martha in *Who's Afraid of Virginia Woolf?*, which she admits she was too young to play but which gave her an opportunity to "go to the dark side of myself … the most exciting thing for me, and I got to do it in spades for that role." More successful was her portrayal of the mother in Michel Tremblay's *For the Pleasure of Seeing Her Again* at the Grand Theatre in London. Once again she tapped into her working-class Québécois roots to give us an eccentric, funny, perverse, and ultimately very moving portrayal. "I was basically revisiting my entire family…. My mother and also my aunts. It was tough and wonderful and full of life." When I saw it I cried, a rare experience for me in the theatre.

It was probably inevitable that Louise would want to sing the songs of Édith Piaf, to whose tough life and emotional openness she could readily respond. In a British play about Piaf, Jane Lapotaire had avoided the best-known songs and sung only some of the less familiar tunes in her repertoire, but not so with Louise, who tackled "La vie en rose," "Hymne à l'amour," and "Non, je ne regrette rien" head on and without apology. She has said, "I tried not to copy her. My voice is not like hers. But I was true to her stylistically and idiomatically. To be honest I played my great aunt Alice. She was a hell of a character and looked much like Piaf." Louise herself, however, did not look much like Piaf, who was small and shapeless and invariably wore a black dress. Louise, slim and elegant, with her snow-white hair and spangled dresses, her extravagant gestures and expressive facial expressions, made no attempt to impersonate the French singer. Rather, she captured the spirit and the emotional rawness of the celebrated chanteuse, her courage and her pain.

461

In between his stage appearances, Carver appeared as a guest on a number of TV shows: *The Twilight Zone*, *War of the Worlds*, and *Street Legal*. His next major film appearance was in Marc Michel Bouchard's *Lilies* (1996), where he played the Countess, the deluded mother of the two young lovers. This film was based on a play in which the inmates of a prison act out their fantasies, but it loses much of its power when their fantasies are allowed to be shown cinematically in fully realized costumes and settings. Carver was totally convincing as a woman losing her mental equilibrium but deeply concerned for her son's happiness. Then, as Ichabod Crane in the *Legend of Sleepy Hollow* (1999), Carver gave a comedic performance that provided a completely new take on this stock character, once more a person out of step with his community.

In 2004, Rhombus Media filmed *Elizabeth Rex* with the original cast that had presented Timothy Findley's play at Stratford. Carver took on the role of Ned Lowenscroft, a young actor dying of a venereal disease who confronts Queen Elizabeth I, played by Diane D'Aquila. The Queen has always had to act as a man and suppress her romantic feelings; Ned has played women on stage but has had to hide his homosexual nature and suppress his deepest yearnings. He wants to mourn his soldier lover who has

Ned Lowenscroft with Diane D'Aquila in Elizabeth Rex

recently been killed; Elizabeth refuses to mourn her lover, the Earl of Essex, who is about to be executed for treason. At the climax of the drama Elizabeth says to Ned, "If you will teach me how to be a woman, I will teach you how to be a man." It is perhaps Carver's most fully realized cinematic performance.

Physically, Brent Carver is slight, nimble, and quick. He has particularly expressive hands. His face is distinctive, somehow both weathered but also still fresh, with bright blue eyes, strong creases around the mouth, and a wide and ready smile. It is not the face of a leading

man, yet it suggests both innocence and experience. Now in his 60s, he looks not so much younger as ageless.

In spite of his wide range of dramatic and comic roles in the theatre, Carver's reputation rests primarily on his musical interpretations, especially at Stratford. In Brian Macdonald's rollicking rendition of *The Pirates of Penzance* at Stratford, his spirited rendition of "Oh! better far to live and die," which contains the famous lyrics "It is, it is a glorious thing to be a Pirate King!", stole the show and had the theatre audience frequently demanding a repeat of the number. He would go on to play the sleazy, decadent Master of Ceremonies in *Cabaret*, with Sheila McCarthy as Sally Bowles, and the beset-upon but buoyant Tevye in *Fiddler on the Roof*, who struggles with his strong-willed daughters who want to marry for love and the Cossacks who set fire to his shtetl and finally drive him and his family out of it in an interpretation that owed nothing to the corpulent, grimacing Tevye of Zero Mostel, Carver expressed both the joy and perplexity of this outsized creation of Sholem Aleichem on his own terms.

463

In 1993, Carver won the leading role in the musical *Kiss of the Spider Woman*

The Master of Ceremonies in Cabaret *with a simian partner*

The Countess in Lilies

after Richard Thomas dropped out. He had already been seen in the United States, playing Ariel to the Prospero of Anthony Hopkins in *The Tempest* in Los Angeles. *Spider Woman*, which was directed by Harold Prince, opened in Toronto and played in London before it went to Broadway, with Brent playing Molina, the gay window-dresser who fantasizes in a Brazilian jail cell about a vampy film actress Aurora; her most famous character is the Spider Woman, who kills with a kiss. In Molina's cell is a political prisoner Valentin, who confesses he is in love with a girl Maria. The jailers offer to let Molina visit his ailing mother if he will disclose the whereabouts of Valentin's lover. Molina refuses, is beaten up, and eventually shot. The final sequence offers a heaven-like vision where Molina is surrounded by all the people in his life. The Spider Woman appears and delivers the fatal kiss. Carver later said, "My favourite part of the role was singing 'She's A Woman.' When I got to 'How Lucky Can You Be?' I felt like Liza Minnelli." For his bravely open-hearted and emotionally tortured performance, Carver was awarded a Tony. He dedicated it to Susan Wright.

Susan was probably Carver's greatest friend. A gifted and vivid actor and singer, she had a bawdy sense of humour and an outsized enjoyment of life. In her short career at Stratford she played a number of comic roles: Mistress Quickly,

Molina in The Kiss of the Spider Woman *with Chita Rivera*

Susan Wright as Shirley Valentine

Adriana in *The Boys from Syracuse*, Éliante in *The Misanthrope*, Mistress Page in *The Merry Wives of Windsor*, and Aunt Essie in *Ah, Wilderness!*, as well as more serious dramatic parts: Paulina in *A Winter's Tale* and Marie-Louise in Michel Tremblay's *Forever Yours, Marie-Lou*. Her greatest triumph was as Mother Courage in 1987, in which she revelled in the salty, cynical Brecht songs. Carver played her son Eileff. In December 1991, she was staying in Brent's house in Stratford when a fire broke out and she died in the blaze. It was a staggering loss for Brent. I still remember him at her memorial singing "When the Red, Red Robin Goes Bob-Bob-Bobbin' Along". He often quotes her saying, "What an actor needs is courage, confidence and compassion." Carver certainly has all three.

Louise continued to appear in productions of Broadway shows: *The Roar of the Greasepaint—The Smell of the Crowd*; *And the World Goes 'Round*; *I Love You, You're Perfect, Now Change*. In September 2009, she appeared at Carnegie Hall singing the role of Ulrika in a concert version of the musical *Kristina*, with songs composed by Benny Andersson and Björn Ulvaeus of the pop group ABBA. The next year she reprised the role at the Royal Albert Hall in London.

Soon after, she tried out for the role of Josephine in a musical about Napoleon. She didn't get the part, but the director

Francesca Zambello realized that she would be perfect in a musical she was to direct the next year. Donna in *Mamma*

As Donna in Mamma Mia *in Toronto and New York*

465

Mia was built around popular ABBA tunes. She is a free-spirited, middle-aged woman living on a Greek island who is preparing for her daughter's wedding. The girl wants her father to give her away. The only problem is that Donna is uncertain which of the three lovers she had some twenty summers ago is the actual father. The piece is a romp with serious underpinnings. Louise with her comic gifts was perfectly cast as the rueful, fun-loving Donna. She belted out the ABBA songs, particularly "Dancing Queen," with verve, but the show-stopper was her rendition of "The Winner Takes It All," which she sang with the heartfelt pathos of a Piaf ballad. It would become one of her signature tunes.

The show played to packed houses when it opened at the Royal Alex in Toronto. The audience who knew the ABBA tunes waited to see how they were fitted into Donna's story and applauded wildly as they recognized each song. The show went on tour in the United States, with Louise playing the lead across the continent and eventually on Broadway, where she was nominated for a Tony. I caught it one evening and phoned Louise to let her know. She invited me to a party the next afternoon at Sardi's, where her picture was being mounted on the wall alongside the great stars of the American theatre. It was there I met her new husband Joe Matheson.

Before she met Joe, Louise's romantic life had not been particularly happy. While playing in *Les Misérables* she lived with her co-star Michael Burgess. She had a number of later partners, including a married man and a man who left her to join the army. Before long, however, all these relationships seemed to go sour. She admitted she had "lousy taste in men." Barry Flatman, with whom she boarded in a house in Riverdale after one of her break-ups, said, "She was so brave, so honest. She is the woman I should have married."

It was shortly after that she met Joe and entered into a new kind of partnership. Joe was a singer and dancer who performed in various shows, including *Jersey Boys*. He was in no sense dependent on Louise, but they enjoyed performing together, particularly in *For the Pleasure of Seeing Her Again*. They bought a farm near Alliston and thoroughly enjoyed country life. Joe was a

Ne me quitte pas

466

romantic suitor, buying her gifts on Valentine's Day. When he got a gig in Halifax, Louise drove halfway across the country with their dog to be with him.

Increasingly, Louise has given concerts in between shows, some-times backed by a full orchestra, sometimes only by her pianist, Diane Leah. Her repertoire was varied but always included songs sung in French. She liked to include comic numbers such as "A Great Way to Lose a Man" or "Some People" jux-taposed with ballads: "Send in the Clowns" and "The Man That Got Away." She joked and quipped and got her audience laughing, and then tore at their heartstrings. Her outfits were sexy and sometimes outrageous. She loved bright colours, sequins, gold lamé. And always her gestures were broad and exuberant, her facial expressions tellingly comic.

Louise continued to tour, singing for audiences across the country. One of the concert tours she enjoyed the most was to northern Ontario where she had been born. She sang in gyms, church basements or Legion halls. She was delighted that her audiences were appreciative and enthusiastic. She had made a record, which she flogged at these perform-ances, by composing ditties to well-known tunes:

ESPANOLA (to the tune of Mr. Sandman)
Thanks one and all
I've never sung in a Legion Hall
I've never changed in a kitchen, that's true
It's been a rainbow of emotions too

WA-WA (to the tune of Blue Moon)
We started out in Toronto
Drove miles how many, I don't know
But now it's time that we should go
I have a thought for you to end this evening
Before you leave tonight on your way through
Perhaps pick up a CD that I'm selling
And you can take my singing home with you

Louise has made three records: *All My Life Has Led to This* and *Songs My Mother Taught Me* are a mix of English and French standards. Her latest disc *La Vie en Rouge* ("Pink is too pretty") is made up entirely of French songs. She can also be heard on the cast recording of *Could You Wait?*, a show she co-wrote with Joe and her accompanist Diane Leah.

Brent would continue to play in musicals, including *Parade* on Broadway, based on a real story in which Carver as Leo Frank, a Jewish worker in a match factory, is accused of raping and mur-dering a girl; after many complications he is tried and eventually lynched. It is a

467

powerful piece and once again Carver gave a compelling performance that was nominated for another Tony. He would go on to animate the character of Gandalf in David Mirvish's musical version of *The Lord of the Rings* at the Royal Alexandra in Toronto, which was not a success. "When I first heard the music, I thought it could be amazing but… I had to cram in all this exposition. What could I do?" He declined to go with the show to London: "I can't play any role for too long. I start to say, no, no, no more." In the summer of 2015, he began rehearsals for a new musical, *Evangeline*, with music by Ted Dykstra, to be produced at Charlottetown and Edmonton and in which he plays a priest, Father Felician, who is pivotal to the story of the expulsion of the Acadians from New Brunswick.

Louise has made no secret of her ambition to play all the leading roles in Broadway musicals for which she feels she could be suitably cast. At Massey Hall she played Annie in *Annie Get Your Gun*, in a semi-staged production with full orchestra directed by Donna Feore. Although she described the musical as "hokey," her exuberance carried the day, whether she was belting out "You Can't Get a Man With a Gun," "Doin' What Comes Natur'lly" or "I Got the Sun in the Morning," which entered her repertoire and, in her words, "still

provides one of my goose-bump moments." Donna Feore hoped that it might lead to a fully staged production, but so far this hasn't happened.

Louise's next major role in a musical was Mrs. Lovett in *Sweeney Todd* in Calgary. Again she was channelling her dark side in this macabre piece. The song about the human content of the pies she bakes using the flesh of the demon barber's victims was rendered with ghoulish glee: "I love to cook and bake. I got to roll out pastry every night as I sang those incredibly ghoulish words. A gift." Her clear articulation made every word of the intricate lyrics audible. But she has pointed out that although she admires Sondheim's virtuosity, she thought she was not old enough yet to tackle two favourite tunes, "The Ladies Who Lunch" and "I'm Still Here."

Soon afterwards, she appeared in *Love and Loss and What I Wore* with Andrea Martin, in which she matched Martin's comic verve and didn't sing a note: "I got to sit on stage and watch my fellow performers. I loved just sitting in the dressing room with those amazing women. It was the warmest, friendliest show I've ever done."

The two roles she had always wanted to play were Auntie Mame and Mama Rose in *Gypsy*. In 2012, she finally played *Mame* at Goodspeed Theatre in

468

Louise Pitre and Brent Carver

As Mrs. Lovett with John Fanning in Sweeney Todd *in Edmonton*

Connecticut. She got to sing two favourite songs: "If He Walked Into My Life" and "Bosom Buddies" with Judy Blazer. And then in the winter of 2014 she played in *Gypsy* in Chicago, where she exercised what the *New York Times* described as "her terrific pop belter's voice in the tradition of Ethel Merman."

In between stage shows Louise has found time to appear in several movies and TV shows: Lifetime's *A Christmas Wedding*, *Recipe For a Perfect Christmas*, *MVP*, *Flashpoint*, and a CBC biopic in which she plays Céline Dion's mother. She has also hosted a TV show, *Star*

Portraits, on Bravo, in which she interviewed a variety of Canadian entertainment celebrities. Her recent Toronto appearances include *The Toxic Avenger*, a political satire in which she played Mayor Babs Belgoody and Ma Ferd, and then a children's play, *A Year with Frog and Toad*, at the Lorraine Kimsa Theatre for Young People. She won Dora awards (her third and fourth) for both performances.

She followed this with a one-woman show, *On the Rocks*, at Theatre Passe Muraille in September 2013. Louise wrote the book herself, working with

Auntie Mame *at the Goodspeed Theatre in Connecticut*

470

dramaturge and director Jen Shuber, whom she had met when she choreographed *A Year with Frog and Toad*. As usual her accompanist was Diane Leah: "We're all women working together and I love it." The show deals unashamedly with Louise's life as a kid, a high-school student, and a performer. She was frank about her early predicaments trying to establish herself as a musical performer, her disastrous experiences with men, and the disturbing emotions she felt as she watched her parents disappear into the

As Mama Rose in Gypsy *in Chicago*

irreversible darkness of senile dementia. She wrote not only the script but also the songs and some of the lyrics herself. The tunes are recognizable as being influenced by the musicals she has played in, especially *Les Misérables* and *Mamma Mia*, with a touch of Sondheim thrown in. For the most part they are lyrical and their titles, such as "The Power of Dreams" and "If I can See It (I Can Believe It)," suggest the emotions on which the show was built.

Louise in performance: On The Rocks

Louise faced her audience head on, her silver hair cropped short, wearing a black tailcoat in the tradition of the archetypal music-hall performer. She cracked jokes, made faces, and then burst into song. Louise's willingness to expose herself, to share her feelings, her sense of the ridiculous, and her pathos was immediately affecting. Her opening-night audience gave her two standing ovations. Let's hope this show will be picked up and reach a wider audience.

471

In the meantime she demonstrated her skills as an interviewer and presenter at the Pan Am Games in Toronto before going to Edmonton with husband Joe to play, of all things, the Snake in a new musical of *The Little Prince*, based on the children's classic by Antoine de Saint-Exupéry, with music by Nicholas Lloyd Webber (son of Andrew). Louise goes on reaching out to and delighting her audiences with her salty humour and her passionate performances of original material—as well as some of the greatest songs of the twentieth century.

Louise in performance: "if I can see it…"

Unlike Louise, Brent has always been very reticent about his personal life. When asked he quotes Hamlet: "You would pluck out the heart of my mystery." He feels that his personal emotional journey is nobody's business but his own. In an interview with Richard Ouzounian, he admitted that he has sometimes been in love but that these passions were fleeting. The most important thing in his life is his work in theatre. Though he has often turned down offers, he loves to work and seemingly never stops. He has said that he feels lucky to have been able to make a living doing what he loves.

He continues to do cabaret-style evenings with songs, most recently at Soulpepper and for The Art of Time Ensemble at Harbourfront in Toronto. Seemingly relaxed, he may sing for anywhere from 50 to 90 minutes without a break, sometimes wandering around the stage between numbers, moving to the musical beat. He employs restrained gestures but expressive facial expressions. Each song is a mini-play, acted out and emotionally satisfying. His repertoire is varied: contemporary songs mixed with occasional folk tunes like "The Minstrel Boy" or "All Through the Night." He often includes European songs by Charles Trenet, Kurt Weill, and of course Jacques Brel. (He returned to this show, one of his earliest successes, at Stratford in 2012.) As Brent has put it, "All of life is in his songs, the happiness,

472

the sadness, the hope, the despair. And you get to experience all of it in one night." At the Art of Time concert he surprised his audience by singing the Beatles' "Honey Pie." And he included two bittersweet numbers that are part of his standard repertoire, the Austrian interwar song "Just a Gigolo" and a rueful Noël Coward lyric that might well stand as a summation of Carver's own life as a performing gypsy:

> I believe that since my life began
> The most I've had
> Is just a talent to amuse.
> Heigh-ho, if love were all.

Brent Carver in cabaret performance

WIZARD

Robert Lepage

One afternoon in the mid 1980s, I received a phone call from Ken Gass, telling me that there was an absolutely stunning theatre piece playing in an abandoned church on Avenue Road and urging me to go to see it. It proved to be a one-man show about a French-Canadian guy travelling to Europe. The actor was Robert Lepage. He was charming, inventive, and funny and I managed to arrange to meet him for an interview. He had a very distinctive look: an almost meaty face dominated by huge eyes that seemed to look out on the world with insatiable curiosity, shrewd in a down-to-earth way, a look he shares with many of his fellow Québécois, including Jean Chrétien. He was completely devoid of hair, the result of an unusual childhood illness, a condition the late American director Mike Nichols also suffered from. Like Nichols did, Lepage wears a toupee, but unlike Nichols, Lepage has not gone to the trouble of pasting on fake eyebrows.

We talked over coffee; he was open and articulate, his English only very slightly accented but a bit hesitant. He confessed that from an early age he had been fascinated by geography. His earlier play *Circulations* sprang in large part from this interest. It was a theme that would recur frequently in his future work. By chance I had met his close friend Richard Fréchette in a bar a few weeks before. This provided us with something to talk about that was personal without being overly intimate. We seemed to hit it off. I wrote a piece about him and his show for the *Toronto Star*, probably the first article about him to appear in an English-language newspaper.

There was a psychological theory current in the 1960s and 1970s that art was the product of alienation. "Outsiders" were the people who produced Art. Their otherness was like the grain of sand inside the shell of the oyster that resulted in the formation of a pearl. Robert Lepage possessed this alienation in spades: his alopecia, the disease that caused his hair loss, also caused him to be shy and withdrawn; as a teenager he suffered from depression and worry about his sexual ambiguity. He sought escape by turning to theatre at school. At the age of seventeen he entered the Conservatoire in Quebec City, where he was told he had no talent as a naturalistic actor. Upon graduation he studied in Paris with Alain Knapp. Back in Quebec, he linked up with the small company Théâtre Repère (which translates as "Signpost") at a time when their entire budget for a show consisted of fifty dollars. With this meagre sum he created *Circulations*, winning an award at La quinzaine internationale du théâtre de Québec before touring it across the country.

My first encounter with his work was *Vinci*, a work that expanded on his earlier play. In this one-man show, Lepage appeared in the first act as an ingenuous Quebecker who wanted to visit Europe in search of the work of Leonardo. His

deft manipulation of a slide-rule at one point was a magical piece of theatrical ingenuity. In the second act he appeared in a wig and high heels as a Parisian streetwalker looking uncannily like the Mona Lisa. In the final scene he was again the young traveller turning up in a Roman bath-house. When he turned his head he became an older man whose jaw and cheek were covered in shaving cream, giving him the aspect of the great Renaissance painter. This was magic achieved with a few props and a huge dollop of imagination. He held the stage not just by these witty transitions but by the sheer magnetism of his personality.

The next year he came to Toronto with his production of *The Dragon Trilogy*, a six-hour journey spanning more than half a century, beginning in the tiny Chinese community of Quebec

The Dragon Trilogy

City in the early years of the twentieth century and expanding as the characters work out their destiny on two continents. The piece had an air of mystery; facts and connections were hidden at first. The staging was simple, the lighting dim and the pace often slow, allowing for speculation as the striking visual images dissolved and then recurred in unexpected ways.

The play was trilingual: French, English, and Cantonese, an aspect of Lepage's vision that would turn up often in his future productions. Although he would set his plays in various countries and uses several languages, he has said that he does not aim to be international but rather universal. At the centre of all of his plays is an artist figure, who is usually Québécois. This figure is in some sense Lepage himself, who embarks on a journey of discovery that takes him into unexplored territory, both geographical and emotional.

I saw his next major production, *Tectonic Plates* at Harbourfront. It involved a huge swimming pool; the actors swam and dived. Lepage's fascination with water would recur frequently in his work. It also involved a piano and was deeply concerned with Romantic music. I saw the play again in Ottawa after he had toured with it in Europe. It was barely recognizable as the same piece, it had changed so much. At that time

Lothaire Bluteau, actor

475

Lepage refused to allow any videotape recording of his work, claiming that it was constantly in flux as he and his actors experimented from night to night, adding and discarding business and text as new ideas occurred to them.

It was inevitable that Lepage would turn up in film. He appeared as René, an out-of-work actor who joins the amateur company assembled by Daniel, a young actor hired by church authorities to re-enact the Crucifixion, in Denys Arcand's movie *Jésus de Montréal* (1989). The film is structured so that the events in Daniel's life parallel those experienced by Jesus. Although it embodies a stinging critique of the Roman Catholic Church,

476

Lepage clowning in Jesus of Montreal *with Rémy Girard*

it was a huge success in Quebec and later in the rest of Canada, establishing Arcand as a major filmmaker who would go on to make some of the most important Québécois films of the 1990s.

Not surprisingly, Lepage made a film himself a few years after he acted for Arcand. *Le Confessional* (1995) is a thriller, an homage to Alfred Hitchcock, who appears in the back-story making a

Robert Lepage

film in Quebec City, as he actually did in the 1950s. The story is complex and shifts between 1990 and a past forty years earlier. The central character, Pierre Lamontagne, is played by Lothaire Bluteau, who was so moving as Daniel, the young actor who played the Christ-figure in Arcand's movie. Pierre returns to Quebec for his father's funeral, reconnects with his half-brother and other members of his family, and gradually unravels a mystery that has eluded them for all those long years. The film is highly critical of the Church, setting its authoritarian hierarchy alongside the seamier side of life in the old city. The relationship of the two brothers is complex and would turn up in other Lepage works in the future. (I learned that Lepage has a brother, also an artist, a well-known photographer.)

The Far Side of the Moon (2003) explores this fraternal relationship further. Philippe, the central character, grieves for the loss of his mother as he competes with his brother. Lepage plays both siblings, who are caught up in following the exploits of the Soviet space program, which has created a satellite that orbits the moon, revealing its scarred and pitted other side, never before seen by the earth's inhabitants. Philippe ponders the emptiness of this lunar landscape as he tries to fathom his own loneliness and answer the question, "Are we *all* alone?"

Connectivity, in fact, is very important to Lepage. He has stated that one reason he prefers theatre to any other creative medium is that even in a one-man show the actor is part of a community. He sees theatre as a collaborative art. Although he may start working on a new piece by simply taking an object or an idea and

477

Lepage in drag with a puppet child in The Far Side of the Moon

gradually, intuitively allowing images to accrue around it, he shares this process with others: co-writers, technicians, even critics. As he proceeds, strange pairings occur to him: Jean Cocteau and Miles Davis in *Needles and Opium*, Chopin and Jim Morrison in *Tectonic Plates*. He has said that the artist must have the humility to let these elements enter his work, just like the Inuk who looks at a rock and gradually lets it show him the creature that exists within it, so that he can shape it into a sculpture. The guiding imagination that perceives and connects these images as they build up in his creations would seem to be unique to Lepage.

In 1989 he became artistic director of the French division of the National Arts Centre in Ottawa, working with a resident company of actors. Here he became familiar with the work of William Shakespeare, impressed like all great directors with the scope and com-

Lepage at the heart of the circle in Needles and Opium

plexity of the sixteenth-century playwright. In Ottawa he directed productions of *Coriolanus*, *A Midsummer Night's Dream*, and *The Tempest* in translation. His work would lead to an invitation for him to direct for the National Theatre in London, the first North American to do so.

My friend Pia Kleber, who was the director of the University College Drama Program at the University of Toronto, was a great admirer of Lepage's work and asked me if I thought he might agree to direct a student production. We had lunch with him, and to my surprise he agreed. I think he wanted to try his hand on a low-profile production in English before he embarked for London and the publicity that would inevitably surround his work there. The play he chose was *Macbeth*. When he set up auditions, a great many women showed up but very few men. He decided to cast all the women as men and the boys as the lady and the witches. Martha Mann, who designed the production, was astonished at how well Lepage had prepared. His approach was highly textual and he knew Shakespeare's script as if he had done many previous productions. Even though he lacked adequate rehearsal time, his version of the Scottish play was excitingly original, exposing relationships between characters, particularly Macbeth and his wife, in a new light.

478

Robert Lepage

Unfortunately the introduction of a good deal of syncopated sound sometimes drowned out the words. This may well have been because he lacked the sophisticated technical backup he was accustomed to.

Lepage's production of *A Midsummer Night's Dream* at the National Theatre in Great Britain involved a muddy pond in which most of the characters became

A Midsummer Night's Dream

smeared and streaked with dirt. It was both hailed and reviled, but Lepage was recognized as a major talent and he would continue to work in the English capital. Soon after he created a new version of *A Midsummer Night's Dream* in French in Quebec, centring the play on a sylvan watering hole from which the fairies appeared and into which they disappeared. He went on to create *Elsinor*, his one-man version of *Hamlet*, in which he played all the major characters himself, often disappearing for seconds to reappear as someone else.

In the late 1990s, much of his energy was devoted to the creation of epic works. In 1994 he founded Ex Machina, a multidisciplinary production company involving musicians, visual artists, writers, and actors but also technical experts. Lepage has always been fascinated by the technical aspects of production and by technologies generally. He would go on to incorporate more and more elaborate devices into his works using film, projections, and music. He has said that he wishes to erase the boundaries between theatre and film and explains that a modern audience is highly sophisticated because of the exposure of its members to television, rock music, and the internet with its blogs and tweets. There is a tremendous challenge for the artist to keep up with his audience, let alone get ahead of them. Lepage installed his clos-

479

est collaborators in an abandoned fire hall in the old city of Quebec, which he christened La Caserne. It would become a production centre for every form of creative activity.

His next major work was *The Seven Streams of the River Ota*, a nine-hour piece that intertwines multiple stories in a variety of styles, from farce to high drama. Lepage and his actors developed this epic over a period of years, touring and playing sections of it until finally the complete version was presented in Montreal. In the course of touring, Lepage spent time in Japan. His ideas about theatre were strongly influenced by the work he saw there, with its mixture of stylized precision and fluid improvisation, traditional ritual and comic invention. Japan's influence is very evident in his film *Nô*, which contains one section from *The River Ota* and conflates a story involving Japanese theatre with the separatist referendum in Quebec—another example of Lepage's imaginative juxtaposition of unlikely elements to create a surprising and satisfying narrative. As he has said, "One must never overestimate an audience's culture level or underestimate its intelligence."

Lepage would continue to appear in films, again with Denys Arcand and a number of other Québécois directors, often in small roles. Typically he contributes a comic cameo. He also has

directed other films, a version of his own stage shows, *Le Polygraphe* and *Far Side of the Moon*, as well as John Mighton's *Possible Worlds*, his first English-language feature. In it a man and a woman go through a series of scenes exploring aspects of their ever-changing relationship. He has recently followed up with the film *Triptych*, an adaptation of his stage show *Lipsynch*.

For the 400th anniversary in 2008 of the founding of Quebec City, he devised *The Image Mill*, the biggest outdoor architectural projection ever made in the world, using the huge surface of the Bunge grain elevators on the banks of the Bassin Louise as a giant screen. The forty-minute show was not just an historic tableau, but also an amusing illustration in three dimensions of the city's past, present, and future. It consisted of a collage of icons, sounds, and ideas covering four epochs in the development of Quebec City: the age of waterways and exploration, the age of roads and settlement, the age of railroads and development, and the age of air travel and communication, once again tapping into Lepage's ongoing fascination with evolving technology.

His primary focus would continue to be live performance, and he developed a series of long performances pieces. *Lipsynch*, for example, lasts for nine hours. It explores all aspects of the

480

Robert Lepage

human voice, from a baby's cry to the performance of an opera diva. The play begins in an airplane when a woman dies in childbirth and one of the other passengers, an opera singer, decides to adopt the baby. Their relationship is played out over the next seven decades as the child becomes a rock singer. It narrates the intertwined stories of seven other characters in French, English, Spanish, and German. *The Geometry of Miracles*, a less demanding piece, explores the life and work of Frank Lloyd Wright. *The Andersen Project*, another one-man show, is built around *The Dryad* and *The Shadow*, stories penned by the Danish writer. Lepage inhabits a variety of characters, from a French impresario to the girl imprisoned in the tree. The program lists some thirty collaborators who contributed to the show.

The Blue Dragon, a sequel to *The Dragon Trilogy*, was written in collaboration with Marie Michaud, who performs in it along with Lepage. It is set in modern-day Shanghai and explores the complex relationship of two characters from the earlier play against the rapid expansion of the city, a thriving metropolis though still burdened by state police and rigid censorship. The play offers the audience a choice of three endings, played out in rapid succession. All of Lepage's recent plays have toured extensively, typically opening in various

As Hans Christian Andersen

European capitals: London, Madrid, Copenhagen, as well as playing in Canadian and American cities.

Needles and Opium is one work that has stood the test of time. It juxtaposes three characters who seemingly have little in common: Robert, a Québécois actor who is in Paris to do a voice-over assignment while trying to recover from a break-up with a lover; Jean Cocteau, who has just returned from a visit to New York, where he has been lionized by *LIFE* magazine although he feels they have totally misunderstood his work, while at the same time he is trying to recover from an addiction to opium; and Miles Davis, the black American trumpeter who is combatting his obsession with the French singer Juliette Gréco with an increasing consumption of alcohol and heroin. The three characters never meet, but their parallel stories are played out in hotel bedrooms, recording studios, and the streets of Paris and New York. The two sides and floor of a huge cube that rotates and revolves become these various venues, while a battery of projections of cityscapes and human figures and faces are projected. Visually the show is both filmic and surreal, hallucinatory and constantly changing, while a complex sonic montage plays out in counterpoint.

The characters engage in the mundane business of sleeping in a bed, talking on the telephone or into a microphone, and taking a bath, but they also undergo hypnotism, roll in the gutter, and fly through the air. They appear and disappear through openings in the cube as their stories overlap as if in a dream. Originally Lepage played the piece as a one-man show. Now he has turned two of his roles over to another actor who speaks in both French and English, and a black actor who impersonates Davis and seemingly plays the trumpet. The piece has toured not only in North America but around the world. It is a stunning example of Lepage's unique fusion of the

As Miles Davis in Needles and Opium

performing arts—theatre, cinema, music, and literature—in a dynamic fusion that both demonstrates and comments on the processes and perils of creativity.

Lepage has branched out from theatre to create other spectacles, too. At the invitation of Guy Laliberté he has devised several productions for Cirque du Soleil, including *KÀ*, a narrative set in imperial China and permanently installed in Las Vegas, and *Totem*, based on many of mankind's founding myths. He has also designed tours for the rock artist Peter Gabriel. Recently he appeared in a ballet, performing with two trained dancers, as an eighteenth-century master swordsman and French spy who lived much of his life dressed as a woman. *Eonnagata* opens with a dazzling display as Lepage rapidly swings two swords around his head in constantly changing light. It recalls his earlier ingenuity with a slide-rule in *Vinci*, only on a much grander scale. After this brilliant opening spectacle, however, the rest of the piece proved to be something of a letdown.

Lepage's foray into the opera world has been more successful. It began when Richard Bradshaw invited him to stage two short operas, Bartók's *Bluebeard's Castle* and Schoenberg's *Erwartung* for the Canadian Opera Company in Toronto in 1993. The result was a strikingly original visual interpretation that stunned audiences and critics alike. It went on tour and catapulted Lepage into the front rank of opera designers and directors, particularly for new work. In London he staged Lorin Maazel's *1984*, based on George Orwell's dystopian novel. Soon after he directed the rarely staged *La Damnation de Faust* by Berlioz for the Metropolitan Opera in New York, using acrobats swinging on ropes to represent the demons of hell. The production was also seen in Paris and Tokyo. In Toronto he staged Stravinsky's *Nightingale*, filling the orchestra pit with water so that the singers could float in little boats modelled on Asian sampans and incorporating Japanese- and Indonesian-style puppets to help tell the story. He has given a highly original staging of Stravinsky's dissonant opera *The Rake's Progress*, with a libretto by W.H. Auden, in Brussels and San Francisco.

Lepage's most ambitious project to date was his design and staging of all four operas comprising Wagner's Ring cycle at the Metropolitan Opera. This involved the construction of a vertical structure of moveable metal planks that twisted and shifted to suggest the various locations required to tell the story. The planks were lighted in a dazzling variety of combinations, including interactive videos that featured animated animals and birds. It offered many stunning stage

483

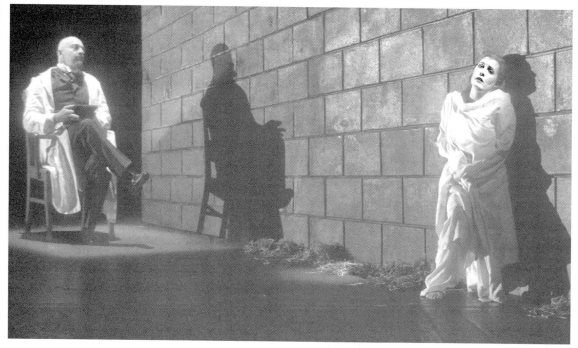

Erwartung *in Toronto*

484

pictures. The production, which ran between 2010 and 2012, put paid to the nineteenth-century presentations with winged helmets and flying horses, although some sections did not entirely succeed in evoking the magic of Wagner's grandiose conception.

More successful was the production at the Met of Thomas Adès's *The Tempest*, based on Shakespeare's play. Lepage had already directed a dozen productions of the play. He set the piece in an old opera house more or less modelled on La Scala in Milan. It had fanciful costumes that mixed the primitive garb of the creatures of a tropical island

with the elegant costumes of the early nineteenth century: braided uniforms and flowing gowns. This fanciful piece

Caricature of Lepage designing Wagner's Ring cycle at the Metropolitan Opera

is perhaps more suited to Lepage's temperament than the *Sturm und Drang* of Wagner's masterpiece.

Lepage is a risk-taker who will seemingly take on any challenge. Yet some years ago I was present at a session we set up with Richard Monette during which Pia Kleber tried to persuade

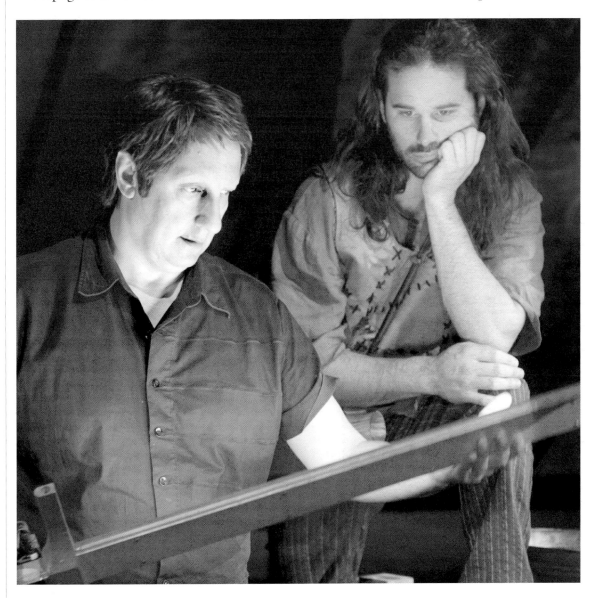

Directing the documentary Wagner's Dream

Lepage to direct at Stratford. He turned down Monette's offer. As usual he had done his homework and realized that he would not comfortably fit into the rigorously controlled scheduling at Stratford, where a director is allowed to have his full cast only one day in three and where he would have to relinquish a good deal of control to the demands of the repertory system.

For the 2015 Pan Am Games in Toronto he presented his latest one-man show, *887*, in which he delves into his own memories of childhood and asks why we remember certain seemingly irrelevant things and forget much more vital ones. The play also focuses on oblivion, the unconscious, and the memories that fade over time and whose limits are compensated for by digital storage, mountains of data, and virtual memory. It asks the question why, in this era, is theatre, an artform based on the act of remembering, still relevant?

Owing to his successes and reputation, Lepage now has access to almost unlimited funding. The costs of his production of the *Ring* topped $16 million, and it is known that Guy Laliberté gave him carte blanche for his work for Cirque du Soleil. It is arguable that he was better off when he had to work his magic with more limited means; it is also arguable that he is prone to take on too many projects, sometimes five or six simultaneously. Yet it is not that he has become grandiose or greedy: the last time I saw him on a street in New York he was walking to work at Lincoln Centre wearing faded jeans and a t-shirt.

Lepage has received many honours. He is a Companion of the Order of Canada, the recipient of the Governor General's Award for Lifetime Artistic Achievement, the European Commission's Theatre Prize, and several Genie awards for his films. In 2013 he became the tenth and youngest recipient of the Glenn Gould Prize. John Ralston Saul, one of the jurors on the Prize committee, commented, "Here's someone who, in half his life, has done more than most people could ever dream of doing." Who knows what future enchantments

EXPLORER

Sarah Polley

In the late 1950s I was assistant director to Herbert Whittaker at the University Women's Alumnae Theatre of an O'Neill play, *A Touch of the Poet*. The female lead was being played by a very pretty and sensuous young woman, Diane Buchan, who I soon realized was married to a guy I had known slightly in high school. The major male role was being played by a young English actor, Michael Polley. I sometimes drove Diane home after rehearsal, and although we didn't really discuss it I soon realized that there was something going on between her and Michael. Not too long after the production I learned that Diane had divorced her husband and moved in with Michael.

Although we more or less lost touch, it turned out that John, her son by her first husband George Buchan, was a classmate of my son Guy at Northern Secondary School. Thus I learned that Diane had become a casting director with my friend Anne Tait at CBC. Diane had two children with Michael, one of

whom, Mark, became a child actor in Gordon Pinsent's TV series *A Gift to Last*. After a few years, Diane and Anne set up their own casting agency and one of their major clients was Kevin Sullivan, who had been one of my students. Diane and Anne had a roster of talented protégés. Diane promoted and for a time managed a comedy group The Kids in the Hall. I realized when I worked for the two women briefly that Diane was a force to be reckoned with. When she realized she was pregnant for the third time since leaving her first

Diane Buchan

husband, I recall her saying, "I really shouldn't be having this baby, but now it's too late." The baby was born and was christened Sarah.

Diane continued to work with Anne on casting for Kevin, who decided to follow up on his highly successful film *Anne of Green Gables*, starring Megan Follows, with a family drama, *Road to Avonlea*. Again it would be set in Prince Edward Island in a farming community and would involve many of the characters from the Anne movies. But Megan was now a grown woman and Kevin wanted a heroine who was younger. It was perhaps inevitable that Diane would propose Sarah for the role of Sara Stanley, though

it was apparently motivated by Sarah's insistence, inspired by the success of her older brother. She had already made a film for Kevin, *Lantern Hill*, also based on a work by Lucy Maud Montgomery.

Young Sarah rapidly proved to be an ideal choice for Kevin's new series. She had blonde hair and fresh-faced Anglo good looks, but also a certain innately feisty personality, which perfectly fitted in with the character than Kevin had envisaged at the centre of his new show. One of her colleagues in the show, R.H. Thomson, when asked what it was like working with her, remarked, "Her outstanding quality, in a word—independence." The series was picked up for American distribution by Disney and became enormously successful, running for several seasons and containing enough episodes for it to go to syndication. It was and continues to be shown around the world, and its principal actors

Sara Stanley in Road to Avonlea *with Jackie Burroughs and Mag Ruffman*

continue to receive residuals to this day.

Sarah adapted to the life of a child actor, at least initially, with seeming ease. She learned her lines, developed a capacity to work with other actors, and possessed a natural quality when she faced the camera. She would later comment that she really didn't have a childhood, but that she did not hold that against her parents. Paralleling the plot of the series, her mother Diane died of cancer when Sarah was in her early teens. At this point Sarah never spoke out about whatever negative feelings she might have had about Diane. After all, the desire to work in film was hers. I recall a few years later having a drink with Anne Tait when we spotted Sarah who, at Anne's invitation, joined us. Under her breath Anne hissed, "For God's sake don't talk about her mother."

Sarah continued to work in the *Avonlea* series but eventually left it, complaining about the Americanization imposed on the scripts by the Disney organization. By this time the press had picked up on her growing fame and labelled her "Canada's sweetheart." (At least they didn't call her "Canada's answer to Shirley Temple.") Sarah had become a financially independent young woman with the capability of picking and choosing whatever projects she might agree to work on. Not surprisingly, after the success of *Road to Avonlea*, Sarah was

An older Sara Stanley with Gema Zamprogna

489

in demand as an actress for both film and stage work. In 1994, at the age of fifteen, she played the lead in *Alice Through the Looking-Glass* at the Stratford Festival. She had already proved that she was a gifted film actress who could register her thoughts without having to articulate them, but now she showed herself an effective stage actress who could convey her feelings to a live audience of hundreds and speak Lewis Carroll's often intricate and formally patterned words with clarity and conviction. The production was repeated two years later and only failed to be shown in Toronto because Sarah needed to have an operation to correct a spinal condition she had already lived with for several years.

She had already appeared in a number of films, a TV series, *Ramona*, about the adventures of an eight-year-old girl, and *Baron Munchausen* (1988), Terry Gilliam's epic comedy based on a German fable about a teller of extravagantly tall tales,

in which she performed with her father and the eminent British actors John Neville and Eric Idle. Already at the age of nine she was highly observant. She would say in a later interview that she was aware of all the behind-the-scenes politics and manipulation that were going on during the shooting of this large-scale, big-budget movie. She would also say that she thought the experience of being a child actor working constantly

490

Alice Through the Looking Glass *at Stratford*
with Keith Dinicol, Bernard Hopkins and Mervyn Blake

inevitably left psychological scars.

Soon after she left *Avonlea*, she made *Guinevere* (1999), in which she plays a young misfit from a wealthy family who has an affair with Stephen Rea, an older photographer who teaches her about life and art before she discovers that he has had affairs with a number of other young women and kicks him out. She had graduated from being a smart and opinionated child to a romantically involved young woman. Her strongly marked character and opinions remained very much in evidence.

Once again her screen personality seemed to reflect events in her personal life. As a young actress with a heavy shooting schedule, her school attendance had been erratic. She did attend Subway, an alternate public school, and later Earl Haig Collegiate. She picked up new information and ideas quickly but found the experience of high school repressive, conformist, and boring. Michael Polley once told me that as a teenager she soon became highly self-sufficient. She quit school and pursued politics; her views became increasingly left-wing. She had already been something of an activist when in 1991 she was invited to an awards ceremony by Disney and appeared wearing a Peace sign protesting the Gulf War. Disney asked her to remove the sign but she refused. She worked closely with several politicians in the New Democratic Party, particularly Toronto mayor David

as Selma in Beowulf and Grendel

491

Miller. Her political acting out slowed down, however, when an encounter with the police at a demonstration at Queen's Park in Toronto directed against the policies of the Conservative premier Mike Harris resulted in the loss of some of her back teeth.

Sarah remained based in Toronto and worked in a number of Canadian projects: the children's TV series *Straight Up* and two adult films for filmmaker Atom Egoyan: *Exotica* (1994), a psychological thriller set in a strip club, and *The Sweet Hereafter* (1997), about the effects of a fatal bus accident on a small town, in

492

With Tom McCamus in The Sweet Hereafter

which Sarah played the aspiring singer Nicole Burnell. She sang covers of the Tragically Hip's "Courage" and Jane Siberry's "One More Colour," as well as the title track, which she co-wrote with Mychael Danna. She followed this with a role in Don McKellar's first film *Last Night* (1998), about a varied group of people facing what they believe will be the end of the world. The cast included almost every well-known Canadian actor and attracted a good deal of favourable attention, establishing McKellar as an important up-and-coming director. She had already appeared in David Wellington's initial film *Joe's So Mean to Josephine* (1996), and Thom Fitzgerald's breakthrough movie *The Hanging Garden*

Sarah Polley

(1997), which proved not only her willingness, but also her ability, to recognize and work with directors setting out on the beginning of their careers.

At the same time Sarah was active on the international film scene. She was cast in the big budget film *Almost Famous* but dropped out to make the much smaller Canadian feature *The Law of Enclosures* (2000) for John Greyson, followed by *My Life Without Me* (2003), as a young woman with a husband and two children who learns she is soon to die. Both films reflect her serious involvement in political and social issues. She also made the American feature *Go* (1999) with rising American star Katie Holmes, a remake of the horror flick *Dawn of the Dead* (2004), and *The Secret Life of Words* (2005) with Tim Robbins and Julie Christie, followed by *Mr. Nobody* (2009), another science-fiction film in which she plays a woman

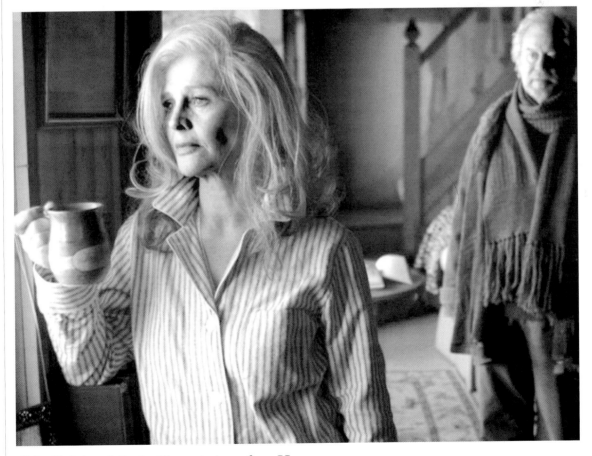

Julie Christie and Gordon Pinsent in Away from Her

suffering from deep depression. Appearing on her first late-night interview show in Los Angeles she was confident, quick-witted, and hip, instantly connecting with her audience.

Back in Canada she was cast in the third season of the theatrical comic TV drama *Slings and Arrows* as a young actress, once again working with her father Michael Polley. By 2014 she had appeared in some forty films, about half of them Canadian productions. She had established herself as an actor with the valuable ability to give her directors a sense of the inner life of the character she was portraying. Although she would not budge when her principles were challenged, she was not temperamental in the manner of Bette Davis or Tallulah Bankhead. She looked younger than her age and had a natural beauty that had nothing to do with Hollywood glamour or fashionable trends. She could appear elegant but also simple and understated. Her thoughtful intelligence is quickly evident in her interviews, and her judgment was recognized by her fellow artists and also by the powers that be in the industry, a fact demonstrated by her invitation to act as a juror at the annual Film Festival at Cannes in 2007, at the age of twenty-eight.

In 1999 she directed her first short films, *The Best Day of My Life* and *Don't Think Twice*. In 2001 she attended the directing classes at the Canadian Film Centre that Norman Jewison had established on the former Bayview Avenue estate of Toronto industrialist E.P. Taylor. Both her early short films were about personal relationships, and this would become her major theme. In them Sarah worked with established actors, gaining from them convincing emotional performances. *The Best Day of My Life* was shown at the Toronto International Film Festival and the Venice Film Festival, giving Sarah immediate credibility as a director and setting her up for her first feature.

Away From Her (2006) was based on a short story, *The Bear Came Over the Mountain* by Alice Munro. Sarah persuaded Julie Christie, with whom she had worked on two films—*No Such Thing* and *The Secret Life of Words*—in the 1990s, to play Fiona Anderson, the aging wife who drifts into Alzheimer's disease. With these two famous women and Atom Egoyan acting as her producer, she was able to attract the necessary funding. She has praised Egoyan as the director who has had the greatest influence on her, partly because he has such a warm feeling for the actors he works with. She wrote the screenplay for this first feature herself and planned the production carefully. She would later comment that she could only afford to rent a crane for one day, so she had to be sure she got the footage she needed in that limited time.

But her great accomplishment was in drawing out richly detailed and moving performances from Christie and the veteran Canadian actor Gordon Pinsent, who played the baffled but sympathetic husband who watches his wife become involved with another man at the nursing home where she is in residence. The cast included a number of accomplished performers, including Olympia Dukakis, Wendy Crewson, Clare Coulter, and Kristen Thomson, and Michael Murphy who played Aubrey, the mute patient who is the new object of Fiona's affection. There are moments of comedy, but it is the emotional reality of the film that gives it depth and impact. It was shown at both the Toronto and Sundance festivals and won seven Genie awards as well as being nominated for two Academy Awards—a stunning debut for a film director.

Her next film, *Take This Waltz* (2011), a title derived from the song by Leonard Cohen, concerned the conflict in the life of a married young woman who becomes involved with a neighbour and eventually leaves her husband to be with him. Although the movie is set in Toronto, Sarah worked with American actors Michelle Williams and Sarah Silverman as well as Canadians Seth Rogan and Luke Kirby. It is both lighter and less moving than *Away From Her* but has its own fresh originality. it had a respectable financial success and largely favourable reviews. The *Daily Telegraph*'s reviewer commented, "Her film is flush with beauty and truth, and is unerringly, unnervingly accurate on love, desire and friendship," while *The Empire*'s critic wrote, "Sarah Polley's second film is a masterfully painted portrait of an ordinary marriage under threat, dominated by a central performance of exquisite subtlety and observation." The film is also a sort of romantic tribute to the city of Toronto, which Sarah knows intimately and for which she has a great affection.

Once again Sarah's work reflected circumstances in her personal life. In 2003 she married film editor David Wharmsby,

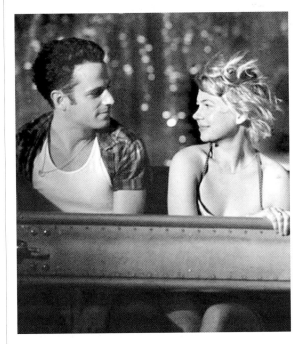

Luke Kirby and Michelle Williams in Take This Waltz

495

her long-time companion and, in the words of a close associate, "her best friend." Perhaps not surprisingly she proposed, getting down on her knees in a public park to do so. But she came to feel their relationship lacked passion, and they divorced in 2008. Three years later she married David Sandomierski, a law clerk, and they have two daughters. Nevertheless, when questioned Sarah has affirmed that the screenplays she has written are not consciously biographical but are largely based on observation of people she knows.

She took a break from acting after appearing in the movie *Trigger* (2010), written by Bruce McDonald and Daniel MacIvor, about two rock-and-roll women who meet up in their 30s. She has stated that she would not give up on acting and that as an actress she wants to advance and deepen her work and try for something new rather than rely on the qualities she realizes she has often been cast for. But before returning to the screen as a player she released the astonishing film *Stories We Tell* (2012). From about the age of eighteen, Sarah became curious as to who her real father might be after her siblings teased her about the fact that she bore no physical resemblance to Michael. Her mother Diane had gone to Montreal in the spring of 1978 to act in a play, and it was there that she became pregnant. Michael visit-

ed her while she was there and indeed their fading passion seems to have rekindled, but Diane also had affairs with her leading man Geoff Bowes and with Harry Gulkin, a Quebec film producer whose best-known film is *Lies My Father Told Me* (1975). Sarah questioned Bowes and went to Montreal to meet Gulkin. A DNA test confirmed him as her biological father.

Stories We Tell is a documentary about her pursuit of the truth about her parentage. Working with associates at the National Film Board, she learned a great deal about making non-fictional films. She assembled old footage of home movies involving members of her family at home or on holiday, and then also shot some scenes involving her dead mother Diane, played by actress Rebecca Jenkins, with Peter Evans playing Michael. She also interviewed Michael and members of her family, her siblings Mark and Joanna, half-brother and -sister John and Susy Buchan, casting directors Anne Tait and Deirdre Bowen, Gulkin, Bowes, and a variety of other real people who knew or worked with Diane in order to flesh out the story. It is an extraordinary achievement and a fascinating look at the ways in which people remember the past and reflect on it, as well as having an extremely complex and original structure. Sarah is not upset if people find it confusing, because she

496

Sarah Polley

believes it stimulates discussion about the nature of remembered truth. About this film she has stated, "If there's one thing I have learned it's to embrace the mess of life. None of us knows what our stories truly are." This attitude again reflects the influence of Egoyan.

During the hiatus she has made for herself to look after her two young daughters, she has been said to be working on a number of projects, including an original script of her own invention, a version of *Little Women* by Louisa May Alcott; *Looking for Alaska*, adapted from the novel by John Green; and *Alias Grace*, based on the novel by Margaret Atwood. Although she has expressed some disillusion with Canadian filmmaking, especially since the commercial mandate came in effect at Telefilm, she has said, "It is important for me to stay in Canada. I used to think it was because I thought it was important to build up an indigenous film industry—but now I realize I'm incapable of living anywhere else. I'm a real homebody."

It remains to be seen where Sarah will go from here. She established herself in the front rank of Canadian film directors by the age of twenty-seven. She has been praised not just for her talent, but also for her integrity and her sacrifice of a big Hollywood career in order to work in Canada. Although some people involved in the industry see Canadian filmmaking

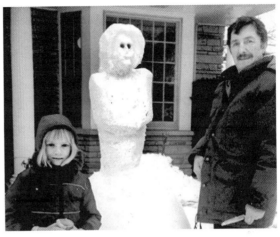

Young Sarah with Michael Polley

Sarah Polley, film maker

as a failed industry, Sarah's experience has proven that it is possible to work in Canada and pursue an individual vision. She is a model of what can be done by someone with intelligence, a strong individual sensibility, determination, and the skills acquired over three decades of involvement in the process of filmmaking on both sides of the camera. Her accomplishments to date and her optimistic outlook bode well for the future of the art of cinema in Canada and wherever else she may choose to work.

498

ACKNOWLEGEMENTS

This book has been a labour of love shared with my designer V. John Lee. As someone said of our earlier collaboration *Romancing the Bard*, "the pictures alone are worth the price."

The actors profiled, those that are still alive, have been very willing to unpack their memories of not only their own experiences but those of their colleagues. And in some cases their surviving children and friends have contributed additional recollections.

I am grateful to the Stratford Festival, especially to Nora Polley, to the Toronto International Film Festival, especially to Kristen MacDonald and the Toronto Public Library, especially to Kathryn Chirametti and to Caitlin Dyer at The National Ballet of Canada for making their photographic archives available to us. Also to John Pennino at the Metropolitan Opera archives in New York. And to Kristina Howard who helped me with permissions for photographs.

I have been greatly encouraged by the interest of David Mirvish, in whose theatres many of these artists have appeared.I am particularly grateful to my copy editor Martin Boyne, who not only pointed out various inaccuracies, but provided many positive suggestions and encouraging comments. Useful ideas were also supplied by Kirk Howard of Dundurn Press and Marc Cote of Cormorant Books. Thanks to Inta Erwin at the Breakout Educational Network. And to my friend Edgar Cowan at Mosaic Press who helped to make the book a reality.

The distribution of this book has been greatly assisted by the advice of John Karastamatis at Mirvish Productions, Anita Gaffney at the Stratford Festival and Jesse Wente at TIFF.

BIBLIOGRAPHY

Bishop-Gwyn, Carol. *The Pursuit of Perfection: a Life of Celia Franca*. Toronto: Cormorant Books, 2012.

Caux, Patrick, and Bernard Gilbert. *Ex Machina: Creating for the Stage*. Vancouver: Talonbooks, 2007.

Dewhurst, Colleen, with Tom Viola. *Colleen Dewhurst: Her Autobiography*. New York: Scribner, 1997.

Forrester, Maureen. *Out of Character*. Toronto: McClelland & Stewart, 1986.

Fouquet, Ludovic. *The Visual Laboratory of Robert Lepage*. Trans. Rhonda Mullins. Vancouver: Talonbooks, 2014.

Garebian, Keith. *William Hutt: a Theatre Portrait*. Oakville, ON: Mosaic Press, 1990.

———, ed. *William Hutt: Masks and Faces*. Oakville, ON: Mosaic Press, 1995.

Green, Michelle. *David Earle: A Choreographic Biography*. Toronto: Dance Collection Danse, 2005.

Harron, Don. *My Double Life*. Toronto: Dundurn Press, 2012.

Joni Mitchell: The Complete Poems and Lyrics. New York: Three Rivers/Crown, 1997.

Kubernick, Harvey. *Leonard Cohen: Everybody Knows*. Milwaukee: Backbeat Books, 2014.

Lillie, Beatrice. *Every Other Inch a Lady: an Autobiography*. New York: Doubleday, 1972.

Marom, Malka. *Joni Mitchell: in Her Own Words*. Toronto: ECW Press, 2014.

Massey, Raymond. *A Hundred Different Lives*. New York: Little, Brown, 1979.

———. *When I Was Young*. Toronto: McClelland & Stewart, 1976.

Monette, Richard, with David Prosser. *This Rough Magic: the Making of an Artistic Director, a Memoir*. Stratford, ON: The Stratford Shakespearean Festival of Canada, 2007.

Neufeld, James. *Lois Marshall: a Biography*. Toronto: Dundurn Press, 2010.

———. *The Power to Rise: the Story of the National Ballet of Canada*. Toronto: University of Toronto Press, 1996.

Plummer, Christopher. *In Spite of Myself*. New York: Alfred A. Knopf, 2008.

Simmons, Sylvie. *I'm Your Man: the Life of Leonard Cohen*. New York: HarperCollins, 2012.

Stonechild, Blair. *Buffy Sainte-Marie: It's My Way*. Markham, ON: Fifth House Publishers, 2012.

Tynan, Kenneth. *Profiles*. London: Nick Hern Books, 1989.

Williams, Jeannie. *Jon Vickers: A Hero's Life*. Lebanon, NH: Northeastern University Press, 1999.

Williams, Richard. *The Animator's Survival Kit*. New York: Faber & Faber, 2009.

PHOTO CREDITS

LILLIE
p.3 Vandamm • p.7 Wallace Litwin.

MASSEY
p.15 Alex Kahle • p.27 Vitagraph, Inc. • p.28 Michael Powell, The Archers • p.29 Warner Bros. Pictures • p.30 NBC Universal • p.31 Friedman-Abeles • p.32 Drawing by Grant Macdonald, The Agnes Etherington Art Museum, Queens University

MALLETT
p.39 Stratford Festival Archives • p.46 Fortunato Aglialoro Other images: collection of the Toronto Public Library

GELINAS
p.56 (Upper) Stratford Festival Archives, Herb Nott & Co. • p.56 (lower) by Grant Macdonald Other images: Pascal Gelinas, Courtesy of Productions Gratien Gelinas.

REID
pp. 61, 63, 69, 80 & 87 Stratford Festival Archives, Peter Smith & Co. • p.67 Toronto Public Library, Crest Collection • p.70 Stratford Festival Archives • p.71 Stratford Festival Archives • p.72 Broadhurst

Theatre, NY • p.73 Paramount Pictures • p.74 American Film Theatre • p.76 Shaw Festival Archives • p.77 Stratford Festival Archives, Robert C. Ragsdale • p.79 Stratford Festival Archives

VICKERS
pp. 81, 84, 87, 88, 89, 91, Metropolitan Opera Archives, photographer Louis Melancon • p.93 Courtesy of the Royal Opera House, Covent Garden • p.96 Opera Quebec

FRANCA
p.97 Ken Bell • p.99 John Lindquist • pp. 101, 102 & 103 (left) National Ballet Archives • p.103 (right) Andrew Oxenham • pp.106, 107 & 109 National Ballet of Canada Archives, Anthony Crickmay • p.110 National Ballet of Canada Archives

HUTT
pp. 111 & 134 Stratford Festival Archives, Michael Cooper • p.113 Drawing by Grant Macdonald, The Agnes Etherington Art Museum, Queens University • p.115 Toronto Public Library, Crest Collection • p.116 Lutz Dille, David Gardner collection, Thomas

Fisher Library • p.118 drawing by Grant Macdonald, Stratford Festival • p.119 Stratford Festival Archives, Peter Smith & Co., • p.123 Stratford Festival Archives, Douglas Spillane, • p.125 Stratford Festival Archives, Robert C. Ragsdale • p.128 Stratford Festival Archives • pp. 131, 132 (left) Stratford Festival Archives, Cylla von Tiedemann • p.132 (right) Cylla von Tiedemann, Soulpepper

FORRESTER /MARSHALL
p.135 p.136 Get Stock, Toronto Star Archives • p.138 p.141 courtesy of Gina Dineen • p.143 Ken Bell • p.144 (New Zealand newspaper caricature) • p.146 Bach Aria Group • p.148 Edmonton Opera • p.149 Stratford Festival Archives, Robert C. Ragsdale • p.108 Jack Deleno

WILLIAMS
p.155 Tom Sito • p.153 Martin Hunter Collection • p.155 Walt Disney Productions. • pp. 157 & 158 Richard Williams Collection • pp. 159 & 160 by permission of Faber and Faber, from The Animator's Survival Kit • p.162 Frank

Herrmann • pp. 163, 164 & 166 Richard Williams Collection • p.165 Touchstone Pictures and Amblin Entertainment • p.168 Illustration by Richard Williams, courtesy of Faber and Faber

HENRY/LEBLANC
pp .169, 189 (left) & 190 Stratford Festival Archives, Cylla von Tiedemann • pp. 170, 172 & 182 Toronto Public Library, Crest Collection • pp. 174, 176, 177, 181, 184 & 185 (left) Stratford Festival Archives, Robert C. Ragsdale • p.175 Stratford Festival Archives, Peter Smith & Co. • p.178 Stratford Festival Archives, Zoe Dominic • p.179 Stratford Festival Archives, Jim Hockings • p.185 (right) Stratford Festival Archives, Cylla von Tiedemann • p.189 (right) Soulpepper Theatre, Cylla von Tiedemann

PLUMMER
p.191 Erin Samuell • pp. 194, 196 & 197 (left) Stratford Festival Archives, Peter Smith & Co. • p.197 (right) Grant Macdonald drawing, Stratford Collection • p.201 p.203 Stratford Festival Archives, Inge Morath • p.205 (top)

Paramount Pictures • p. 205 (bottom) Courtesy of American Shakespeare Theatre • p.206 Stratford Festival Archives, Cylla von Tiedemann • p.207 Stratford Festival Archives, V. Tony Hauser • p.208 Stratford Festival Archives, David Hou • p.209 (top) Sony Pictures Classics • p.209 (bottom) Olympus Pictures

DEWHURST
p.211 Michele Singer/ Outline Press • p.212 Martin Hunter Collection • p.213 Courtesy of the estate of Colleen Dewhurst • p.214, 215 & 216 New York Public Theater Collection at the New York Public Library, George E. Joseph • p.217 (left) Peter Cunningham • p. 217 (right) Martha Swope / TIME, Inc. • p.218 Billy Rose Theatre Collection, New York Public Library Collection, Friedman-Abeles • pp.219, 220 & 221 (below) Copyright Kevin Sullivan Productions • p.221 (top) CBS, Inc.

COLICOS
p.223 Getty CBS Photo Archive • p.225 (top) inter-net • p.225 (bottom) Stratford Festival Archives • p.226 & 228 Stratford

Festival Archives, Peter Smith & Co. • p.227 Stratford Festival Archives • p.229 Getty. Central Press) • p.230 Courtesy of MGM Pictures • p.231 GettyImages CBS Photo Archive) • p.232 internet

STRATAS
pp .233, 236, 237 & 238 The Metropolitan Opera Archives, Winnie Klotz • pp. 239 & 241 Estate of Franco Zeffirelli • p.240 Copyright Kevin Sullivan Productions • p.242 Courtesy of the Paris Opera

MONETTE
p.243 Toronto Public Library, Crest Collection • p.244 Keith Clark, Richard Monette collection • p.245 Stratford Festival Archives, Peter Smith & Co. • p.247 New Shakespeare Company, Richard Digby Day • p.248 (left) Aviva Slesin, Richard Monette Collection • p.248 (right) St. Lawrence Centre, by permission of The Canadian Stage Company • p.249 Robert A. Barnett, Tarragon Theatre • pp.250 (left), 251 & 252 (top), Stratford Festival Theatre, Robert C. Ragsdale • p.250 (right) Stratford Festival Archives, Zoe Dominic • pp. 252 (bottom) & 257

Stratford Festival Archives, Michael Cooper • p.254 Stratford Festival Archives, David Cooper • pp. 256 & 258 Stratford Festival Archives, Cylla von Tiedemann • p.259 Stratford Festival Archives p.260 Mark Monette

SAINTE-MARIE
p.261 p.262 p.264 Rowland Scherman, US National Archives • p.265 (Michael Ochs Archive, Getty Images) • p.266 (left) Buffy Sainte-Marie • p.266 (right) PBS Television • p.268 NBC Television

CUNNINGHAM/EARLE
pp. 269 & 272 Toronto Public Library, Toronto Children Players Collection • p.271 David Earle Collection • p.273 Courtesy of the National Ballet School • pp. 277, 279, 284, 288 & 291 Collection of the Acme Dance Company • p.281 (top) Lois Greenfield • pp. 281 (bottom) & 283 Andrew Oxenham • p.282 Frank Richards • p.286 John Lauener • p.287 Cylla von Tiedemann • p.292 Michael English • p.294 Martin Hunter Collection

MITCHELL/COHEN
p.295 p.296 Frank Prazak,

Library and Archives Canada • p.298 York University Library, Toronto Telegram Collection • p.300 Sue Sullivan p.301 Leonard Cohen Collection • p.302 p.303 Danny Fields • p.304 • p.305 Joel Bernstein • p.307 Perla Batalla • p.309 Eija Arjatsalo • p.310 p.311 Aaron Harris, Canadian Press Agency • p.312 courtesy of John Uren

THOMSON
p.313, 314, 315, & 317 Martin Hunter Collection • p.320 Martin Hunter Collection, Hart House Theatre • p.322 (left) CBC Archives • p.322 (right) Copyright Kevin Sullivan Productions • p.324 (left) • p.324 (right) • p.325 CBC Archives • p.326 Stratford Festival Archives, Robert C. Ragsdale • p.328 Cylla von Tiedemann • p.329 (left) Segal • p.329 (right) Cylla von Tiedemann • p.329 (left) p.329 (right) p.332

BUJOLD
p.333 Paul Almond p.335 Fildebroc • p.337 NBCUniversal • p.339 Michael Cacoyannis • p.340 Canadian Film Development Corporation • p.342 Morgan Creek

Productions • p.343 (left) Park Ex Pictures, Attila Dory

BEATTIE
pp. 345, 351, 353 (top) & 362 Terry Manzo • p.346 & 347 Martin Hunter Collection, Hart House Theatre • p.349 Stratford Festival Archives, Jim Hockings • p.353 (bottom) Ian Jackson • p.356 Martin Hunter Collection • p.357 Stratford Festival Archives, Michael Cooper

BURROUGHS
pp. 359 & 366 Toronto Dance Theatre • p.361 Toronto Public Library, Crest Theatre Collection • p.363 Don Owen • p.367 Courtesy of Mirvish Productions • p.368 Stratford Festival Archives, Robert C. Ragsdale • p.369 John Walker • p.371 Peter O'Brian • p.373 Copyright Kevin Sullivan Productions • p.374 Peter O'Brian • p.375 Check out Tales of the City Producer

FEORE
p.377 Stratford Festival Archives, David Cooper • pp. 378, 380 (bottom), 381 & 384 Stratford Festival Archives, Michael Cooper • pp. 379, 386 & 388 Stratford Festival Archives, David

Hou • p.380 (top) National Theatre School • p.383 Park Ex Pictures, Atilla Dory • p.385 Stratford Festival Archives, Cylla von Tiedemann • p.387 (top) BBC Productions • p.387(bottom) NBCUniversal

TENNANT
pp. 389 & 394 Anthony Crickmay • p.392 Courtney G. MacMahon • p.395 Getstock, Toronto Star Collection • p.396 Martha Swope • pp .398 & 404 (left) Andrew Oxenham • pp.399 & 402 David Street • p.400 Cylla von Tiedemann • p.404 (right) Ken Bell • p.406 Jorge Gavilando

OUIMETTE/McCAMUS
pp. 407, 413 (left & right), 414 (right), 415, 416 & 418 (left) Stratford Festival Archives, Cylla von Tiedemann • p.408 Shaw Festival Archives, David Cooper • p.409, 414 (left), 418 (right) & 422 (top) Stratford Festival Archives, David Hou • p.410 Nelvana pp. 411 & 421 (left) Rhombus Media • p.412 Tarragon Theatre Michael Cooper • p.417 SFA • p.420 Fireworks Entertainment, Marvel Studios • p.421 (right) Liz Lauren,

Goodman Theatre, Chicago • p.422 (bottom) Stratford Festival Archives, Michael Cooper

McKENNA
pp. 423, 424, 426 (left & right), 433 (left), 437 & 438 Stratford Festival Archives, David Hou • p.428 Manitoba Theatre Centre • p.429 Centaur Theatre, Montreal, Lydia Pawelak • pp. 430 (top) & 433 (right) Stratford Festival Archives, Cylla von Tiedeman • p.430 (bottom) & 431 Stratford Festival Archives, Michael Cooper • p.434 Stratford Festival Archives • p.435 Vancouver Playhouse • p.436 Erin Samuell

SCHULTZ
pp. 439 & 446 Stratford Festival Archives, Cylla von Tiedemann • pp. 441 (left & right) & 443 Stratford Festival Archives, Michael Cooper • p.447 (left & right) Guntar Kravis • pp. 448, 449, 451 & 452 Cylla von Tiedemann

PITRE/CARVER
pp. 453, 454, 466 & 471 (top & bottom) courtesy of Louise Pitre • p.455 Vince Talotta, Toronto Star File • p.457 Stratford Festival Archives, Robert C.

Ragsdale • pp. 458 & 465 Mirvish Productions • p.459 Norflicks Productions • p.460 Citadel Theatre • p.462 Stratford Festival Archives, V. Tony Hauser • p.463 (left) Stratford Festival Archives • p.463 (right) Triptych Media • p.464 (right) Robert C. Ragsdale, Grand Theatre, London • p.469 Citadel Theatre, Edmonton • p.470 (left) Goodspeed Theatre, Connecticut • p.470 (right) Goodman Theatre, Chicago • p.472 Courtesy of Brent Carver

LEPAGE
p.473 Darren Calabrese, Canadian Press • p.474 Claudel Huot p.475 • p.476 • p.477 (left & right) Sophie Grenier • p.478 Alistair Muir • p.479 Neil Libbert Royal National Theatre in London) • p.481 Erick Labbe • p.482 Claudel Huot • p.484 (top) Mark Johnson as the Psychiatrist and Krisztina Szabo' as the Woman in the Canadian Opera Company production of *Erwartung*, 2015. Michael Cooper • p.484 (bottom) • p.485 Veronica Redgrave

POLLEY
pp. 487 & 488 (top), 495 &

504

497 (top & bottom) Courtesy of Sarah Polley • p.488 (bottom) & p.489 Copyright Kevin Sullivan Productions • p.490 Stratford Festival Archives, Cylla von Tiedemann • p.491 Eurasia Motion Pictures • p.492 Atom Egoyan • p.493 Foundry Films

505

516

Bright
Particular
Stars

Canadian Performers